LITERATURE AND THE QUESTION OF PHILOSOPHY

EDITED AND INTRODUCED BY
ANTHONY J. CASCARDI

The Johns Hopkins University Press
Baltimore and London

Excerpts from "The Gift Outright," by Robert Frost, are from *The Poetry of Robert Frost*, edited by Edward Connery Lathem. Copyright 1942 by Robert Frost. Copyright © 1969 by Holt, Rinehart and Winston. Copyright © 1970 by Lesley Frost Ballantine. Reprinted by permission of Henry Holt and Company.

This book has been brought to publication with the generous assistance of the Andrew W. Mellon Foundation.

The Johns Hopkins University Press, 701 West 40th Street,
Baltimore, Maryland 21211
The Johns Hopkins Press Ltd., London

The paper used in this publication meets the minimum requirements of American National Standard for Information Sciences—Permanence of Paper for Printed Library Materials, ANSI Z39.48-1984.

Library of Congress Cataloging-in-Publication Data

Literature and the question of philosophy.

Bibliography: p.
1. Literature—Philosophy. I. Cascardi, Anthony J.,
1953–
PN49.L519 1987   801   86-21461
ISBN 0-8018-3418-x (alk. paper)

Contents

Acknowledgments

All of the essays included in this volume were written specifically for it and are published here for the first time, with the exception of Arthur Danto's "Philosophy as/and/of Literature" (copyright, the American Philosophical Association), which first appeared in *Grand Street* (Spring 1984). Martha Nussbaum's contribution is a revised and expanded version of a paper which was originally published in the *Journal of Philosophy* (October 1985), which holds copyright. Stanley Rosen's "The Limits of Interpretation" is appearing simultaneously in a collection of his essays entitled *Hermeneutics as Politics* (Oxford University Press), and Berel Lang's "Postmodernism in Philosophy" appeared in *New Literary History* (Autumn 1986).

As editor it is my pleasure to acknowledge the many forms of assistance received in the preparation of this book. The University of California, Berkeley, has been generous in providing research assistance funds. Richard Macksey took interest in the project at an early stage, and Eric Halpern guided it through the editorial process at Johns Hopkins. Carol Ehrlich undertook the difficult task of aligning the various texts. To them and to the authors, whose faithfulness and commitment are realized here, I offer public thanks.

Introduction

Collections of critical essays commonly begin with an introduction of some thirty or forty pages in which the editor of the volume sets forth the premises tacitly understood by the various contributors, thereby exposing, without arguing for, the program or ideology they all share. The present volume dispenses with the conventional omnibus introduction in favor of a series of interstitial notes designed to mediate among thirteen disparate voices in the larger interdisciplinary conversation of literature and philosophy. Beginning with Arthur Danto's general essay on the interrelationships between these two fields, and proceeding in a roughly historical fashion from Harry Berger, Jr.'s, essay on Plato to Berel Lang's essay on postmodernism, this volume purports to give a fair sampling of some of the liveliest of the most recent work of North American scholars in this area.

The very nature of this project precludes ideological summary, for it is first and foremost characterized by the diversity of voices and positions competing within it. My contention in assembling this collection has been that such diversity does not preclude the possibility of dialogue and, moreover, that such dialogue should be made available to all who would care to seek it out. Thus, one will not find in these essays any secret campaign in favor of one or the other of the many critical terms currently in vogue. There is no collective apologia for historicism, for idealism, for *différance*, or for the aesthetics of reader-response. What there is, by contrast, are thirteen individual voices, each of which speaks to the problematic interrelations of literature and philosophy at some point near the forefront of their mutual concerns. The appropriate image for the present volume is thus less that of the "book" than that of the roundtable discussion. In such a conversation, all the speakers are unlikely to agree on conclusions; indeed, they are likely to disagree on premises as well. Nonetheless, they share an understanding that the interrelationship of literature and philosophy throughout their history has been problematical, and they recognize where the most fruitful areas of investigation are apt to lie.

The effort to establish a dialogue between literature and philosophy will depend for its specific character on the exact nature and range of the issues that are thought to stand between them. Thus, while the conversation initiated here may preclude any initial (or terminal) summary, the essays may be situated with respect to one another and to the problem they collectively address. If there is no single "metanarrative" that unifies them, the compass of their shared concerns is limited only by the angle of one's historical view. For the problem of literature and philosophy in their relationship to one another may be seen as continuous with the entire "history of Western metaphysics" from Plato to the present age, and as coextensive with those institutions (e.g., "literature," "philosophy") which that metaphysics founds. In book 10 of the *Republic*, Plato refers to an "ancient quarrel" between literature and philosophy, but it is to his treatment of that quarrel that most discussions in the West in fact look back. Plato moves to exclude the poets from his Republic, but as Dalia Judovitz shows in her essay on Plato and Descartes, the marginalization of poetry within the Republic marks something deeper than a thematics of rivalry might suggest. The founding of the institution named "philosophy," which is imaged in the founding of the new state, is here accomplished by the exclusion of the "literary" from its bounds. The "mark of absolute difference" which Plato seeks to establish between philosophy and literature (indeed, between philosophy and all the other arts) is itself, as Judovitz says, "the trace of a series of differential operations that reinscribe and retrace the figure of philosophical discourse."

The differentiation of "literature" and "philosophy" would indeed be absolute were it not for the fact that philosophy is itself unable to produce a coherent theory of the differences that separate it from literature. As Peter McCormick demonstrates in his essay, "Philosophical Discourses and Fictional Texts," neither a theory of speech-acts based on such notions as "semantic markers" or "illocutionary force" nor a theory of genre is able to distinguish categorically between fictional and philosophical texts. Indeed, there are good reasons for construing at least some of the texts we customarily call "philosophical" as fictions of a peculiar sort. Within philosophy we witness the return of the literary, as of the repressed, in the guise of dialogue, fable, and myth. The presence of these "literary" qualities has in fact been acknowledged by Plato scholarship since at least the work of Paul Friedländer and Leo Strauss, even if it has been systematically ignored by those analytical philosophers who attempt to draw on Plato.

In the essay entitled "Levels of Discourse in Plato's Dialogues," Harry Berger, Jr., confronts this conventional view with the charge that the notion of the "literary" nature of the Platonic dialogues thereby invoked cannot be coherently maintained. Either the dialogues are regarded as literary (more accurately, "dramatic") and aspire to the condition of closure, but laudably fail to produce closed solutions to the problems they broach, or the ironic nature of the individual dialogue as a literary form is maintained, and the will to closure is displaced onto some conception of the coherence of the dialogues as a group. In either case, claims for the "literary" nature of the dialogues are severely undercut by the search for a systematic Platonic *doxa*. As Berger says, to presuppose that there exists a recoverable "teaching" or Platonic system in the dialogues is to succumb to that desire which Heidegger and Derrida have analyzed under the rubric of the "metaphysics of presence." Of equal interest here is the break that Berger makes with Heidegger and Derrida: whereas they seek to locate the origin of the metaphysics of presence in Plato, Berger produces a reading of the dialogues in which they are seen to anticipate Heidegger and Derrida in a critique of that same metaphysics. I would perhaps add that, as a result of such a reading, deconstruction turns against itself; the very notions of "Western metaphysics" and the "metaphysics of presence" are revealed to be strategic concepts, the effect of which is to configure the relationship between philosophy and literature as a function of the crucial deconstructive term, "difference" (*différance*).

To say this much is, if not exactly to produce a critique of "difference" from within, then at least to indicate that the program for the deconstruction of philosophy corresponds to a determinate conception of "literature" and its affiliates ("writing," "text") and of the ideology they share. Where philosophy is seen as aspiring to "closure," to "system," or to knowledge as possession or full presence, literature will be defined as that which is disruptive of closure and productive of (sexual, racial, historical, etc.) difference, as the province of desire, displacement, delay, deferral, or lack. In an analogy that is apposite here, Mary Bittner Wiseman takes Roland Barthes's partly autobiographical essay on photography (*La chambre claire*) as a long excursus on that kind of writing which subverts philosophical discourse. What Barthes

calls the "scandal" of photography lies in its transgression of the customary association of the real with the present by virtue of the fact
that this apparently realistic art can testify only to the past existence of
objects. Photography thus also undermines the Cartesian notions of
the self as subject and of the world as its representation, which the
notion of presence underwrites. It is more closely related to the Diderotian aesthetics of the gesture, the performance, and the *tableau
vivant* than to classical (Cartesian) representation. As Barthes says,
representation suppresses performance, just as it also suppresses the
gesture and the mask: "representation is when nothing emerges, when
nothing leaps out of the frame: of the picture, the book, the screen."

Photography is thus the radicalization of writing (and, in particular,
of modern writing) because in it signs are removed from the assertive
field of force on which philosophical discourse depends and in which
they are used to enjoin belief. Like theatricalized writing, its signs are
acted, or perhaps more accurately, they are performed. And yet the
camera lens is not an extension of the human eye; its role is neither to
humanize the world nor (what amounts to the same thing) to repro-
duce through light the point of the subject's gaze. Rather, the mode of
photography is that of an automatism; it is a mode of automatic writing with light in which it has proved possible to achieve something
that literature itself could not: the decentering of the physical world
and of the material presence of objects before the lens.

This extreme form of writing is valuable as an image of what literature might be were it fully to clear free of those constraints that "philosophy" imposes on it. In the absence of such a limit-case, however,
the history of literature has been intricately bound up with those concepts (e.g., "author," "representation," "intention") which the Platonic and Cartesian notions of "presence" and "subjectivity" found.
Accordingly, the majority of the contributors to this volume are more
circumspect in their projects. Rather than concentrate on that moment in which the human is eclipsed, in which both "literature" and
"philosophy" are transformed into (automatic) writing, and in which
the modern is overtaken by postmodernism, they devote themselves to
the intermediate-range tasks of revising, clarifying, and purifying the
central range of concepts in terms of which the relationship of literature to philosophy has historically been viewed. In the concluding essay of this collection, Berel Lang describes postmodernism as that age
in which nothing is above suspicion; in another description, it is the
age in which nothing is beyond belief. The essays that precede his are
themselves the products of postmodernism insofar as they take up with

healthy suspicion the questions of hermeneutics (Dutton, Nehamas, Rosen), ethics (Altieri, Cascardi, Nussbaum), and aesthetics (Cascardi, Halliburton, Nussbaum); but none of these places literature in a position that inherently contravenes the demands of philosophical belief.

Alexander Nehamas, for instance, breaks with the Foucauldian will to dispense altogether with such concepts as "work" and "author" by arguing that these may coherently be understood as the constructs of interpretation, rather than as absolute points of departure for it. Authorship may not follow the model of "knowledge as possession," and the author may not be the sole proprietor of the meaning of his words; he may be considered as an "artificial person," which is to say as a character who acts in the production and reception of texts. But he may also be reconstructed as a plausible variant of who the writer may historically have been. In a related essay, Denis Dutton demonstrates the uncanny resilience of the concept of "intention" and its importance for the construction of almost any reasonable account of the meaning of a work. Yet at the same time he seeks to specify the legitimate field over which such a concept may be applied, in this case by broadening it beyond the province claimed for it by romanticism. If "romantic intentionalism" conceives the artist first and foremost as one who speaks, and as one whose words thereby have the meaning with which he alone invests them, then Dutton follows Wittgenstein far enough to say that the picture of meaning as a function of intention, and of intention as an inner, subjective state, must be replaced by the notion that meaning is accessible through public and historical conventions and rules. Dutton breaks with standard conventionalism at roughly the point where Wittgenstein in the *Philosophical Investigations* speaks about the folly of seeking rules for following conventions and rules. At this point, the knowledge accessible through a familiarity with the rules reaches its limit: contravention of the rules can no longer be described as an instance of error within the framework of the rules, but only as choosing the inappropriate set of rules, as stepping into the wrong (hermeneutic) circle. Consider Peter McCormick's essay once again in this regard. In the effort to distinguish fictional from philosophical texts, one proceeds from a search for an exhaustive list of the markers characteristic of each class of texts to a search for a single rule (a "law of genre") for the interpretation of the significance of these differences. But since neither such a list of differences nor such a law for their interpretation can be formulated theoretically, it is more profitable to think of "genre" as a function of the natural sense of types and kinds, a product of the intuitive rather than the theoretical mind.

The example of Wittgenstein has often been invoked in support of the "antitheoretical" program of contemporary literary criticism, but as several of the essays in this volume suggest, theory can never entirely be repressed. Consider in this regard Stanley Rosen's essay, "The Limits of Interpretation." Rosen conducts a strenuous argument not so much against the notion of "theory" as in favor of the proposition that theory necessarily has limits. He suggests that a theory of interpretation, qua theory, with the features of coherence and closure, is impossible to achieve and must be supplemented by something akin to the "natural sense" mentioned above (e.g., intuition or insight). If one thinks along Wittgensteinian lines, the question that theory proves unable to answer is *what to do* once we have reached the heights (or the depths) marked out by silence and the theoretical "ladder" has been thrown away. Or, if one thinks along more strictly metaphysical lines and chooses Hegelian terms, the question remains that of how to gain an absolute entrance into the Absolute; yet, despite its will to closure and its remarkable powers of totalization, this is the question that Hegelianism does not address. As Rosen says, the problem is not with theory (or "method") as such but with our attitude toward it: the metaphysics of method, which receives its canonical formulation in Descartes, is, in Rosen's words, "the attempt to replace the judicious selection of methods by a comprehensive method of selection. In the case of hermeneutics, it is the attempt to replace or to fortify the judgment of the reader with a methodology for the selection of methods of reading." The search for method, and the reliance on the (scientific) conception of knowledge as the possession of the foundations of truth, manifest themselves as a loss of faith in what Husserl in *Ideas* and Northrop Frye in connection with Shakespearean comedy and romance have each called the "natural" perspective. My own essay on "romantic" responses to Kant works toward a recovery of the natural along related lines. This requires surpassing the appeal to a "pretheoretical" attitude, just as it also requires transcending the Wittgensteinian conception of knowledge as the "post-theoretical" familiarity with tacit rules, which ultimately issues in silence. Rather, I regard the natural as at once an epistemological, a moral, and an aesthetic project, and I propose that for romanticism, at least, it may be understood as an articulation of the self in its relations with the world and with others which goes beyond the sublime.

The notion of a sublime rooted in idealism which at some point gives way to the natural is imaged in those "forms of life" in which we are able to know everything about others that we can and in which we are free to pursue whatever forms of passionate attachment to others such knowledge would allow. It corresponds on the aesthetic and moral planes to that point at which theory must be supplemented by practical wisdom or prudence. These latter terms are central to Martha Nussbaum's essay on literature as a form of moral imagination. Based largely on a reading of Henry James's *Golden Bowl*, Nussbaum's analysis of the relationship between literature and moral philosophy relies on Aristotle's *Nicomachean Ethics* and on the contrast between scientific knowledge and prudential wisdom presented there. If scientific knowledge consists, in Aristotle's words, in "judgment about things that are universal and necessary" and follows from "first principles" (1140B), then practical wisdom offers proof of the fact that antifoundationalism does not necessarily issue in skepticism, nihilism, or the anxieties of indeterminacy. Practical wisdom is a reasoned state (although not only a reasoned state); it is a virtue, and if it does not admit of demonstration this is because the very objects of its knowledge—human goods—are things whose first principles are variable. With this basis in Aristotle more or less understood, Nussbaum succeeds in showing that literature in general, and the novel in particular, may be considered as a form of moral philosophy. Insofar as the tasks of morality call for *phronēsis*, or practical wisdom, and rely on a range of activities customarily associated with the "aesthetic" (e.g., vision, imagination, attention, and insight), they are exemplarily fulfilled by the novelist.

The range of moral action which Nussbaum discusses in terms of practical wisdom is taken up toward rather different ends in Charles Altieri's essay on the relationship between literary theory and "expressivist ethics." With reference to the contemporary projects of such thinkers as Stanley Cavell, Alasdair MacIntyre, Robert Nozick, Angel Medina, and Charles Taylor, Altieri begins by distinguishing the claims of the ethical from those of the moral. If the moral in Kantian philosophy is marked as that region in which all subjects are treated under a rubric of equivalence, and if the moral agent is correspondingly recognized by the capacity to generalize the "I," then the ethical addresses the question of how the empirical subject chooses his or her own good. In its appeal to Wittgenstein's delimitation of the ethical by the "aesthetic," i.e. by the peculiar modalities in which personal (ethical) identity is modeled and engaged, this outline of an "expressivist" ethic crosses the boundary between pure and practical reason which troubled Kant. By confronting the question of how the "I" disposes the will, which defines its particular hold on the world, the notion of an expressivist ethic is powerful enough to embrace the Wittgensteinian critique of subjectivity without at the same time being drawn into pure anticognitivism or into an "antitheoretical" stance.

At several points in the essays that follow, the interests of literature and philosophy cross over into the realm of aesthetics. Signal instances occur in the studies of Nussbaum and Altieri and in my own essay, "Romantic Responses to Kant." Yet the aesthetic as such is given special foregrounding in David Halliburton's theory of "constitution": "Endowment, Enablement, Entitlement." Written in a spirit that owes something to Kenneth Burke, Halliburton begins from the pragmatism of C. S. Peirce and proceeds to demonstrate what it might mean to substitute a metaphysics that puts aesthetics in first place for one that takes epistemology as "first philosophy." Epistemology is conveniently described as the theory of knowledge, and as Heidegger has said, since Descartes and Kant a theory of knowledge has preceded a theory of the world. What Halliburton intends by "constitution," then, is a response to Cartesian and Kantian metaphysics and to their Platonic underpinnings, for it is not a "theory of knowledge" but a "theory of the world." When Plato described the relationship between the realm of appearances and that of ideas, he described a "founding" relationship in which the visible world is subordinated to the realm that transcends it and that it reflects. Following Heidegger in "The Question Concerning Technology" (and, implicitly, the Nietzschean revolt against Platonism, which Heidegger takes up), Halliburton recalls that the Platonic notion of *eidos* on which this understanding of "foundations" is based was itself the product of a reversal in that thinking according to which the *eidos* was regarded as the outward aspect that a visible thing presents to the eye. Insofar as Halliburton follows Heidegger and Nietzsche in their "aesthetic" critique of Platonism, the position that he outlines is "antifoundational," while it is "foundational" as well. More accurately, it seeks to replace a theory of "foundation by ideas" with a theory of "foundation by functions," or, as Kenneth Burke might have said, with a theory of "ratios," of which that of "endowing" (founding) is itself one.

Halliburton's recollection of the importance of the aesthetic at an early juncture in his essay leads to a reconsideration of "foundational" thought and thus complements the revision of foundationalism carried out by a number of the authors represented in this book. Taken together, their work may be regarded as a large-scale response to the proposition that the rejection of foundationalism must lead to an antitheoretical posture. Collectively, this work shows that the theoretical impulse of contemporary literary theory has been transformed into an inquest of literature by philosophy, and that literature, rather than theory, itself constitutes a philosophical inquest. Philosophy has shown that at some point theory reaches its limit and is eclipsed by (literary) practice. For its part, literature has taught that "philosophy" can no longer be conceived as the enterprise that Descartes, Kant, and Hegel described as the search for totalizing theories of knowledge or of the Absolute. If the essays gathered here may be taken as proof, literature and philosophy are not separable enterprises, and the dialogue that they constitute is not about to end.

I
Philosophy
as/and/of
Literature

What are the boundaries between philosophy and literature? What would it mean to see the philosophical corpus as composed of (literary) texts or, conversely, to take a philosophical interest in literature? At a time when literary theory has widened the notion of "text" to include virtually any cultural artifact, it comes as little surprise to regard philosophy too as a form of writing. And yet such a move stands at a sharp angle to the prevailing thrust of analytical philosophy, which, as Arthur Danto characterizes it, has sought to align itself with the sciences and to dissociate itself from the arts. Philosophers are taught to direct their interest to the arguments of Plato's dialogues or Descartes's *Meditations* (arguments that may, it is suggested, be reduced to logical formulae), which means that the dialogic, meditational, and other "literary" features of these works of philosophy are bound to be dismissed. But would the reinterpretation of philosophy as a form of literature have any significant philosophical impact? This is a question that must necessarily be left suspended until something further can be said about what it might mean to take a text *literarily*, which, as Danto discusses in the final portion of his essay, involves answering questions about the nature of reading. (Cf. Harry Berger, Jr.'s, essay on levels of discourse in Plato's dialogues, which may be taken as a further investigation into what it might mean to view works of philosophy as texts, and also Dalia Judovitz's essay on Plato and Descartes, which takes up the problem of the distinction of philosophy and literature as seen from within two seminal philosophical texts.)

When analytical philosophy has seriously addressed the question of literature, the problem of fictional reference has been its principal concern. In discussing fictional reference here, Danto does not aim at new solutions. His purpose is rather to suggest that philosophical interest in literature is not exhausted in the semantic relationship between literature and the world. Semantic theories of reference succeed, Danto says, at the expense of distorting the world; its candidate referenda are "as bizarre a menagerie of imaginabilia as the fancy of man has framed." They limit literature's possible connections to the world to such (semantic) matters as reference, truth, instantiation, exemplication, and satisfaction, whereas the place of literature could only adequately be measured by some account of its persistent importance to cultures across time. Semantic explanations of literary reference are, moreover, versions of what contemporary literary theory has roundly condemned as the Referential Fallacy. From this view, which Danto wishes to show is both incomplete and extreme, literature does not refer to reality at all, but at best refers only to other literature. Thus, a concept of intertextuality is advanced "according to which a literary work is to be understood, so far as referentiality facilitates understanding, only in terms of other works a given work refers to, so that no one equipped with less than the literary culture of the writer up for interpretation can be certain of having understood the work at all." If analytical philosophy, which centers on the problem of reference, can be said to view the text "vertically," then the intertextualist may correspondingly be said to view the text "horizontally." Danto urges that these axes be supplemented by a third, the axis of the reader, if we are to produce an account that might do justice to the importance of literature in our lives.

Danto's essay is marked throughout by a concern for the relevance of literature, which goes unaccounted in both the analytical-semantic and the intertextual accounts. As he says at one point, "Literature seems to have something important to do with our lives, important enough that the study of it should form an essential part of our educational program." It is the problem of the relevance of literature, over and above the problem of literary reference (seen either semantically or intertextually), which Danto tackles in the final section of his essay. He does so by appealing to the fact that texts may be said in some significant way to be meant for the reader: each reader of a text, each "I" who reads, is activated (some might want to say "engaged") by the text as a *particular* "I," so that each text may be said to be about the reader. Here, the thrust of Danto's argument overlaps with Sartre's in *What Is Literature?* and with the theories of *Rezeptionsaesthetik* and reader-response produced more recently by Wolfgang Iser and Hans Robert Jauss. The novel suggestion of Danto's essay in relation to their work lies in its final appeal to the philosophical text, as modeled on Descartes's *Meditations*, "where the reader is forced to co-meditate with the writer, and to discover in the act of co-meditation his philosophical identity." Considerations such as these introduce questions of authenticity, influence, and originality, which are customarily excluded from analytical philosophy's concerns.

Philosophy as/and/of Literature

Arthur C. Danto

> By displaying what is subjective, the work,
> in its whole presentation, reveals its purpose
> as existing for the subject, for the spectator
> and not on its own account. The spectator
> is, as it were, in it from the beginning, is
> counted in with it, and the work exists only
> for this point, i.e., for the individual
> apprehending it.
> —Hegel, Aesthetik, trans. T. M. Knox

Philosophy seems so singular a crossbreed of art and science that it is somewhat surprising that only lately has it seemed imperative to some that philosophy be viewed as literature: surprising and somewhat alarming. Of course, so much has been enfranchised as literature in recent times that it would have been inevitable that literary theorists should have turned from the comic strip, the movie magazine, the disposable romance—from science fiction, pornography, and graffiti—to the texts of philosophy. This is in virtue of a vastly widened conception of the text which enables us to apply the strategies of hermeneutical interpretation to bus tickets and baggage checks, want ads and weather reports, laundry lists and postage cancellations, savings certificates and address books, medical prescriptions, pastry recipes, olive oil cans, and cognac labels—so why not meditations, examinations, and critiques? Admittedly this is not the exalted sense of literature we have in mind in speaking of philosophy as an art, but even if we retain the normative connotations of the term, there is something disturbing in the fact that this particular face of philosophy should have now become visible enough that we should have been enjoined to treat its texts as a particular literary genre. For after all the imperatives that have governed the transformation of philosophy into a profession have stressed our community with the sciences. Were a kind of semiotic egalitarianism to direct us to regard as so many texts the papers that regularly appear in the *Physical Review*, their literary dimension must seem deeply secondary, as ours has always seemed to us to be; so to treat it suddenly as primary has to be unsettling.

Philosophy-as-literature carries implications in excess of the claim that philosophical texts have at times a degree of literary merit. We take a remote satisfaction that some of us—Strawson, Ryle, and Quine, let alone Santayana, Russell, and James—write distinguished prose, and we would all regard as astute a teacher of English who took pages from any of these as compositional paradigms. Still, our tendency is to regard style, save to the degree that it enhances perspicuity, as adventitious and superfluous to that for the sake of which we finally address these texts: as mere *Farbung*, to use Frege's dismissive term. So to rotate these texts in such a way that the secondary facets catch the light of intellectual concern puts what we regard as the primary facets in shadow; and to acquiesce in the concept of philosophy-as-literature just now seems tacitly to acquiesce in the view that the austere imperatives of philosophy-as-science have lost their energy. Considering what has been happening to texts when treated in recent times, our canon seems suddenly fragile, and it pains the heart to think of them enduring the frivolous sadism of the deconstructionist. But the perspective of philosophy-as-literature is an uncomfortable one for us to occupy, quite apart from these unedifying violations.

Consider the comparable perspective of the Bible-as-literature. Certainly it can be read as such, its poetry and narrative responded to as poetry and narrative, its images appreciated for their power and its moral representations as a kind of drama. But to treat it so is to put at an important distance the Bible considered as a body of revelations, of saving truths and ethical certitudes: a text of which a thinker like Philo could believe that everything in it and nothing outside of it is true. So some fundamental relationship to the book will have changed when it sustains transfer to the curriculum as "living literature." Of course some aspect of its style has from the beginning of its historical importance played a role in biblical epistemology. The language of the Koran is said so to transcend in its beauty the powers of human expressiveness as virtually to guarantee its own claim to have been dictated by an angel and to be, not even metaphorically, the word of God: so its style is taken to be the best evidence for its truth. Biblical writing, by contrast, was taken to be the record of human witnesses, and much of it was so offensive to literary taste that it had to be true. A second-century apologist writes, "When I was giving my most earnest attention to discover the truth I happened to meet with certain barbaric writings ... and I was led to put faith in these by the unpretending cast of the language." Origen, admitting the stylistic inferiority of Scripture by specific comparison with Plato, finds in this evidence that it is exactly the word of God, since if written by men it would be classier: its rudeness is a further weapon for confounding the wise. "However roughly, as regards mere authorship, my book should be got up," Poe has his fictional hero write in the arch foreword to *The Narrative of Arthur Gordon Pym*, "its very uncouthness, if there were any, would give it all the better chance of being received as truth." That plain prose has a better chance of being received as true is a stylistic maxim not unknown in adopting a philosophical diction—think of Moore—but my point is only that there is a profound contrast between taking the Bible as literature and viewing it as the Word, and I would suspect disjoint classes of passages to become prominent depending on which view we take. The remaining music of the Bible must count as small compensation when the truth-claims made on its behalf are no longer felt to be compelling, and something like this contrast arises with philosophy-as-literature set against philosophy-as-truth. On the other hand, it provides an occasion to reflect on how philosophical truth has been regarded if we approach philosophy for the moment as though it were a genre of literature: it enables us to see how we constructed truth when we hadn't thought of ourselves as producing literature. And so we may reflect on the ways in which the dimensions of our professional being are connected.

For a period roughly coeval with that in which philosophy attained professionalization, the canonical literary format has been the professional philosophy paper. Our practice as philosophers consists in reading and writing such papers; in training our students to read and write them; in inviting others to come read us a paper, to which we respond by posing questions which in effect are editorial recommendations, typically incorporated and acknowledged in the first or last footnote of the paper, in which we are exempted from such errors and infelicities as may remain and thanked for our helpful suggestions. The journals in which these papers finally are printed, whatever incidental features useful to the profession at large they may carry, are not otherwise terribly distinct from one another, any more than the papers themselves characteristically are. If, under the constraints of blind review, we black out name and institutional affiliation, there will be no internal evidence of authorial presence, but only a unit of pure philosophy, to the presentation of which the author will have sacrificed all identity. This implies a noble vision of ourselves as vehicles for the transmission of an utterly impersonal philosophical truth, and it implies a vision of philosophical reality as constituted of isolable, difficult, but not finally intractable problems, which, if not altogether soluble in fifteen pages more or less, can be brought closer to resolution in that many pages. The paper is then an impersonal report of limited results for a severely restricted readership, consisting of those who have some use for that result, since they are engaged with the writers of the papers in a collaborative enterprise, building the edifice of philosophical knowledge.

It is perfectly plain that the implied vision of philosophical reality, as well as of the form of life evolved to discover it and the form of literature in which it is suitable to represent it, is closely modeled on the view of reality, life, and literature which composes what Thomas Kuhn has instructed us to think of as normal science. Mastery of the literary form is the key to success in the form of life, bringing tenure and the kind of recognition which consists in being invited to read papers widely and perhaps in attaining the presidency of one or another division of the American Philosophical Association. These practical benefits aside, no one could conceivably be interested in participating in the form of life defined by the literary form in issue, were it not believed that this is the avenue to philosophical truth. It is less obviously a matter of agreement that philosophical truth is defined by this being believed to be the way to find it.

It is not my purpose here to criticize a form of life in which I after all participate, nor to criticize the format of speech and writing that, after all, reinforces the virtues of clarity, brevity, and competence in those compelled to use it. I only mean to emphasize that the concept of philosophical truth and the form of philosophical expression are internally enough related that we may want to recognize that when we turn to other forms we may also be turning to other conceptions of philosophical truth. Consider the way in which we address our predecessors, for example. Much of what I have read on Plato reads much as though he, to whom the whole of subsequent philosophy is said to be so many footnotes, were in effect a footnote to himself and were being coached to get a paper accepted by the *Philosophical Review*. And a good bit of the writing on Descartes is by way of chivying his argumentation into notations we are certain he would have adopted had he lived to appreciate their advantages, since it is now so clear where he went wrong. But in both cases it might at least have been asked whether what either writer was up to can that easily be separated from forms of presentation that may have seemed inevitable, so that the dialogue or meditation flattened into conventional periodical prose might not in the process have lost something central to those ways of writing. The form in which the truth as they understood it must be grasped just might require a form of reading, hence a kind of relationship to those texts, altogether different from that appropriate to a paper, or to what we sometimes refer as a "contribution." And this because something is intended to happen to the reader other than or in addition to being informed. It is after all not simply that the texts may lose something when flattened into papers: life may have lost something when philosophy was flattened out to the production and transmission of papers, noble as the correlative vision is. So addressing philosophy as literature is not meant to stultify the aspiration to philosophical truth so much as to propose a caveat against a reduced concept of reading, just because we realize that more is involved even in contemporary analytical philosophy than merely stating the truth: to get at that kind of truth involves some kind of transformation of the audience, and the acquiescence in a certain form of initiation and life.

I cannot think of a field of writing as fertile as philosophy has been in generating forms of literary expression. Ours has been—to use a partial list I once attempted—a history of dialogues, lecture notes, fragments, poems, examinations, essays, aphorisms, meditations, discourses, hymns, critiques, letters, summae, encyclopedias, testaments, commentaries, investigations, tractatuses, *Vorlesungen*, *Aufbauen*, prolegomena, parerga, pensees, sermons, supplements, confessions, sententiae, inquiries, diaries, outlines, sketches, commonplace books, and, to be self-referential, addresses, and innumerable forms that have no generic identity or that themselves constitute distinct genres: *Holzwege*, Grammatologies, Unscientific Postscripts, Genealogies, Natural Histories, Phenomenologies, and whatever the *World as Will and Idea* may be or the posthumous corpus of Husserl, or the later writings of Derrida, and forgetting the standard sorts of literary forms— novels, plays, and the like—which philosophers have turned to when gifted those ways. One has to ask what cognitive significance is conveyed by the fact that the classic texts of China are typically composed of conversational bits, a question vividly brought home to me when a scholar I respect complained that it is terribly hard to get any propositions out of Chuang Tzu: for this may be the beginning of an understanding of how that elusive sage is to be addressed, and what it means to read him. Responding to a review of *The Realm of Truth* by his amanuensis, Santayana wrote: "It is well that now you can take a holiday: which doesn't exclude the possibility of returning to them with freshness of judgement and apperception. Perhaps then you might not deprecate my purple passages, and might see, which is the historical fact, that they are not applied ornaments but natural growths and *realizations* of the thought moving previously in a limbo of verbal abstractions."

It is arguable that the professional philosophical paper is an evolutionary product, emerging by natural selection from a wild profusion of forms Darwinized into oblivion through maladaptation, stages in the advance of philosophy toward consciousness of its true identity, a rockier road than most. But it is equally arguable that philosophers with really new thoughts have simply had to invent new forms with which to convey them, and that it may be possible that from the perspective of the standard format no way into these other forms, hence no way into these systems or structures of thought, can be found. This claim may be supported, perhaps, by the consideration that pretty much the only way in which literature of the nonphilosophical kind has impinged upon philosophical awareness has been from the perspective of truth-or-falsity. The philosopher would cheerfully consign the entirety of fiction to the domain of falsehood but for the nagging concern that there is a difference between sentences that miss the mark and those that have no mark to miss and are threatened in consequence of prevailing theories of meaning with meaninglessness. Some way must therefore be found for them to have meaning before they can be dismissed as false, and pretty much the entirety of the analytical—and I may as well add the phenomenological—corpus has been massively addressed to the question of fictive reference. Literature sets up obstacles to the passage of semantical theories, which would go through a great deal more easily if literature did not exist. By assessing it against the concept of reference, literature derives what intellectual dignity philosophy can bestow, with the incidental benefit that if literature is merely a matter of skillfully relating words to the world, and if philosophy is literature, literature is meaningful, providing it can show how. And philosophy's way of relating literature to reality may make philosophy-as-literature one with philosophy-as-truth.

This is scarcely the place to tell the chilling tale of fictional reference, in part because it seems not to have reached an end, there being no accepted theory of how it works. But if there ever was an argument for philosophy as a kind of literature, it might be found in the extravagant ontological imagination of semantical theorists in proposing things for fictive terms to designate. Since *Don Quixote* is meaningful, "Don Quixote" must refer, not to some specific addled Spaniard in La Mancha, but to Don Quixote himself, a subsistent entity, which *Don Quixote* can now be about in just the way it would if he were indeed an addled Spaniard in La Mancha. How such subsistent entities confer meaning, or at least how they explain the fact that we grasp it, was never particularly explained, causal transactions between the domain of subsistent entities and existent entities such as we being surely ruled out of question. This problem is aggravated when we purge the universe of fictive beings by waving a quinian wand which changes names into predicates, Don Quixote becoming the x that quixotizes all over the y that lamanchas. The prodigality complained of in manufacturing entities to order is evidently unnoticed when it comes to manufacturing predicates to order, and the change from *Gegenstände* to *Gedanke* leaves the question of meaning and its being grasped about as dark as ever. Nor is the matter especially mitigated when we allow *Don Quixote* to pick a possible world to be about, for the relationship of it to ours and finally to us remains as obscure as that between Don Quixote and us when he was a homeless wraith, an ontological ghost wandering in worlds undreamt of by poets.

From this point of view Professor Goodman's elegant theory of secondary extensions is particularly welcome, first from the perspective of ontology, since secondary extensions are composed of things we can put our hands on, like inscriptions, and second from the point of view of epistemology, since pictures play a prominent part in the secondary extension of a term and we in fact begin our adventures into literature with picture books. It does on the other hand throw an immense semantical burden on illustrated editions and the like and tangles us in puzzles of its own, since the set of pictures ostensibly of the same thing may look so little alike that we may have severe doubts as to what their subject would look like if it existed, while pictures of altogether different subjects may look so alike that we could not tell them apart were they to be real. Whether we must ascend to tertiary extensions and beyond, and how these would solve our further problems, are matters not to be taken up here, for the question I want to raise is why, whichever of these theories is true, we, as readers, should have the slightest interest in *Don Quixote* if what it is about is an unactualized thin man in a region of being I would have no reason to know about save for the interventions of semantical theory: or if it were about the x that quixotizes (there being none) or a set of possible worlds other than my own, or primarily about nothing but secondarily about such things as a set of engravings by Gustave Doré.

I raise the question because literature, certainly in its greatest exemplars, seems to have something important to do with our lives, important enough that the study of it should form an essential part of our educational program, and this is utterly unexplained if its meaning is a matter of its reference, and if its candidate referenda are as bizarre a menagerie of imaginabilia as the fancy of man has framed. And it may be that when we show the kind of connection there is, there will not be a problem of the sort to which semantical theory has been so elaborate a response. Well, it may be said, this might simply remove literature from the sphere of philosophical concern, a welcome enough removal but for the fact that it might remove philosophy itself from the domain of philosophical concern if philosophy itself is literature. And my insinuation has been that the sorts of things philosophy has laid down to connect literature in order to give it meaning—*Gegenstände*, intensions, fictive worlds—are themselves as much in need of ontological redemption as the beings to whose rescue they were enlisted: Don Quixote, Mr. Pickwick, Gandolf the Grey. To believe we can save fiction by means of fiction is one of the endearing innocences of a discipline that takes pride in what it likes to think is its skeptical circumspection.

Semantical theory does the best it can in striving to connect literature to the world through what after all are the only kinds of connections it understands: reference, truth, instantiation, exemplification, satisfaction, and the like. If this means distorting the universe in order that it can receive literary representations, this has never been reckoned a high price for philosophy to pay but a creative opportunity, and it remains to the credit of this enterprise that it at least believes *some* connection between literature and the world is required. In this it contrasts with literary theory as currently practiced, which impugns philosophical preoccupations with semantical ligatures as but a further instance of what one leading theoretician dismisses as the Referential Fallacy. Literature does not refer at all to reality, according to this view, but at best to other literature, and a concept of *intertextuality* is advanced according to which a literary work is to be understood, so far as referentiality facilitates understanding, only in terms of other works a given work refers to, so that no one equipped with less than the literary culture of the writer of a work up for interpretation can be certain of having understood the work at all. There is certainly something to this view if Northrop Frye is correct in claiming of Blake's line "O Earth, O Earth return" that "though it contains only five words and only three different words"—five tokens and three types, as we might more briskly say—"it contains also about seven direct allusions to the Bible." The author of the Referential Fallacy, whom I prefer for somewhat complex reasons to refer to simply as R (he after all speaks for his profession) assures us that "the poetic text is self-sufficient." But "if there is external reference, it is not to reality—far from it! Any such reference is to other texts." This extreme view merits some examination, if only for its vivid opposition to the standard philosophical view.

Consider one of his examples, the last line of Wordsworth's poem *Written in March*, which goes, "Small clouds are sailing,/Blue skies prevailing,/The rain is over and done." This line, together with the title, might lead the reader to suppose that the poem refers to the end of winter and expresses the poet's gratitude that spring has come at last— but this easy reading is, according to R, quite seriously and fallaciously wrong: it refers in fact to *The Song of Songs*, from which Wordsworth's line is taken verbatim, and is in fact a fragment of the biblical line that begins "For lo! The winter is past . . ." Now it can hardly be doubted that Wordsworth knew *The Song of Songs*, and it is certain that literary scholarship, in explaining the sources of the poem, will refer to it as an ultimate source for the last line. Perhaps every line or phrase in a poem may be explained with reference to something in the literary culture of the writer. But not every literary effect necessarily refers to its causes, and there is a considerable difference between understanding a poem, which may require understanding its references when it makes them, and understanding the provenances of a poem, which is quite another matter: it is specialist knowledge, and likely incidental to understanding a poem.

Let me offer an illustration from another art, in part to make my argument more general, in part to confirm a claim about pictorial semantics. Raphael's beautiful *Madonna della sedia* is composed within a circular frame—a *tondo*—not, as Gombrich points out, because Raphael one day seized a handy barrelhead in order to paint an innkeeper's daughter who charmed him, together with her pretty child, as Madonna and Infant, which is the tour guide's lovely explanation; but rather because, like many of his contemporaries, Raphael was excited by some recently exhibited drawings of Leonardo, among them some circular compositions. Every painter in the region would have known about those drawings, and hence the provenance of Raphael's painting, but for all that Raphael was not referring to the drawings that inspired him. By contrast, the American painter Benjamin West did a portrait of his wife and son in *tondo* form, her garment the garment of Raphael's Madonna, not as a copy of but in *reference to* Raphael's painting. It was an exceedingly pretentious reference, depicting his wife as Madonna, his child as the Baby Jesus, *his* painting as *The madonna della sedia*, and himself as Raphael. But to understand the painting is to understand those allusions, for he is representing his family *as* the Holy Pair *as* depicted by Raphael, and a very self-exalting metaphor is being transacted. (What a humiliation to have had this hopeful vision deaccessioned by the Reynolds's collection in exchange for a merely typical Thomas Cole!)

It was a triumph of art historical scholarship to demonstrate the unmistakable use made by Manet of an arrangement of figures in an engraving by Marcantonio Raimondi in setting the figures in his *Déjeuner sur l'herbe*. This by no means excludes the possibility, or rather the fact, that Manet was representing friends of his, wits and demimondaines, enjoying an elegant outing. Of course it is a different painting depending upon whether he was referring to or merely using Raimondi's work. If he was referring to it, then his subject is *that* outing *as* a feast of the gods, which is the subject of the original engraving. Raimondi was the most famous engraver of his age (as well as a notorious forger), but in Manet's world he was doubtless too obscure for such an allusion to be made, by contrast perhaps with biblical references in Wordsworth's world; and probably obviousness is a condition of allusion as banality is a condition of validity in the enthymeme. But even so Manet's use of that engraving must be distinguished from a use made by the American painter John Trumbull, in his famous portrait of General Washington with his horse, of a certain preexisting form of horse-representation. Far from being the finely observed depiction of Washington's elegant steed, Washington's horse, as shown, is but one in a long historical sequence of similar horses which Leo Steinberg has traced back to a Roman cameo, and which probably could be traced even farther. Still, it is Washington with his horse that is being referred to, and not any member of this series, each of which but conforms to a pattern. The pattern, which may be an example of what Gombrich speaks of as a *schema*, is a very satisfactory way of representing horses, which are, as we know, very difficult to observe—until Muybridge nobody knew whether all four legs were altogether off the ground in the gallop—and yields up a kind of representational a priori of a sort whose narrative and lyrical counterparts may be found in literature; and, though this is not my topic, there may be profound similarities to scientific representations as well.

In all these cases and countless others, reference to the world works together with references to other art, when there are such references, to make a complex representation; so why should or must it be different in the case of Wordsworth? R writes thus: "The key word—*winter*—absent from Wordsworth, is the matrix penetrating every Spring detail in the poem . . . now perceived as the converse of an image that has been effaced, so that the poem is not a direct depiction of reality, but a negative version of a latent text on the opposite of Spring." This is the kind of hermeneutic contortion that earns interpreters of literature distinguished chairs in universities—the kind that argue, for example, that *Hamlet* is a negative version of a latent text about Fortinbras, the *true* hero of the play, which is perceived now as comedy rather than tragedy, since the hero is alive at the end, thus making Shakespeare a clever forerunner of Tom Stoppard. But my concern is not to argue with the interpretation but with the "so" to which R is not entitled: a proper interpretation would have to show why Wordsworth referred to the season through the medium of a biblical allusion if in fact it was an allusion and not a cliché of the sort that has simply entered language the way so much of *Hamlet* has that a student is said to have criticized it for being too full of clichés, though a pretty exciting story. And what of *The Song of Songs* itself, if poetry: is it about winter, or, to use the other option offered us, altogether self-contained?

In a famous letter to his mistress, Louise Colet, Flaubert lays out his own ideal as an artist: "What I should like to write is a book about nothing, a book dependent upon nothing external, which would be held together by the internal strength of its style, just as the earth, suspended in the void, depends upon nothing external for its support: a book which would have almost no subject, or at least in which the subject would be invisible, if such a thing is possible." Flaubert's astronomy is appalling, and if R is right he could not have failed of his purpose, all literature, just so far as it is literature, being about nothing. Or at best it is about other literature, work holding work in referential orbit, to give Flaubert a happier physical metaphor, but basically untethered to reality. The question is, what considerations recommend the guaranteed irrelevancy of literature to life?

"In everyday language," the author of the Referential Fallacy writes, "words seem to refer vertically, each to the reality it seems to render, like the labels on a barrelhead, each a semantic unit, while in literature the unit of meaning is the text itself. The reciprocal effect of its words on one another, as members of a finite network, replaces the vertical semantical relationship with a lateral one, forged along the written line, tending to cancel the dictionary meanings of the words."

Now I want to applaud the concept of a text as a network of reciprocal effects. Not original with R, of course, it has entered our world from European sources, making an immense impact upon literary theorists while leaving philosophy so far untouched. I feel that were the concept of the text to become as central in analytical philosophy as the sentence has been since Frege gave it primacy, or as the term has been since Aristotle, a vast world for philosophical research will have opened up. For the concept of the text is considerably wider than literary texts alone. It applies to musical compositions and to architectural structures, art forms whose referentiality has been in occasional question, and to personalities, whole lives in the biographical sense of the term, families, villages, cultures, things for which the question of referentiality has hardly been raised at all. And the expression "a network of reciprocal effects" will come to be exchanged for a class of relationships as various as and perhaps as important as those that bind sentences into arguments and that have been so massively explored in contemporary philosophical thought. Even so, it is altogether compatible with being united through a network of reciprocal effects that a literary work should refer, as it were extratextually, though the reference may be complicated as much by intra- as by intertextual references. The Prelude and Finale of *Middlemarch* refer reciprocally, as well as to the novel they frame, and both refer or allude to Saint Theresa, herself not a text save in so wide a sense as to make R's theory timid and disappointing. They refer to her to provide a metaphor for Dorothea Brooks—Miss Brooks as erotic ascetic perhaps—proving that her character has remained constant through two marriages, and saying finally something deep about the narrow space there after all is for being different from what we are.

But this goes well beyond what philosophers have wanted to say in supposing *Middlemarch* refers, say, to a world of its own or to some fleshless subsistent woman, Dorothea Brooks. And it goes well beyond what R will allow, who leaves us with the same question philosophical discussions of fictional reference did, namely why should we be interested in *Middlemarch*? Why, since not ourselves literary scholars, should we concern ourselves with these intricate networks of reciprocal effects? "Because they are there" was not even a good reason for climbing mountains, but I am struck by the fact that philosophers seem only to understand vertical references and literary theorists, if R is right, only horizontal ones. On this coordinate scheme it is difficult to locate literature in the plane of human concern at all. Clearly we need a z-coordinate; we must open a dimension of reference neither vertical nor horizontal reference quite reveals, if we are to get an answer.

"The distinction between historian and poet is not in the one writing prose and the other verse," Aristotle writes, helpfully as always. "You might put the work of Herodotus into verse and it would still be a species of history." Though he neglects the reverse possibility, I take Aristotle to mean that one ought to be unable to tell by mere examination of a text whether it is poetry or something else, which gives my own question an immediate philosophical structure. The form of a philosophical question is given—I would venture to say always but lack an immediate proof—when indiscriminable pairs with nevertheless distinct ontological locations may be found or imagined found, and we then must make plain in what the difference consists or could consist. The classical case is matching dream experience with waking experience in such a way that, as Descartes required, nothing internal to either mode of experience will serve as differentiating criterion. So whatever internal criterion we in fact, and, as it happens, pre-analytically, employ will be irrelevant to the solution of the problem, for example, that dreams are vague and incoherent. For dreams may be imagined, and possibly had, which are as like waking experience as we require to void the criterion. So the difference must come in at right angles to the plane of what we experience, and philosophy here consists in saying what it can be. Kant discovers the same thing in moral theory, since he imagines it possible that a set of actions should perfectly conform to principle and yet have no moral worth, because that requires a different relationship to those principles than mere conformity, and outward observation cannot settle the matter. And Adeimanthus furnishes the stunning example that generates the *Republic*, that of a perfectly just man whose behavior is indiscriminable from that of a man perfectly unjust: the example requires that justice be orthogonal to conduct, and entails as uniquely possible the kind of theory Plato gives us. Other examples lie ready to hand. The present state of the world is compatible with the world being any age at all, including five minutes old, and nothing on the surface of the world will arbitrate without begging the question. A mere bodily movement and a basic action might appear exactly alike, just as what we take to be an expression of a feeling may be but a kind of rictus. Nothing open to observation discriminates a pair of connected events, to use Hume's distinction, from a pair merely conjoined. And in my own investigations into the philosophy of art, I have benefited immensely from Duchamp's discovery that nothing the eye can reveal will arbitrate the difference between a work of art and a mere real thing that resembles it in every outward particular. So any proposed distinction based upon perceptual differences, even in the visual arts, will have proved, as with the Linnaean system in botany, to be artificial, however useful in practice. Duchamp consigned all past theories to oblivion by proving that the problem was philosophical. And here is Aristotle, telling us that the difference between poetry and history does not lie on the surfaces of texts, and that distinguishing them is not an ordinary matter of classification but a philosophical matter of explanation.

It is indeed not at all difficult to imagine two quite sustained pieces of writing which belong to relevantly distinct genres, without there being so much difference as a semicolon. I once imagined a pair of indiscriminable texts, one a novel, one a piece of history. My colleague Stern, suppose, comes across an archive containing the papers of a Polish noblewoman of the last century, who died, characteristically, in a convent. Incredibly, she was the mistress of Talleyrand, Metternich, the younger Garibaldi, Jeremy Bentham, Eugène Delacroix, Frédéric Chopin, and Czar Nicholas of Russia, though the great loves of her life were George Sand and the nubile Sarah Bernhardt. Published by Viking, it wins the Pulitzer Prize in history in the same year as a novel with exactly the same name wins it in literature—*Maria Mazurka, Mistress to Genius*. The novel was written by Erica Jong, who was inspired to invent a heroine who dies appropriately in a convent, but who in her time had been the mistress of Talleyrand, Metternich, the younger Garibaldi, Jeremy Bentham, Eugène Delacroix, Frédéric Chopin, and Czar Nicholas of Russia, though the great loves of her life were George Sand and the nubile Sarah Bernhardt. Jong's novel, unfortunately, is too improbable, has too many characters, sprawls all over the place, as Jong is wont to do these days, and bears critical comparison with Stern's marvelous book, which manages to keep track of all its characters, is tightly regimented given the diversity of materials, and contains not a fact in excess. So Jong's book, to the despair of the author and Random House, is soon remaindered, and for $2.98 you can get a lot of pages which cannot be told apart from Stern's book, on special at $19.99 through the History Book Club—though none of Stern's readers would be caught dead reading a mere novel. Stern's book, of course, refers vertically, while Jong's, being a novel, is a network of reciprocal effects, and self-sustained or nearly so, characterized only by horizontal reference. I realize I am slipping out of philosophy into literature, but the point is that whatever is to mark the difference must survive examples such as these.

Aristotle's famous suggestion, of course, is that "poetry is something more philosophical and of graver import than history, since its statements are of the nature of universals, whereas those of history are singular." It is plain that this difference is not registered grammatically or syntactically, if the example just constructed is possible, and in the Aristotelian spirit. So there must be a way in which Jong's book, for all its failings, is universal, and in which Stern's book, splendid as it is as historiography, remains for just that reason singular—about that specific woman in just those steamy liaisons. On the other hand, there must be some way in which Jong's book, if universal and hence more philosophical than Stern's, is not quite so philosophical as philosophy itself is. Otherwise the problem of construing philosophy as a form of literature would be solved at the cost of so widening philosophy, since nothing could be more philosophical than it, as to compass whatever Aristotle would consider poetry. In whatever way philosophy is to be literature, if it is to be literature at all, it must respect whatever differences there may be with literature, which is not philosophy, however necessarily philosophical it has to be in order to be distinguished from mere history.

My own view is that philosophy wants to be more than universal; it wants necessity as well: truth for all the worlds that are possible. In this respect it contrasts with history, or for that matter with science, concerned with the truths of just this particular, uniquely actual world, and happy if it can achieve that much. My contention here has been that philosophical semantics renders literature true of possible worlds, to lapse into the vernacular, in such a way that it would be history for any of them if actual instead of ours. *Gulliver's Travels* would just be anthropology for a world in which there were Lilliputians instead of Melanesians. This, I am afraid, is very close to Aristotle's own view, history dealing, according to him, with the thing that has been, while poetry is concerned with "a kind of thing that might be." And that sounds too much like being true of a possible world for me to be comfortable with it as an analysis. I nevertheless believe that literature has a kind of universality worth considering, different from this, and I shall now try to say what it is in my own way, recognizing that if philosophy is also literature, it might have to be universal and possibly even necessary in two kinds of ways.

The thought I want to advance is that literature is not universal in the sense of being about every possible world insofar as possible, as philosophy in its nonliterary dimension aspires to be, nor about what may happen to be the case in just this particular world, as history, taken in this respect as exemplificatory science, aspires to be, but rather about each reader who experiences it. It is not, of course, about its readers as a book about reading is, which happens incidentally to be about its readers just as a subclass of its subject, but rather in the way in which, though you will look for him in vain, Benjamin West's pretentious family portrait is about him. He does not show himself in the manner of Velásquez in Las Meninas, but still, the painting is about Benjamin West *as* Raphael *as* painter of the Holy Family, through an allusive and metaphoric identification: he informs the work as a kind of *dieu caché*. A literary work is about its readers in this metaphoric and allusive way, in an exact mirror image of the way West's painting is about him. In Hegel's wonderful thought, the work exists for the spectator and not on its own account: it exists, as he says, only for the individual apprehending it, so that the apprehension completes the work and gives it final substance. The difficult claim I am making can be put somewhat formally as follows: the usual analysis of universality is that $(x)Fx$ is via the mechanisms of natural deduction equivalent to a conjunction of all the values on x, true in the event each is F. The universality of literary reference is only that it is about each individual that reads the text at the moment that individual reads it, and it contains an implied indexical. Each work is about the "I" that reads the text, identifying himself not with the implied reader for whom the implied narrator writes but with the actual subject of the text in such a way that each work becomes a metaphor for each reader: perhaps the same metaphor for each.

It is a metaphor, of course, in part because it is literally false that I am Achilles, or Leopold Bloom, or Anna or Oedipus or King Lear or Hyacinth Robinson or Strether or Lady Glencora; or a man hounded by an abstract bureaucracy because of an unspecified or suspected accusation; or the sexual slave O; or the raft rider responsible to a moral being whom an unspeakable nation refuses to countenance as a man; or the obsessive narrator of the violence of my ancestors, which is my own violence, since their story is in the end my story; or one who stands to Jay Gatsby as Jay Gatz stood to the same dream as mine of "love, accomplishment, beauty, elegance, wealth" (which is a list I just found in a marvelous story by Gail Godwin). It is literature when, for each reader I, I is the subject of the story. The work finds it subject only when read.

Because of this immediacy of identification, it is natural to think, as theorists from Hamlet onward have done, of literature as a kind of mirror, not simply in the sense of rendering an external reality, but as giving me to myself for each self peering into it, showing each of us something inaccessible without mirrors, namely that each has an external aspect and what that external aspect is. Each work of literature shows in this sense an aspect we would not know was ours without benefit of that mirror: each discovers—in the eighteenth-century meaning of the term—an unguessed dimension of the self. It is a mirror less in passively returning an image than in transforming the self-consciousness of the reader who in virtue of identifying with the image recognizes what he is. Literature is in this sense transfigurative, and in a way that cuts across the distinction between fiction and truth. There are metaphors for every life in Herodotus and Gibbon.

The great paradigm for such transfiguration must be Don Quixote, Cervantes having to be credited not only with the invention of the novel but with discovering the perversion of its philosophy. Quixote is transformed, through reading romances, into an errant knight while his world is transformed into one of knightly opportunities, wenches turning into virgins and innkeepers into kings, nags into steeds and windmills into monsters. Yet it is a perversion of the relationship between reader and romance because Quixote's own sense of his identity was so antecedently weak that he failed to retain it through the transformation, and his own sense of reality was so weak that he lost his grip on the difference between literature and life. Or he read poetry as though it were history, so not philosophical but particular. He would be like those who, through reading Descartes, seriously come to believe that "they are kings while they are paupers, that they are clothed in gold and purple while they are naked; or imagine that their head is made of clay or that they are gourds, or that their bodies are glass." Or that there is an Evil Genius, or that there is no world or that the belief in material objects is misguided. These are failures to distinguish philosophy from life, whose counterpart in Cervantes induces an illusion so powerful that the distinction is lost: which may be a formula for happiness—living in an illusion—making *Don Quixote* genuinely comic.

I have encountered the tragic obverse of this, where one's sense of self is strong but one's sense of reality has become desperate through literature having thrown a bitter discrepancy into the relationship between the two. I knew a lady who discovered the truth from Proust's novel that she really was the Dutchess of Guermantes, as unavailing, in her case, unfortunately, as the Prince's knowledge of who he really is, when a spell has nevertheless required that he live in the investitures of a frog. *Her* land was Combray and the Faubourg St. Germain, an air of wit and exquisite behavior and perfect taste—not the Upper West Side, falling plaster, children with colds, a distracted husband, never enough money, and nobody who understood. Her moments of happiness came when reality on occasion agreed to cooperate with metaphor, when she could coincide with an alien grace, too ephemeral alas, leaving her with the dishes to clear and the bills to pay and a terrible exhaustion. Unlike Quixote, her illusions were never strong enough to swamp reality, only in a sense to poison it; and while she maintained that her greatest happiness consisted in reading Proust, in truth he only caused her anguish.

I should like to place the theorist R alongside these two readers of fiction, one of whom happens to be in fiction as well, since R himself could be a fictional being and the Referential Fallacy a fiction within a fiction, both of them created by me. In fact both the theorist and article are real. R is a man of great pride and passion, who has lived through times of extremity and has known, as much as anyone I know has known, the defining tribulations of the full human life. Surely he cannot have been drawn to literature simply to be a reader of literature through literature to literature, unless, like the professor in Mann's *Disorder and Early Sorrow*, he meant to draw a circle in order to exclude life. If it were a piece of literature, the Referential Fallacy would offer a metaphor of extreme dislocation, putting life as a whole beyond the range of reference, displaying an existence lived out in an infinite windowless library, where book sends us to book in a network of reciprocal relationships the reader can inhabit like a spider. Imagine that it had been written by Borges, whose life was almost like that, and included in *Ficciones!* But it in fact is by R and it gives us a misanalysis rather than a metaphor; it refers vertically to readers whose relationship to texts it gets wrong, rather than to the reader of the text whose life it metaphorically depicts. If this address were art, it would be a mirror only for R, who seeing his own image reflected back, might find his consciousness entrapped and mend his thought.

R's text, which I have sought to view once as literature and once as science, illustrates, since it is about reading, the two ways in which a text might refer to readers, and with these two modes of reference in mind, we may return to philosophy as literature, not by way of treating philosophical texts as literature, which would be merely a conceit if they were not that, as R's text is not that, but by way rather of displaying one of the ways in which philosophy really does relate to life. *One of the ways.* There is a celebrated deconstructionist text that holds that philosophy must be treated as a genre of literature because it is ineluctably metaphoric, when in fact it only becomes interestingly metaphoric when it is first decided to treat it as literature, and that text begs just the question it has been taken by its enthusiasts to have settled. Metaphors have in common with texts as such that they do not necessarily wear their metaphoricity on their surfaces, and what looks like an image may really be a structural hypothesis of how a reality we heretofore lacked words for is to be understood. One mark of metaphors is their ineliminability, a feature that makes them para-intensional if not fully intensional. But in philosophical as in scientific writing, what looks like a metaphor in the beginning ends as a fact, and it may be eliminated in favor of a technical term, as Locke begins with the natural light—with "the candle within us"—and ends with the technical term *intuition.* So what appear to be metaphors, what have been taken by deconstructionists to be metaphors, belong to philosophy as science, rather than to philosophy as literature.

There is a view abroad, credited to Nietzsche, that in metaphor we have the growing edge of language, assimilating by its means the unknown to the known, where the latter must originally have been metaphor now grown cold and desiccated and taken for fact. It is difficult to understand how, on its own view, this process got started, but I think it must be appreciated as a transvaluational and necessarily paradoxical view, like saying that the first shall be last or that the meek shall inherit the earth, giving poetry the place science has presumed was its own. But it is a view lent credibility by the fact that structural hypotheses look enough like metaphors to be taken for metaphors by theorists resolved to view an activity like philosophy as largely if not altogether metaphorical. It is my own thought that philosophical texts are kept alive as metaphors when they have long since stopped seeming plausible as structural hypotheses, a tribute to their vivacity and power, their status as literature being a consolation prize for failing to be true. But this is to overlook the way in which philosophy functions as literature does, not in the sense of extravagant verbal artifacts, but as engaging with readers in search of that sort of universality I have supposed to characterize literary reference: as being about the reader at the moment of reading through the process of reading. We read them as literature in this sense because, as Hegel said, they exist for the reader who is "in them from the beginning." The texts require the act of reading in order to be complete, and it is as readers of a certain type that philosophical texts address us all. The wild variety of philosophical texts implies a correspondingly wild variety of possible kinds of readers, and hence of theories of what we are in the dimension of the reading. And each such text finds a kind of ontological proof of its claims through the fact that it can be read in the way it requires.

The most conspicuous example of such a text is obliged to be the *Meditations*, where the reader is forced to co-meditate with the writer and to discover in the act of co-meditation his philosophical identity: he must be the kind of individual the text requires if he can read it, and the text must be true if it can be read. He finds himself there, since he was in it from the beginning. How astonishing I find it that precisely those who insist that philosophy is merely a genre of literature offer readings of Descartes so external that the possibility of their being universal in the way literature demands is excluded from the outset. To treat philosophical texts after the manner of Derrida, simply as networks of reciprocal relationships, is precisely to put them at a distance from their readers so intraversable as to make it impossible that they be about us in the way literature requires, if my conjecture is correct. They become simply artifacts made of words, with no references save internal ones or incidental external ones. And reading them becomes external, as though they had nothing to do with us, were merely there, intricately wrought composites of logical lacework, puzzling and pretty and pointless. The history of philosophy is then like a museum of costumes we forget were meant to be worn.

The variety of philosophical texts, then, subtend a variety of philosophical anthropologies, and though each text is about the reader of it and so is a piece of literature by that criterion, it does not offer a metaphor but a truth internally related to the reading of it. Even now when textual innovativeness has abated in philosophy and all texts are pretty much alike, so much so that the address to the reader has thinned almost to nothingness, the reader in the act of reading exercises some control over what the text says, since what the text says must be compatible with its being read. A text, thus, that set out to prove the impossibility of reading would have a paradox of sorts on its hands. Less flagrantly, there are texts in philosophy, current reading among us, which if true would entail their own logical illegibility. It is inconceivable that philosophers would have fallen into such incoherences if they had not, as it were, forgotten that their texts, in addition to being representations of a kind of reality, were things to be *read*. We pay a price for forgetting this in the current style of writing, since it enables us to depict worlds in which readers cannot fit.

The propensity to overlook the reader goes hand in hand with the propensity to leave beings of the sort readers exemplify outside the world the text describes. Contemporary philosophies of mind, language, humanity, may be striking examples of an oversight encouraged by a view of philosophical writing which makes the reader ontologically weightless, a sort of disembodied professional conscience. Science, often and perhaps typically, can get away with this, largely because, even when about its readers, is not about them as readers and so lacks the internal connection philosophical texts demand because they are about their readers *as* readers. So philosophy is literature in that among its truth conditions are those connected with being read, and reading those texts is supposed then to reveal us for what we are in virtue of our reading. This revelation is not metaphorical, however, which is why I cannot finally acquiesce in the thought that philosophy is literature. It continues to aim at truth, but when false, seriously false, it is often also so fascinatingly false as to retain a kind of perpetual vitality as a metaphor. It is this that makes our history so impossible to relinquish, since the power is always there, and the texts engage us when we read them vitally as readers whose philosophical portraits materialize about us as we enter that place that awaited us from the beginning.

2
Philosophy and Poetry: The Difference between Them in Plato and Descartes

In Arthur Danto's essay on the relations between philosophy and literature one can see how philosophy has, in some of its modes, from time to time been guilty of regarding literature as superfluous: the "literary" dimension of a philosophical text is regarded as expendable; it may be eliminated without jeopardizing the philosophical content (the arguments) of the text. This is an extension of the related view, to which Danto also replies, which regards literature itself as superfluous within the discourse of human culture. In some celebrated works, however, the relations between philosophy and literature have been considerably more strained than this. Perhaps the most famous is Plato's *Republic,* in which the constitution of the new state (which, as Dalia Judovitz says, "heralds the coincidence of the order of philosophy and the order of the *polis*") requires the exclusion of the poets. In Plato's view, this is because poets speak about things they do not know. The exclusion of poetry is both possible and necessary by virtue of the definition of knowledge as it takes shape in the *Republic,* the *Ion,* and *Theaetetus:* "As a form of knowledge, poetry will also be shown to lack a certain pragmatic character, since its only model of acquisition and communication can be glimpsed through inspiration. Thus poetry is presented as a form of knowledge that one has without possessing it."

The Platonic effort to distinguish philosophical knowledge is the first systematic attempt to constitute philosophy in terms of its absolute difference in relation to all other domains of knowledge, including poetry, painting, and music. It functions centrally in the foundation of philosophy as an epistemological discourse. At the same time, it may be said to contribute to the foundation that is attempted again in Descartes and in Kant. (In my essay on romantic responses to Kant, I discuss some ways in which romantic thinkers tried to reclaim the philosophical status of the aesthetic domains; this may be regarded as part of their more general will to describe our relationship to the world as founded on something other than epistemology.)

Drawing on insights first framed by Hans-Georg Gadamer, Judovitz goes on to explain how the displacement of poetry by philosophy requires not only the elimination of poetry but, as Gadamer says, "an attack on the foundations of Greek culture and on the inheritance bequeathed to us by Greek history." Insofar as Plato's imaginary foundation of the ideal state is guided by ethical and moral concerns, poetry must be excluded on the grounds that it proposes an ethos that is untranslatable into praxis. Insofar as poets lay claims to knowledge, their knowledge is something that they have but do not possess. In contrast, Plato lays the groundwork for epistemology in his insistence that knowledge involve the mastery of a field as a general domain, not simply mastery of objects within that field. As modeled in the Platonic dialogues, it is the philosopher, not the poet, who possesses this kind of knowledge. With this we have a description of Plato's constitution of philosophy as a separate discourse and of the establishment of epistemology as "first philosophy." The model of knowledge at work in the dialogues suggests itself as superior to knowledge gained through the visual arts, which stands conceptually for representations. Yet in order for this model to work, one has to grant the instrumental nature of the dialogues as well as their literary or "poetic" effects—effects Plato would otherwise ignore: "The denunciation of poetry is supplemented by the recognition of the instrumental character of the dialogue as a genre, and of the intervention of style that dissimulates the activity of representation by conceiving it in purely instrumental terms, which are discarded like the skin of arguments." In a phrase that links her essay with Danto's concern for the reader of the text, and with Harry Berger, Jr.'s, study of levels of discourse in the Platonic texts, Judovitz says, "Speaking from inside the body of the dialogue—and thus by extension, the body of the reader—these figures act upon him and turn him into a ventriloquist. Alcibiades, in the Platonic text, speaks about Socrates' speech and turns him into a ventriloquist."

The turn from Plato to Descartes may seem precipitous; however, there are similarities linking them that, as Judovitz points out, warrant the comparison. Like Plato, Descartes was concerned with the absolute differentiation of philosophical discourse, but in the case of Descartes this differentiation requires a break not from poetry but from philosophy itself; specifically, it is a break of philosophy from its past. Whereas Plato regards poetry and the visual arts as unphilosophical,

Descartes similarly reduces the rest of philosophy and consigns it to the province of the merely "historical." The specifically philosophical pretension of the "I" of the *Meditations* is registered, for example, by its unwillingness to accept any knowledge but that which might be self-certifying. Here Descartes resembles Plato in his effort to constitute philosophy as a system, which for Descartes means the establishment of a system of representations grounded by his new invention, the subject. In order for the Cartesian project to succeed, however, the "I" of the *Meditations* must also succeed in acting as a model and in engaging every reader of the Cartesian text.

Judovitz focuses in the conclusion of her essay on this paradoxical exclusion of the literary from the Cartesian conception of philosophy—paradoxical because the Cartesian texts so manifestly work by virtue of literary figures and effects: "The disappearance of literature from its oppositional position to philosophy [in Descartes] in no way means that this conflict has been overcome, for this difference still marks its character. The qustion of style that haunts the very definition of literature also haunts the definition of philosophy." However, in Judovitz's view, philosophical discourse is not constituted so much by any particular style but rather by its implicit or explicit opposition to the very notion of style which so problematically defines literature.

Philosophy and Poetry: *Dalia Judovitz*
The Difference
between Them in
Plato and Descartes

Philosophy and poetry, Plato tells us in the *Republic* (bk. 10), have a very "old quarrel."[1] Plato alludes to this conflict after he has actually excluded poetry and poets from his republic, only to suggest that this longstanding enmity is not reflected in his own criticism. And yet, poetry, that "bitch that growls and snarls at her master," is consistently and systematically under attack throughout the Platonic dialogues.[2] The radical separation and exclusion by philosophy of poetry, its provocative and paradoxical character, cannot merely be reduced to a thematics of rivalry. The opposition that Plato sets up between the two is more than a rhetorical device intended to show off the merits and ultimate superiority of philosophical discourse. Rather, Plato's critique of poetry corresponds to his attempt to differentiate finally between philosophical and poetic discourses, with the aim of establishing philosophy as the discourse of knowledge. Moreover, the exclusion of poetry is also paradigmatic of the constitution of the Republic itself. Hans-Georg Gadamer contends that Plato's critique of poetry can be understood "only within the total refounding of the new state in words of philosophy."[3] In other words, the institutionalization of philosophical discourse as the only proper discipline of knowledge must be understood in the context of the foundation of the institution, par excellence, of Plato's new state. The latter heralds the coincidence of the order of philosophy and the order of the city-state (*polis*), that of theory and praxis.

The effort to distinguish philosophical knowledge from all other ways of knowing—poetry, painting, and music—becomes the first systematic effort to define philosophy in an absolute sense: as the "mark of differentness" (to use Plato's term) from all other domains. It is my contention that this conflict (*diaphora,* or difference) can be shown to function as the constitutive operation in the foundation of philosophy as a metaphysical discourse. But this mark of absolute difference, which Plato seeks to establish between philosophy and all the other arts, is itself the trace of a series of differential operations that reinscribe and retrace the figure of philosophical discourse. However, the hierarchical exclusion, difference, and domination of poetry by philosophy in the Platonic text represses the very rhetorical and discursive structures that define it.

In Descartes's works, the Platonic conflict between philosophy and literature becomes a conflict within philosophy itself. In seeking to found a new philosophical language based on mathematics, Descartes rejects (in *Rules for the Direction of the Mind* and in *Discourse on the Method*) not only literature but also all philosophy because of its inability to attain certitude. The difference that Plato sought to establish between philosophy and literature will be shown to be paradigmatic of the *difference operated by epistemology* put forth by Descartes in his effort to define a new or modern philosophy. The initial expulsion of poetry from the *Republic* is echoed by Descartes's radical exclusion of all previous philosophical authors. In the *Rules,* Descartes remarks that his knowledge based on criteria of certitude reduces previous philosophies to the status of history: "Neither, though we have mastered all the arguments of Plato and Aristotle, if we have not the capacity for passing a solid judgment on these matters, shall we become philosophers; we should have acquired the knowledge not of a science, but of history" (*Rule* 3, HR, 1:6).[4]

Descartes's distinction between philosophy as science and philosophy as history becomes his mark of a difference that informs in a more general sense the ontological character of Cartesian metaphysics.[5] For this difference now comes to signify Descartes's own interpretation of Platonic metaphysics: being as subject and being as represented object.[6] The Platonic difference between philosophy and literature is reinscribed by Descartes as a fundamental difference between subject and object that now marks the character of being as *ratio* according to epistemological requisites. But Descartes's own arguments against the philosophy that precedes him, like Plato's arguments against poetry, are based on and produced by means of metaphor and rhetorical figures, that is, by the use of fiction. Literature consequently mediates and conditions the very character of both Platonic and Cartesian metaphysics.

My analysis begins by outlining the three major issues involved in the conflict of philosophy and poetry. First, I examine Plato's critique of the status and efficacy of poetry as a discourse of knowledge. In *Ion,* the *Republic,* and *Theaetetus* Plato tries to demonstrate that poetry does not involve true knowledge of things, since poets speak about "things they do not know." Second, as knowledge, poetry is shown to lack a certain pragmatic character, since its model of acquisition and communication is that of inspiration. Thus, poetry is presented as a form of knowledge that one has without possessing, a distinction Plato elaborates in the *Theaetetus.* Third, poetry is considered throughout the *Dialogues* to lack a certain communicative and pragmatic mastery of the world; in modern terms, a technological grasp and possession of the world. This explains the impossibility of translating its ethos into a praxis. Paradoxically, the expressive power of poetry is thus at issue, inasmuch as for Plato poetic skills (*technē*) are divinely rather than artistically inspired.[7] Moreover, Plato considers the poet to be the embodiment of the deceptive nature of poetic knowledge, since he is described as a derivative being, an interpreter of divine inspiration, an oracular mouthpiece of a knowledge to which he cannot gain access and which he cannot communicate or master.

Having criticized poetry as a form of knowledge, Plato proceeds in book 10 of the *Republic* to critique poetry by an analogy to painting. Plato's failure to address poetry and poetic language is most visible in his particularly derogatory definition of poetry as a third-removed imitation, one inferior both to the thing itself and to the semblance of the thing as created by artisans. By examining the analogy of poetry and painting I show that Plato's critique of poetry relies upon, and is subtended by, an even more fundamental opposition of the visual and the poetic. This latter opposition, although unaccounted for in the argument, lends its rhetorical veracity in order to restrict, and finally exclude, the poetic. The allegory of the cave, for instance, in the *Republic* (bk. 7) can be shown to function as the means or apparatus that makes visible the problem of knowledge, that of the opposition of essence and appearance, without any elaboration of its own instrumental, visual, and perceptual role as metaphor and allegory.

Once excluded from the *Republic,* poetry comes to haunt the very definition of philosophical discourse. This raises the question of what distinguishes the discourse of philosophy from poetry. Although Plato asserts that Socratic language is ordinary language and that the dialogue is only a way of questioning what one knows in order to find out how truly ignorant one is, I would like to show the extent to which Platonic discourse is marked by its poetic, metaphorical, and rhetorical character. In the *Symposium,* Socratic discourse produces a new mythology, one that leads to the idealization of both Socratic method and its figurehead, Socrates. Consequently, poetry reappears surreptitiously in the *Republic* disguised as the only admissible poetry, that of edification, elegy, or panegyric about the gods, and by extension, the heroes, the philosophers-founders of the new state, Plato and Socrates.

In conclusion, I consider the implications of the necessary displacement of the poetic discourse by the discourse of philosophy. The effort to separate philosophy and poetry involves, as Gadamer points out, not only the destruction of poetry, but more important, "an attack on the foundations of Greek culture and on the inheritance bequeathed to us by Greek history."[8] As Gadamer suggests, a great deal is at stake, since the effort to reinterpret the relation of philosophy and literature menaces our concept of tradition and its so-called rational origins. Moreover, the Platonic rejection of poetry opens up the possibility of denouncing the very notion of tradition. The violence exercised by philosophy against literature in Plato will thus return to haunt the structure of modern philosophy. Modern philosophy, as inaugurated by Descartes, bears the mark of this double inscription of difference: first between poetry and philosophy, and then within philosophy, as a break with philosophical tradition.

I

The question of whether poetry is an art, as opposed to philosophical knowledge, constitutes one of Plato's fundamental concerns. What is at issue is not merely the exclusion of poetry and certain other arts from the Republic (*polis*) but also the problem of the epistemological status of poetry. What kind of knowledge might poetry represent? Is it theoretical or practical in nature? Is it related to skill (*technē*) or inspiration? These are the problems that inform Plato's rejection of poetry in the *Dialogues*. Poetry's relation to truth will be found to be thrice removed in the *Republic* (bk. 10), and inadequate, since its relation to the original is more derivative than that of other arts or skills (*technē*) such as handicrafts, medicine, or education.[9] I begin by examining whether poetry is truly a form of knowledge by referring to Plato's arguments in *Ion* and book 10 of the *Republic*.

Socrates opens the dialogue *Ion* with the rhetorical admission that he envies the rhapsode Ion (a professional performer and interpreter of Homer) because his art requires him to be conversant with many poets, including Homer, the most divine of all, and also because the rhapsode must understand the lines and act as an interpreter of poetic thought as well.[10] This apparent recognition of the art of poetry and interpretation soon becomes the pretext for a critique not only of the knowledge represented by poetry but also of the interpreter as a paradigm of the poet, himself only an interpreter of divinely inspired knowledge. Socrates proceeds first to critique Ion's specialized knowledge of Homer, since he is shown neither to know nor to be interested in any other poets. This leads Socrates to question the universality of the rhapsode's knowledge, and by extension, later in the dialogue, the poet's knowledge as well. The question "Does Homer treat of matters different from those that all the other poets treat of?" (531c) is answered negatively, with the qualification that they "all treat of the same subjects, yet not all in the same fashion" (532a). Having admitted this difference of style in poetic speech, Socrates is, however, unwilling to pursue its consequences. What Socrates here evades is the problem that poetry is not about universals, since poetry makes tangible the inseparable character of ideas and their representation. The discursive and stylistic heterogeneity of poetry is not accounted for by Plato, bent as he is on defining philosophy as a discipline independent of its discursive medium. He associates knowledge with homogeneity of discourse and method. This search for homogeneity is based on the paradigm of the state, an institution where like individuals will speak of like subjects in the same way, thereby fostering the illusion of an unmediated and transparent relation of theory and practice, the citizen and the state.[11]

Socrates goes on to show that Ion's knowledge of Homer is illusory because it is neither true knowledge nor art, since art would give Ion the power to discourse equally well on all the poets. The question of whether there is an art of poetry as a whole (532c) is tied to the methodological question of whether the "inquiry is the same whenever one takes an art in its entirety" (532c). In other words, Plato's rejection of poetry as an art involves its lack of guiding inquiry and consistent methodology. Plato's critique of the art of poetry involves applying it to criteria more suited to art interpreted as a handicraft (*technē*) than to knowledge. Thus poetry is found to be profoundly unsystematic in both its object and its procedure, its subject and its style. The inability to describe poetry as a theory of knowledge, one circumscribed by epistemic constraints that would objectify its domain and delimit its style or methodology, leads Socrates to conclude that neither the rhapsode (third-removed interpreter) nor the poet (second-removed interpreter) can be ascertained as possessing an art. Rather, they are both respectively possessed by a divine power that informs them, making them thrice removed from the truth. They are both considered to be "interpreters of interpreters" (535a).

For the poets tell us, don't they, that the melodies that they bring us are gathered from rills that run with honey, out of the glens and gardens of the Muses, and they bring them as the bees do honey, flying like the bees? And what they say is true, for a poet is a light and winged thing, and holy, and never able to compose until he has become inspired, and is beside himself, and reason is no longer with him . . . Therefore since their making is not by art, when they utter many things . . . each is able to do well only that to which the Muse has impelled him. (534b)

Socrates' conclusion is that if it were by art that the poets know how to treat a subject, they would know how to deal with all the others as well. The poet is thus presented as a creature whose inspiration and method preclude reason and therefore a true knowledge of things.

In *Ion,* Socrates goes on to specify that for him art means the knowledge of a particular thing. He marks the difference among the arts by their respective names, designating the specialized domain and object of knowledge of each. This "mark of differentiation" (537d) separates the arts according to their objects and thus endows them with a technical meaning insofar as each art designates the possession of a particular knowledge, somewhat along the lines of handicrafts (cf. the distinction between arts and *technē*). However, the problem of poetry, like that of the art of the rhapsode, is that it pertains to all other arts—those of the charioteer, the general, the doctor, and so forth. Socrates, however, rejects the possibility of poetry as a generalized but heterogeneous knowledge of the world as sheer deception.

But the fact is, Ion, that if you are right, if it really is by art and knowledge that you are able to praise Homer, then you do me wrong. You assure me that you have much fine knowledge about Homer, and you keep offering to display it, but you are deceiving me. Far from giving the display, you will not even tell me what subject it is on which you are able, though all this while I have been entreating you to tell. No, you are just like Proteus; you twist and turn, this way and that, assuming every shape, until you finally elude my grasp and reveal yourself as a general. And all in order not to show how skilled you are in the lore concerning Homer . . . But if you are not an artist, if by lot divine you are possessed by Homer, and so, *knowing nothing* speak about many things and fine about the poet, just as I say you did, then you do no wrong. (541–42a; emphasis added)

Socrates' triumph is to demonstrate to Ion his lack of true knowledge, since his art of poetic interpretation is so Protean that it assumes the shape of any art. He denounces the illusion fostered by poetry that it has knowledge of all other arts, and of the poet as knowledgeable about all matters. At the end of the dialogue, Ion is given the choice of being known as an "unjust man" or as "near divine." It is not difficult to imagine Ion's choice, "near divine." But in so choosing, Ion has, in fact, been forced to renounce his very identity as an artist. This leads Socrates to conclude, "This lovelier title, Ion, shall be yours, to be in our minds *divine* and not an *artist,* in praising Homer" (542b; emphasis added). By claiming that Ion is divinely inspired, rather than an artist, Socrates condemns the artist to renounce his relationship to language as a medium that imitates, mediates, and transforms the world. The "near" divine status of the poet would reduce him to a purely passive instrument and deprive him of his technical grasp and artistry. By reducing poetry to an oracular genre, one in which the divinely inspired poet is deprived of his own voice, Plato frees philosophy from the challenge of truly considering the problem of knowledge posed by poetry. The character of poetic art is thus ascertained in terms later defined by Aristotle's description of the Sophist as possessing not true art but merely the "effects of art."[12]

In the *Republic* Plato further specifies the derivative and mimetic character of poetry: "The poet, knowing nothing but how to imitate, lays on with words and phrases the colors of several arts in such a fashion that others equally ignorant who see things only through words will deem his words excellent" (10.601a–b). It is only as imitation that poetry can effect and combine knowledge of several different arts and skills. But such an art for Plato is purely an illusion, one that lacks a conceptual grasp of things and is reduced to a false semblance of what one "sees through words." Poetry is thus defined as an art that represents things it does not know and cannot come to know. By analogy to painting, poetic language is presented in paradoxical terms as a false language whose elusive transparency is an actual obstacle to true knowledge. Poetic representation misleads the reader into a false perception of truth, since for Plato poetic representation is always imitation and thus derivative in character from the original.

The problem of the status of poetry in relation to knowledge is further elaborated by Plato when he discusses the inability of poets or rhapsodes to comment on their own work. The paradox is that the knowledge made visible by the poet is a knowledge that he cannot systematically represent as commentary. The poet's inability to comment on his own work leads Socrates to believe in the poet's ignorance. Poets do not compose their poems with knowledge, since they are unable to discuss them, to comment upon them (*Apology,* 22b). The lack of a systematic commentary about poetry is considered to be the sign of the invalid nature not only of poetic art, in general, but also of its practitioner and producer, the poet. Having discredited both, Socrates shifts to the last test of his argument—the fact that poetic knowledge cannot be translated into an actual praxis, a concrete knowledge about a particular discipline. Although he speaks about war, public service, and so forth, Homer is consulted neither to command nor to educate, nor can he be credited with creating a school to transmit to posterity a "certain Homeric way of life" (600a–b). The lack of institutional framework and pragmatic consequences of the poetic art is brought forth as ultimate evidence of the inefficacy of poetry as knowledge. Socrates asks, "If Homer had really been able to educate men and make them better and had *possessed not the art of imitation but real knowledge,* would he not have acquired many companions and been honored and loved by them?" (600c; emphasis added). The fact that poetry in presenting a way of life (*ethos*) does not also present a practice and pedagogy, a methodology functional in an institutional framework, is brought forth as further proof that the poetic art is an art of the dispossessed. Poetry is thus discredited as an art of false semblance that only simulates knowledge without actually possessing it.

Hence the possession of knowledge for Plato involves institutional and civic consequences, that is to say, the implementation of ideas in the context of the state.

Plato's interrogation of poetry as knowledge brings to the fore the epistemological question of the very definition of knowledge. What is knowledge—and is having knowledge different from possessing it? Plato's critique of poetry already implicitly involves this distinction insofar as he posits the possibility of knowledge in a derivative sense through imitation, but not its true possession. Having knowledge and possessing it are for Plato two different matters: possessing knowledge is like possessing a coat—when one is not wearing it, one possesses it without having it about oneself (*Theaetetus,* 197c). Possessing knowledge is therefore tied to special access to knowledge, an enclosure that guards ideas like birds in an aviary, as Socrates explains in the *Theaetetus:* "Now consider whether knowledge is a thing you can possess in that way without having it about you, like a man who has caught some wild birds—pigeons or what not—and keeps them in an aviary he has made for them at home. In a sense, of course, we might say that he 'has' them all the time inasmuch as he possesses them, mightn't we?" (197c-d). The possession of knowledge refers less to knowledge, in particular, than to the particular conditions of its possibility—in other words, to epistemology. Socrates resorts to arithmetic as the analogy of the science as the kind of knowledge he envisions as possession: "That, I take it, is the science in virtue of which a man has in his *control* pieces of knowledge about numbers and can hand them over to someone else" (*Theaetetus,* 198b; emphasis added).[13] The mathematical analogy brings out a new aspect of knowledge, since the possession of knowledge is associated with its economy, the sense of what is contained, communicated, and exchanged.

The derivative character of poetic knowledge as an interpretation of an interpretation and the secondary position of the poet as interpreter rather than artist and creator are highlighted most vividly in Plato's comments in the *Republic* regarding the analogy of poetry to painting.[14] The actual exclusion of poetry rather than painting from the *Republic* indicates a different attitude towards the two domains, one that will be turned strategically against poetry in order to exclude her from the education of the state. If it were a question of imitation alone, surely painting would provide as many reasons for exclusion as poetry. Alexander Nehamas questions Plato's reliance on painting by pointing out that the early history of the term "to imitate" (*mimesthai*) suggests that the term was originally connected with speech and poetry, rather than with painting.[15] Nehamas's seminal discussion of how "imitation" is interpreted by Plato specifically as pictorial imitation informs my own discussion of the difference (*diaphora*) between philosophy and poetry. Plato's reduction of poetry to an art subsidiary to painting leads to the exclusion of poetry as an inferior art of pure semblance or appearance. Plato's judgment of poetry in terms of visual mimesis by analogy to painting necessarily relegates it to a secondary position. Poetry, as Plato shows, can do only what painting already does derivatively, that is, give a third-removed representation of reality. In the pages that follow, I examine the strategic relation of poetry to painting and its epistemological implications. Plato's use of visual metaphors and his allegory of the cave will be at issue insofar as they are instrumental in establishing the difference between philosophy and literature.

In the *Republic,* book 2, Plato discusses the problem of educating children through fables. He contends that Homer and Hesiod composed and related false stories that distort the true nature of the gods by representing them as rivalrous, vengeful, adulterous, unjust characters. At this point Plato compares poetry unfavorably to painting by suggesting that such poetry bears no resemblance to its divine model. Rather, the Protean representations and forms of poetry disguise the gods in the "likeness of strangers." Not only does poetry not reflect the divine model, but it threatens to contaminate the nature of the gods themselves, for it suggests intentional deception on the part of the gods (381e) or the poet. Poetry is consequently allied to allegory and fiction, both of which estrange man from perceiving the true nature of God. Knowing things through poetry is like seeing "likenesses of letters reflected in the water or mirrors; we shall never know them until we know the originals" (402b). Poetry is thus compared to a fluid mirror whose distorted semblance can give no access to the objects or forms that it reflects. Like the poet who is a mirror of divine inspiration, or the rhapsode who interprets poetry, poetic images cannot provide, for Plato, a way of knowing things. Knowledge in this sense implies the knowledge of originals, which might exist independently of their reflection in the mirror as representation.

In book 10, Plato further develops the analogy of poetry to painting. He compares the poet as creator to the handicraftsman. The problem of representation, of the relation of the original to the copy, is shifted to that of the creator. The problem, Plato points out, is not the craft of poetry but the fact that all representation including visual representation is appearance. He proposes the example of the craftsman who recreates the world with a mirror. "You could do it most quickly if you should choose to take a mirror and carry it about everywhere. You will speedily produce the sun and all the things in the sky, and speedily the earth and yourself and the other animals and implements and plants and all the objects of which we just now spoke. Yes, he said, the appearance of them, but not the reality and the truth" (596e).

The ease with which the craftsman can create the world about him is associated with the facile and illusory nature of the imitation he practices. It suggests that the imitator knows nothing about the reality he imitates, only the appearance; consequently, "it is merely play and not anything serious" (602b). This devaluation of visual imitation as play with appearance functions as the paradigm of the other producer of images, that of the painter. Plato's analogy reduces the painter to the craftsman, presenting him as the passive recorder of the world without considering the nature of the medium of painting. But painting is not purely a reflective surface, or mirror, but rather a medium of representation. Nehamas's question regarding Plato's definition of imitation through painting rather than poetry brings us to the crux of the problem. The analogy to painting brings out the illusory character of representation as well as its derivative character as an interpretation of appearance. Plato's shift of register to painting transposes the question of poetry and distances it from philosophy. His strategic displacement of poetry through painting inscribes an irreducible difference between philosophy and literature exactly at the point they both share as a medium of representation, that of language. Plato's stratagem for excluding poetry works only because his arguments about poetry and painting have distanced poetry irremediably from philosophy. By deferring the discussion of the similarity of poetry and philosophy, Plato succeeds rhetorically in distinguishing between the two. The mark of difference that he has created has less to do with his actual argument than with the rhetorical distance he has established between philosophy and poetry. Plato most powerfully summarizes this difference when he urges the painter to give up "fashioning phantoms" in order to devote himself to the real thing (599b) and, by extension, to undermine the poetic enterprise.

The superiority of painting over poetry as a mimetic genre is transitional, since Plato now proceeds to critique visual representation in terms of its illusory character.

Then the mimetic art is *far removed* from the truth, and this, it seems, is the reason why it can produce everything, because it touches a small part of the object and that a phantom, as for example, a painter, we say, will paint us a cobbler, a carpenter or other craftsman, though he himself has no expertness in any of these arts, but nevertheless if he were a good painter, by exhibiting *at a distance* his picture of a carpenter he would deceive children and foolish men, and make them believe it to be a real carpenter. (598b–c; emphasis added)

The success of painterly illusion here becomes the mark of the failure of painting, since it signifies the distance that separates it from both the truth and the viewer. This double distance produces a space whose figure is intended to establish the estrangement of the viewer from illusory fascination. The plenitude of illusion in painting is tied to the very lack of its total relation to things, since it touches or refers to a small aspect of the object, and that already illusory (a phantom). The distance between the object and the painter is thus augmented, thereby creating an irradicable difference between painting as an art and philosophy as knowledge. Thus, painterly imitation is emptied of all significance and substantiality, either as practice or as product.[16] Moreover, the conflation and confusion of appearance as both object and product of imitation forecloses the inquiry into the artistic status of the poet as producer.

The poet is ambiguously represented as either an imitator or a maker of images once removed from painting ("imitation of appearance"), but in either case he knows nothing about that which he either imitates or produces. But this lack of knowledge is described as dangerous. The poet's only true craft is the exploitation of a confusion in the soul about essence and appearance and "falls nothing short of witchcraft" (602d). The poet, like the painter, addresses the lowest part of the soul, the one incapable of measuring and weighing. Consequently he threatens to destroy its rational part. Plato specifies: "Precisely in the same manner we shall say that the mimetic poet sets up in each individual soul a vicious constitution by fashioning phantoms far removed from reality, and by currying favor with the senseless element that cannot distinguish the greater from the less, but calls the same thing now one, now the other" (605b). Both the painter and the poet endanger the rational part of the soul. However, only poetry menaces the "polity" (608b) of the soul, and by extension, that of the state (*polis*). The exclusion of poetry thus takes on political overtones. It is no longer simply a matter of illusion or false semblance, but rather of endangering rationality itself, the possibility of attaining true knowledge.

Plato's final argument against poetry is that poetry, unlike philosophy, cannot defend herself. In other words, poetry is denied self-reflexive status; her speech is double. Poetry is both exposition and commentary, presentation and re-presentation. Instead of speaking for herself, philosophy will speak for her: "We will gladly have the best possible case made out for her goodness and truth, but so long as she is unable to make good her defense we shall chant over to ourselves as we listen to the reasons that we have given as a counter charm to her spell" (607e; 608a).

The trial of poetry, the consideration of her legitimate status within the state, leads to her exclusion, since she cannot even participate in the exchange required to make her case. The muteness of writing as opposed to living speech becomes the sign of the inferiority of writing that needs, as Plato tells us in the *Phaedrus,* "its parent to come to its help, being unable to defend or help itself" (275e).[17] This is because poetic writing does not know how to "address the right people." Hence, it is not surprising that Plato chose the dialogue as a genre because of its capacity to simulate a live conversation. If Plato in the *Republic* reproaches poetry for her silence, this is because he has already demonstrated her inability to know either the world or herself. Once again, the difference between philosophy and literature is falsely established, not in terms of what they share, but through the hierarchical differences that Plato creates. Like a woman, or better a child, philosophy must silence poetry and break her spell through speech, "chant" of reasons. However, Plato fails to point out that the chant of philosophy at the very moment of its distinction from poetry threatens to become poetry.

In the *Phaedrus,* Plato pursues the issue of the silence of poetry by declaring that painting too shares that silence. "The painter's products stand before us as though they were alive, but if you question them, they maintain a most majestic silence. It is the same with written words; they seem to talk to you as though they were intelligent, but if you ask them anything about what they say, from a desire to be instructed, they go on telling you just the same thing forever" (275d). The effort to address painting is met with a "majestic silence," and poetry's intelligibility is illusory, since no actual dialogue with her can take place. Thus poetry is inferior to painting because its discourse creates the illusion of speech and exchange without, however, fostering true exchange, as philosophy aspires to do. Plato's exclusion of poetry rather than painting can now be understood. Poetry must be expelled because it pretends to speak. Painting can remain in the *Republic* exactly because it will never speak, preserving its "majestic silence" as an image. Poetry's "false" speech thus challenges the very legitimacy and prerogative that Plato seeks to establish for philosophy. While painting produces images through colors and material, poetry does so through speech. As Gadamer observes, "The poet turns *himself* into the tool of his art."[18] It is a liability to the poet that he is at once *speaker* and *speech*, so that poetic speech is double, concealing the poet (cf. Plato's reproach to Homer regarding direct and indirect discourse). Plato's contention of the muteness of poetry is thus challenged by the proliferation of voices that speak through poetry. Plato's narrow interpretation of dialogue in terms of conversation fails to account for the ongoing polyphonic dialogue in which poetry is already engaged.

Plato's exclusion of poetry is all the more interesting once we consider his own position as a writer. In book 7 of the *Republic,* through the allegory of the cave, Plato presents an appeal to both poetry and painting. The allegory of the cave is the fable of the condition of the soul that lacks education. The fable's philosophical function is justified in advance by analogy to the mathematician's use of visual forms. Plato explains that mathematicians

talk about them, though they are not thinking of them, but of those things of which they are a likeness, pursuing the inquiry for the sake of the square as such and the diagonal as such, and not for the sake of the image of it which they draw. And so in all cases. The very things which they mold and draw, which have shadows and images of themselves in water, these things they treat in their turn only as images, but what they really seek is to get sight of those realities which can be seen only by the mind. (*Republic,* 6.510d-3)

Mathematicians use visible forms as schemata in order to embody a conceptual reality. Their status as representations is denied by their instrumental function, that of conveying ideas. Plato's reflection on the use of visual figures helps the reader situate the allegory of the cave. Its figurative aspect is framed by its function as a construct, a schema, and in modern terms, an apparatus.[19] The allegory of the cave does not purely illustrate; rather, its representation is also a stage. This can be seen in Plato's comparison of the prisoners to the spectators at a puppet show (514b). The allegory of the cave stages the problematic status of representation, which for Plato is merely the shadow of reality, thus eliding its instrumental character in the production of reality. The prisoners of the cavern cannot proceed beyond visual evidence in order to decide the true status of the images. Not having a true basis for judging the reality about them, the prisoners are lost in the endless illusory reflections that further disorient them in a game of infinitely recessed mirrors and trompe l'oeil. The names they give to the things about them are like the echo that resounds in the cave, mistakenly associated with the passing shadows. Thus the prisoners "would deem reality to be nothing else than the shadows of the artificial objects" (515c). The proliferation of false appearances in the cave thus appears like the proliferation of images in literature. The poet, like the prisoner in the cavern, names things without knowing them, falling prey to the very illusions he imagines he has mastered. Rather than possessing knowledge about them, the poet is prisoner of their illusory projection; he mistakes the echo for the original, the simulacrum for the real.

In the allegory of the cave, the soul's journey to knowledge is presented in terms of an ascent and a habituation to light and the development of correct vision. Once again vision is defined in a conceptual rather than a perceptual sense. The kind of vision that Plato refers to here is the vision of the intellect, which uses the visible form as a schema for truth. This vision is analogous to the sight of the sun "in and by itself," no longer mediated through shadows, phantasms, or reflections in water (516b). The vision of the sun is also equated with seeing the idea of the good, but as unmediated by representation, a direct vision whose character is almost that of a perception. Plato describes this preparation of the soul for the contemplation of essence as a new art of vision: "Even so this organ of knowledge must be turned around from the world of becoming together with the entire soul, like the scene-shifting periactus in the theater, until the soul is able to endure the contemplation of essence and the brightest region of being. And this, we say, is the good, do we not?" (518c–d). This new art of vision, like Plato's allegory itself, uses visible form, that is, the sun, to communicate the actual idea of the good. The use of the metaphor of vision must not be mistaken for visual sensation tied to deception, shadow, and appearance. Rather, this vision is transcendent, like an "art of conversion of the soul" (518d) that restages the direction of the soul's gaze from its exterior to its interior objective. However, this process of redirection of the soul's gaze, described as "scene-shifting periactus in the theater," is itself hidden by the correspondence between the sun and the idea of the good. This moment of blindness corresponds to the plenitude of the perception of true essence, or the good, figured only as an absence in Plato's text. This absence becomes the site of the most extensive projection in philosophy, since Plato equates the sun with the idea of justice and the good, and with the defeat of idols.

Socrates, the author of the allegory, is also presented as the fighter of shadows in an exercise of sparring that strangely evokes the very structure of the Platonic dialogues. Socrates describes how the liberated prisoner of knowledge attempts to legitimize his vision: "He is compelled in courtrooms or elsewhere to contend about the shadows of justice or the images that cast shadows and to wrangle in debate about the notions of these things in the minds of those who have never seen justice itself" (517d–e). Like Achilles, who refuses the shadowy world of Hades, Socrates contests the images of shadows of justice in order to set straight its definition. The allegory of the cave uses vision not merely as an analogy but also as an apparatus of projection in order to portray the mechanisms of true vision, embodied by intellectual and philosophical discourse. Plato's critique of painting and poetry in mimetic terms as purely derivative is intended to reinforce the distinction between philosophy and poetry. Philosophy is the only true vision, since its intellectual character transcends perception.

Plato, however, does not account for the representational impact of his allegory, which relies upon vision only in the narrow sense of intellectual rather than perceptual vision. Plato's use of poetry in the allegory of the cave, as metaphor and stage for his ideas, must be recognized. His allegory emerges as the figure of the discourse of philosophy. The representational aspects of the allegory are occulted by its projected impact, by its transcendental and idealist ideology.[20] Thus a fundamental mark of difference is produced, a distance that separates philosophy from its counterparts, painting and poetry. This difference is the mark of knowledge provisionally defined in the *Theaetetus* as "correct belief and knowledge of a differentness" (210a). However, what is represented as the difference between philosophy and all the other arts is nothing more than the mark of a series of differences and displacements that constantly reinscribe and retrace the figure of philosophical discourse. But these very differences come to constitute through their displacements and deferrals the mark of an absolute difference. The myth of this pure origin or moment of distinction is necessary to Platonic philosophy, since it seeks to create the myth of its autonomy and superiority.

What, then, is the discourse of philosophy? Plato describes philosophical writing in the *Phaedrus* as a writing that is different from poetic writing. He who has knowledge cannot simply represent his ideas. To do so means that he is not much better than the poet. "Then it won't be with serious intent that he writes them in water or that black fluid we call ink, using his pen to sow words that can't either speak in their own defense or present the truth adequately" (276c–d).

Because of its medium, philosophy has to distinguish its own character from that of all other discursive (poetic) representation. The diacritical mark of the separation of philosophy and poetry is set up by

Plato in terms of genre and style. The Platonic dialogue as a vehicle for representation of his ideas creates the illusion of presence, of dialectical exchange.[21] The dialogue, because of its generative capacities, its illusion of direct conversation, is distinguished from other kinds of purely descriptive writing. The dialogue is equated with farming and sowing: "The dialectician selects a soul of the right type, and in it he plants and sows his words founded on knowledge, words which can defend both themselves and him who planted them, words which instead of remaining barren contain a seed whence new words grow up in new characters, whereby the seed is vouchsafed immortality, and its possessor the fullest measure of blessedness that man can attain unto" (276–77a). Thus the dialogue as genre, as style, traces the ultimate difference that separates it from poetic written discourse: it is a discourse that pretends to speak and also to defend itself. It is a dialectical genre that suggests the possibility of transcendence: illusory space of conversation, personality, character, and presence. The dialogue is a seed whose differential character marks the soul itself, generatively, as the site for the production of "new characters." Thus the original difference established between philosophy and poetry/painting, necessary for the absolute foundation of philosophy as the discourse of knowledge, is recouped by Plato as a difference of style. For the dialogue is the only legitimate site of generation and immortality, the proper medium for insemination (sowing the signs).

To have a precise description of the function of dialogue in Plato's work, it is important to consider Alcibiades' description of Socrates and Socratic discourse in the *Symposium:* "What he reminds me of more than anything is one of those little sileni that you see on statuary stalls; you know the ones I mean, they're modeled with pipes and flutes in their hands and when you open them down the middle there are little figures of gods inside. And then again, he reminds me of Marsyas the satyr" (215a–b). Alcibiades' analogy highlights the contrast between exterior resemblance to sileni and interior richness, hiding figures of gods. Socrates, himself the "midwife" of other people's ideas (as he suggests in the *Theaetetus*), is presented as the container and repository of godlike ideas. Alcibiades' allusion to Marsyas, the satyr, is particularly interesting, since Marsyas was the representative of the double pipe, an instrument used in Bacchic orgies. Alcibiades pursues his comparison, observing that Socrates can elicit the same effects as Marsyas without any instrument at all, "with nothing but a few simple words, not even poetry" (215c–e). The effect of Socrates on Alcibiades, or anyone who repeats his words, is that of being "staggered," "be-

witched," or smitten with a "sacred rage." The dialogue as an instrument, as the double pipe, turns the soul "upside down"; it moves the
hearer to a "philosophical frenzy" (218b), like a dancing Corybant.
The effect of the dialogue on the hearer is that of dialectic, the movement to and fro, like the movement of the dance of the priests of Cy-
bele. This movement unhinges the soul and leads to the overturning of
its unquestioned philosophical ideas. This movement is the result of
godlike images inside Socrates, the manifestation of its truth.

Alcibiades then ties his description of Socrates to the representational properties of philosophical discourse. He adds:

Which reminds me of a point I missed at the beginning; I should have explained how his arguments too, were exactly like those sileni that open down
the middle. Anyone listening to Socrates for the first time would find his arguments simply laughable; he wraps them up in just the kinds of expressions
you'd expect of such an insufferable satyr. He talks about pack asses and black-
smiths and shoemakers and tanners, and he always seems to be saying the
same old thing in just the same old way, so that anyone who wasn't used to his
style and wasn't very quick on the uptake would naturally take it for the most
utter nonsense. But if you open up his arguments, and really get into the skin
of them, you'll find that they're the only arguments in the world that have any
sense at all, and that nobody else's are so godlike, so rich in images of virtue, or
so peculiarly, so entirely pertinent to those inquiries that help the seeker on
his goal of true humility. (221d; 222a)

Alcibiades' description of Socratic—and by extension, Platonic—
discourse helps us understand its mechanisms. The skin of the argument, its lack of poetic pretension, is compensated by the style of
speech: the dialogue. Hiding within it are the godlike images of virtue
that propel the movement of the dialogue, that control the speaker.
Like the sun in the cave allegory, the figures or images of gods compel
the viewer to an instant recognition of their absolute truth. The dialogue speaks to the reader directly because its speech becomes that of
the reader. The Platonic text thus presents through the performative
aspect of dialogue the simulation of an impossible truth—the identity
of Socrates' speech and the reader's opinion. The reader becomes a
mouthpiece for a dialogue that in effect creates his persona as character
in the text. The compelling character of the Socratic dialogue, its truth
effect, is thus as much the result of style as the actual content of what is
said. Alcibiades' recognition of the instrumental character of the dialogue as a genre reveals the significance of the intervention of style.
Although excluded from philosophical discourse, poetry thus returns,
if only in the guise of style to mark its own difference. This difference

is, however, no longer the stable difference that Plato used to found the identity of philosophy, but rather the difference that marks always already its discourse insofar as it is composed of metaphors, rhetorical figures, and its dialogical format. This difference is made by the voice of literature in the dialogue that philosophy would like to establish with itself.

II

The sudden shift from Plato to Descartes might seem at first unjustified. However, any close reader of Descartes must acknowledge Descartes's profound debt to Plato. This debt is incurred at many levels, in terms of his use of metaphors, rhetorical strategies, and concepts. Suffice it to note briefly that almost all of Descartes's major concepts in the *Rules* (mathematics, enumeration), in the *Discourse* (architecture, the critique of literature, argument of perfection, etc.), and in the *Meditations* (waking/dreaming, illusion/reality, use of rhetorical figures, etc.) are informed by the Platonic dialogues, especially the *Theaetetus* and the *Republic.* In the analysis that follows I am not interested in showing Descartes's borrowings from Plato. Rather, I would like to show how Descartes incorporates into his own strategy the conflict that we have seen between philosophy and poetry in Plato. For Plato's exclusion of poetry in the *Republic* is echoed by Descartes's exclusion of all philosophy that does not obey his epistemic criteria. As shown earlier, philosophy before Descartes is disparaged as pure history, losing its truth value, since it does not obey the rules for certitude. Descartes's critique of traditional philosophical language is based on an idealization of mathematics that can already be found in the Platonic text. Like Plato, Descartes considers philosophy above all a theory of knowledge. However, by choosing mathematics as the norm and basis for a new philosophical language, Descartes reinterprets philosophy and reduces it to a more technical perspective. His philosophy is no longer concerned with truth, beauty, or ideas, but rather with the conditions of interpretation of truth as certitude. Truth in Descartes has become normative and propositional. Certitude is merely a statement of adequation to a given norm. The original conflict of philosophy and poetry in Plato is barely perceptible in Descartes's comments on his education in the *Discourse,* where he denounces the lack of certitude in literary knowledge. Descartes's search for new foundations of knowledge excludes literature, only to turn to philosophy. But this philosophy is no longer philosophy as traditionally defined by the schools. Rather, it is a new philosophy whose first principles involve a recasting of philosophy into epistemology. Descartes's criteria for certitude establish the priority of a theory of knowledge, of its conditions of possibility (axioms) that must precede any actual knowledge of the world. Descartes thus establishes a difference in the heart of philosophy, one that relegates all previous philosophy to history. Descartes's use of architectural metaphors in the *Discourse* and of hyperbolic doubt in the *Meditations* provides insights into his use of literature to found his metaphysical system. Like Plato's philosophical position, that of Descartes will be shown to emerge from the metaphorical and rhetorical aspects of the text. It is important to remember, however, that Descartes's use of certitude has been most instrumental in redefining philosophy according to mathematics so as to exclude—apparently forever—literary and previous philosophical considerations. Thus Descartes's interpretation of philosophy marks a break with the tradition. The modernity of philosophy is constituted by this difference that now separates philosophy irrevocably both from itself and from literature.

In the *Discourse,* Descartes resorts to an architectural method to describe the necessity of his project of finding truth in the sciences. He claims that there is less perfection in works composed in several portions and carried out by several masters than in those on which one individual alone has worked. He explains:

Thus we see that buildings planned and carried out by one architect alone are usually more beautiful and better proportioned than those which many have tried to put into order and improve making use of old walls which were built with *other ends in view.* In the same way also, those ancient cities which, originally mere villages, have become in the process of time great towns, are usually badly constructed in comparison with those which are regularly laid out on a plain by a *surveyor who is free to follow his own ideas.* (HR, 1:88; emphasis added)

Descartes's analogy to architecture and planning seems clear enough. What is interesting is to determine its strategic function in the formulation of his concept of philosophical discourse. By emphasizing how "difficult it is to build upon the works of others" (i.e., those of other philosophers), Descartes announces his intent to begin anew, according to his own plans. The problem is that he cannot incorporate previous traditions into his own philosophical system, since, as he claims, they were built with "other ends in view." Descartes's philosophy has, however, only one end in view—that of rebuilding philosophy according to his "rational scheme." Descartes's architectural metaphor is based on Plato's passage in the *Republic* (bk. 6), where he compares the construction of the perfect city to the work of a painter using a divine model (500e). This analogy adds a special dimension to Descartes's analogy because it allows us to understand Descartes's interpretation of the function of his philosophy. For Descartes, the perfect city is no longer built on a divine model, but rather upon a self-made and self-invented rational model. Plato's divine model (the supra-sensible) is now reinterpreted according to a manmade model as a mathematical axiomatic position, a set of self-made laws which legislate all access to knowledge.

In order to impose this new model, Descartes must begin with a clean slate. While he admits the improbability of reform of knowledge in an institutional sense, Descartes also posits the possibilities of reforming all his own options. He explains:

It is true that we do not find that all the houses in a town are razed to the ground for the sole reason that the town is to be rebuilt in another fashion . . . But as regards all the opinions which up to this time I had embraced, I thought I could not do better than endeavour once for all to sweep them completely away, so they might later on be replaced, either by others which were better, or by the same, when I had made them conform to the uniformity of a rational scheme. (HR, 1:89)

Once again, what is interesting is Descartes's reinscription of another Platonic *topos,* the reformer, who "will take the city and the characters of men, as they might a tablet, and first wipe it clean—no easy task" (6.501a). The tabula rasa becomes for Descartes the city that, once razed to the ground, must be rebuilt. However, unlike Plato, Descartes admits the implausibility of such a project in an institutional sense: "I argued to myself that there was no plausibility in the claim of any private individual to reform a state by altering everything and by overturning it throughout, in order to set it right again" (HR, 1:89). Thus Descartes restricts the sphere of his discourse away from institutional concerns toward the private, individual ones. And yet, what appears initially as a reduction of the philosophical sphere of influence from the state to the individual emerges as an attempt to enforce and ground that position in a more convincing and pervasive philosophical manner. The localization of reform within the individual marks the shift away from the state (*polis*) as the city of men to the city as a metaphor of a single man and a single plan.

Descartes's reinscription of the Platonic metaphor also documents his radical reinterpretation of philosophy. For the city in question is the edifice of philosophy, one that Descartes would like to replace with his own plan, his own discourse. Unlike Plato, Descartes is not content to exclude literature and the other arts from philosophy; he also wants to exclude the tradition of philosophy. The exclusion of earlier philosophy ("razed to the ground") corresponds to his effort to constitute a new philosophy, the first meditations upon a clean slate. Plato's effort to constitute the discourse of philosophy at the expense of poetry and the arts is now reinterpreted in more radical terms. Cartesian philosophy operates an even more violent exclusion upon the body of philosophy in order to disengage its own discourse from the tradition as the only proper discourse. It is this operation of differentiation, the epistemological reinterpretation of philosophy, which posits the ground for a new philosophy. This mark of difference between philosophy and history endows modern metaphysics with its specific ahistorical character. This difference can best be summarized as the effect of subjectivity upon the world and its reduction to an object. As an object the world now takes on the character of a picture.[22] The ontological difference that defines the Platonic text—that of being (the suprasensible) from being (the sensible)—was sustained by the difference operated on the order of discourse by the exclusion of poetry. Descartes's reinterpretation of knowledge stabilizes the Platonic difference so that ontology becomes purely epistemology.

To gain an even more precise sense of Descartes's reinterpretation of Platonic metaphors and, by extension, Platonic philosophy, we turn to his comment in the *Discourse* (pt. 6), where Descartes alludes to the cave metaphor as a way of assessing the impact of his own philosophy:

In this they seem to me like a blind man who in order to fight on equal terms with one who sees, would have the latter to come into the bottom of a very dark cave. I may say, too, that it is in the interest of such people that I should abstain from publishing the principles of philosophy of which I made use, for being so simple and evident as they are, I should in publishing them, do the same as though I threw open the windows and caused daylight to enter the cave into which they have descended to fight. (HR, 1:125)

Descartes's use of the cave allegory is not surprising, since he is resolving here the Platonic problem of the relation of essence to appearance. He believes that his rational system settles, once and for all, the question that haunts the seventeenth century—the problem of illusion.[23] Descartes pictures himself as the ultimate architect who engineers the abolition of the cave altogether by putting in windows and throwing them open. The fact that the cave functioned allegorically in

Plato as a means of setting up and projecting the problem of defining knowledge and truth and its separation from the illusion associated with poetry is not recognized by Descartes. His effort to install windows corresponds to the creation of a new kind of philosopher—the subject—who stands, through his new definition of the sun (truth based on mathematics), outside that which constitutes philosophy, that is, outside its metaphors. Descartes's new principles are the windows, the luminous and liminal difference that signifies the displacement of one philosophical system by another. These windows now open onto the modern world, a world framed by representation and subtended by the position of the subject. The Platonic difference between the supra-sensible and the sensible, philosophy and literature, is now reinscribed by the fundamental difference produced by the reinterpretation of philosophy from an epistemological and subjective position. The windows in the cave stand as the model of a new concept of representation which disguises the criteria of its representability inside the very concept of representation, which now appears as a purely transparent and neutral medium.[24]

Descartes's profound reliance on the figurative and rhetorical aspects of literature can be seen in all his texts. His reiteration of the themes of dreaming, waking, madness, deception, and illusion in the *Meditations* demonstrates more than a mere transposition of metaphors from literature to philosophy. Paradoxically, these metaphors have already been given currency in the Platonic text, especially the *Theaetetus,* and have been part of its constitutive scenario. Descartes's attempt to overcome these metaphors means actually using them in order to produce a discourse that excludes them.

The rhetorical consideration of the function of hyperbolic doubt highlights the so-called metaphysical foundation of the Cartesian system. As the cornerstone, hyperbolic doubt hides within its figurative structure the paradox of the definition of the *cogito* as determined reason and unreason. This aperture of the hyperbole toward indeterminacy, made possible by the rhetorical (fictional) character of the hyperbole, is quickly reinscribed by Descartes within his system of certainty and the so-called chains of reasons. For Derrida this dialogue between that which exceeds totality and the closed totality constitutes the proper character of the philosophy inaugurated by Descartes. He observes, "*At its height,* hyperbole, the absolute opening, the uneconomic expenditure, is always reembraced by an *economy* and overcome by economy."[25] This circumscription of hyperbolic doubt, its transitional appeal to indeterminacy in order to achieve mere determinacy (certitude), constitutes the paradoxical character of Descartes's metaphysical system. This paradox will mark not only the definition of the *cogito* and its relation to the world, but—what is more significant—its relation to history. For the dialogue instituted by Descartes between the hyperbole and the finite structure implies new concepts of both philosophy and history and, in that sense, of the history of philosophy.[26] For the hyperbole, "the uneconomic expenditure," is always contained and overcome by economy, the limited interplay between infinite and indefinite. However, the uneconomic expenditure signified by the hyperbole is itself the result of its rhetorical and figurative function. For this excess, produced in the domain of philosophy, totalizing it, is itself made possible by another order, that of the rhetorical figure of the hyperbole, in other words, fiction or literature. But this order is never itself represented or accounted for within Descartes's philosophical system. Although Descartes's arguments are obsessed with fiction (the "new" world in the *World,* the *Discourse* as a fable, or the evil genius and even the style of the *Meditations*), the instrumental character of these literary interventions in the formulation of a new metaphysical foundation is not acknowledged pragmatically as having in fact made possible the illusion of the absolute nature of his philosophical position.[27] Like Plato, Descartes refuses to consider the metaphorical and rhetorical intervention of poetry at the very heart of philosophy. He sets up the fiction of philosophy as an autonomous field where truth is defined as objectivity, that is, as a truth beyond language, metaphor, and poetry.

In Descartes's work, Plato's famous conflict between philosophy and literature is hidden by the effort to differentiate the new philosophy from history. And yet, the disappearance of literature from its oppositional position to philosophy in no way means that this conflict has been overcome, for this difference still marks its character. The question of style that haunts the very definition of literature also haunts the definition of philosophy. Plato's dissatisfaction with Homer for having created the Greek world through poetry was resolved by his renaming that world in a new style, through philosophical categories elaborated in the *Dialogues.* Descartes's dissatisfaction with Plato and Aristotle is resolved by his redefinition of truth in a new style, that of mathematical adequation. Thus the difference of style haunts the very definition of philosophy as a discipline proper. As Tom Conley notes, the style of philosophy—whether a dialogue, a discourse, or a meditation—always makes a difference. "Style was to be understood as inscription, as marking in a literal sense rather than as a metaphor of decor. With this supplemental view of the craft, the 'styles' of philosophy and literature would be of the same stamp."[28] But this difference is neither dialectical nor oppositional. Rather, style implies difference, a dialogue that is not oppositional but polyphonic. The difference made by style does not reduce philosophy to literature. Rather, the difference between philosophy and literature becomes a difference not from without but within, one that stamps their respective characters without trivializing their interplay.

Notes

1. *The Collected Dialogues of Plato*, ed. Edith Hamilton and Huntington Cairns, Bollingen Series 71 (Princeton: Princeton University Press, 1961). The dialogues that I shall be referring to have been translated by the following: Hugh Tredennick (*Apology*); Lane Cooper (*Euthyphro*); R. Hackforth (*Phaedrus*); Michael Joyce (*Symposium*); Paul Shorley (*Republic*); Francis M. Cornford (*Theaetetus*); A. E. Taylor (*Laws*); henceforth designated by essay and paragraph number.

2. I am using here Plato, *The Republic*, trans. and ed. Desmond, 2d ed., rev. (London: Penguin Books, 1974), 607b–c, 438.

3. Hans-Georg Gadamer, "Plato and the Poets," in *Dialogue and Dialectic: Eight Hermeneutical Studies in Plato*, trans. and introd. P. Christopher Smith (New Haven: Yale University Press, 1980), 48.

4. *Philosophical Works of Descartes*, trans. and ed. Elizabeth S. Haldane and G. R. T. Ross, 2 vols. (1911; reprint, Cambridge: Cambridge University Press, 1967), 1:6; henceforth designated as HR, volume, and page number.

5. For an elaboration of Descartes's distinction between philosophy and history of philosophy see Judovitz, "Autobiographical Discourse and Critical Praxis in Descartes," *Philosophy and Literature* 5 (Spring 1981): 100–105.

6. For an analysis of Plato's and Descartes's interpretations of Being and being, see Martin Heidegger, "The Ontological Difference," in *Nihilism*, vol. 4 of *Nietzsche*, trans. Frank A. Capuzzi and ed. David Farrell Krell (San Francisco: Harper & Row, 1982), 150–58.

7. Heidegger points out that originally art, fine art, and handicraft were designated by the same word—*technē*, and that it does not designate making or producing, but rather knowledge. See *The Will to Power as Art*, vol. 1 of *Nietzsche*, trans. David Farrell Krell (San Francisco: Harper & Row, 1979), 80–82. See also Catherine Rau, *Art and Society: A Reinterpretation of Plato* (New York: Richard R. Smith, 1951), 77–79.

8. Gadamer, "Plato and the Poets," 46.

9. Cf. Rau, *Art and Society*, 77–81.

10. For a more general discussion of the problem of poetic inspiration in *Ion*, see Whitney Oates, *Plato's View of Art* (New York: Scribner, 1972), 32–42.

11. For a discussion of the *Republic* as political education, see Gadamer, "Plato and the Poets," in *Dialogue and Dialectic*, 39–72.

12. Cf. Aristotle, *On Sophistical Refutations*, trans. Hugh Tredennick (Cambridge: Harvard University Press, 1938), 184a, 2.

13. Cf. Francis M. Cornford, *Plato's Theory of Knowledge: The Theaetetus and the Sophist in Plato* (Indianapolis: Bobbs-Merrill, 1957), 135–36. He also points out that from the *Meno* onward, knowledge is not a thing that can be "handed over" (135).

14. For a discussion of Plato's relation to the painting of his time, see Rau, *Art and Society*, 45–48.

15. Alexander Nehamas, "Plato on Imitation and Poetry in *Republic* X," in *Plato on Beauty, Wisdom, and the Arts*, ed. Julius Moravcsik and Philip Temko (Totowa, N.J.: Rowman and Littlefield, 1982), 56–59.

16. Nehamas, "Plato on Imitation and Poetry," 62–63.

17. For an analysis of the role of writing and the problem of filiation in the *Phaedrus*, see Jacques Derrida, "Plato's Pharmacy," in *Dissemination*, trans. Barbara Johnson (Chicago: University of Chicago Press, 1981), 87–94.

18. Gadamer, "Plato and the Poets," 60.

19. Cf. Jean-Louis Baudry's analysis of the analogy of the cave and the filmic apparatus in "Cinéma: Effets idéologiques produits par l'appareil de base," *Cinéthique* 7/8 (1970): 1–8.

20. Baudry, "Effets idéologiques," 7.

21. See Gadamer's examination of dialogue and dialectic in "Plato's Unwritten Dialectic," in *Dialogue and Dialectic*, 124–55.

22. See Martin Heidegger, "The Age of the World Picture," in *The Question Concerning Technology and Other Essays*, trans. William Lovitt (New York: Harper & Row, 1977), 115–54.

23. See Sylvie Romanowski, *L'illusion chez Descartes: La structure du discours cartésien* (Paris: Klincksieck, 1974).

24. For an analysis of the questions of subjectivity and representation in Descartes, see Judovitz, *Subjectivity and Representation: The Origins of Modern Thought in Descartes* (Cambridge: Cambridge University Press, 1987).

25. Jacques Derrida, "Cogito and the History of Madness," in *Writing and Difference*, trans. Alan Bass (Chicago: University of Chicago Press, 1978), 61–62.

26. See Derrida's distinction between history and historicity in "Cogito and the History of Madness," 60.

27. Cf. Jean-Luc Nancy's analysis of fiction and fable in Descartes in "Mundus est Fabula," *MLN* 93 (French Issue), (1978): 931.

28. Tom Conley, "A Trace of Style," in *Displacement: Derrida and After*, ed. Mark Krupnick (Bloomington: Indiana University Press, 1983), 79.

3
Philosophical Discourses and Fictional Texts

When contemporary literary theorists have turned to philosophy for guidance about the nature of literary texts, they have on a number of occasions looked to the philosophy of speech-acts, especially when the nature of fiction is at stake. According to the theories developed by J. L. Austin in *How to Do Things with Words* and by John Searle in *Speech Acts*, when we speak we may also be said to do things with words. In the case of fictional texts, however, we are confronted with utterances that do not accomplish what they ordinarily might. As we shall later see, Mary Wiseman takes this as a central fact in her essay on the utopias of language in connection with Roland Barthes. Somehow, the conditions for the efficacy of these speech-acts are suspended, or the acts are embedded in other such acts so that the usual illocutionary forces do not obtain. Following the theory that Peter McCormick outlines here, it could be said that in the case of fictional utterances we are not confronted with illocutionary acts themselves but only with representations of them. As early as the Renaissance, Philip Sidney invoked a kindred idea when he said that the poet "nothing affirmeth."

In looking to philosophical theories of speech-acts for guidance in understanding the nature of fictional texts, however, it would be wrong to assume that such theories are necessarily adequate to their description. One would expect a theory to be able to distinguish philosophical texts (which we presume to be nonfictional) from fictions; but if one compares a series of fictional and philosophical texts, as McCormick does here, it appears that speech-act theory is unable to tell them definitively apart. We find good reasons for taking philosophical texts not just literarily (e.g. admiring the prose of Santayana or Quine) but as fictions, albeit of a peculiar sort.

In order to distinguish philosophical from fictional texts, one might supplement the theory of speech-acts by a notion of genre. One might invoke a rule or "law" of genre (as Derrida would say) made to keep the genres apart. The standard account of fictionality as provided by a theory of speech-acts would have to accommodate a theory of genre; but if McCormick's arguments are convincing, then whatever use the notion of genre may have as a hermeneutical model of understanding, genre cannot be taken as a rule, and so cannot be thought of as an adequate supplement to the speech-act account of the difference between fictional and philosophical texts. This of course leaves open the possibility that one might seek some account of the difference between fiction and philosophy which might not depend on the idea of "rule" and kindred terms at all.

McCormick takes the literary features of certain philosophical texts as sufficient to undermine the speech-act theory, which purports to differentiate them from literary texts. If this is in fact the case, we may further revise the standard speech-act account, which seems a relatively unfruitful line of approach, or we may openly admit the fictional nature of philosophical texts and demand a fuller investigation of their fictional status. If McCormick's suggestions are right, this program will leave us with a richer account of the fictional than we currently possess. At the same time, such a program might reveal something far closer to the heart of philosophy's worries and concerns—to wit, why "no richer account of the fictional can be expected without an account of why the real itself would seem to be partly fictional." An erasure of the boundaries between philosophy and fiction is, I take it, one of the consequences of the contemporary interest in the question of "texts." In Harry Berger, Jr.'s, exemplary readings of Plato, the distinction between fiction and philosophy disappears; accordingly, we are shown how the reading of a work of philosophy may be significantly enriched if we agree to regard it simply as a "text."

Philosophical Discourses and Fictional Texts

Peter McCormick

A truth is then prescribed: to study the
philosophical text in its formal structure, in
its rhetorical organization, in the specificity
and diversity of its textual types, in its
models of exposition and proclamation—
beyond what were previously called genres—
and also in the space of its mises en scène,
in a syntax which would be not only the
articulations of its signifieds, its reference to
Being and to truth, but also to the handling
of its proceedings and of everything invested
in them. In a word, the task is to consider
philosophy also as "a particular literary
genre."
—Derrida, Margins of Philosophy,
trans. Alan Bass

In examining the differences between fictional and nonfictional—especially philosophical—texts, my procedure will be to construct a current account of just how this distinction may be understood, to test this account in terms of three putatively nonfictional texts taken from eighteenth-century philosophical aesthetics, and finally to reflect briefly on the alternatives that result from this examination. My suggestion will be that we have good reasons for construing at least some of those nonfictional texts we call philosophical as fictions of a peculiar sort.

I

Below is an excerpt from *Doctor Zhivago*. Very early in the novel the boy, Yury Zhivago, accompanies his uncle, Nikolay Nikolayevich, to the country. There Nikolay converses with his friend Ivan Ivanovich.

They passed the hothouses, the gardeners' cottage and some stone ruins of obscure origin. They were talking about new talent in the world of letters and scholarship. "Of course one does meet brilliant men," said Nikolay Nikolayevich, "but they are isolated. The fashion nowadays is all for groups and societies of every sort.—It is always a sign of mediocrity in people when they herd together whether their giving loyalty is to Soloviev or to Kant or to Marx. The truth is only sought by individuals, and they break with those who do not love it enough. How many things in the world deserve our loyalty? Very few indeed. I think one should be loyal to immortality, which is another word for life, a stronger word for it. One must be true to immortality . . . But you're frowning, my poor man.[1]

The first question I wish to investigate is just what makes this obviously thoughtful text fictional. One recent view, which I shall call the standard view,[2] is a contemporary variation on Sidney's defense of poetry against the Puritans: what makes a text fictional is that it "nothing affirmeth." In modern parlance, Pasternak does not perform illocutionary acts; rather, he represents the performance of an illocutionary act.

The cardinal notion of an illocutionary act invoked here is relatively familiar. However, some conventions allow speakers to make a single utterance do double duty. Those familiar with the conventions of e.g. christening a ship, which is to say with certain specifiable social, psychological, and physical conditions governing a particular utterance and with certain rules for the production of a well-formed utterance, are able both to communicate with other persons and at the same time to confer a name on a newly launched ship. In making an utterance of a certain type, a speaker both performs an act of communication and at the same time conventionally generates an act of christening. With some simplification, the first act is called a locutionary act and the second an illocutionary one. An utterance, moreover, can be an act of writing or of gesturing as well as one of speaking. Since a locutionary act can generate an illocutionary one only if all the requisite conditions and rules for the generation of that kind of illocution are satisfied, some putative illocutionary acts may be incomplete. And when a locutionary act is performed in such a way as to invite a hearer or a reader to recognize the concomitant production of an illocutionary act without satisfying all the conditions and rules required for the generation of such an act, the result is a quasi-illocutionary act, or what the standard account calls a fictive illocutionary act.

In the case of fictive illocutionary acts, two elements are crucial. First, the text must include sufficient markers (sentences in the form of assertions) which clearly invite the hearer's or reader's supposition that appropriate conditions and rules might generate an illocutionary act. Second, the text must also include sufficient markers (a subtitle like "a novel") which clearly indicate that some of the appropriate conditions are lacking and/or that some of the rules are not being followed. The result is a text that includes utterances representing genuine illocutions while not itself actually presenting genuine illocutions. Such utterances are instances of what the standard account calls "fictive discourse," that is, "discourse in which there is a make-believe illocutionary action, but in fact no such action is performed."[3]

We need to look at several aspects of this initial formulation more closely; accordingly, here is my first formulation of one standard view: (1) What makes a text fictional is its representations of the performances of illocutionary acts.

This view of fiction focuses on the nature of a particular text and not just on how a reader or a community of readers in a culture takes a text. For even though some community of readers may approach virtually any text within a certain set of common expectations so that the text is taken as fictional, it is another and more difficult matter to say whether virtually any text may appropriately be taken as fictional.[4] Just as not any text can properly be described as literary, so too not any text can properly be described as fictional. It is true that the fictional text, like the literary one, is a language game set within a frame.[5] And of course someone somewhere may always choose to set any language game whatsoever within a frame, perhaps by viewing the game at issue from a particular perspective or with a certain attitude. But in the standard view these facts do not entail that any text whatsoever is fictional. For the fact that a text may be considered as fictional does not make the text a fiction. Further, the fact that someone may take any text as fictional does not entail that a community of educated readers in a culture may take any text as fictional. Thus some texts, in this view, cannot be properly taken as fictional at all.

The standard view incorporates a particular interpretation of what a text is. A text here is construed as an oral or written "syntactically ordered string of words in a language" (Beardsley, "Fictions," 293). More precisely, the text is "not an individual inscription or utterance but a text-type, of which inscriptions and utterances are instances."[6] A text is produced in order to perform an illocutionary act, that is, an essentially rule-governed act of a particular act-type like promising, inviting, regretting, lying, and so on. Fictional texts as opposed to nonfictional ones represent the performance of such illocutionary acts where the term "represent" is used by analogy with its use in the visual arts. Thus a fictional text is said to represent those performances in the way that a painting is said to depict a scene. "It is a matter," this account goes, "of selective matching—some shapes, colors, line-segments, regional qualities, or gestalts are captured and perceived to be those characteristic of the kind of object or event depicted" (Beardsley, "Fictions," 295). So, the sense of representation which is central in fictional texts is representation not as denotation but as a selective similarity relationship between symbol and referent.

The standard view also tries to address the question of whether any objective features distinguish fictional from nonfictional texts. Most discussion so far has focused on fictional prose narratives and lyric poetry. The accent has not fallen on external markers like the subtitle "a novel" indicated earlier but on internal markers only. And the working assumption continues to be that, although the aesthetic intentions may suffice to distinguish such texts as literary, they do not suffice to distinguish them further as fictional.

Five such features stand out. One mark of fictionality is said to be the use of indirect discourse about the mental states of characters. Such a practice implies an omniscient narrator. And no nonfictional speaker can rightly claim omniscience. Thus the occurrence of an illocutionary speech-act in such contexts must be construed not as the performance of such an act but as its representation. Another mark is the use of narrated monologues, which transforms performances of illocutionary acts into their representations. For such monologues contract the past and future tenses of verbs into a fictionally present time. Third, some putative descriptions of particular events in fictional texts are not required to satisfy the same epistemic conditions that govern descriptions in nonfictional texts. A further objective mark of fictionality is said to be the presence in fictional texts of nonreferring names or descriptions, that is, sentences containing names or descriptions of what does not exist. The illocutionary acts at issue in such sentences can only be represented and not actually performed. Finally, still another mark of the fictional text is the aspect of address without access. The author of a fictional text, while wishing to communicate by the very fact of writing and publishing such a text, deliberately withdraws from the occasions and circumstances that would allow personal access to an individual reader. "We hear a personal voice," this account goes, "but we know that it cannot be speaking to us, since we have not received the text from the author, but found it in a library or book-store or magazine" (Beardsley, "Fictions," 303).

With these observations in hand, I shall now detail the initial statement of the fictionality theory more fully. Thus, (2) what makes a text fictional is the presence in the text-type itself of certain markers and the operation of certain external and internal conditions that together ensure that a community of readers in a culture (*a*) takes the relevant sentences as illocutionary performances, (*b*) recognizes that at least some requisite conditions are not fully satisfied, and (*c*) accordingly goes on to construe these illocutions not as one final performance but as represented ones in the sense of selectively matched ones only.

If this is a fuller statement of the standard theory, what are the central qualifications? First, some fictional texts may be used to perform illocutionary acts, for example to make a political statement by being read aloud at a political rally. But such a use does not change the nature of the text; it remains a representation of the performance of such acts and not a performance in its own right. More interesting is the case in which the composition of a fictional text is used to perform an illocutionary act. For example, in writing a fictional text the author is understood to be inviting his or her readers to consider certain fictional entities in a particular set of fictional states of affairs.[7] Here again, however, the composition of such a text, just as its performance, can be an illocutionary use of a text that itself is not an illocution.

Second, the standard theory does not include the claim that fictions contain *only* representations of illocutionary acts; some fictions include both representations of such acts and the acts themselves. But the theory does include the related claim that the speakers in fictional works and not the authors perform the illocutionary acts in question. This claim, however, remains very general in that no attempt is made to explain just how speakers' statements in fictional texts can be absolved from bearing authors' intentions (Wolterstorff, ibid.).

Still, the function of the distinction is clear. For the speakers most often direct their illocutionary acts at characters in a work and hence cannot assume responsibility for the seriousness of such acts. And by merely representing illocutionary acts instead of performing them the author need not assume such responsibilities—hence the notion that fictional texts involve the suspension of speakers' responsibilities.

A third qualification turns on the distinction between a text being fictional and one becoming fictional. The standard theory attempts to do justice to both kinds of works, the readily recognizable and the puzzlingly experimental. Thus the basic task is to plot "a comprehensive, yet limited and explicit set of characteristics that both identifies and describes fictional works" (Krukowski, 328).

A text is fictional if it exhibits most but not necessarily all of such characteristics. But this set of characteristics is not fixed. And, as times change, innovatory pieces may provoke the addition of further elements to the original set. A text then becomes fictional by exhibiting some traditional characteristics and forcing interpretive communities to consider adding novel elements to the original set of characteristics (Krukowski, 324).

A fourth qualification touches on the structure of fictional works. For the standard theory of the fictional to hold, not all fictional works need to be structured as first-person narratives. This case, of course, is the central one in such a theory because first-person narrative illustrates very clearly just how the distinction between fictional speakers' performances and authors' performances arises. But other fictional texts are in fact structured in other ways. It is sufficient for the standard theory that many but not all fictional texts, whatever their basic structure, exhibit the fundamental distinction between those illocutionary acts that fictional speakers perform and those performances that authors represent (Wolterstorff, 316).

A fifth qualification is the distinction between what an author may represent about characters in a fictional text and what he or she may represent about himself or herself in a fictional text. For "just as we can assert of ourselves what is not true, so too can we fictionalize of ourselves what is not true" (Wolterstorff, 316). This distinction is important, for it addresses the often-remarked fact that at least some sentences in any fictional text can be parsed satisfactorily only on the hypothesis that they in part reveal something about the teller of the tale and not just about the speaker in the tale. "Literary discourse," this thesis reads, "cannot be viewed solely as telling a story. Discourse has significance beyond story" (Wolterstorff, 318). And part of this significance attaches not just to the figure of the narrator but also to the author specifically in the guise of fictionalizing something about himself or herself in the various stances of pretending.

A final qualification turns on just who or what is doing the representing in the text. For even when we gloss representing as a selective similarity relationship, we need to distinguish between what the author represents and what the text represents. In the standard view, the author initially represents what the text ultimately goes on to represent in a process called "the detachment of reference." The author intentionally devises and uses various modes of referring. However, "once the convention becomes understood and accepted in a community, the locus of reference is shifted from the person to the object used to refer and unintentional reference becomes possible" (Beardsley, "Fictions," 296–97). This qualification allows the standard view to accommodate the usual kinds of concerns which arise about so-called intentional fallacies, failures of reference, pretended reference, and so on.

With these qualifications in mind I now restate the fuller account more carefully: (3) What makes a text fictional is the nature and not the use of certain markers and conditions of a text-type structured in no one way other than such as to ensure that a community of readers in a culture takes those among the many cardinal sentences of the text which are speakers' illocutionary performances in a certain way. These illocutionary acts are taken as putative illocutions, finally incomplete ones, and therefore not authorial but textual representations of illocutions understood inside the continuing history of an interpretive community. Thus, what makes Pasternak's text fictional is the nature of certain linguistic and epistemic marks that ensure that the readers of the text *Doctor Zhivago* construe that text's supposed illocutions as representations and not as performances.

II

What we have so far is an account of what makes a text fictional. This explanation is a standard one in the sense that, without being the only view available, it remains one of the few comprehensive and influential accounts on record which continues to solicit sympathetic critical qualifications. The form of the description I have been elaborating will surely be put to further critical testing, but in its present form it already incorporates much of the most recent criticism. In short, we have an explanation that, whatever its weaknesses, can be taken as a serious working view of what constitutes fictionality.

I am now in a position to take up my second and central task, that of scrutinizing several philosophical texts from the perspective of what presumably makes them nonfictional. Accordingly, I propose to examine three eighteenth-century philosophical texts from a seminal period in the philosophy of art which trace the notion of taste across the successive figures of (*a*) the tasteful critic, (*b*) the judge of taste, and (*c*) the connoisseur. They are excerpts from Hume's "Of the Standard of Taste" (1757), Kant's *Critique of Judgment* (1790), and Hegel's Berlin lectures on art (the 1820s). Each philosophical text, we can assume, is a nonfictional one, and each is a representative example of excellent work on the part of the philosopher concerned. Further, it is best to choose expository prose pieces and to leave aside the more ambiguous pieces such as Plato's *Dialogues*, Augustine's *Confessions*, Anselm's prayers in the *Proslogion*, Descartes's *Meditations*, the *Dialogues* of Berkeley and Hume, and Mill's *Autobiography*. My procedure is to examine such texts in the light of the standard account. The working hypothesis to be tested is that these philosophical texts are nonfictional in the sense that they do not come under the standard account of fictionality.

The Tasteful Critic

Though the principles of taste be universal, and, nearly, if not entirely the same in all men, yet few are qualified to give judgement on any work of art, or establish their own sentiment as the standard of beauty. The organs of internal sensation are seldom so perfect as to allow the general principles their full play, and produce a feeling correspondent to those principles. They either labour under some defect, or are vitiated by some disorder; and by that means, excite a sentiment, which may be pronounced erroneous. When the critic has no delicacy, he judges without any distinction . . . the finer touches pass unnoticed and are disregarded. Where he is not aided by practice, his verdict is attended with confusion and hesitation . . . where he lies under the influence of prejudice, all his natural sentiments are perverted. Where good sense is wanting, he is not qualified to discern the beauties of design and reasoning . . . Under some or other of these imperfections, the generality of men labour; and hence a true judge in the finer arts is observed . . . to be so rare a character: strong sense, united to delicate sentiment, improved by practice, perfected by comparison, and cleared of all prejudice, can alone entitle critics to this valuable character; and the joint verdict of such . . . is the true standard of taste and beauty.[8]

Hume's text, from his 1757 piece "Of the Standard of Taste," is generally understood as part of a nonfictional, indeed a philosophical, work. The philosophical character of the text is said to be evident in the preeminently argumentative style in which the text is elaborated. The speaker begins with a carefully qualified thesis. He proceeds to adduce reasons in support of the thesis. These reasons are not merely stated; they are ordered in such a way as to make their point evident. Further qualifications are noted. The central elements are gathered into a summary conclusion, and a further argumentative discussion is motivated.

The text, of course, is not just argumentative, for readers usually respond as well to several of its striking literary features. For example, the text turns on a well-observed contrast between two characters, the critic and the judge. Both finally give way to a third character, the judicious critic, who unites the key elements of his predecessors. Another literary feature is the rhetorical use of careful parallelism in the construction of the sequence of three relative clauses, each beginning with a "where" and all reaching a minor crescendo at the very center of the text. However, the standard claim goes, even if the text has literary elements, it is still, at least on the initial formulation of the standard view of fictionality, to be judged as nonfictional. The reason quite simply is that Hume's text does not include any representations of illocutionary acts.

But, on reflection, this verdict seems too simple. Even though we must grant that the text includes no such explicit representations, still the use of identifiable characters, even in a third-person narrative, might be taken together with other factors as warrant enough for inferring that the text includes implicit representations of illocutionary acts. Such a case, of course, needs detailed support. But without trying to provide that support just now, I think there is at least the possibility of arguing such a case.

A standard theorist might not require us to go so far, however, for he has at hand a simpler move. He may allow the possibility of implicit representations of illocutionary acts and yet still claim that the possibility is not actualized in Hume's text because that text does not conform to the second and fuller statement of his theory. Consider this move in more detail in the light of a second philosophical and putatively nonfictional text, this time on the nature of the judgment of taste.

The Judge of Taste

The delight which we connect with the representation of the real existence of an object is called interest. Such a delight, therefore, always invites a reference to the faculty of desire . . . Now, where the question is whether something is beautiful, we do not want to know, whether we, or anyone else, are, or even could be, concerned in the real existence of the thing, but rather what estimate we form of it on mere contemplation (intuition or reflection). If anyone asks me whether I consider that the palace I see before me is beautiful, I may, perhaps, reply that I do not care for things of that sort that are merely made to be gaped at . . . All this may be admitted or approved; only it is not the point now at issue. All one wants to know is whether the mere representation of the object is to my liking, no matter how indifferent I may be to the real existence of the object of this representation.[9]

Kant is at pains here, in his 1790 *Critique of Judgment*, to show how the quality of the attention we pay to the object of a judgment of taste (e.g., "this picture is beautiful") differs from that which we pay to the object of any other kind of judgment (e.g., "this picture is expensive"). Just as in the Hume text, we can note a number of features that seem to distinguish the text as philosophical and hence as presumably nonfictional—a sustained argumentative structure, a fastidiousness about distinctions, the recourse to a technical vocabulary, a high resolution in the level of analysis, and so on. By contrast, however, literary elements with few exceptions (one example is the use of a brief illustration) are noticeably lacking: where are the characters, where is the plot, where are the rhetorical and persuasive uses of language?

Reading this text, a standard theorist might press his earlier point. Thus even though some implicit representations of illocutionary acts might possibly be teased from such a text, the efforts would be insufficiently justified. Consequently, the so-called implicit representations should be judged implausible. For on the second and fuller account of the standard theory, this text does not exhibit the marks of those conditions and constitutive rules that invite uptake on the part of cultivated readers. This uptake normally results in the recognition that certain illocutionary actions can be construed "by filling in the gaps of the text in a reasonable way" (Beardsley, "Fictions," 307). But here he fails. Accordingly, the original verdict that the standard theorist brings down on the Hume text is now extended to the Kant text also on the same but more detailed grounds—both philosophical texts are judged to be nonfictional.

But while no longer too simple, the verdict now seems shortsighted. Granted that Kant's text lacks virtually all the literary elements that might have invited Hume's readers to infer the possibility of his text's implicitly representing illocutionary acts, still Kant's text turns in part on a remarkably suggestive syntactic feature that the verdict of "nonfictional" has overlooked—the play of personal pronouns.

Kant's text in fact abounds in variations not only in the selection of pronouns but in the specification of their referents. Notice first the variety: the movement is from "we" to "anyone" and again to "one." And now notice the various referents of those pronouns. One pronoun ("we") refers to both the speaker and the implied readers of the text; another ("anyone else") refers to everyone who could be in the situation at issue; one pair ("me" and "I") refers to the author; another pronoun ("one") also refers to the author; still another ("I") refers to the speaker; and finally we have a pronoun ("everyone") that refers to all those rational persons who concur with the conclusions of Kant's argument.

This analysis is, of course, elementary, although it could easily be developed in greater detail. But even as it stands, reflection on the play of pronouns raises a serious question about the satisfactoriness of the standard theorist's second try at bringing down the verdict of "nonfictional" on philosophical texts. For even without examining the consequences of change of person or shifts in quantification or modal variations, this pronominal play is itself suggestive enough to solicit uptake on the part of some community of cultivated readers. Hence some marks, *pace* the standard theorists, do seem present in the text and thus can be construed as allowing the inference that the text implies the representation of illocutionary acts even if it does not explicitly incorporate these representations. Accordingly, a question arises whether such a text as this one is properly construed as fictional or nonfictional. Or, we may ask in Derrida's terms, "to what extent does traditional philosophical discourse . . . derive from fiction?"[10]

The usual answer to this question is that Kant's text and philosophical texts generally are instances of serious discourse and consequently must be construed as nonfictional. To construct the text otherwise is, in Searle's terms, to assimilate "the sense in which writing can be said to be parasitic on spoken language with the sense in which fiction, etc., are parasitic on nonfiction or standard discourse. But these are quite different. In the case of the distinction between fiction and nonfiction, the relation is one of logical dependency. One could not have the concept of fiction without the concept of serious discourse."[11]

This answer, however, turns on certain assumptions that may not go unchallenged. Thus, someone may point out the unexamined opposition between serious and nonserious discourse. And indeed Derrida writes that "one could with equal legitimacy reverse the order of dependence. This order is not a one-way street [*à sens unique*] (how can the serious be defined as postulated without reference to the nonserious, even if the latter is held to be simply external to it?) and everything that claims to base itself upon such a conception disqualifies itself immediately" (Derrida, 248). But this point itself turns on one's accepting the legitimacy of Derrida's characteristic play with oppositions, and Searle regrets this kind of move.[12]

It may not be possible to resolve this kind of disagreement. But before facing that eventuality we need to recognize that the controversy about the fictional and the nonfictional turns on different interpretations of what is meant by "serious discourse." And the key to that discussion is just how we are to understand the implication that serious discourse makes truth-claims.

The standard theorist, however, may still rejoin that, despite the objections raised to a verdict of nonfictionality based on the first two formulations of the standard theory, philosophical texts may finally be seen to be proper instances of the nonfictional if we appeal to the third and most detailed formulation. Thus, granted that some philosophical texts include markers that may seem to invite fictional uptake, still the *relevant* markers for fictional texts are not present in philosophical ones. Consider this final rejoinder in the context of one last philosophical text, this one not on the standards or judgment of taste but on its limits.

The Connoisseur

Since the work of art is not . . . meant merely in general to arouse feelings (for in that case it would have this aim in common, without any specific difference, with oratory, historical writing, religious edification, etc.), but to do so only in so far as it is beautiful, reflection on the beautiful hit upon the idea of looking for a peculiar *feeling* of the beautiful, and finding a specific *sense* of beauty. In this quest it soon appeared that such a sense is no blind instinct, made firmly definite by nature, capable from the start in and by itself of distinguishing beauty. Hence education was demanded for this sense, and the educated sense of beauty was called *taste* which, although an educated appreciation and discovery of beauty, was supposed to remain still in the guise of immediate feeling.[13]

Like those of Hume and Kant, this text from Hegel's 1820s Berlin lectures on art exhibits some of the generally recognizable features of philosophical prose—an argumentative structure, the careful consideration of alternative views, the use of historical material for speculative turns, indications of the evolution of an abstract idiolect (in and by itself, Hegel says, the concern for validity), and so on. And once again like Hume's text, but not like Kant's, Hegel's makes some room for such literary elements as the movement of a narrative, the use of rhetorical devices, a sensitivity for the use of historical and period echoes. But, the standard theorist would urge, this text includes no explicit representations of illocutionary acts. Nor does it include any of those relevant linguistic markers that would authorize proper fictional uptake. The pronouns are not at play here. And even should someone try to make something of the interesting shifts in tense halfway through this text, closer analysis would, the claim is, be able to explain away such shifts in terms other than those of the requisite markers for fiction. So, once again, the original verdict should remain unchanged—philosophical texts are nonfictional, but now it is justified by an appeal to the carefully qualified features of the standard view's third formulation.

The verdict is no longer either simple or short-sighted. But again after reflection I still do not think it will do, for the verdict now seems blinkered. Even in such cases as the Hegel text where either the requisite markers are missing or no discrete markers are present at all, the text can still, I believe, work such effects on some community of cultivated readers that it may properly be taken in part as fictional. Here the signal may be construed in two ways. Either a reader attributes to the text nonperceptual properties such as "having been composed by students and not by Hegel himself" or "being intended to illustrate Hegel's mature thoughts" and accordingly construes the generalizations in the text as implied representations of illocutionary acts. Or a reader observes in the text diffused signs rather than discrete markers—recall the juxtaposition of the central generalizations with the evocative personification of genius in the suggested metaphorical guise of the Russian spirit driving Napoleon back from Borodino—these signs are contextualized in such a way that they can once again be taken as implied representations of illocutionary acts. In either case it remains an open question whether the absence of specific linguistic markers of fictionality is sufficient warrant for construing such a text as nonfictional, for some markers are epistemic and not just linguistic ones. And epistemic markers may be other than explicit; they may in fact be implicit. Thus the justice of the repeated verdict of nonfictionality on these representative philosophical texts remains in doubt.

Still, the text makes at least one basic assertion for which it provides some justification, namely the claim that the connoisseur has replaced the person of taste. Accordingly, the question arises whether such a claim can be understood as true or false. Thus a strategy begins to take shape. For if the claim can be appraised as true or false, then sufficient warrant is in hand for construing the text as "serious discourse" and hence as an instance of the nonfictional.

The usual answer to this question is, "Yes, the text does make a claim; the claim can be assessed as true or false; and in fact, for the simple reason that times have changed since Hegel read his Berlin lectures in the 1820s, the claim here is obviously false." I might add that the claim is obviously false in just the way Searle means when he writes that "Derrida has a distressing penchant for saying things that are obviously false" ("Reiterating the Differences," 203). But such a verdict is not uncontroversial. Derrida replies: "Whenever I hear the words 'it's true,' 'it's false,' 'it's evident,' 'evidently this or that,' or 'in a fairly obvious way,' I become suspicious. This is especially so when an adverb, apparently redundant, is used to reinforce the declaration . . . the notion of evidence, together with its entire system of associated values (presence, truth, immediate intuition, assured certitude, etc.), is precisely what *Sec* [Signature Event Context] is calling into question" (175–76).

This reply, however, seems to assume what it is trying to refute, namely that some reliable argumentative basis for distinguishing between true and false claims is available. If this basis is neither evidence nor the other matters Derrida mentions, nonetheless Derrida implies that there is at least some basis. But that view is exactly what is in question. Searle goes after this point in "The World Turned Upside Down" when he writes that "on the question of truth, [Jonathan] Culler wants to have it both ways . . . [saying] that truth is a kind of fiction and that 'truth is both what can be demonstrated within an accepted framework and what simply is the case, whether or not anyone could believe it or validate it.'"[14] Polemics being what they are, however, Searle's criticism is attacked in turn as a misrepresentation,[15] only to be reaffirmed in even stronger terms. A "purely textual analysis of the works" he has cited, Searle replies, would show that deconstructionists like Derrida are not, as one of their defenders claims, "almost obsessively occupied with truth." "Authors who are concerned with discovering the truth are concerned with evidence and reasons, with consistency and inconsistency, with logical consequences, explanatory adequacy, verification and testability" (Searle, ibid.).

But surely this is a rather special version of truth. Moreover, it is only one of a variety of versions which have been explored in the history of philosophy from Plato to Nietzsche. And, besides being traditionally controversial, this narrow version of truth is newly controversial today. Hence it cannot be accepted as presented here, as "obviously" supported by a firm consensus, an orthodoxy by which any philosopher today who claims competence is to be judged.

Texts that make truth-claims, then, cannot be judged simply as fictional texts when the kind of truth at issue turns out to be unrecognizable in Searle's view of truth.[16] In short, the current view of Hegel's text and philosophical texts generally as nonfictional cannot be correct. For just as in the case of Kant's text, where the issue was how to construe the sense of the predicate "serious discourse," so too here, where the issue is one of parsing the proposition "this text makes a truth-claim," recent controversies about poststructuralists confront us with the likelihood that our current proposals may turn out to beg the question. Whether a text can be said to be making a truth-claim reverts to a still prior question about whether the text in question is cognitive.

III

In this final section I would like to consider a key objection to this presentation, formulate the alternatives my view would seem to leave us with, and then suggest several considerations that might urge us to pursue one of these alternatives more strenuously than others.

Objections may be brought to bear on the perspective I have been sketching so far about what is said to make a text fictional. Someone may wish to insist on the need for a more sophisticated account of speech-acts. Another may want a more detailed discussion of the place in my presentation of so-called markers and their conditions and rules. And still someone else may require a more thorough analysis of the cardinal distinctions between implicit and explicit representations of illocutionary speech acts. Each of these critical concerns is reasonable. Yet each seems to be more a request for detail than a fundamental objection. For although one might fail to satisfy these requests, then again one might succeed. So dissatisfaction with the level of my analysis, while legitimate, is not a basic objection.

The standard account of fictionality I have constructed here, someone might argue, is seriously flawed in omitting altogether the notion of genre. Without complementing the speech-act analysis with a relevant discussion of genre, we wind up with an account of fictionality which is either overingenious or simply counterintuitive. The account is overingenious because it depends on what seems to be a continuing and probably unending series of technical amendments designed to obviate an equally inexhaustible supply of counterexamples. And the account is counterintuitive because it works against the grain of our habitual practice of initially categorizing most if not all texts in terms of some loose sense of kinds, sorts, and types—in short, of genres.

The following is an example of this objection:

To account for fictional discourse, we need not postulate a separate but equal set of linguistic rules; we need only postulate one rule—the pretence-of-reporting rule. The rule knowledge required to focus or interpret fictional discourse is identical with that required for non-fictional [discourse] with the exception of this one rule. Let's call this rule *a genre rule* to distinguish it from grammatical, propositional-act, and illocutionary-act rules . . . fictional and non-fictional discourse share the grammatical and speech-act rules of the language.[17]

This view, when cast in the form of an objection to the standard account of fictionality, cannot be sidestepped with dismissive remarks about inappropriateness. For the objection already incorporates many of exactly those features of the standard account which I have been relying on for my construction. The objection in fact is an internal one, phrased with the help of the central terms in the theory it challenges, and hence quite robust. But can this objection overturn the standard account?

Granted that the central term in the objection is vague, can we unbalance the objection by applying critical pressure to the peculiar indeterminacy in the way the vague notion is used? For notice that this basic objection not only includes distinctions between broad and narrow genres, discrete and overlapping ones, and genres and subgenres, but even between coincident genres. "Sonnets," this account reads in another place, "can be either fictional or non-fictional discourse. Wordsworth's are fictional; Elizabeth Barrett Browning's nonfictional; Shakespeare's in doubt. The genre rules that constitute sonnets—specifying phonological, semantic, and graphic features—are neutral to fictionality" (Brown and Steinmann, 153). Such a generous view of genre has its liabilities, but I need not analyze them here—for again critics may appeal to some principle of charity in alleging that, given the occasion, the theory of genre their objection turns on could in principle be sufficiently detailed. Of course charity can turn into license, but obligingly I may say that it does not in this case.

What may allow an effective reply to this basic objection is neither vagueness in its central term nor indeterminacy in the uses of that notion but the incoherence of its cardinal feature—the pretense-of-reporting rule.

We know roughly what this curious expression refers to—namely, the recent view that fictional storytellers, unlike nonfictional ones, are engaged in pretense. Instead of describing, reporting, asserting, evaluating, judging, and criticizing, writers of fiction are merely pretending to describe, report, assert, evaluate, judge, criticize, and so on. Thus when we read a text that includes an apparently genuine description but that we already know antecedently is a fictional text, we are to construe that putative description as a pretended one only. For the claim is that sentences that constitute those putative descriptions are in fact to be understood as prefixed with some such phrase as "In the fiction such and such . . ." or "In the novel such and such . . ." Further, this prefixing must itself be understood against the so-called background beliefs actually operative in a culture at a certain time.

Thus the prefixing plus the background beliefs is the prerequisite for the pretense on which the genre of this text turns.

This view of fictional discourse as pretended discourse is not naive; a number of important works in recent years have made use of refined versions of this notion. But despite its sophistication, the appeal to such a view in support of objections to the standard account of fictionality is threatened with incoherence. The problem lies in the conjunction of a questionable account of pretense with an open-ended use of the term *rule*. For the basic objection turns on the expression "the-pretense-of-reporting-rule." I can leave the narrowness of this formulation (why just reporting and not asserting, affirming, denying, etc.?) without comment. But I cannot leave unremarked the suggestion of equivocation in the use of the word *rule*. For if this objection is to work, we must make room for grammatical rules, utterance-act rules, propositional-act rules, illocutionary-act rules, sets of linguistic rules, and the pretense-of-reporting rule, which we are told is also to be called genre rule. One needs to know whether all these rules are, or indeed can be, rules in the same sense. The question becomes all the more critical when we note that this objection already explicitly includes a distinction between at least two kinds of rules, regulative and constitutive ones.

My critical question is not uncharitable; it arises from linking talk about grammatical rules with talk about propositional rules. Such rules exist. But we know that they are different in at least three respects—these rules not only pertain to quite different kinds of things and incorporate quite different contents but they are said to be rules in arguably quite different senses of the word. If, however, the suggestion of equivocation arises with respect to how the concept of rules is to be understood in this familiar and standard distinction, the suggestion of equivocation arises even more strongly in the unfamiliar and deviant talk here about a "pretense-of-reporting-rule." In linking talk of rules with, as the journals show, a highly questionable account of pretending, such talk is unfamiliar. And it is deviant in that its proponents resort to stipulation in categorizing this rule—"Let's call this rule a genre rule," they write.

I want to suggest, then, that this serious and basic objection to the standard account of fictionality is nonetheless ineffective because it allows good grounds for doubting its coherence. The notion of genre is clearly central for any account of fictionality, and presumably a standard account must eventually make some room for some such notion. But unless more cogent reasons than the ones adduced here can be brought forward in its support, the present objection is not substantive.

To summarize: I have constructed a standard account of what makes some texts fictional. Further, negating this view does not seem to account for the putative nonfictional character of several representative philosophical texts. And I have investigated and finally found unacceptable a fundamental objection to the standard account. We are left therefore with several alternatives.

We may, on the one hand, construe philosophical texts as counterexamples to the negation of the standard account. The consequence is that we persist in taking philosophical texts as nonfictional on some as yet to be explained intuitive basis but not on the basis of the present theory of fictionality. The task, then, is to get on with the long-range project of revising the standard account still further so that in some future statement of that account virtually all counterexamples, at least of a philosophical sort, will be obviated. We may, on the other hand, construe the philosophical texts as subsumable under the standard account. The consequence, then, is that we begin to read at least some philosophical texts with an eye to their fictional components. Accordingly, the task is to take up the much more immediate job of revising our traditional and still largely intuitive accounts of the nature of a philosophical text. Still other alternatives can, of course, be formulated. But with at least these two alternatives before us I want to suggest that the second is more promising.

It is true that further work on revising the standard account should and presumably will yield important intellectual clarifications. And the expected results will include a greater sophistication in the theories of the fictional, the practices of criticism, the teaching of literature, and perhaps even the production of literary works of art. But given the technical level already required for the statement of the standard account, even in the simple form I have settled for here, the relative slowness with which theoretical breakthroughs occur in philosophy, and especially the intrinsic difficulty in any definitional strategy of obviating virtually all those endless objections that the sophisticated use of counterexample strategies can generate, it is not evident that important enough results will be available for some time.

Consider, however, the kind of results one might expect relatively sooner from a program devoted to investigating the fictional character of philosophical texts. The results do not initially depend on further technical progress in the articulation of the standard account. Even in the present form of this account, a number of interesting features can be noted in philosophical texts. What makes these features interesting is not just their linguistic character but their epistemic aspect. For these features would seem to call for some immediate revisions in how we traditionally appraise philosophical texts for their truth or falsity, their validity or invalidity, and their soundness or unsoundness. In short, these features invite more careful accounts of what we take to be not just the rhetorical structure but the so-called informal logical structure of philosophical texts.

Fictional aspects of philosophical texts are also interesting because they suggest the presence of similar kinds of features in other nonfictional texts. For example, nonextensional predicates also attach to such central texts in a society as legal documents, religious materials, scientific accounts, moral justifications, and psychoanalytic reports. The promise is that explicating the fictional aspects of philosophical texts and their relevant consequences for the description, evaluation, and appreciation of those texts can be generalized to produce similar consequences in our readings of other, perhaps more socially valuable, putatively nonfictional texts.

Besides promising relatively speedy results in rethinking our understanding of the informal epistemic and logical structure of such texts and the relatively easy generalization of some such results to the reassessment of the character of other kinds of nonfictional texts, pursuing the analysis of the fictional aspects of philosophical texts also promises central revisions in our traditional understanding of what fictionality is. The character of philosophical texts is such that they must be turned against the models used in their analysis. Like literary works of art, philosophical texts may not, on peril of dissolution, be reduced to the status of examples for theories. We do not yet agree on how the opposite of the fictional is to be specified. Such an agreement would have to turn on some account of the real. And that task itself, as the history of metaphysics reminds us, generates texts that are peculiar hybrids of the fictional and the nonfictional. Part of the promise of such a program is not just a fuller and perhaps richer account of the fictional than what we have so long and narrowly labored with, but a formulation of the reasons why no richer account of the fictional can be expected without an account—or shall we say story?—of why the real itself would seem to be partly fictional.

In concluding, I would return to Derrida's remark that "the task is to consider philosophy also as 'a literary genre.'" How are we to take such a view? Some would argue that once we construe philosophical texts as literary and go on to take the "literary text" as nothing more than the play of signifiers, then what initially prompted us to take up such books and read, namely their claims to tell the truth, simply evaporates (Danto, "Writing," 1036). But we may understand Derrida's remark here differently:

Derrida does not think that philosophy is a literary genre in the sense that there is a genre of texts (called "literature") of which philosophical works (along with novels, lyrics, epics, etc.) are species. On the contrary he has argued that it is impossible to distinguish and clearly demonstrate different genres of writing. What we ordinarily recognize as philosophy and what we ordinarily call literature are linked by their common submission to the conditions of writing . . . It does not follow, therefore, . . . that to read philosophy as literature is to discount its concern with truth, or that the interest of a philosophical text evaporates once its claim to tell the truth has been disturbed by deconstructive analysis. It is indeed just that claim to tell the truth and the preoccupation with truth which are most interesting to a deconstructive reader of philosophical texts. (Mackey, "Reply," 1280)

My concern has been to suggest that current questions of speech-act theory and genre which may arise in connection with philosophical texts lead back to questions about whether such texts are fictional or nonfictional. Currently, this distinction is based on a prior set of considerations about whether a text can properly be construed as making truth-claims, and about what is customarily called "seriousness," as the celebrated debates of John Searle and Jacques Derrida make clear. However, since the sense of truth most often invoked in talk about truth-claims is a narrow sense of truth as truth-functional, the issue of seriousness would lead to the problem of how the cognitive character of a text is to be understood. Here again we currently find disagreement among those who interpret cognitivity strongly, in terms of a text as a source of knowledge (and knowledge as justified true belief), and those who would insist on the weaker but richer view of a text's cognitive character as its capacity to be a source of insight or enlightenment. This latter view, I think, amounts to the notion that any philosophical text can be taken as trying to tell the truth in the sense that, regardless of its genre, it may be a serious work that sometimes results in the enhancement of perception, the deepening of self-understanding, and the small occasional, progressive, and incessant transformations of our habitual and unreflective dealings with a so-called real world.

Notes

1. B. Pasternak, *Doctor Zhivago* (New York: New American Library, 1958), 18.

2. This view is not, of course, the only one available.

3. M. Beardsley, "Aesthetic Interaction and Fictive Illocutions," in Paul Hernadi, ed., *What Is Literature?* (Bloomington: Indiana University Press, 1978), 161–77.

4. See M. Beardsley, "Fictions as Representation," *Synthese* 46 (1981): 291–314.

5. See Stanley Fish, *Is There a Text in This Class?* (Cambridge: Harvard University Press, 1980), passim.

6. See L. Krukowski, "Commentary," *Synthese* 46 (1981): 325–30.

7. See N. Wolterstorff, "Response," ibid., 315–24.

8. Excerpt from David Hume, "Of the Standard of Taste," in G. Dickie and R. Sclafani, eds., *Aesthetics* (New York: St. Martin's Press, 1977), 601–2.

9. Excerpt from Immanuel Kant, in Dickie and Sclafani, 644.

10. Jacques Derrida, "Limited Inc. abc . . . ," *Glyph 2: Johns Hopkins Textual Studies* (Baltimore: Johns Hopkins University Press, 1977), 217.

11. John Searle, "Reiterating the Differences: A Reply to Derrida," *Glyph 1: Johns Hopkins Textual Studies* (Baltimore: Johns Hopkins University Press, 1977), 207. See also Richard Rorty, "Philosophy as a Kind of Writing: An Essay on Derrida," *New Literary History* 10 (1978–79): 141–60, and his earlier essay "Derrida on Language, Being, and Abnormal Philosophy," *Journal of Philosophy* 74 (1977): 673–81.

12. John Searle, "The World Turned Upside Down," *New York Review of Books,* 27 October 1983, 76–77.

13. G. W. F. Hegel, *Introduction to the Berlin Aesthetics Lectures of the 1820s,* trans. T. M. Knox (Oxford: Oxford University Press, 1979), 34–36.

14. Searle is citing Culler's *On Deconstruction* (Ithaca: Cornell University Press, 1982), 154.

15. R. Mackey, "An Exchange on Deconstruction," *New York Review of Books,* 2 February 1984, 47.

16. See Arthur C. Danto, "Writing and Its Spokesman," *TLS,* 30 September 1983, 1035–36; R. Mackey, "Reply," *TLS,* 18 November 1983, 1279–80; and Danto's "Rejoinder," *TLS,* 9 December 1983, 1374.

17. R. L. Brown and M. Steinmann, Jr., "Native Readers of Fiction," in Hernadi, *What Is Literature?,* 152, 157.

4
Levels of Discourse in Plato's Dialogues

If the essays of Danto and Judovitz suggest some of the ways in which philosophy is inescapably "literary," Harry Berger, Jr.'s, essay, "Levels of Discourse in Plato's Dialogues," deals squarely with those who claim to discover the literary dimension of the Platonic dialogues in their dramatic nature. Here we are very far indeed from a reading of the dialogues which presupposes that Plato expounded a systematic metaphysics and which accordingly searches the dialogues for the Platonic system (on this see E. N. Tigerstedt, *Interpreting Plato* [1977]). Berger suspects a close link between the search for Plato's "system" and a preference for oral teaching among these interpreters of Plato, the "Indirect Listeners." In Berger's view, Plato shares a critical view of the metaphysics associated with this desire for (oral) presence, the blame for which has been laid on Plato by Heidegger and Derrida.

It is perhaps more difficult to respond to the tradition of "Direct Listening" to Plato's texts. The Direct Listeners, who are largely indebted to Leo Strauss, are confident of their ability to identify which among the various *logoi* discussed by Socrates and the others in the dialogues are indeed Plato's opinions. In order to accomplish this task, this group of commentators has elaborated numerous explanatory schemes (e.g., allegorical, genetic, developmental, systematic) in terms of which they have tried to elicit "the presence of the master, the coherence of his meaning, and the disclosure of his mind." This tradition is, in Berger's view, afflicted by deep confusion and self-contradiction: in spite of themselves, their practice is subversively influenced by the very theory they reject. They regard the dialogues as achieving literary or dramatic closure ("literary" and "dramatic" being roughly the same) while at the same time remaining open-ended in terms of the problematics they explore.

The body of Berger's essay falls in two parts. In the first he offers two exemplary readings, one of the *Theaetetus* and the other of the *Ion*. His purpose is to demonstrate a reading of Plato which responds to that feature of the dialogues to which Danto pointed in his essay on the relations of philosophy and literature: their status as writing—that is, as texts that must perforce be read. However, "reading," in Berger's view, does not necessarily imply the transmission of authority (or authorized meaning) from the text or from personages figured in it to the reader. We find texts that deny closure (in Berger's formulation, "the boundary conditions of the text are underdetermined by the boundaries and interior of the dramatic encounter"). Thus while lines of force may flow from text or personage to reader, this need not be so; in the *Ion*, for example, these relationships undergo reversal: Ion's hold on his audience is, in Berger's words, "the reflex, the mirror image, of their hold on him . . . The audience is actually the first link in the chain, the magnetic source that moves upward and backward from rhapsode to poet to god."

To the extent that Berger's readings of Plato avoid making dramatistic assumptions about the texts, they suggest that a serious reevaluation of the dominant strain of commentaries on Plato associated with Leo Strauss is in order. This second major project requires a reconsideration of the mimetic postulates underlying the dramatistic model of the Platonic text as developed, for instance, by Jacob Klein and Paul Friedländer, as well as of the suppositions of Stanley Rosen, who, in Berger's view, posits the ironic character of the dialogue as a literary form while relying heavily on assumptions about the systematic coherence of the dialogues as a group.

Following up his early comment that the preference for Plato's oral teaching and a search for Plato's system are twin aspects of that single desire which Heidegger and Derrida have called the "metaphysics of presence," Berger turns to Derrida himself in order to suggest the extent to which a critique of this metaphysics of presence may already be found within the Platonic dialogues. Derrida was the first to suggest that the dialogues privilege the argument and drama they represent only in order then to problematize them. And similarly, Derrida's essay on the *pharmakon* works toward freeing the "textual system" from the "author function." But these strategies then allow Derrida to continue to use such concepts as "author" and "Plato," even if *sous rature*: "Derrida tries to avoid 'blaming' on the author a necessary inability to control the ambivalence originally inscribed in the very notion—*pharmakon*—that grounds and evokes the Platonic discourse, for example, 'all these significations nonetheless appear, and, more precisely, all these words appear in the text of "Plato." Only the chain is concealed, and, to an inappreciable extent, concealed from the author himself, if any such thing exists.' Yet [the essay] 'Plato's Pharmacy' persistently raises a question about the proprietary relation of authors and speakers to their discourse, a question it strives to suppress." (For a complementary discussion and alternative understanding of the "proprietary function," see Alexander Nehamas's essay in this volume, "Writer, Text, Work, Author.") Berger thus places Derrida in the line of those who must reify the authorial intentions of the Platonic text and who, in so doing, undermine whatever is significant in our talk about "texts" and "writing." "In the final analysis," Berger says, "Derrida's reifying repetition of appeals to the erased Plato's intentions has the effect of preventing his 'Plato' from seeing and doing what he, Derrida, sees and does." In Berger's reading of the dialogues, "Plato" himself anticipates the problematic that we customarily associate with Derrida.

Levels of Discourse in Plato's Dialogues

Harry Berger, Jr.

"The soul is tripartite." "The soul is immortal." "There are Forms." "The One and the Indefinite Dyad are the ultimate ontological principles." These propositions and others are often written down as opinions of Plato. Those who have written them down know whereof they write because they believe they have either indirectly or directly heard Plato speak. The Indirect Listeners are those who circumvent Plato's writings and rely on the "basically indisputable testimony of Plato's pupils" as to the content of the master's oral doctrines.[1] Why do I call them Indirect Listeners? Because they read as if listening to the words of those whose knowledge can be trusted, since they in turn—the pupils—listened to the words of Plato, who must have known what he was talking about and wanted to pass it on to them. Indirect Listeners argue that the writings are unreliable sources of the doctrine for "the hermeneutic reasons given by Plato himself in the *Phaedrus* and Seventh Letter," and that "Plato's first principles, as he himself often said, can only be understood in depth via the long course of oral dialectic" (ibid., 27). It is not yet clear to me how, given this assumption, any reasons derived from writings ascribed to Plato can be admitted as evidence of anything "Plato himself" thought or said, so long as the ascriber has not himself taken the long course. Nor is it yet clear how this Listener has been able to determine that Plato "himself often said" something, or determine how many times he said it, and where, apart from the unreliable writings, these several utterances are recorded.

What is reasonably clear, or what has been made so by E. N. Tigerstedt's critique of these Indirect or Esoterist Listeners, is that strict reliance on the traces of Plato's "oral teaching" seems intimately related to the "conviction that . . . Plato expounded a systematic metaphysics."[2] Though Gaiser insists against Tigerstedt that "systematic thinking" need not be "equated with rigid dogmatism . . . as if there was no such thing as an open or dialectical system" (29), his own brief sketch of the system (12–13) makes it appear anything but open or dialectical. In his version, Plato's lecture on the Good, which he claims contained the substance of "dialectical discussions" previously reserved for "an inner circle of pupils" (25), provides the sort of Final Answer and Full Disclosure that can resolve doubt by submitting all problems to the regime of a mathematical world model.

The point I want to emphasize, before turning from the Indirect to the Direct Listeners, is that the close link between the preference for oral teaching and the search for Plato's system is symptomatic: these are two aspects of a single desire, the desire that Derrida, following Heidegger, has analyzed under the rubric of "the metaphysics of presence." I shall return to this point, since my thesis is that Plato, or at least the author of Plato's dialogues, or at the very least the text of Plato's dialogues as I read it, shares with Heidegger and Derrida a critical view of the metaphysics of presence, which has always been blamed on the name of Plato.

The Direct Listeners are those to whom Plato speaks in his writing through Socrates and the other major interlocutors (Parmenides, the Eleatic Stranger, Timaeus, the Athenian Stranger). The tradition of Direct Listening[3] goes back to antiquity and is still flourishing, and its various schools or subtraditions are united under the flag of what has come to be known as the "mouthpiece theory." Mouthpiece theorists have had to show ingenuity in auditing the accounts of Platonic ventriloquism, since the dialogues abound in contradictions and inconsistencies that are not easy to reconcile. Hence in order to determine which *logoi* among the many discussed by Socrates and the others are Plato's opinions, they have elaborated various explanatory schemes—allegorical, genetic or developmental, systematic—in terms of which they have tried to elicit the presence of the master, the coherence of his meaning, and the disclosure of his mind. Typical of their claims is the statement of a recent and particularly dogged proponent, Terence Irwin, that in *Plato's Moral Theory* he is giving "an exposition of Plato's views," citing "textual evidence as fully as I can, to show that I am discussing some views he really holds."[4] Though his appetite for full citation is slender and quickly satisfied, he is—like other mouthpiece theorists—confident of his ability to distinguish the real views of the Platonic Socrates from those of Plato and to document the successes and failures of Plato's defense, rejection, and revision of Socratic ethics. Plato's views are important, he concludes, even though "much of what he says is false, and much more is confused, vague, inconclusive, and badly defended" (4).

I do not intend to discuss the failures of the mouthpiece theory here, because at this late date that would be redundant. Direct Listeners have not suffered from lack of critical attention, but they display an impressive ability to remain deaf to those who argue, as Leo Strauss did in 1964, that "Plato conceals his opinions," that the Platonic dialogues "must be read like dramas," and that the utterances of fictional speakers directly reflect their author's views no more in Plato's case than in Shakespeare's.[5] Irwin, who does not list Strauss in his bibliography, writes as if no such critical tradition existed, forcing an unfriendly reviewer to remind us once again that there is no warrant for taking any speaker's utterance "to be something 'Plato said'—as in the standard misleading locution."[6] It is possible to show that if logical and thematic analysis of the dialogues is undertaken from a standpoint outside of the mouthpiece theory, some of the limits imposed by the theory can be avoided, and the contributions of its practitioners enhanced. But my purpose here is to examine a particular kind of confusion, perhaps of self-contradiction, manifest in the work of several leading critics of the mouthpiece theory, and to suggest that in spite of themselves their practice is subversively influenced by the theory they reject. I offer as a clue to this problem a statement by Irwin's reviewer: the dialogues have "literary or dramatic closure *and* remain intellectually open-ended or *problematic*" (133). My focus in the following critique will be on the phrase "literary or dramatic," and especially on the function of the "or," which identifies rather than distinguishes the two. But because this critique presupposes a reading of Plato which is eccentric in relation to the traditions of commentary, I shall offer some brief samples of interpretation before undertaking the critique.

Passages: Some Textual Preludes

In the course of putting Theaetetus through the paces of a Protagorean theory of perception, Socrates speaks in the following way of the exchange that occurs between the perceiver and the object perceived.[7] As we read the passage, let us imagine that he is not talking about a perceived object but about another percipient, a perceived person— one who is also perceiving, which includes hearing as well as seeing: The result of the exchange "is that we . . . *are* or *become*, whichever is the case, in relation to one another, since we are bound to one another by the inevitable law of our being, but to nothing else, not even to ourselves. The result, then, is that we are bound to one another; and so if a person says anything is, he must say it is for, or of, or toward something, and similarly if he says it becomes; but he must not say or let others say that it is, or becomes, just in and by itself" (160b–c). This language continually glances away from its epistemological context toward an ethico-rhetorical context; the account fits the logocentric relation of dialogue as well as—in fact, better than—the perceptual coupling that is its nominal subject. Socrates will go on to refute the Protagorean theory of perception. But the Protagorean theory of logocentric bondage will be confirmed by the inescapable constraints of Socrates' own practice, and so, at a different level, Protagoras—or whatever he embodies—will refute Socrates. In this example, the perceptual account comes to work as a displacement, a metonymic condensation, of the larger, more complex human relationship of which the perceptual relation of bodies and their extensions is a part.

This conclusion is implicit in Gail J. Fine's analysis of Socrates' dream (201e–202c), "according to which there are no accounts of some things, which are therefore unknowable." Plato (i.e., Socrates) "argues that knowledge involves mastery of a field, an ability systematically to interrelate the elements of a particular discipline." The dream theorist distinguishes between letters and syllables, "between primary elements . . . and the compounds . . . formed from them. Compounds, but not elements, are knowable, although elements are nameable and perceivable." Fine argues that Socrates attacks "this awkward result of the dream theory," that is, that although "knowledge requires . . . accounts that must end somewhere . . . it emerges that the final resting place will be unknowables." He shows that there can be some knowledge of grammatical or musical elements by "locating them within a systematic framework interconnecting and interrelating them" and that this "interrelation account" is "fundamental to knowledge of any sort of entity, elementary or compound. Knowledge always requires the ability to interrelate—not merely to list—the parts of a thing (if it has parts) to one another, and to relate one entity, elementary or compound, to others within the same systematic framework." Thus Plato (i.e., Socrates) "abandons the dream's conviction that accounts end somewhere; instead, they continue on circularly within a given field."[8]

While accepting the general sense of Fine's conclusion, I would like to head it in a different direction. Socrates argues against the proposition that "the final resting place will be [elementary] unknowables" by opening up the boundaries of any "given field." What is wrong with the dream theory is precisely its downward or reductive thrust from compounds to elements, and the corrective is to reverse the thrust, situate unknowables at the periphery, and treat them as only relatively unknowable. The position is roughly that taken by Quine in arguing against "the dogma of reductionism," which

survives in the supposition that each statement, taken in isolation from its fellows, can admit of confirmation or infirmation at all. My countersuggestion . . . is that our statements about the external world face the tribunal of sense experience not individually but only as a corporate body . . . The totality of our so-called knowledge or beliefs, from the most casual matters of geography and history to the profoundest laws of atomic physics or even of pure mathematics and logic, is a man-made fabric which impinges on experience only along the edges . . . A conflict with experience at the periphery occasions readjustments in the interior of the field. Truth values have to be redistributed over some of our statements . . . But the total field is so underdetermined by its boundary conditions, experience, that there is much latitude of choice as to what statements to reevaluate in the light of any single contrary experience. No particular experiences are linked with any particular statements in the interior of the field, except indirectly through considerations of equilibrium affecting the field as a whole.[9]

The implicit move Socrates repeatedly makes in the *Theaetetus* is to open up any "technical" or logical element of discussion so that it reflects or epitomizes wider and more complex contexts of interaction, exchange, conflict, and praxis. "Plato's" point, according to Fine, is that, for example, knowing a word "involves not just spelling it correctly some number of times, but also the ability to handle its constituents in a variety of contexts" (388), and this pushes in principle beyond grammar, linguistics, logic, and epistemology to the ethico-political contexts of experience within which they arise and with whose pressures and conflicts they are inscribed. To reverse Quine's emphasis, the dialogue shows how the boundary conditions of "experience" impinge on "particular statements in the interior of the field." And it is partly in this sense that "we are bound to one another." But as in any contextualist argument, the drawing of boundaries and the specifying of what counts as an element will be relative and variable. There is no way to close off the search and stabilize what Fine calls a "systematic framework" or "given field." Within the field bounded by the dramatic encounter represented in the text of the *Theaetetus*, Socrates is again, as in the *Meno*, defeated. But the boundaries of the field of the text reopen the encounter to the experience of future readerships. To reverse Quine's emphasis once more, the boundary conditions of the text are underdetermined by the boundaries and interior of the dramatic encounter. Reading may indeed be made to conform to the dynamics of an effluence theory that transmits authority and authorized meaning, for example, from Socrates to Eucleides to his slave to Terpsion, or from Socrates to Plato, or from Plato to us. But it need not necessarily do so. It may move in the other direction as well.

When the famous myth of the magnet in Plato's *Ion* is tested against the actual rhapsodic motives and practices the dialogue reveals, its lines of force undergo reversal. For the myth tells us that the stone magnetizes a sequence of dactyls, moving from the god or muse through the poet to the rhapsode or actor and finally to the audience.[10] Yet, although Ion likes the idea that he is engodded and out of his senses while performing, he confesses at one point that in the midst of his madness he carefully checks his audience to make sure they are with him, since his financial health depends on their approval. Like Hippias, Protagoras, and other well-heeled and well-traveled performers questioned by Socrates, Ion's success comes from giving his auditors what they want. In other words, his hold on the auditors is simply the reflex, the mirror image, of their hold on him. For them he concocts a selective version of Homer—and therefore of Homer's muse and god—which caters to their desires. Thus the audience is actually the first link in the chain, the magnetic source that moves upward and backwards from rhapsode to poet to god. Socrates tells Ion that the many call this source the stone of Heracles—a glamorous, diffusely mythic name—but he attributes the name *magnet* to his disenchanted contemporary, Euripides. This is a polarity that suggests with great precision the conflict between the two perspectives on the process, one

the product of a mystified golden age, the other the product of a modernist iron age.

In addition to the god or muse in the mystified version and the audience in the ironic version, there are two other problematic sources
and mediations of power. One mediation occurs between Socrates and
Ion, for although the myth of the magnetic poet and muse travels from
Socrates to Ion (as if Socrates is Ion's god and muse) and is demystified
at Ion's expense but without his knowledge, Ion keeps on going, as his
name suggests, presumably to other rhapsodic triumphs. The Socratic
narkē fixes him only for a short spell; Socrates cannot finally shake
Ion's confidence, penetrate his ironclad desire not to know, or maneu-
ver him into self-refutation; he cannot be said to win his contest with
Ion except in the eyes—*the eyes*—of the reader. Socratic narcosis has a
deeper and more enduring effect on Plato's readers than on many of
Socrates' interlocutors. And yet the text *can* break the magnetic chain.
For it is precisely as a reader that I interpret his manhandling of Ion
not as a victory for Socrates but as a defeat. The second mediation of
power is therefore a complex one that occurs between the interlocutors
and the text, and between text and reader. Neither Ion nor Socrates
mentions the real source of the power that inspires and speaks through
them: Plato's text and its interpreters. Textuality reverses the chronological lines of force (or "influence") that move from Socrates through
Plato to us, sending them back from readers through the Platonic text
to its representation of Socrates.

Most of what I have just written is part of an interpretation available not to Socrates' interlocutor in the *Ion* but only to Plato's readers,
an interpretation whose failure to materialize within the imaginary encounter, the field of *dramatic* play, is conspicuously featured in the
field of *textual* play where it does materialize. Thus the *Ion* can be read
as a dialogue or agon between its speakers and its text. For the text tells
us something about itself in adumbrating the limits of a form of discourse—Socratic *logos*, constrained by its oral conditions—which only
textual representation can recuperate, or supplement, or transcend.
Ion's victory over Socrates—the victory of Ionic culture and its
power—is secured by the very density that makes him the butt of the
dialogue. If Plato's myth of Socrates delivers Socrates from Ion, it also
delivers us from Socrates' charismatic presence through the mediation
of the text that ironically preserves it. Plato's text replaces the Homeric
or Ionic golden age with a Socratic golden age, plays on our ironic but
still paradisal desire for the all-knowing *pharmakeos* who is the absent
father of Platonic writing. But this desire is aroused only to be foiled by

a text that "speaks" against Socrates as well as through him. The father generated and desired by the Platonic text continually beckons and allures through the writing that continually rejects his beloved presence and thus creates the space for its own existence.

Stoppages: Some Critical Postludes

As the sample readings just given will show, my position is not that of those who privilege the logical or—roughly speaking—"philosophical" interpretation of the Platonic dialogues. However, to the extent that these readings illustrate an approach to Plato which also avoids making "dramatistic" assumptions about the text, they suggest that a serious reconsideration of the dominant strain of commentaries on Plato associated with the "Straussians" is in order.

In the preface to his translation of the *Republic*, Allan Bloom asserts that "in order to understand a man or what he says both . . . [speech and deed] must be taken into account. Just as no action of a man can be interpreted without hearing what he says about it himself, no speech can be accepted on its face value without comparing it to the actions of its author."[11] This dictum informs the following methodological injunction:

Every argument must be interpreted dramatically, for every argument is incomplete in itself and only the context can supply the missing links. And every dramatic detail must be interpreted philosophically, because these details *contain the images of the problems* which complete the arguments. Separately these two aspects are meaningless; together they are an invitation to the philosophic quest. (xvi, emphasis added)

The arguments center on problems that are both imaged and completed by the dramatic details. "Completed" does not prejudice the relation between argument and drama as much as "imaged" does: the dramatic completion could conceivably be expected to qualify or even contradict the argument, but "to image" connotes "to imitate." If the text is analytically divided into action and speech, or drama and argument, or if the speech itself is divided into—to use Austin's terms—its performative and constative aspects, it is arbitrary to postulate a mimetic rather than, say, an ironic relation between the divisions. The consequences of this mimetic postulate will be unpacked from the next set of examples.

The general form of the mimetic postulate has been developed by Jacob Klein on what is essentially a theatrico-dramatic model. Like Bloom, Klein explores the idea that answers to questions raised but not decisively resolved in the spoken discussion may be "gathered, if not from the words, then from the action which the—written—dialogue 'imitates.' "[12] The process by which indirect or implicit answers are "given in a written text by the very action it presents" confers on the dialogues "their dramatic or mimetic quality," also "the quality of completeness" which is set "against their unfinished (aporetic) character in terms of the verbal argument" (17). Klein goes on to distinguish different "mimetic devices" or "mimes"—ethological, doxological, and mythological, only the first two of which are relevant here. Ethological mimes are "imitations of actions in which the speakers reveal themselves both in character and in thought, . . . to use Aristotle's phrase, in which they show their souls 'naked,' to quote Plato himself"—this ascription to Plato of a Socratic *logos* (cf. *Protagoras*, 351a–b, *Charmides*, 154d) is rare for Klein, who is careful not to treat Socrates as a mouthpiece.[13] In "doxological mimes . . . the falsity or rightness of an opinion is not only argued in words but also manifested in the character, the behavior, and the actions of the speakers themselves" (18). I shall return to Klein's argument a little later; at this point all I want to emphasize is that his formulation of the mimetic postulate bases itself on Aristotle's dramatic model of character in action, that he assigns the written text the job of completing the unfinished oral discussion by its representation of "the drama itself, the 'deed,' the 'work,' the *ergon*" (ibid.), and that he follows Schleiermacher and others in arguing that the written dialogue, "being indeed an 'imitation of Socrates,' actually continues Socrates' work" by appealing to us, "the listeners or readers," to participate in the discussion (7, 18). In a later study, Klein puts the last point more forcefully: "We, the readers, are also listeners and must participate, as silent partners, in the discussion; we must weigh and then accept or reject the solutions offered and must comment, as well as we can, on what is at stake."[14]

Klein acknowledges his debt to Paul Friedländer, who defends Platonic writing as a copy justified by the original it represents. Friedländer describes the relation between Socrates and Diotima in the *Symposium* as "an *ironic division* . . . between the seeker for truth and a power that, shining through him, is also above him."[15] And he postulates that Plato is similarly divided between his commitment to an art of mimetic writing and the "nature" of a model "completely committed to oral discourse": "the figure of Socrates signifies the central plane in Plato's world view" and also "conceals the final goal envisaged by Plato" (158, 165, 170). Though the written word "contradicts the basic Socratic-Platonic principle" that "philosophy is possible only as an exchange between two people" (113), Plato resolves the contradiction by imitating Socratic conversation and appropriating Socratic ignorance in such a way as to represent "the inexpressibility of . . . 'the good' " through his image of "the living person of the master" (169–70). Thus, in Friedländer's view, writing criticizes itself for its failure to be genuine speech, and justifies itself only to the extent that it can transcend its secondariness by adumbrating the lost presence in the charismatic image of a Socrates made newer and more beautiful. For this reason, the reader who wishes to hear what the dialogue would truly say must approach it dramatically as well as philosophically, ignoring no details of staging, gesture, or action, and then inquiring into "the symbolical meaning of the spatial setting and the physical happenings" (161).

Like Friedländer, Leo Strauss appeals from the interpretive criteria that, institutionalized in academic departments of philosophy, rule that Plato's works must be rendered down to a set of discussable arguments, to criteria that strangely resemble those institutionalized in departments of literature after World War II. These are the criteria of the New Criticism: autonomy, organicity, ambiguity, mimetic virtuality. They valorize the "surface" as well as the "depth" of the dialogue, that is, the integrity of the "whole," and they demand that we read it as drama, read it as if we were present and as if the speakers were speaking to us. Of course, not everyone will know how to listen to "good writing," which, since it "must imitate . . . good conversation, . . . must be addressed primarily to . . . men more or less well known" to the speaker or author; yet, unlike the speaker, the writer must make that "conversation" accessible "to a multitude wholly unknown to Plato and never addressed by Plato himself."[16] Hence, to unveil the Platonic presence, or at least to initiate us into the Lower Mysteries of the teaching, there is need of a Straussian Interpreter who understands the proper way of reading or listening.

The Platonic dialogue, if properly read, reveals itself to possess the flexibility or adaptability of oral communication. What it means to read a good writing properly is intimated by Socrates in the *Phaedrus* when he describes the character of a good writing. A writing is good if it complies with "logographic necessity" . . . which ought to govern the writing of speeches: every part of the written speech must be necessary for the whole; the place where each part occurs is the place where it is necessary that it should occur; in a word, the good writing must resemble the healthy animal which can do its proper work well. The proper work of a writing is to talk to some readers and to be silent to others. (53)

The proper work of reading is to restore "the original three-dimensionality" of the drama by apprehending "the 'speeches' of all Platonic characters in the light of the 'deeds'"—that is, of "the setting and action," the conspicuous silences, and the unmentioned "facts" hinted at "partly by the unthematic details and partly by seemingly casual remarks" (60).

The difficulty of sustaining so "austere" a standard, which demands that we not "ascribe to Plato any utterance of any of his characters without having taken great precautions" (60, 59), is illustrated in the passage quoted above. For if proper precautions are taken, it becomes clear that Socrates' opinions about good writing need not, perhaps cannot, be ascribed to Plato. This is partly because they are accommodated to, limited by, reflective of, the intransigent self-deceptions of his interlocutor. Strauss himself insists that "in no Platonic dialogue do the men who converse with the main speaker possess the perfection of the best nature" (54). The consequences—to confront Strauss's term with Derrida's—is that Socrates is forced to submit to logo*centric* necessity: he must adapt his speech to the imperfect interlocutors in his presence. This being the case, the "true" Socratic-Platonic teaching can emerge only in the paradigmatic textuality of the written "whole," and the three-dimensional logocentric experience that is the subject of imitation is called into question. If the logic of Strauss's argument is followed out, it leads to the conclusion that the "good writing" need not merely imitate the original drama it represents; it may present itself as a critique of that representation. But Strauss blocks this conclusion with the mimetic postulate: good writing imitates good speaking and its dramatic setting. Platonic writing imitates Socratic speech. Strauss, like Klein, is careful to dissociate Socrates from Plato. The name "Plato" is sparingly used in his chapter on the *Republic*. Only once does he slip and identify Socrates' opinion with Plato's (119). The result, however, is that Socrates has simply come to replace Plato, and where Strauss finds inconsistencies in his argument that are not provoked by his interlocutors, he can only speculate that similar difficulties must have confronted Plato (92–93). Thus, in spite of his precautions, the ghost of the mouthpiece theory haunts his account.

No one has argued more trenchantly or eloquently against the sins of the mouthpiece theorists than Strauss's student Stanley Rosen. Rosen insists that "Plato says nothing in his own name" and that it is essential to pay "rigorous attention to the dramatic context of an argument as a key to Plato's intentions."[17] A slight prospective doubt about the success of Rosen's ability to maintain Plato's anonymity is raised by "Plato's intentions." And indeed, Rosen writes as if something he calls "Plato's teaching" is discernible and statable even though hidden from the inattentive reader. This teaching can be approached via two paths, close study of the individual dialogue and a "synoptic grasp of the Platonic corpus," a grasp of "the full range of Plato's thought" (xxxvi). More specifically, though Rosen of course never says this, the attentive reader is likely to discover that Plato's teaching has the form given it by Rosen's analytic scheme of the Platonic Whole, and that this scheme supplies the esoteric doctrine or "the unspoken dimension of the dialogues" (xix). I am going to devote more space to Rosen's work than I have to the commentators discussed above. The reason is that a comparison between Rosen's programmatic statements and his practice illustrates with great force—partly because his critical self-awareness is so acute—the dilemmas and inconsistency structurally inherent in the dramatistic project.[18]

Rosen's view of the Platonic Whole appears to elaborate some suggestions made by Strauss. The following statement by Strauss, though vague and figurative, suggests that although he rejects both systematic holists and developmentalists he is closer in spirit to the former than to the latter, and this provides a clue to Rosen's allegiances:

Plato's work consists of many dialogues because it imitates the manyness, the variety, the heterogeneity of being. The many dialogues form a *kosmos* which mysteriously imitates the mysterious *kosmos*. The Platonic *kosmos* imitates or reproduces its model in order to awaken us to the mystery of the model and to assist us in articulating that mystery. There are many dialogues because the whole consists of many parts. But the individual dialogue is not a chapter from an encyclopaedia of the philosophic sciences or from a system of philosophy, and still less a relic of a stage of Plato's development. Each dialogue deals with one part; it reveals the truth about that part. But the truth about a part is a partial truth, a half truth. (*City and Man*, 61–62)

This conception, somewhat mystifying as it stands, has been articulated into a more detailed and practical form by Rosen, with occasionally dubious consequences.

Rosen holds that although in the variety of its cognitive and rhetorical modes each dialogue "imitates the whole of human existence," it does so in a unique manner, so that we could not hope "to extricate the full range of Plato's thought from any one dialogue." The parts of the whole affect and complete each other. Thus "the teaching of the *Symposium*, once it has been understood, points toward dialogues like the *Parmenides* and *Sophist*." The *Symposium* portrays its themes "in pre-philosophical language, or in terms of concrete existence," and it contains "the seeds of Plato's philosophical teaching, which are implanted in his account of the forms of the psyche. By virtue of that fact it is an essential part of his philosophical teaching; that is, the results of the *Parmenides* and *Sophist* are themselves incomplete unless taken together with the results of the *Symposium*" (*Plato's "Symposium,"* xxii, xxxv–vi). Rosen's seed metaphor has developmental implications that are no doubt unintended, but the lapse suggests the difficulty of avoiding that line of explanation. His purpose is to oppose it by positing the ironic character of the dialogue as a literary form and thus to affirm Plato's philosophical anonymity. But when he begins to extricate the "full range of Plato's thought" he lays out a scheme of the whole that suggests Plato is less anonymous to Rosen than to others.

Rosen distinguishes two fundamental methods, "ways," or "paths" of philosophy, which are also "the two fundamental inflections" of eros, and which are roughly analogous to poetry and mathematics in the broad sense. These paths determine his classification of dialogues. The *Symposium*, for example, embodies the poetic way, the *Republic* and *Philebus* include both, while in the *Sophist* and the *Statesman* "the principal interlocutors are mathematicians and an Eleatic Stranger, a student of Parmenides." In the Eleatic dialogues, "the mathematical character of philosophy is not merely emphasized but exaggerated, and any attempt to interpret them must take this fact into account."[19]

Given this scheme, it should be possible to approach the *Symposium* and the *Sophist* as different but equal expressions—complementary parts—of Plato's philosophical whole. At the same time, it should be possible to do this without prejudging the relative distance from Plato of Socrates and the Eleatic Stranger. "All dialogues the same distance from Plato" need not entail "all principal speakers the same distance from Plato." But when Rosen moves from the level of theory to that of practice, this distinction is not firmly maintained; the principles he lays down are subjected to a good deal of pressure and barely survive. This may be exemplified by his treatment of Socrates, his treatment of the irony principle, and his implicit evaluation of the Eleatic dialogues.

For Rosen, "the most important theme of the *Symposium* is the hybris of Socrates, as well as the problem raised by his peculiarly unerotic nature," and he stresses the importance of recognizing "the sense in which it is a criticism as well as an encomium of Socrates. The complete portrait of the philosopher's psyche emerges only when we reflect upon the difference between Socrates and Plato" (*Symposium*, xxxv); "Plato" here is presumably a synonym for "the complete body of interpreted dialogues." But in the *Republic*, Rosen argues, Socrates is less visible as a figure objectively characterized through the attention directed toward him by other persons in the dialogue, and he appears to be less hybristic. Rosen explains this as necessitated by the different theme of the *Republic*, that is, justice: "Plato decided to suppress or transform Eros in the course of describing the just city" because "Eros is connected with private striving and immoderation." Therefore he "disguises or camouflages philosophical Eros by emphasizing the impersonal aspect of philosophy, in which it is related to or very much resembles *mathematics*" ("Role of Eros," 466). But philosophical eros is present "within the depths" of the dialogue (471), which combines the two emphases—poetry and mathematics—separated in the *Symposium* and the *Sophist*.

This view of the central position of the *Republic* in Rosen's scheme, and of the relative restraint in the portrait of Socrates, produces an inconsistency: in spite of his emphasis on Plato's anonymity and on the dramatic principle, Rosen occasionally looks through Socrates as if he were a window. For example, shortly after remarking that "Socrates vindicates philosophy," he mentions "Plato's defense of philosophy" (459). In this essay, as opposed to his study of the *Symposium*, the names of Socrates and Plato are more often than not interchangeable, and the portrait of the philosopher king is assimilated to both. Rosen writes that "Socrates in particular and the philosopher-king in general are never referred to as hybristic or shown as acting in a hybristic manner" (457), and he repeats this identification several times (458, 460, 469), ignoring Socrates' emphasis on the philosophic soul's hybristic sense of *megaloprepeia*.[20] Here the operation of the mimetic postulate draws the three figures—Plato, Socrates, and the philosopher—closer together.

Rosen brings the principle of irony to bear against those who have difficulty reconciling the doctrines they find in the dialogues with those they find in the epistles attributed to Plato. The charge that the letters are spurious is met by arguing that, since the dialogues are ironic, why shouldn't the letters be ironic in the same way? Yet he occasionally uses the genuineness of the letters as an excuse to ignore his own stricture on irony and to treat them as sources of Platonic doctrine: "Plato carefully says [in *Ep.*, 7] that his teaching on the highest or most serious matters 'cannot be stated like the other kinds of knowledge'" (xv). This is combined with other texts to prove that under certain conditions his highest teaching *can* be stated and understood, and that it is in fact the core of the dialogues. The point Rosen is making oddly reinforces the assumption that enables him to make it. But what if Plato was being "carefully" ironical? On what authority does Rosen cap his account of the hidden and open aspects of the dialogue with the claim that he has clarified Plato's opinion as stated in the second epistle: "We can now see more clearly why Plato would say that philosophy cannot be written like other forms of knowledge, and that his dialogues are about a Socrates 'become beautiful and young'" (xx)? Rosen's own interpretations seem to be the principles that determine which of Plato's statements may have their potentially ironic quality bracketed so that they can qualify as true doctrine.

This tendency is especially noticeable in *Plato's "Symposium"* in the employment of references to the Eleatic dialogues and *Timaeus*. Thus Timaeus's opening remarks on procedure are cited as if they could serve as Platonic guidelines (209), and in succeeding paragraphs Rosen appeals five times to texts from the *Sophist* for the same purpose. Criteria drawn from the *Sophist*, for example, are used to validate Rosen's critique of Agathon:

Agathon was right to wish to exhibit the nature of Eros but wrong to combine logos with poetry. Some other method for praising Eros must be employed. Agathon's speech was a poem or myth which pretended to be a logos: it was the speech of a Sophist [here, a reference to *Sophist*, 239c4ff., in which the Stranger tells how the Sophist hides and challenges the epithet *image-maker*]. And indeed, the problem of how to describe Eros, let alone praise it, is closely related to the problem of how to say what is not, or to attribute being to nonbeing [here, a reference to 241b1-2, in which Theaetetus complains that the Sophist forces us into this paradoxical attribution]. Hence the connection between the teachings of the Sophists and speech about Eros. (211)

Elsewhere analyses and distinctions from the *Sophist* are used to elucidate passages from the *Symposium* (109ff., 295) after they have been correlated with analogues from other dialogues—for example, "the division of image-making is a refinement of the lowest segment of the divided line" (295). And in his methodological introduction Rosen borrows both ideas and authority from the Eleatic Stranger:

It must never be forgotten that, even in the most abstract discussions, the form of the dialogue as writing or publication corresponds to the political or communal nature of discourse. Similarly, the synoptic or architectonic character of dialectic corresponds to the technique of politics, or the royal art of weaving [cf. *Statesman*, 306a1ff.] . . . Whatever else it may be, dialectic as practiced by the Socratics has the political end of communion or general agreement, a fact which is constantly emphasized by the chief speakers in the Platonic dialogues [cf. *Sophist*, 218c1-3, *Statesman*, 258d1, 260b7]. (xxiii–xxiv)

Each of these references also includes references to other dialogues in which Socrates makes similar points. There are serious problems with this procedure, in which passages by different speakers are superimposed to provide a consensus, which is then ascribed to Plato. Rosen's practice of citing analogies in support of his own opinions tends to give references to the ideas of the *Republic* Socrates or the non-Socratic spokesmen the status of criteria. When he writes that *x* in the *Symposium* is like *y* in the *Timaeus* or the *Sophist*, the force of the analogy is not mere agreement but rather authorization: *x* is thereby marked as a Platonic opinion. This means that for all practical purposes Rosen has suspended the irony principle in these cases and has assumed that the *Timaeus* and the Eleatic dialogues, like the epistles, can be used as Platonic doxographies.

Something quite odd begins to emerge from these explorations of dramatistic commentary: the mouthpiece theory against which the commentators inveigh returns like the repressed, but returns in a strange form that reveals not only the originary structure of the theory but also the common assumption that unites both proponents and critics of the theory. This assumption is clearly displayed in Klein's extension of the mimetic postulate from relations within the dialogue (drama and argument) to relations between Socratic speech and Platonic writing: "A properly written text will tend to transform the unavoidable deficiency of writing into a lever of learning and understanding." It can do this by "imitating a discussion" in such a way as to accentuate "the character of incompleteness" that is, "the best inducement for its continuation" (*Meno*, 17). "The ultimate goal of the dialogues is to make us repeat and continue the questioning" (*Trilogy*, 6). Furthermore, insofar as "partial or ambiguous answers" are completed or clarified in the tacit code of dramatic action, the written dialogue "reflects the character of Socrates himself, whose life and death speak still louder than his words." The mimetic interplay of speech and action, *logos* and *ergon*, "provides the texture into which we, the listeners or readers, have to weave our thread" (*Meno*, 17–18). Since what Klein obviously means is "we, the readers as listeners," the textual metaphor (thread-weaving) is as ironic as it is confusing. And Klein's allegiance remains divided between his strenuous objections to the mouthpiece theory and his lingering desire to know what Plato really said:

No Platonic dialogue can be said to represent what might be called, and has been called, the "Platonic Doctrine"; a dialogue may hint at genuine and ultimate thoughts of Plato, the thinker, but they are never set before us with complete clarity. An unimpeachable source provides us with more direct information about Plato's thinking than he himself ever put down in writing; this source is Aristotle, who . . . heard what Plato himself *said*. (*Trilogy*, 1)

Klein's extension of the mimetic postulate seems partly motivated by this logocentric desire to hear Plato speak, and his thesis that readers should continue the dialogue as participants betrays the peculiar feature of the mouthpiece theory to which I alluded above: its apparent or explicit structure is the reverse of its true or implicit structure. In the explicit structure, Socrates and the other major speakers are Plato's mouthpieces. Yet notice that the model in terms of which the major speaker's utterances are ratified as Plato's opinions is speech-centered, not text-centered: we imitate the speaker's interlocutors, revive or repeat an "original" discussion by responding as if directly addressed. We have, however, an advantage over the fictional interlocutors in that we can observe and hear them from the standpoint of a theatrical audience. The writing that preserves and imitates this drama is thus constituted as a transcription, a transparent image. And what this implies is that if "Socrates" names the speaker's position and "Plato" the writer's, then "Socrates" is not "Plato's" mouthpiece. Rather, "Plato" is "Socrates'" mouthpiece, or "mouthpiece," that is, scribe.

The situation is no different, only a little more complex, when Plato's thought is distinguished from Socrates' on the basis of what Timaeus or the Eleatic Stranger asserts; or when, of diverse positions taken by Socrates in different dialogues, some are authorized as Plato's but not the historical Socrates', others as Socrates' but not Plato's—or, alternatively, some as the "earlier Plato's," others as the "later Plato's"; or when, as in Irwin's odd way of reading the *Republic*, some of Socrates' utterances are treated as objects of Plato's criticism, while others are treated as genuine Platonic statements.[21] Whenever opinions, explanations, or procedures of argument are transferred from one or another speaker to the author, what Plato thought is determined strictly on the basis of speech-acts. Writing then becomes reduced to the medium by which the author's utterances are preserved for a wider audience that includes posterity. Any interventions and revisions produced by the difference between speech and writing, and by the differences within writing itself, are screened out. Direct acquaintance with the writer's opinion is presumed on the basis of direct acquaintance with his speakers—on the basis of a reading that abjures its peculiar textual privileges in order to simulate a hearing. Thus what the explicit structure of the mouthpiece theory offers its dramatistic critics is a false target, a false category, from which they can easily dissociate their own practice. But when the category is analyzed to produce its inversion in the implicit structure in which it is embedded, the resultant category includes the critics along with their targets. Dramatistic interpretation cannot therefore avoid being infiltrated by assumptions and practices to which it is programmatically opposed. Though it takes more into account and is more sensitive to context than practice governed by the explicit theory, it remains inconsistent, pulled one way by the desire to avoid the failures of the explicit theory, and another way by the desire to recuperate the presence of the author and to arrive at knowledge of his "teaching."

The dramatistic notion of "context" itself poses problems. On a superficial level, it seems to have been developed primarily in terms of the Socratic dialogues, with their obvious interlocutory drama. But it would be hard to imagine, for example, how Bloom would apply to the *Timaeus* his dogma that "every dramatic detail must be interpreted philosophically," since, as soon as Timaeus begins his discourse, "every dramatic detail" vanishes. What elements of mimetic action could Klein adduce from what appears to be an uninterrupted lecture? The speech of Timaeus is taken by many to be a full disclosure of Plato's ideas about cosmology and to provide a touchstone of Platonic theory by which to judge the statements of other speakers: Friedländer, Klein, and Rosen all use it this way, often in the face of their own warnings against such a practice.[22] Is it *because* the speech is uninterrupted that strictures against mouthpiece readings can be wholly or partly suspended, or that dramatistic criteria fail to apply? And given the intermittent scruples of, for example, Klein and Friedländer, what *literary* principles determine which of the opinions uttered by Timaeus are not to be identified as Plato's? Shouldn't the deployment of the dramatistic approach be fully consistent regardless of the kind of text to which it is applied? Shouldn't mouthpiece readings always be blocked, whether the text is superficially a direct dialogue, a monologue, or an indirect (narrated) dialogue?

What lies behind the inconsistent practice of dramatistic interpreters? To attribute it to conflicting desires, as I did above, is to commit the error I have been criticizing, since "desire" metaphorically evokes the presence of the authors whose texts, not psyches, are my topic. It would be better to borrow Paul de Man's terminology of blindness and insight: a certain insight "could only be gained because the critics were in the grip of . . . [a] peculiar blindness: their language could grope toward a certain degree of insight only because their method remained oblivious to the perception of this insight," and as a result their "critical stance . . . is defeated by their own critical results."[23] De Man attributes this dilemma not to any particular errors on the part of the critics but to the fundamentally "rhetorical nature of literary language" (141) and to the endless "dialogue between work and interpreter" (32): "since interpretation is nothing but the possibility of error, . . . a certain degree of blindness is part of the specificity of all literature" (141).

What, then, is the relation of blindness to insight in the dramatistic critics under discussion? The theoretical orientation of Friedländer, Strauss, Klein, and their followers generated insights that significantly advanced our understanding of the dialogues, and did so by insisting on the privileged character of a dramatic mimesis that could not be fully appreciated without the most scrupulous attention to the text. Yet this act of foregrounding the drama seems to have been made possible only by remaining blind to the ways in which textuality proclaims its difference from, its independence of, its superiority to, the conversations it pretends to represent. The aesthetic decision to read the text as drama, and the ethical decision to idealize the Platonic Socrates to the status of a quasi-mouthpiece, seem reciprocally to reinforce each other. The very critics who probe most deeply into the relations between the logocentric dilemma and what Strauss calls "logographic necessity" fail to follow through on their inquiry. A widespread symptom of this failure is the tendency to use the terms "dramatic" and "literary" interchangeably, as in the following sentence from Kenneth Dorter's recent interpretation of the *Phaedo*: "Let us reflect on the drama as well as the arguments, bearing in mind that the literary as well as philosophical exegesis must be grounded in textual evidence."[24] Notice that the sentence actually picks out three levels of discourse—textual, dramatic, and logical—although Dorter's analysis as a whole consistently conflates the textual, the literary, and the dramatic. I submit that *literary*, *dramatic*, and *thematic* name three levels of discourse, that the dramatic is an abstraction from the literary, and the thematic is an abstraction from the dramatic. Analysis of the logic of argumentation in the dialogues occupies a narrow segment of the thematic level.

Other terminologies could also be used to mark some of these distinctions: Austin's "illocutionary" and "constative," for example, could replace "dramatic" and "thematic," respectively, while Derrida's "grammatocentric" and "logocentric" could stand in for "textual" or "literary" and "dramatic," and, on this model, logical analysis might be called "logicocentric." Interpretation dominated by the mouthpiece theory remains at the thematic level, while the dramatistic interpreters tend to move back and forth among all three levels, sometimes separating the thematic from the dramatic but very seldom (because of their reliance on the mimetic postulate) distinguishing between their textual and their dramatic analyses. This is more than a mechanical failure. It prevents them from attending to what I think is a central theme of Platonic discourse, namely, the structural inadequacy and ethical dangers inherent in any method of teaching, and indeed in any institution—whether educational, political, social, or more broadly cultural—committed to the dramatic or logocentric level of discourse and grounded in the speaking presence of institutional actors. Within this general critique, there is an especially pointed and poignant critique of Socratic method and the Socratic presence.

My argument, then, is that the only way to block the influence of the mouthpiece theory in its two forms, explicit and implicit, is to drive the wedge deeper between the textual and dramatic levels of analysis, to make that division rather than the division between theme and drama the critical one, and to reorganize the semantic and semiotic interplay among the three levels from a standpoint more firmly based in operations particular to reading, operations not transferable to a reading that simulates listening.

To approach Plato in terms of a dialectic between oral and written discourse is to situate the interpretive project in a more general discussion that has been going on for some time. I refer to the hermeneutic theories of Gadamer, Ricoeur, Benveniste, and others, and more specifically to Ricoeur's two basic propositions about the changes produced by the transfer of a text from speech to writing: (1) emancipated or "distanciated" from speech, speaker, and author, the text becomes autonomous, is appropriated by readers (or readerships—"interpretive communities," as Stanley Fish calls them), and opens itself up to the endless conflict of interpretation; (2) in this process, the intentional control of speaker and author over their texts diminishes, and the margin or surplus of unmeant meaning increases. It is interesting that the student of Plato who has been most influential in drawing our attention to the dialectic between oral and written discourse has not profited from this hermeneutic tradition: Eric Havelock reads the dialogues as documents in which Plato directly ventriloquates his own arguments and opinions through the major speakers. He contradicts much in his own thesis by approaching the Platonic text logocentrically, that is, he fails to see that Socrates is represented in the dialogues as laboring under the same set of logocentric constraints as those of the

Homeric culture Plato has Socrates criticize. Havelock argues that dialectic in its original and

simplest form . . . consisted in asking a speaker to repeat himself and explain what he had meant. In Greek, the words for explain, say, and mean could coincide. That is, the original function of the dialectical question was simply to force the speaker to repeat a statement already made, with the underlying assumption that there was something unsatisfactory about the statement, and it had better be rephrased.[25]

Repetition, then, is an aid not only to memory but also to criticism and interpretation. If the statement could be separated from the movement of speech, could be stilled and preserved, it would not have to be repeated, and critical rephrasing could go on in a relatively "disinterested" context, that is, one that could put out of play the interest and self-protectiveness that make the speakers confronted by Socrates reluctant to submit their speech, behavior, and values to the rigorous examination enjoined by the gadfly. Havelock's argument is that the Socratic procedure produces the germinal form of the abstraction and distanciation which, in Ricoeur's model, emancipates the text. But Havelock's practice blocks the emancipatory movement by reembedding the author in the speaker and the writing in the speech.

Derrida was the first to suggest that the written text does not merely privilege the argument and drama it represents, but represents and privileges them in order to problematize them. But whether his practice is consistent with his thesis remains to be seen. In "Plato's Pharmacy" he tries very hard to deconstruct the problematic of the *pharmakon* in purely structural terms. Though his inquiry is centered in the *Phaedrus*, it plays outward over the *oeuvre* as a whole, constituting a "chain of significations" that transgresses the boundaries of individual texts. This system is dissociated from

the intentions of an author who goes by the name of Plato. The system is not primarily that of what someone *meant-to-say* . . . Finely regulated communications are established, through the play of language, among diverse functions of the word [*pharmakon*] and, within it, among diverse strata or regions of culture. These communications or corridors of meaning can sometimes be declared or clarified by Plato when he plays upon them "voluntarily," a word we put in quotation marks because what it designates, to content ourselves with remaining within the closure of these oppositions, is only a mode of "submission" to the necessities of a given "language." None of these concepts can translate the relation we are aiming at here. Then again, in other cases, Plato can *not* see the links, can leave them in the shadow or break them up. And yet these links go on working of themselves.[26]

Thus Derrida, while freeing the "textual system" of the *pharmakon* from the author function, places under erasure the "crude" oppositions ("conscious and unconscious, voluntary and involuntary") invoked by the appeal to that function. The aim of this move, of course, is to enable him to go on using these oppositions *sous rature*, for how else would it be possible to dissociate the system from authorship in order to show how "Plato," and after him his followers and commentators and translators, close down on the system, try to impose on it a privileged sense which the text subverts as it proliferates the malady "Plato" tries to remedy?

Inevitably, however, the strategy of erasure must fail, if only because the accumulation of intentional references dulls its effect. Derrida tries to avoid "blaming" on the author a necessary inability to control the ambivalence originally inscribed in the very notion— *pharmakon*—that grounds and evokes the Platonic discourse, for example, "all these significations nonetheless appear, and, more precisely, all these words appear in the text of 'Plato.' Only the chain is concealed, and, to an inappreciable extent, concealed from the author himself, *if any such thing exists*" (129, my italics). Yet "Plato's Pharmacy" persistently raises a question about the proprietary relation of authors and speakers to their discourse, a question it strives to suppress. For it makes a difference whether we ascribe a particular sequence of speech acts to, for example, Timaeus, Socrates, the Eleatic Stranger, or Critias as their property, a property that qualifies and characterizes them, or whether we ascribe it directly to "Plato" or "his" text. Once we decide to reinstate the boundaries of individual dialogues dismantled by the deconstructive project, we confront the problem of determining the relationship of Timaeus to Socrates and (thus) of both to "Plato," and it makes no difference whether or not the Plato we discuss is under erasure if one reader's erased Plato differs from another's. Derrida sometimes identifies what "Plato thought about" (126) with what the Eleatic Stranger or Timaeus or the Athenian Stranger says, as if their sayings and missayings all play with equal authority into the weave of the text, are not differentiated from it by structural irony, so that if the Eleatic Stranger stops the movement of the *pharmakon* in the interest of his diacritical obsession, it follows that "the opposites or differences are stopped by Plato" (127). Elsewhere he asserts that "writing appears to Plato . . . as that process of redoubling in which we are fatally (en)trained: the supplement of a supplement, the signifier, the representative of a representative . . . Plato maintains *both* the exteriority of writing *and* its power of maleficent penetration, its ability to affect or infect what lies deepest inside" (109–10).

I think that in the final analysis Derrida's reifying repetition of appeals to the erased Plato's intentions has the effect of preventing his "Plato" from seeing and doing what he, Derrida, sees and does. My "Plato" differs in the greater extent to which "he" anticipates the Derridean problematic. But it does so only because I have followed Derrida's lead, and therefore I should unsay, or unwrite, what I have just written, for in "blaming" Derrida, or in blaming "Derrida," I commit the error of which I accuse him. I misrepresent him as another interpreter of Plato's texts when in fact he refuses this privilege to trace the deep-structural necessities woven through the text within which the "intentions" of "Plato" are sometimes, but only sometimes, inscribed. It is precisely this grammatological project that makes available both the generative insight and the interpretive terms of another reading: one that traces the way the written dialogue represents deep-structural necessities woven through the speech within which the intentions of a presence who goes by the name of Socrates are sometimes, but only sometimes, inscribed.[27]

Notes

1. Konrad Gaiser, "Plato's Enigmatic Lecture 'On the Good,'" *Phronesis* 25 (1980): 7.

2. E. N. Tigerstedt, *Interpreting Plato* (Stockholm: Almquist & Wiksell International, 1977), 89.

3. My reason for employing the locution "Direct Listening" will emerge later.

4. Terence Irwin, *Plato's Moral Theory* (Oxford: Clarendon Press, 1977), 3.

5. Leo Strauss, *The City and Man* (Chicago: University of Chicago Press, 1964), 59.

6. V. Tejera, "Methodology of a Misreading: A Critical Note on T. Irwin's *Plato's Moral Theory*," *International Studies in Philosophy* 10 (1978): 132.

7. This paragraph is taken from Berger, "Facing Sophists: Socrates' Charismatic Bondage in the *Protagoras*," *Representations* 5 (Winter 1984): 67–68.

8. Gail J. Fine, "Knowledge and Logos in the *Theaetetus*," *Philosophical Review* 88 (1979): 368, 369, 370, 378, 385.

9. Willard Van Orman Quine, *From a Logical Point of View*, 2d ed., rev. (1961; reprint, New York: Harper & Row, 1963), 41–43.

10. This discussion of the *Ion* is for the most part taken from Berger, "The Origins of Bucolic Representation: Disenchantment and Revision in Theocritus' Seventh *Idyll*," *Classical Antiquity* 3 (1984): 1–2 and 34–35.

11. Allan Bloom, *The Republic of Plato* (New York: Basic Books, 1968), xviii.

12. Jacob Klein, *A Commentary on Plato's "Meno"* (Chapel Hill: University of North Carolina Press, 1965), 16.

13. He occasionally stumbles, however: see 112, 116, 122, 150, 166, and 171—all, significantly, in a digressive chapter on epistemological theory in which he violates his own principles by decontextualizing and conflating passages from Socrates' accounts of the sun, the line, the cave, and the philosophers' education.

14. Jacob Klein, *Plato's Trilogy: "Theaetetus," the "Sophist," and the "Statesman"* (Chicago: University of Chicago Press, 1977), 1.

15. Paul Friedländer, *Plato: An Introduction*, trans. Hans Meyerhoff (1958; reprint, New York: Harper & Row, 1964), 1:150.

16. Strauss, *City and Man*, 54.

17. Stanley Rosen, *Plato's "Symposium"* (New Haven: Yale University Press, 1968), xiii, xi.

18. Cf. Tigerstedt, *Interpreting Plato*, 78–79, for a somewhat different way of situating what I take to be Rosen's inconsistency.

19. Stanley Rosen, "The Role of Eros in Plato's *Republic*," *Review of Metaphysics* 18 (1965): 453.

20. Cf. Berger, "Plato's Flying Philosopher," *Philosophical Forum* 13 (1982): 385–407.

21. Irwin, *Plato's Moral Theory*, 177–248.

22. Cf. Paul Friedländer, *Plato: The Dialogues, Second and Third Periods*, trans. Hans Meyerhoff (Princeton: Princeton University Press, 1969), 355–82; Klein, *Plato's "Meno*," 192–93, 199ff.; Rosen, *Plato's "Symposium"*: footnotes on 148, 183, 210, 211, etc., are explanatory glosses that use the *Sophist* as if its teaching were Plato's and could be extracted from context to illuminate Plato's "prephilosophical" drama; on 188–89, 209, 217–18, and 230, the *Timaeus* is used as a doctrinal touchstone with which to criticize Agathon on the Symposium. In *Plato's "Sophist*," Rosen's attitude toward the relation of the Stranger's procedures to Plato's remains, as I have tried to suggest, irresolute and at times cryptic.

23. Paul de Man, *Blindness and Insight: Essays in the Rhetoric of Contemporary Criticism* (New York: Oxford University Press, 1971), 106.

24. Kenneth Dorter, *Plato's "Phaedo": An Interpretation* (Toronto: University of Toronto Press, 1982), 4.

25. Eric Havelock, *Preface to Plato* (Cambridge: Harvard University Press, 1963), 208–9.

26. Jacques Derrida, *Dissemination*, trans. Barbara Johnson (Chicago, University of Chicago Press, 1981), 95–96.

27. I would like to thank A. J. Cascardi for assistance in revising this essay.

5
From the Sublime
to the Natural:
Romantic Responses to Kant

At one point in *Experience and Nature*, John Dewey gave an account of the influence of Greek aesthetics on the development of Western metaphysics from the perspective of the concept of form. "Form," he said, "was the first and last word of philosophy because it had been that of art . . . It conveys an intimation of potentialities completely actualized in a happier realm, where events are not events, but are arrested and brought to a close in an eternal self-sustaining activity. Such a realm is intrinsically one of secure and self-possessed meaning. It consists of objects of immediate enjoyment hypostatized into transcendent reality. Such was the conversion of Greek esthetic contemplation effected by Greek reflection." In modern times, however, the relationship between philosophy and the aesthetic object has been marked more by their division than by their coalescence. One may attribute this largely to a shift in the conception of form, which, first in the writings of Descartes and later in those of Kant, has come to be defined as a matter of representations to the mind. As the following essay seeks to show, there is abundant evidence for this understanding of form in the tradition of modern writing about the sublime; indeed, it could be argued that the sublime in this respect exemplifies the nature of the aesthetic as such, thus reaffirming (in a way that Dewey, writing on Greek thought, could hardly have expected) an alliance between philosophy conceived as representation and the aesthetic domain.

This essay works along two discernable axes and proposes two formulations of what I take to be the romantic interest in the natural, over and above romanticism's interest in the sublime. I take the "natural" first in the widely accepted (Kantian) sense as the totality of appearances governed by law or rule (which in Kant's parlance is the same as the possibility of experience). But I also regard the natural as capable of fulfilling some of the deficiencies which are left by the concept of the sublime. Here I regard the natural contextually, as those circumstances in which we are able to discover everything that we can about the external world, ourselves, and others—in other words, a context free of any necessary deceptions, yet one that need not be controlled by any limit-concept of Absolute Rationality or Consciousness. A related discussion of the natural may be found in Roberto Mangabeira Unger's recent work *Passion: An Essay on Personality* (1984). Whereas Unger is seeking to formulate a theory of personality, however, my purpose is to analyze the structure of our relationship to those objects denominated "beautiful," and especially "sublime," as set forth by such modern philosophers as Kant, Hegel, and Sartre, all of whom require some distance from the aesthetic object and who accordingly posit that object as unnatural or unreal. My specific examples are prompted by Hans Robert Jauss's observations on the history of aesthetic experience as revealed in Petrarch and Rousseau. What Jauss describes as "romantic" aesthesis in Rousseau may, on my account, be regarded as an aesthetic type or mode (the "romantic" as such) which is visible prior to romanticism proper in the genre of romance, as exemplified in Shakespeare's romantic plays. Thus, to look ahead to Charles Altieri's essay on expressivist ethics and to his invocation of Charles Taylor's conception of the romantic, I would suggest that the modes of knowledge and communal relationship there proposed need not be situated according to the Hegelian model of history; they may be located with equal precision on some imaginary *Rota Virgilii* or anatomical (Fryean) conception of the totality of literary genres.

The second axis of my essay, which intersects with the first, involves the characterization of this "romantic" typology in philosophical terms. Here, I take my bearings once again from Kant, who most successfully described our relationship to the world as a function of our knowledge of it. This was part of Kant's way of securing the natural, but if Heidegger is indeed correct, Kant's achievement also had the undesirable consequences of converting nature into an object of knowledge. Following up this Heideggerean suggestion, and tracing it back to pre-Heideggerean responses to Kant, I look at a wider range of motives which might provoke resistance to Kant's first *Critique*. There, our knowledge of the world is achieved only on the condition that we relinquish any claims to know things-in-themselves, which to romantic thinkers and poets seems too high a price to pay, even in return for the natural. Rather than accept the consequences of Kant's critical project, they would prefer to find ways in which poetic imagination or aesthetic experience might reclaim access to things-in-themselves. These may be regarded as the romantic roots of Heidegger's interest in "poetic thinking" in his later phase.

This romantic response to Kant is enticing in its goals, but, as I say in my concluding section, it may have nihilistic consequences, such as an unconditional appeal to the will (more accurately, an appeal to the unconditioned will: "poetic thinking" may too easily be a disguise for the will-to-power). Here, the work of Iris Murdoch and her general critique of the modern philosophical tradition in *The Sovereignty of Good* (1970) is of decisive, if tacit, influence. But rather than discard romantic goals, which I recognize as attractive, my hope is to identify a model that would purify the romantic project of its potentially nihilistic effects. In contrast to Rousseau's *Pygmalion*, which typifies the problems inherent in the romantic mode, I propose a reading of Shakespeare's *Winter's Tale*, which allows for a recovery of the natural—both as (lawful) experience and as a context for our knowledge of others—while trading the nihilistic determinism and the capriciousness of the will for a morality based on faith. The result remains "romantic" to the extent that Altieri's characterization of "expressivism" may be called romantic as well: it is a vision of the moral, but more specifically of the ethical—which is to say that it grants priority to an agent's particular stance toward determinate goods rather than to a program of goods to which all (rational) agents must accede.

From the Sublime to the   *Anthony J. Cascardi*
Natural: Romantic
Responses to Kant

In his "Sketch of a Theory and History of Aesthetic Experience," Hans Robert Jauss describes the writing and influences of Jean Jacques Rousseau—and in particular Rousseau's *Nouvelle Héloise*—as marking an "epochal turn in the history of aesthetics."[1] The romantic turn in the conception of the aesthetic so marked corresponds on his account to a discovery of the sublime in nature, which on his further account entails the perception of nature as a "spectacle" capable of producing in the viewer effects proper to the ancient (tragic) theatre. Such an achievement is explained as the result of a shift in the direction of aesthetic experience, rather than as a modulation in kind. Whereas earlier—in the Petrarchan tradition, to take the example that Jauss himself cites—aesthetic experience was inwardly directed, it is now directed outward, onto nature. In Petrarch and, according to Jauss, in literature until Rousseau, the aesthetic object was sublimated within an essentially self-reflective poetic consciousness; the beloved—or rather the image, memory, or other trace of the absent beloved—was there as a function of the poet's inward state of desire or lack, and nature, if it was invoked at all, became a mirror of what was happening within the poetic self. When, in a typical passage, Petrarch describes Laura as like a laurel whose branches are in turn compared to gems, the hardness and brilliance of this image are, as one recent commentator says, "qualities her image gains from the meditation of the lover."[2]

The incorporation of nature within the poet's subjective experience is what is often meant by reference to the specifically lyric quality of Petrarch's verse, but in order to support such a claim with reference to the *Canzoniere* it would be necessary to add that the poet's "inward" experience is, in certain essential ways, constituted by its relationship to the absent beloved. Jauss cites Petrarch's sonnet 310, which proceeds from the natural world and its accompanying mythology ("Zephyr returns, fair weather in his train / and flowers and grass, and all his gentle brook . . .") to an "inward landscape" in the final stanzas ("To me, alas, return more heavy sighs, / drawn from the heart in that profound distress . . . and ladies in their motion sweet and wise / seem savage beasts that roam a wilderness"); he rightly observes that "lyric aesthesis can seize phenomena of external nature such as the times of the day or the seasons in newly perceived shadings which then become integral parts of a whole that has its center in the name of Laura and often gets its significance only through the symbolism of that name" (76). It is not entirely clear from this why the symbolic values of Laura's name, which Petrarch exploits in paranomasia throughout the *Canzoniere*, should at the same time be central to the aesthetic relationship between the poet and his beloved, but one may venture an explanation on roughly Hegelian grounds. In a famous definition, Hegel described the beautiful as "the sensory manifestation of the idea" ("das sinnliche Scheinen der Idee"), but the beautiful, he also made clear, is a function of the symbolic order, which is to say that it is not entirely sensory but depends on the mediation of the mind. Thus in Hegelian terms the poet worships "Laura" because the idea makes its "sensory appearance" in and through this (symbolic) name. Paul de Man has made the case that Hegel's famous definition is equivalent to his more problematical statement that "art is for us a thing of the past."[3] Petrarch's relationship to Laura illustrates what that equivalence might mean, but it also shows that these two features of aesthetic experience—its quality as "sensory appearance" and also as recollection—remain paradoxical equivalents: throughout the *Canzoniere*, Petrarch is supremely aware of his ability to call to Laura, to name her, but also of his inability to possess her, precisely because his present experience of her can only be a recollection of some sensory experience of the past.

One may object to Jauss's scheme of aesthetic history, and to the respective places given to Petrarch and Rousseau, on any number of grounds. It may, for instance, be said that Jauss's notion of "direction" in aesthetic experience could not be rigorously sustained, and that concepts like "inward" and "outward" in aesthetics should accordingly be abandoned or replaced. Rather than speak of the incorporation of nature within the poet's experience in Petrarch, for example, it might be more accurate to speak of the sublimation of nature, by which I mean the process of raising and purifying nature by aestheticizing it. I will take up this and some related points in what follows, but first I wish to follow Jauss to the following central point. The new (romantic) experience, which made possible the vision of nature as an aesthetic object, and ultimately as an object of the sublime, is said to anticipate a shift of interest during romanticism proper from the functions and concerns of the rational faculties to the aesthetic imagination, such as is described in Joachim Ritter's remarks on Kant: "After the science of nature had embarked on a certain path by restricting itself to 'spelling out' the phenomena with which it deals in the field of possible experience only, the aesthetic imagination takes on the task of making present the idea of the suprasensible which we can no longer recognize in the 'concept of worlds.'"[4] The crucial concept here is that through the aesthetic imagination one might grasp that of which Kant had said in the *Critique of Pure Reason* we could have no knowledge: things-in-themselves, noumena, the realm beyond appearances. If one accepts the opening principle of the first *Critique* that all knowledge begins in experience, then one might see the aesthetic imagination in general, and the category of the sublime in particular, as motivated by the desire to deny a corollary of that principle—that we are limited *to* experience—by seeking to transcend it in the representation of those ideas (e.g., the "suprasensible") which cannot be accommodated within the Kantian conception of a world of appearances.

Such expectations are not entirely incompatible with the nature of aesthetic experience as Kant himself described it in the *Critique of*

Judgment, but the romantic strategy might be thought of as an application of aesthetic experience to the problems generated (and, implicitly, left unsolved) by the *Critique of Pure Reason*. In his explanation of the sublime, for instance, Kant insisted on the role of the imagination and of the representation of images before the mind in attending to this category of experience. "Nature is not judged to be sublime in our aesthetical judgments in so far as it excites fear, but because it calls up that power *in us*," he says; "[n]ature is here called sublime merely because it elevates the imagination to a presentation of those cases in which the mind can make felt the proper intensity of its destination in comparison with herself."[5] Kant began the tradition in aesthetics which takes the beautiful as something essentially unreal, and this tradition reaches, with some modifications, to Sartre's *L'imaginaire* (1940), where it is said that in order for consciousness to constitute something as beautiful, it must first posit that object as unreal.[6] Thus Sartre can say that while we may take an aesthetic attitude toward the real, the real can never be beautiful *as* real. Consequently nature, insofar as it is real, is not a proper aesthetic object, which means that if nature is aestheticized in Petrarch and Rousseau, it is correspondingly rendered unreal. In the *Vorlesungen über die Aesthetik*, Hegel excludes nature from the province of aesthetics and gives reasons that may reveal the paradox implicit in Petrarch's and Rousseau's attempt to sublimate (i.e., raise and purify) nature: the beauty of art, he says, is always higher than that of nature, so to see nature as sublime would be to elevate it beyond the realm of the natural. Artistic beauty is "higher" than nature because natural phenomena are necessary and lawful, while properly aesthetic phenomena are recreations of the mind and hence not bound by nature's laws.

Artistic beauty is *higher* than nature. For the beauty of art is the beauty that is born—born again, that is—of the mind; and by as much as the mind and its products are higher than nature and its appearances, by so much is the beauty of art higher than the beauty of nature . . . even a silly fancy such as may pass through a man's head is *higher* than any product of nature; for such a fancy must at least be characterized by intellectual being and by freedom . . . a natural existence such as the sun is indifferent, is not free or self-conscious, while if we consider it in its necessary connection with other things we are not regarding it by itself or for its own sake, and, therefore, not as beautiful.[7]

Hegel, Kant, and Sartre are in agreement that aesthetic contemplation is "disinterested," which is not to say that it takes no interest at all in an object but that it seeks no end for that object outside itself. Hegel describes this as a situation "devoid of relation to our appetitive faculty," which for Petrarch means that the poet is able to stimulate his desire for the beloved and yet run no risk of destroying the purely aesthetic basis of their relationship by satisfying his desire. I underscore that the Petrarchan poetic self represents itself always to the image, memory, or trace of the absent beloved and in so doing aestheticizes her or, as I prefer to say, sublimates her, elevating her above him by an absolute, aesthetic distance. She is not experienced in direct sensuous manifestation but only as she is called (named) and recalled from this distance. Insofar as the aesthetic relationship to the real is maintained only at the price of an aesthetic distance from the real, aesthesis becomes a relationship in which we must deny the real being of the real. In Petrarch, this becomes evident through the fact that the sublimation of the beloved reaches its highest point coincident with the beloved's death: "Recollection as the lyric medium of absence as discovered by Petrarch, which sublimates the concrete person and sensuous presence of the mistress by making it the unique manifestation of a distance, reaches the highest level of such sublimation with Laura's death—the 'turn' between the first and the second phase of the love in the sonnet sequence: 'only the departed is the truly present.'"[8] (Cf. Hegel, "Art is for us a thing of the past.") If the aesthetic qualities of the beloved are a reflection of the poetic consciousness, then her death may be regarded as following naturally from his aestheticization of her, and that aestheticization is implicitly a denial of her.

Aesthetic distance is emblematized in the form of theater and the frame of a canvas and places the aesthetic object, as Sartre says, always "behind itself," so that "it becomes untouchable, it is beyond our reach; hence arises a sort of sad disinterest in it" (225). It is for this same reason that nature, so seen that it excites feelings of the sublime, may be said to be theatricalized or framed. Jauss cites examples from Rousseau's *Nouvelle Héloise* and Stendhal's *Le rouge et le noir*, where nature seems sublime by virtue of the fact that it is presented as an object to be beheld. In these and similar cases, nature is made a spectacle, an object of sight. Perhaps more striking still are the paintings by Caspar David Friedrich, "Woman in Morning Light" and "Monk by the Sea" (both ca. 1809), in which the figures are positioned as having turned away from the viewer; they stand gazing into the landscape as if looking at a vast stage set. The illumination of the landscape in these paintings is patently theatrical, and the position of the spectators suggests that they stand as surrogates for us, as spectators of the world. However, if Sartre is indeed correct, the unseen facial expressions of these figures, which we might expect to show fascination or absorption, would reflect a "sad disinterest," as if at the *loss* of nature; they would mirror some of the same pathos which is visible in Friedrich's paintings of ruins, such as the "Ruins of the Abbey at Eldena" (ca. 1824) and the "Abbey Oak under Tree" (1810).

To the extent that these examples are representative of romanticism's more or less explicit interest in the role of theater-like representations in the perception of the sublime, they may be said to instance Kant's descriptions, and the third Kantian *Critique* may be said to provide romanticism with a justification of the philosophical use of the sublime. However, Kant had other, moral ends in mind when writing of the beautiful and the sublime. He thought that in the beautiful we discover the purposiveness of nature and that in the sublime we have evidence of its transcendent origins, so that when nature excites in us feelings of the sublime, we conceive it as an ideal world. The sublime engages our moral nature because it thus provides a field for the pure practical reason, which legislates "for itself alone." The moral faculty, which judges the noncontingent, is matched by the aesthetic judgment in the exercise of taste, "the faculty of judging an object or a method of representing it by an *entirely disinterested* satisfaction or dissatisfaction."[9]

Accepting Kant's theories of the beautiful and the sublime based on his understanding of aesthetic distance and disinterest would also mean accepting the fact that there is no such thing as the sublime in nature, if only because on Kant's account the sublime is not in anything but rather is in the mind ("Sublimity, therefore, does not reside in anything but only in our mind" [104, sec. 28]; and romanticism, as Jauss said, sought to direct the aesthetic experience onto nature, which means that it saw nature itself as sublime. Thus accepting Kant's proposition would mean acknowledging romanticism's loss of nature, as well as romanticism's failure in one of the undertakings usually counted among its central successes, namely the recovery of the realm of things-in-themselves by the imagination of a suprasensible world. Indeed, there would be no apparent hope for the recovery of things-in-themselves through the experience of the sublime if it were acknowledged that the sublime is only achieved through representations in the mind. Certainly it would not provide a recovery of the natural, for to perceive nature as sublime is, as we have seen, first to posit it as unreal.

One might from there go on to speculate, along Nietzschean lines, that the recovery of things-in-themselves may not in fact amount to the recovery of anything at all. On Kant's own account, we can apply neither the forms of space and time nor the categories of the understanding to these things. Kant wants to say that they are the (unknowable) causes of appearances ("The non-sensible cause of these representations is completely unknown to us, and cannot therefore be intuited by us as object . . . We may, however, entitle the purely intelligible cause of appearances in general the transcendental object");[10] but by his own stipulation he cannot say that things-in-themselves cause appearances, because causality is valid only within the field of experience and so proves meaningless here. What final justification is there for supposing the existence of a realm of things-in-themselves to be recovered at all? Kant probably thought that without things-in-themselves it would be impossible to preserve the idea of a self-in-itself, and without a noumenal self his ideas of human freedom and responsibility would necessarily fail. This would explain why a Nietzschean aesthetic is inconceivable without a prior "transvaluation" of all values; whether Nietzsche recovered the natural, however, is a subject that would require strenuous debate.

The conflict between romanticism's investment in the sublime and its will to recover a world of things-in-themselves might be rephrased in order to reflect romanticism's interests more sympathetically by asking what would become of the romantic conception of the sublime if this project is to succeed. In what follows, I shall speculate about a possible reply in view of some concrete cases, while bearing the following assumptions in mind. The recovery of things-in-themselves, through aesthetic or any other means, will somehow depend on getting beyond representations; this may be imagined as the will to overcome theater or, more generally, as the will to overcome art. Nietzsche saw it as requiring the inversion of Platonism, which would result in a reversal of the relationship between philosophy and art; Heidegger, complaining that Nietzsche, through Schopenhauer, had fundamentally misunderstood Kant, said that this would require a turn in our thinking and would depend on getting back to "poetic" thought. The romantic project so conceived is designed to transform its imagined objects from the sublime into the natural, so that the recovery of a world of things-in-themselves—which might be called the recovery of the world-in-itself—may then be said to depend on getting *beyond* the sublime. This would provide at least one sense in which the creation of the natural, rather than the sublime, could be counted as a peculiarly romantic achievement. As I shall discuss, the natural thus recovered from the sublime is a world of the moral, and not only the metaphysical, imagination. Contrary to the Kantian conception of morality, however, which conceives of man under two aspects, as living in two worlds, one in which he is determined and the other in which he is free, this is a conception of morality as *conditions*, whose goal corresponds to the romantic metaphysical project, namely the reconciliation of these two worlds.

The first of my cases is Rousseau's dramatization of the Pygmalion myth as a brief *scène lyrique* during the period of romanticism proper (1775); the second, which I will take up again at the conclusion of this essay, is Shakespeare's late romantic play, *The Winter's Tale*, which may be said to have the Pygmalion myth as its subtext. Each presents a vision of the natural as a distinctive achievement, as a moral goal, in part by dramatizing its attainment by passing beyond the sublime. The difference between Shakespeare and Rousseau here, one should aver, lies in what they imagine a morality of conditions actually to be. For Rousseau it is something that depends on genius and the (artistic) will; for Shakespeare it is founded on faith. In this way Rousseau reveals some of the nihilistic consequences of the romantic achievement of the natural—consequences also borne out in the philosophical response to Kant—while Shakespeare's romance might be thought of as working toward a purification of romantic goals.

At the beginning of *Pygmalion*, the sculptor finds himself dispirited, in part as a reflection of the fact that he finds the world itself in a spiritless condition.[11] But if the sublime is a form of nature theatricalized, then there is no reason that what at one moment appears awesome and inspiring should not at another seem uninteresting or even dead; one might simply take this as proof of the fact that sublimity lies, as Kant said, in our representations of nature, not in nature itself. Pygmalion has lost the world to the death of boredom, which is one of the risks entailed in aestheticizing the world. In the descent of Venus, where an inert statue, a stone-cold work of art, is brought to life, the world is redeemed from this death; and while this is a moment of the sublime which yields to the natural, it is nonetheless an achievement subject to the fluctuations of genius and spirit. In Rousseau, and in romanticism generally, the creation of the natural is a task entrusted to the artist—a fact worth recalling when reading Shakespeare, where the creation of the natural requires the abandonment of magic and art.

In *The Winter's Tale*, the return of Hermione to her husband under the guise of a statue that comes to life is similarly an occurrence of the romantic sublime, but it is also a stock instance of the marvelous, a staple of literary romance; it is an event requiring, as Paulina says, that one be ready for "amazement" (5.3.87). The creation of the natural could then be said to be accomplished by going beyond amazement and wonder to whatever (natural) relations these creatures may develop among themselves. In Shakespeare that is something requiring, as Paulina further says, that "you do awake your faith" (95). I shall say something more about how Shakespeare conceives such a form of life, but in view of Shakespeare's insistence on the morality of faith, the conclusion of Rousseau's *scène lyrique* is all the more disconcerting. There, Pygmalion and Galathea exchange bewildered glances and each exclaims, in thorough amazement, "Moi!" "Moi!" One knows that they recognize their dependence on each other as much as if not more than their independence, but one can only wonder how and if they will honor this fact in a life of dedication to each other.

One might describe the relationship of Pygmalion to Galathea as a form of rather exquisite narcissim. She is not so much the reflection as the tangible projection of his highest aspirations and most ardent desires ("masterpiece worthy of my hands, of my heart, and of the gods; it is you, it is you alone: I have given you all my being; I will live for you alone"). How is this narcissism to be explained? In an essay on the self in Rousseau, Paul de Man quotes the following words of Alain Grosrichard, who sees the main purpose of Rousseau's work as making "the representation I have of the world coincide with the representation I convey to others or, in brief, to name myself."[12] This sounds perplexingly like an inversion of Kant's "Copernican revolution" in philosophy, and if it does indeed go beyond Kant it is in the recognition that the desires we have to represent ourselves to others are also desires for the freedom to reinvent ourselves. On de Man's reading of Rousseau, the unified and transcendental self that Kant supposed can never be presupposed. Neither at the start nor at the conclusion of *Pygmalion* is there a stable distinction between self and other, in part because the self is always already divided from within, and so cannot be taken as the unified ground that Kant invokes. But if it is in the nature of the self, on this account, to unseat any of the stable relationships between itself and its representations, either to itself or to others, then its freedom to reinvent itself is bound to be sacrificed at the hands of (self)-deception. The result is the following predicament, which one might take as paradigmatic of the romantic double-bind: on the one hand an acknowledgment of the central importance of personal striving and love, and on the other a deep-seated skepticism about whether the other is, in fact, anything but a mirage of the self. As Roberto Mangabeira Unger describes its consequences in modernist times, "We should rather expect love to be recognized in the end as a refined narcissism or as a futile attempt to escape our solitude, and the image of the beloved to convey only the fantastical projections of our inner cravings."[13] I can think of no more exact description of the significance of Rousseau's *Pygmalion*.

If the natural may be thought of in contextual terms, and not simply materially or formally, as a context that "allows those who move within it to discover everything about the world [and, I would add, about one another] that they can discover" (Unger, 5), then Rousseau's brief *scène lyrique* is manifestly the representation of a failure to achieve the natural. Pygmalion is bound to be deceived by Galathea, in large measure because he takes her as the sum of the desires which he invents for her. And if Pygmalion is representative of the self in Rousseau, then this only points up the larger fact that Rousseau imagines no context in which the self can discover everything about itself that it can; it is always deceived.[14] Jauss might describe Pygmalion's "creation" of Galathea as an example of the "outward" direction of aesthetic experience, but if such terms must indeed be used it would be better to say that this is a further case of poetic "inwardness," granting the fact that it is relatively senseless to speak of "direction" in such a specular relationship as this.

It is perhaps only in light of the moral consequences of romantic goals that one can go on to evaluate some of the more familiar features of the romantic attempt to recover things-in-themselves in the form of a natural world. I will turn to the subject of morality once again, but first I wish to pursue some further discussion of the romantic response to Kant. In *A Study of English Romanticism*, Northrop Frye suggests the following ways in which romantic poets were able to imagine the noumenal world: "In literature the noumenal world becomes a mysterious world hidden within or behind the world of ordinary experience—for while philosophers may be able to escape from such spatial and diagrammatic metaphors as 'within' or 'behind,' poets never make any pretense of being able to do so."[15] By finding the noumenal to be a (hidden) part of ordinary experience, poets sought to collapse Kant's distinction between things-as-known and things-in-themselves. Accordingly, they were encouraged to seek an immediate experience of the noumenal—which is to say, an experience free of the mediations of the a priori forms of the mind. Kant described space and time as a priori forms of sensibility which are among the conditions of any possible experience; they are a priori in the sense that they precede the actual impressions by which an observer might be affected by objects.

Geoffrey Hartman sees certain romantic and modern poets—namely Wordsworth, Hopkins, Rilke, and Valéry—as in search of pure representations, a vision "unmediated" by any a priori forms of understanding, which is to say a vision that takes *itself* as having absolute priority: "In pure representations, the poet represents the mind as knowing without a cause from perception, and so in and from itself; or he will represent the mind as no less real than the objects of its perceiving."[16] The corollary truth implicit in this search is that the mind is necessarily consigned to the "mediacy" of perceived experience; knowledge, one might say, is reception, and it is always indebted to some instrument of mediation such as the eye, the lens of knowledge. Yet this does not mean that the desire for transparent vision is any less intense. "The mind, therefore, being most keenly aware through the dominant eye of that which is the cause of perception, pure representation will, at base, be the urge to construct that ideal system of symbols which relieves consciousness of the eyes' oppression, but assures it of the eyes' luminosity" (128–29).

Insofar as Hartman's cadre of poets seeks out "pure representations," "the mind as knowing . . . in and of itself," they substantially reverse Kant's strategy in the *Critique of Pure Reason*. In the "Refutation of Idealism" section added to the second edition of that work, Kant takes self-consciousness as the basis for a proof of the existence of a world external to the mind, thus defeating the idealist assumption that "the only immediate experience is inner experience, and that from it we can only *infer* outer things—and this, moreover, only in an untrustworthy manner, as in all cases where we are inferring from given effects to determinate causes" (B, 276). Kant presents his proof schematically as follows:

I am conscious of my own existence as determined in time. All determination of time presupposes something permanent in perception. This permanent cannot, however, be something in me, since it is only through this permanent that my existence in time can itself be determined. Thus perception of this permanent is possible only through a *thing* outside me and not through the mere *representation* of a thing outside me; and consequently the determination of my existence in time is possible only through the existence of actual things which I perceive outside me . . . In other words, the consciousness of my existence is at the same time an immediate consciousness of the existence of other things outside me." (B, 275–76).

Insofar as the romantic and modern poets discover the mediacy of all knowledge, they reveal themselves to be children of Kant. In addition to Kant's exposition of space, time, and causality as a priori forms of understanding, which necessarily precede all knowledge, he provides evidence of the same in his figuration of objects and sense as "inner" and "outer," and of knowledge as having "horizons," which presumably only an eye could see. Sight in particular insinuates itself into the realm of the pure understanding in the following account of the illusions that (speculative) reason encounters as it tries to penetrate that realm: "This domain is an island, enclosed by nature within unalterable limits. It is the land of truth—enchanting name!—surrounded by a wide and stormy ocean, the native home of illusion, where many a fog bank and many a swiftly melting iceberg give the deceptive appearance of farther shores, deluding the adventurous seafarer ever anew with empty hopes, and engaging him in enterprises which he can never abandon and yet is unable to carry to completion" (B, 295). Kant's recourse to descriptions such as these might further be taken as evidence that, while the noumenal is claimed to be unknowable, and the noumenon a "negative" or "limiting" concept, the noumenal is not necessarily unfigurable; it might better be said that it is *only* figurable. Thus when Frye speaks elsewhere of romantic imagery as being indebted to Kant's distinction between the phenomenal and noumenal worlds, the emphasis ought to fall on the imagination and on the concept of the image implicit therein: "Poetry creates for the *imagination* a flexible language of symbols, and expands our range of experience accordingly, in a way that sense and reason cannot do" (84, emphasis added). This would of course be one justification of what romantics thought the role of the poetic, or the aesthetic, to be: if not to free us from our limitations to experience *tout court*, then to give us access to a world beyond ordinary experience.

In an additional comment on romanticism's indebtedness to Kant, Frye says that "the shadow of Kant's riddle falls across the whole Romantic movement. The world that we see and understand is not the noumenon, the world-in-itself, but only the world as phenomenon, as adapted to our categories of perception and reasoning. The inference is that *real* reality, so to speak, cannot be known, at least by the subject-object relationship. The proud boast of the subjective reason, that a perfect being must exist because the mind can conceive the possibility of its existence, no longer carries much conviction. The Romantic sense of something outside ordinary experience which nevertheless completes experience, symbolized by 'nature' in Wordsworth and elsewhere, must be something mysterious, because it cannot be directly apprehended" (84). Formulated in this fashion, romanticism leaves the Kantian problematic largely intact, for while we are thus given access to things-in-themselves, nature, so seen, is not at all natural but is an extra-ordinary, super-natural world, one that holds us at a distance and in awe. Yet the achievement of romanticism, if one can take Coleridge's account of the *Lyrical Ballads* as evidence, was not so much to elevate nature in such ways as to provoke wonder at the (ordinary) circumstances and objects we meet every day: "Mr Wordsworth . . . was to propose himself as his object to give the charm of novelty to things of the everyday, and to excite a feeling analogous to the supernatural, by awakening the mind's attention from the lethargy of custom and directing it to the loveliness and the wonders of the world before us."[17] If such a project was necessary, it was in part because, as Heidegger would later say, Kant's idea of the thing-in-itself succeeds at the expense of "mere real things": "from the beginning Kant does not pose the question of the thingness of the thing that surrounds us. This question has no weight for him. He immediately fixes his view of the thing as an object of mathematical-physical science," that is, as the object of a possible experience.[18]

What would, for a romantic, be required in order to escape from the confines of the Kantian problematic would follow more directly from the first part of Frye's observation: in order to clear free of Kantianism we would have to cease to view nature in the way that subjects see objects. This is Emerson's understanding of the purposes of what he calls "transcendental" philosophy, when he speaks of the "transfer of the world into the consciousness," or when in the essay *Nature* he describes the mind as a "transparent eyeball," that is, as a subject that is transparent to, rather than a mirror of, its object. However, Emerson also says that if "subject" and "object" are the only terms we have, then knowledge, which Emerson also calls "marriage," may prove impossible: "Marriage (in what is called the spiritual world) is impossible, because of the inequality between every subject and every object."[19] In Hartman's terms, an entirely "unmediated vision" could prevail only on the condition that we give up the guiding metaphors of the eye and sight. Heidegger in his later phase will continue to advocate the abandonment of subject-object thinking and, with this, a return to authentic (i.e., "poetic") thought. Heidegger also calls this thinking "thanking," which I would venture to say might be understood as a form of reception, or grace. His complaint was that in Kant's "transcendental" philosophy our knowledge passes over to (*transcendit*) objects a priori and in advance, so that we see the object not directly but as it is posited, fixed, or otherwise set up before us, that is, with regard to "the mode of its objectivity (*Gegenständlichkeit*)."[20] Since, as Coleridge says, an object, seen as object, is "essentially dead" (Heidegger might see it as "framed"), then it would take some vitalizing power, which Coleridge calls the imagination in both its primary and secondary forms, in order to reanimate the "objects" of the mind, as for instance Pygmalion sought to do:

The primary imagination I hold to be the living power and prime agent of all human perception, and as a repetition in the finite mind of the eternal act of creation in the infinite I AM. The secondary I consider as an echo of the former, co-existing with the conscious will, yet still as identical with the primary in the kind of its agency, and differing only in degree, and in the mode of its operation. It dissolves, diffuses, dissipates, in order to re-create; or where this process is rendered impossible, yet still, at all events, it struggles to idealize and to unify. It is essentially *vital*, even as all objects (as objects) are essentially fixed and dead. (*Biographia Literaria*,13:167)

The reservations I have expressed about Frye's postulates regarding Kant and romanticism are, perhaps obviously, also reservations about the thesis of "natural supernaturalism" which M. H. Abrams later developed at length. They are not meant to exclude romantic marvel, wonder, or awe, which are accurate enough descriptions of our response to nature when seen as sublime, but they are meant to suggest that the romantic vision of nature as sublime is only partial—specifically, that it is part of the larger project in which romanticism came to see nature (and much else) as natural. The natural may be seen as an achievement that recuperates not only nature but also moral relationships, which may be sacrificed because of an enshrinement of the subject-object split, insistence on the agency and freedom of the noumenal self, or the identification of morality otherwise with the realm of the noncontingent.

What I have been describing as an aesthetic response to the ideas that culminated in the *Critique of Pure Reason* has its parallel in the philosophical response to Kant—which I would see as similarly romantic—which issued in Heidegger's proposal that there ought to be no difference between poetry and (authentic) thought. The romantic project to recover the world-in-itself, which I have said is the recovery of the natural from the sublime, would not have been unnecessary without the *Critique of Pure Reason*; Nietzsche would predicate it only on Socrates' defeat of the Sophists and on the establishment of Platonism as the reigning philosophy. Yet is could not have been formulated thus without the writing and influence of Kant.

Kant saw his project as surpassing the work of earlier philosophers, who had failed to provide knowledge with adequate foundations by failing to question reason itself. In the preface to the first edition of the *Critique of Pure Reason*, Kant begins by saying that "human reason has this peculiar fate that in one species of its knowledge it is burdened by questions which, as prescribed by the very nature of reason itself, it is not able to ignore, but which, as transcending all its powers, it is also not able to answer" (A, vii). This is a strikingly negative gambit, and as Kant himself was aware it would have been easy in this light to over-look the positive accomplishments of the first *Critique*; to do so would be to forget the more important fact that in his efforts to set limits on the scope of human reason Kant claimed to have established reason's security in the world and thereby to have secured the world *by* human reason. "On a cursory view of the present work," he writes in the pref-ace to the second edition, "it may seem that its results are purely *nega-tive*, warning us that we must never venture with speculative reason beyond the limits of experience. Such is in fact its primary use. But such teaching at once acquires a *positive* value when we recognize that the principles with which speculative reason ventures out beyond its proper limits do not in effect *extend* the employment of reason, but, as we find on closer scrutiny, inevitably *narrow* it" (B, xxiv). Kant's cen-tral idea that the limitations of reason are not necessarily failures but are in fact necessary to its success is the basis for his claim to having set reason along "the secure path of a science" (B, xxx); it is the reason he can say that as a result of the first *Critique* "there is not a single meta-physical problem which has not yet been solved, or for the solution of which the key has not yet at least been supplied" (A, xiii).

The idea that reason must limit itself in order to ensure its efficacy, which is at the heart of what was meant by calling his a *critical* philoso-phy, was Kant's alternative to what he regarded as the reigning forms of dogmatism and ignorance, among which he included skepticism and idealism ("Criticism alone can sever the root of materialism, fatal-ism, atheism, free-thinking, fanaticism, and superstition, which can be injurious universally; as well as of *idealism* and skepticism, which are dangerous chiefly to the Schools, and hardly allow of being handed on to the public" [B, xxxiv]). If a natural context can be taken as one that allows us to discover everything about the world that we can, then the *critical* aspect of the *Critique of Pure Reason* may be taken as a sustained effort to create the natural. Since Kant saw that it is characteristically in one species of its knowledge—in its speculative, or pure, form—that human reason is drawn out of its proper bounds, setting limits to reason would also clear the way for faith and the operations of practical reason, hence for morality as well, which were to be his subjects in the second *Critique* and the *Groundwork of the Metaphysics of Morals*: "All objections to morality and religion will ever be silenced, and in this Socratic fashion," which is to say by the critical, rather than the dogmatic, method. Given a context in which we need not be deceived by ourselves, by others, or by the world external to us, there is no need to constrain our impulses of human striving and desire, nor is there reason to withhold our will to collaborate with others. This does not mean that the self will face the world free of any and all risks; practically, human selfishness and desire will result in conflictive social arrangements, among them the societies in which we currently live; but if we can wait until the end of history, we can look forward to universal peace.

Kant imagined that human reason is caught up in a dialectic of knowledge and illusion in which it strives for knowledge and creates illusions for itself. The task of philosophy is then seen as one of unmasking the deceits of reason and so of providing a world—call this a natural world—in whose knowledge we can rest secure. To take only the most famous and general example, it is an illusion to say that we can know things-in-themselves; yet by the very nature of speculative reason we will always be tempted to think of them as something to be known, as lying just beyond or above the range of reason, or as requiring a more encompassing scope than reason can command. And because Kant thought of such transcendental illusions as somehow ineluctable, as unavoidable temptations, he could not countenance the question that might seem the most reasonable of all at this point, Why then continue to speak of things-in-themselves at all? At the same time, Kant's sharp distinction between phenomena or appearances and noumena, or between things-as-known and things-in-themselves, set the task of philosophy as telling us what we can and cannot legitimately claim to know. These two tasks were closely related for Kant because reason is bound to find itself taken in by illusions unless the distinction between things-as-known and things-in-themselves is strictly enforced. Consequently, Kant thought of the world as divided and of philosophy's task as enforcing that division. As shall become clear over the course of what follows, this consequence was a central romantic concern.

It may be objected that these comments on the *Critique of Pure Reason* place undue emphasis on its procedural, critical side. The Kantian definition of the natural, which has entered the tradition, is largely decontextualized, as is Kant's conception of the self. Indeed, the *Prolegomena* does define nature materially as the totality of appearances, and formally, as the totality of rules; these two are intimately related because Kant was convinced that the world of appearances, which is to say of experience, must necessarily follow laws—those of the understanding. However, these decontextualized definitions may be shown to be the reduction of various aspects of the larger epistemological project described above. Knowing Kant's definition of experience, for instance, as a synthetic combination of intuitions, one could follow Strawson and say that Kant's search for an answer to the question "What are the necessary conditions of a possible experience?" was also his search for a natural context of knowledge. With an answer to this question, Kant provided an answer to skeptical doubts about the possibility of ever knowing the external world; and finding an answer to skepticism provided us with a context that can be called natural because, as Kant further says in the *Prolegomena*, "Nature and possible experience are quite the same."[21]

Central to this larger project of the first *Critique*, although by no means coextensive with it, was Kant's refutation of empirical idealism, in place of which he urged a transcendental idealism and an empirical realism. Kant imagined the empirical idealist as a form of skeptic who suggests that we somehow infer the existence of an external world, but do not know it, or that we imagine "outer objects," of which we have no experience. In his effort to secure our knowledge of the world and so to secure what I would call a natural context, he was at pains to show that this cannot be so, and he accomplished the task by an appeal to self-consciousness reminiscent of the Cartesian *cogito*. His rejection of empirical idealism and his theory of transcendental idealism were both reliant on certain assumptions about the unity and self-awareness of the self, which serves strategically as more than a locus for the synthesis of intuitions. For Kant, self-consciousness *required* the existence of an external world, of "objects in space and time": "the consciousness of my existence is at the same time an immediate consciousness of the existence of things outside me" (B, 276).

The effects of this refutation of idealism are significant, perhaps more significant than its means, for they formed the central target of the romantic response to Kant. When Kant said that "in order to arrive at the reality of outer objects I have just as little need to resort to inference as I have in regard to . . . the reality of my own thoughts," and from there went on to explain that this is because "in both cases alike the objects are nothing but representations" (A, 371), his thinking was predicated on the division of worlds into phenomenal and noumenal, which romanticism would attempt to collapse. The caveat that must be entered in Kant's defense is that to think of the world as thus divided, and of things as apportioned between things-in-themselves and things-as-known, does not mean that we cannot know the things of the external world. Kant's transcendental idealism was tied to an empirical realism, so that it would be more accurate to speak of this division as being between things-in-themselves and things-of-the-world, or things-as-known. The totality of things-as-known is what Kant called nature: it is the totality of appearances, which is also to say that it is the possibility of experience; in the *Prolegomena*, he said that "the understanding, because it makes experience possible, thereby insists that the sensuous world is either not an object of experience at all, or else is nature" (64). Our relationship to nature, however, then becomes defined as to an object of (possible) experience, which, if we are to retain Kant's sense of what a possible experience is, means that our relationship to nature is determined by our knowledge of it. Thus Kant's thought became a central moment in what Heidegger, speaking of Descartes, called "modern philosophy," and which he described as that form of philosophizing which began when "a theory of knowledge had to be erected before a theory of the world."[22]

Heidegger's characterization of "modern philosophy" implicitly recognized the central importance that skepticism has assumed since Descartes. In the *Meditations*, Descartes imagines moving from empirical doubts that arise in connection with local failures of knowledge to the skeptical doubt of the possibility of knowledge *überhaupt*. Descartes is worried that because his senses have sometimes deceived him in the past he may never trust them in the future. Similarly, he imagines that doubts about the existence of the far side of the moon (i.e., things that are "hardly perceptible, or very far away")[23] are powerful enough to undermine any possible claim to knowledge. Descartes had said that by attempting to destroy the foundations of knowledge he could determine the strength of the entire edifice. Kant's response to skepticism was, like Descartes's, part of the larger project of providing philosophy with secure foundations, which for Kant meant showing that the world, as an object of possible experience, is and must necessarily be as we understand it. This is because "the understanding does not derive its laws (a priori) from, but prescribes them to, nature" (*Prolegomena*, 62). But in order to secure our knowledge of the world in such a way, Kant had to impose what many would regard as unbearable conditions: our knowledge can only be of the conditioned, never of the unconditioned; that knowledge not only begins in experience but also is limited to any possible experience, which is of a world of appearances; and he had to debar us from ever claiming knowledge of things-in-themselves.

The romantic response to Kant, which began roughly with Schopenhauer and continued at least through Heidegger, showed displeasure with the notion of the thing-in-itself. That displeasure followed largely from this fact: it seems that the price of Kant's achievement of securing the place of human reason, and of securing the world, or the natural, *by* human reason, was nothing less than the loss of the world-in-itself. It is an index of the strength of Kant's influence over philosophy's future that until the present day the romantic project to recover the world-in-itself has been regarded as "poetic" in certain essential ways. If in this sense "poetic" means "unphilosophical," then that is because philosophy since Kant (some would say since Descartes) has taken knowledge of objects as paradigmatic of our relationship to the world. In response, sometimes as if in retaliation, thinkers like Schopenhauer, Coleridge, Emerson, Nietzsche, and Heidegger saw the success of this romantic, "poetic" project as dependent on finding some term other than knowledge to characterize that relationship. The romantic alternative to Kantian "knowledge" drew on concepts of the aesthetic, the poetic, and the imaginative in various ways, and with varying degrees of success. In Coleridge's *Biographia Literaria* and in Rousseau's *Pygmalion*, for instance, the imagination is seen as capable of reanimating a world gone dead—dead, as Coleridge says, from having been converted into an object of knowledge. In the next section, I shall discuss Heidegger's "poetic thinking" as an alternative to Kantian knowledge, which must necessarily proceed via representational ideas. Aesthetic immediacy, which I have discussed above, holds the promise of self-enjoyment in addition to self-knowledge (cf. the following verses from Goethe's *Faust:* "My breast, cured of the drive for knowledge / Shall in the future exclude no pain. / And whatever is given to all mankind / I will enjoy within my inner self").[24] And yet the possibility of fully immediate, unmediated experience seems impossible to achieve: the romantic will dream of immediacy but will always discover the mediations of the mind.

Schopenhauer thought that whatever was unresolved in Kant's metaphysics (e.g., the relationship between things-in-themselves and phenomenal things) was implicit in the a priori forms supplied by our own intellect—space, time, and causality. He said that if we could do away with these forms and somehow still retain a consciousness of things, then those metaphysical problems would accordingly vanish. ("If we imagine these forms for once removed, however, and a consciousness of things nonetheless still present, then these problems would be, not solved, but non-existent . . . For they arise entirely out of these forms, whose object is not an understanding of the world, but merely an understanding of our own aims.")[25] If we could retain a consciousness of things without the mediation of the a priori forms of the mind, then there would be no fissure between things-in-themselves and things-as-known. Schopenhauer proposed to reunite those two realms in two related ways; first, by describing the intellect as physical rather than metaphysical, as originating in the will and existing "only to serve the will" (59), so that metaphysical perplexities could arise only from a "superfluity of intellect exempt from service" to the will (59–60). Second, Schopenhauer equated things-in-themselves with the will ("Thing in itself signifies that which exists independently of our perception, that which actually is. To Democritus it was matter; fundamentally that is what it still was to Locke; to Kant it was = x; to me it is *will*" [55]), so that what would then be necessary in order to recover the thing-in-itself would be only to will it back.

Despite his insistence on the will, or perhaps because of it, Schopenhauer's thought was plagued by dualisms (viz., his vision of the world as will and idea); and his understanding of the body as "objectified" will, while allowing for human freedom, had pessimistic consequences beyond what most would be willing to accept. If we as individuals are embodied wills, then Schopenhauer's vision of character, which describes our moral nature, is as of a fate—closed to possible revision.[26] In a world where these wills, or fates, are bound to collide, happiness can only be measured in negative terms, as a diminution of the suffering produced by the conflict of wills. The ultimate good lies in accepting that the perceived universe, the "world as idea," is itself nothing.

This is nihilism in what might be called its "negative" mode, and in some essential ways it did not move beyond Kant. Although Nietzsche could perversely say that Schopenhauer's thought demonstrated a "cheerfulness that really cheers,"[27] both he and Heidegger proposed to recover the natural by more positive operations of the will. This contradictory project began with Nietzsche's celebration of the will to power and concluded with Heidegger's *Gelassenheit*, which is a relaxation of the will to will and thus a repudiation of striving itself. Both promised an escape from the fatalism that might otherwise follow from a recognition of the primacy of the will to power; Nietzsche's Zarathustra speaks in this regard of "willing backwards," which entails freeing the will from its manifest powerlessness against the past ("'It was': that is what the will's teeth-gnashing and most lonely affliction is called. Powerless against that which has been done, the will is an angry spectator against all things past").[28] The past is, of necessity, part of what Kant described as experience, and insofar as it is wholly determined it might be thought of as paradigmatic of what Kant called the "conditioned." Seeking freedom of the will over the past might issue in radical historicism, but Nietzsche, like the later Heidegger, saw the will as operating on a variation of the pattern of transcendence. Rather than move us above the world and so, they would say, *remove* us from the world, or remove the world from us behind a veil of ideas, the exercise of the will was seen to result in a *return* of the world. Nietzsche called this (eternal) return by the pregnant term "redemption": "The will that is the will to power must will something higher than any reconciliation with time—but how shall that happen? Who has taught it to will backwards, too?" "To redeem the past and to transform every 'it was' into an 'I wanted it thus?'—that alone do I call redemption!" (*Zarathustra*, "Of Redemption," 163, 161).

If Nietzsche celebrated Schopenhauer for his "cheerfulness," he chided Kant for his "pessimism," claiming that Kant kept faith in the realm of the unconditioned in order to secure human freedom, where no such faith was warranted or necessary at all: "In the face of nature and history, Kant was, like every good German of the old stamp, a pessimist; he believed in morality, not because it is demonstrated in nature and history, but in spite of the fact that nature and history contradict it."[29] Moreover, Nietzsche saw Kantian morality as resulting in a deprivation of nature, so that the recovery of nature became a moral project predicated on the abolition of Kant's moral terms. Kant's central idea of morality, as of aesthetics, was that of an interest taken in something "for its own sake alone"; following Kant's moral maxim, one should treat oneself and others never as means but always as ends; following the essential aesthetic convention, one always regards a work with "disinterest." (Charles Altieri provides a more extensive discussion of the parallels between aesthetics and ethics, with particular reference to Kant, in his essay on expressivism, included in the present volume.) However, Nietzsche located a new "end in itself" and a new "unconditioned," both of which he found in nature. Kant thought of nature as showing in its design features that would lead us to conclude that it was created by God, so that while we may in fact *know* nothing of the transcendental realm, we may *feel* it as something, which feeling is a moral intuition. Insofar as we feel it through (aesthetic) contemplation, the sublime, as induced by nature, is the place where aesthetics and morality converge.

Nietzsche's "nature" by contrast was the world of actuality and immanence; yet since Nietzsche was at the same time unwilling to deny its essential illusoriness he also described it as an "aesthetic" phenomenon. Further, to confirm his opposition to Kant, he said that what lies beyond the aesthetic phenomenon is nothing at all (cf. Sartre, who said that the aesthetic object must be posited as nothing, taken as unreal). The contradictory solution Nietzsche proposed, and which riddles *The Birth of Tragedy*, is that the aesthetic offers refuge from the nothingness beyond itself; it offers protection from that death-drive, which an insight into the illusoriness of reality might otherwise instill.[30] As Paul de Man has said of Nietzsche, "The discovery that all empirical reality is illusory is called a tragic discovery; no man, it seems, would be able to withstand its destructive power . . . The one who has reached it is, like Hamlet, frozen forever in the madness of inaction . . . he knows that 'what is best of all lies forever beyond your reach: not to have been born, not to *be*, to be *nothing*. The second best is for you—to die soon.'"[31] There is an alternative to this nihilism which Nietzsche might have countenanced, and that is to seek redemption or rebirth. The only impossibility lies in knowing which of these alternatives to choose, and how to tell them apart, but then the sign of the true romantic is the incapacity to distinguish between pessimism and cheer, boredom and interest, death and rebirth. Some would say that this is a sign of nihilism, too.[32]

More so than Nietzsche, Heidegger—especially in his later phase—was explicit about the role that poetry might play in the recovery of the natural. In a lecture on the anniversary of Rilke's death, entitled "What Are Poets For?" Heidegger's strategy of reply is predicated on the assumption that this question is asked "in a destitute time." If in Kant's or Descartes's terms the recovery of the natural depends on finding foundations for knowledge, then Heidegger measures the "destitution" of the time by the reluctance to admit the fact that knowledge stands without grounds. Heidegger says that we must first experience and then turn from this *Abgrund*, or abyss: "The age for which the ground fails to come, hangs in the abyss. Assuming that a turn still remains for this destitute time at all, it can come some day only if the world turns about fundamentally—and that now means, unequivocally: if it turns away from the abyss. In the age of the world's night, the abyss of the world must be experienced and endured. But for this it is necessary that there be those who reach into the abyss."[33] When Heidegger speaks of the "destitution" of the time, he is referring to the same cultural age as Valéry in his lecture "The Crisis of the Mind" (1919). Both are aware that nature, as seen by the modern mind, is essentially lost; Valéry describes it as a vision in which the "natural whole" appears as nothing ("If I disregard all detail and confine myself to a quick impression, to that *natural whole* given by a moment's perception, I see . . . *nothing!*).[34] But it might be a more accurate representation of their views to say that nature appears as nothing *because* of the way it has been posited by the modern mind, that is, as an object of knowledge. This "objectification" of nature is seen to follow largely from the philosophy of Kant, but Valéry's description, not insignificantly, might be read as a capsule summary of phenomenology, which is what Heidegger eventually sought to overcome. Since phenomenology can only posit our knowledge of things against some ground, then nature becomes simply a back-ground of distraction for our knowledge of things, which is another way to say that it becomes no-thing.

When Heidegger speaks of the "destitution of the time," he is describing a romantic phenomenon that goes by several other names as well: the dis-godding of nature, the twilight of the gods, the dis-enchantment of the world ("Ever since the 'united three'—Herakles, Dionysos, and Christ—have left the world, the evening of the world's age has been declining toward its night. The world's night is spreading its darkness. The ear is defined by the god's failure to arrive, by the 'default of God'" ["What Are Poets For?" 91]). This is a vision that recalls the central romantic myth of the Fall and that, significantly enough, is both a fall *into* knowledge and a fall *from* grace. Heidegger claims that the assistance poetry can provide is to show us how to put thinking (hence knowledge) aside; for Heidegger, this is to make thinking a form of "thanking," which I said earlier might be regarded as a form of grace. In *What Is Called Thinking?* Heidegger explains that this thinking is a form of listening, or reception, and he says that it is "poetic" in some essential ways. If, in the tradition that culminated in Kant, thinking was taken as the formulation of representational ideas, then Heidegger's idea of poetic thinking is somehow to circumvent representations by moving, if not beyond them, then back before they were invented, which for Heidegger means moving back to an original (pre-Platonic) moment in Western thought. Heidegger supposes that at that time poetry was not an aesthetic object, in part because there were no aesthetic objects as such; *poiēsis* and *technē*, he says, were one: "In

Greece, at the outset of the destining of the West, the arts soared to the supreme height of the revealing granted them. They brought the presence of the gods, brought the dialogue of divine and human destinings, to radiance. And art was simply called *technē*. It was a single, manifold revealing . . . The arts were not derived from the artistic. Art works were not enjoyed aesthetically. Art was not a sector of cultural activity."[35]

In his project to overcome Cartesian and Kantian representational ideas, Heidegger claims to be working toward the reconciliation of beauty and truth. He says that poetry has its "own truth," which is called "beauty," and which he interprets in accordance with that tradition in aesthetics which takes the beautiful object as the sensuous appearance of something beyond reach or fundamentally unreal. Consider the following passage from *What Is Called Thinking?* which is representative in this way: "Beauty is a fateful gift of the essence of truth, and here truth means the disclosure of what keeps itself concealed. The beautiful is not what pleases, but what falls within that fateful gift of truth which comes to be when that which is eternally non-apparent and therefore invisible attains its most radiant appearance."[36] The crucial twist that Heidegger added to the classical tradition is that he applied the categories of aesthetics to things that have real being in the world; this is a turn that is in evidence at least from *Being and Time*, with its emphasis on the ways in which Being is disclosed or otherwise revealed. The troubling result was an aesthetic ontology that, as the emphasis on the fatefulness of truth in the passage above helps make clear, issued in nihilism and a *loss* of the world, not the return of things-in-themselves.

Heidegger's aesthetic ontology points up the danger of nihilism, which was woven into the romantic response to Kant. For romanticism proposed the recovery of a noumenal world, which, it was claimed, has been lost through our efforts at knowledge; yet it hoped to regain that world by aesthetic means, which is to say that it had to negate the world as well. If romanticism regarded itself as able to salvage nature from "objectification," it found nothing behind the world; thus in collapsing subject and object, transcendence became indistinguishable from immanence, as in Nietzsche's inversion of Platonism. Indeed, if one follows Nietzsche and takes the recovery of the natural as a moral imperative predicated on the abandonment of Kant's moral ideas, and if one loses the possibility of transcendence or sees this as transcendence to nothing, as Heidegger apparently thought, then nature becomes a creation of the human will, which is a thoroughly nihilistic idea. In view of these consequences, it may be worthwhile to speculate whether romanticism's enticing goals might be achieved by some less costly means. If the recovery of the totality of things-in-themselves is bound to involve thinking of nature morally, then what ought to be required is a preservation of romanticism's goals along with a purification of its means. In discussing Rousseau's *Pygmalion* as an example of the recovery of the natural by passing beyond the sublime, I suggested that this text is riddled with the problems of nihilism, which also afflicted the romantic response to Kant. In contrast to *Pygmalion*, I would return to *The Winter's Tale*, where a morality of faith replaces the morality of the will, thus relieving the romantic vision of its fatefulness, while still preserving its goals.

Less problematically than *Pygmalion*—certainly in greater detail— *The Winter's Tale* may be said to describe the recovery of the natural, in both the material and contextual senses of the term. In *The Winter's Tale*, the natural is both the world's seasonal return and the passionate attachment and collaboration that obtains between husband and wife. If the natural is in need of recovery, if it has been lost, that is primarily because of Leontes' unnatural passion, his jealous imaginings about Hermione, his wife. If a natural context allows us, in the words of Roberto Mangabeira Unger, to discover everything about the world that we can, then Leontes' jealousy generates unanswerable suspicions about his wife and so is a perversion of the natural. She becomes an unnatural object for him, which is to say that she becomes an aesthetic object for him as well. I take the insistent "nothings" of the following speech as Shakespeare's way of suggesting the parallel between Leontes' unnatural passion and the aestheticization of the beloved, and thus also as Shakespeare's way of dissociating himself from the Petrarchan tradition, which sublimates the beloved by distancing her absolutely above the level of the real:

Is whispering nothing?
Is leaning cheek to cheek? Is meeting noses?
Kissing with inside lip?
. . . .
. . . Is this nothing?
Why, then the world and all that's in 't is nothing,
the covering sky is nothing, Bohemia nothing,
My wife is nothing, nor nothing have these nothings
If this be nothing. (1.2.284–86; 292–96)

In this play, the discovery of the natural is made possible through the reunion of the lovers and in their (re)creation of the conjugal. That is a function of their faithfulness to each other, which does not deny but bears tangible witness to their common will. The conjugal is one of Shakespeare's constant preoccupations, but it is especially acute in the romantic plays, where the interests of love must be balanced against both "nature" and "law," and where the temptation is to regard nature as a species of "lawfulness," which in turn legitimizes love. That Hermione's return may be taken as an image of the natural is registered by the insistence at various points of the text in the lawfulness of this apparent marvel. As Hermione descends, Leontes stands in wonder and awe and says, "If this be magic, let it be an art / Lawful as eating" (5.3.110–11). I am reminded of Kant's definition of nature in the *Prolegomena* as a "totality of rules," which is to say, of laws. In the English Renaissance, Richard Hooker said that the "obedience of creatures unto the law of nature is the stay of the whole world."[37] But *The Winter's Tale* reverses the relationship in which the natural is that form of lawfulness which legitimizes passionate love. On the contrary, it is marriage that provides a basis for "lawful obedience" and thus contributes to the creation of a natural world.

Contextually and epistemologically, Shakespeare does not ask us to imagine a relationship in which these characters are capable of knowing absolutely everything about each other. He simply wants to provide a context that will allow them to know everything about each other that they can. He thus accepts the fact that whatever knowledge we may have will be of the conditioned, indeed that it will be *subject to* conditions. These characters must be satisfied by their trust in each other as a prior condition for their satisfaction of their knowledge of each other. As one would only expect, Shakespeare's provision for a natural context of knowledge is matched in the social and moral realms. He does not deny the passions or the will, but seeks a context in which it is possible to pursue all the forms of passionate attachment and collaboration we may have reason to desire.[38]

These remarks on *The Winter's Tale* are meant to suggest some of the ways in which Shakespeare's understanding of marriage and its role in the creation of the natural purified the romantic vision, as well as some of the ways in which Hermione's descent and apparent return to life reverse the denial of the beloved, which, as we have seen, is essential to the process of sublimation in Petrarch's *Canzoniere*. Shakespeare's response to the Petrarchan tradition is largely found in his provision for the reunion of the lovers on earth; he requires that Hermione suffer only a figurative death. As Leontes overcomes his jealous passions and the projections he makes for his wife, he is also able to overcome the "inwardness" that Jauss saw as characteristic of aesthetic experience in its "romantic" moment. As Hermione is reunited with her husband, their lost child, Perdita, is also returned; the purely natural purpose of marriage (procreation) is morally transformed by their acknowledgment of its fruits. The mechanism of Hermione's return, which is that of a descent, might be thought of as a form of transcendence in reverse. The proverbial rising of time here takes the (natural) form of the descent of the generations, so that the fall into human history can be seen as an occasion for thanks and not a curse. Insofar as the natural is something these characters create between them, not only in their will but by their faithfulness to what they have willed, their reunion allows for an escape from romantic nihilism as well. Their relationship is a moral form of the natural, and no longer an occasion of the sublime.

Notes

1. Hans Robert Jauss, "Sketch of a Theory and History of Aesthetic Experience," in *Aesthetic Experience and Literary Hermeneutics*, trans. Michael Shaw (Minneapolis: University of Minnesota Press, 1982), 80.

2. Robert Durling, "Petrarch's 'Giovene Donna Sotto un Verde Lauro'," *MLN* 86 (1971): 9.

3. Paul de Man, "Sign and Symbol in Hegel's *Aesthetics*," *Critical Inquiry* 8 (1982): 761–75.

4. Joachim Ritter, *Subjektivität* (Frankfurt: Suhrkamp Verlag, 1974), 156–57.

5. Immanuel Kant, *Critique of Judgment*, trans. J. J. Bernard (New York: Macmillan [Hafner Press], 1951), sec. 28, p. 101.

6. Jean-Paul Sartre, *The Psychology of Imagination* (1948; reprint, London: Methuen, 1972), 222.

7. G. W. F. Hegel, *Vorlesungen über die Aesthetik*, trans. Bernard Bosanquet, in *G. W. F. Hegel on Art, Religion, Philosophy*, ed. J. Glenn Gray (New York: Harper Torchbooks, 1970), 23.

8. Jauss, "Sketch of a Theory," 75.

9. Kant, *Critique of Judgment*, sec. 5, p. 45.

10. Immanuel Kant, *Critique of Pure Reason*, trans. Norman Kemp Smith (1929; reprint, New York: St. Martin's Press, 1965), A, 494.

11. For example: "Tyr, ville opulente et superbe, les monuments des arts dont tu brilles ne m'attirent plus, j'ai perdu le gout ou je prenais a les admirer." I follow the edition of Paris, 1821 (Fouquet), Jean Jacques Rousseau, *Oeuvres*, 6:345.

12. Paul de Man, *Allegories of Reading* (New Haven: Yale University Press, 1979), 163.

13. Roberto Mangabeira Unger, *Passion: An Essay on Personality* (New York: Free Press, 1984), 38.

14. Cf. de Man's essay on the self in Rousseau's *Narcisse* and *Pygmalion* (*Allegories of Reading*, 160–87). De Man posits a self in Rousseau which is always already divided and indistinguishable from the "other." Another way of describing this self, in line with literary-theoretical terminology, would be to say that it acts to disrupt closure in Rousseau's texts. De Man says, for instance, that "the concluding scene [of *Pygmalion*] is not in fact a conclusion but one more vacillation in a sequence of reversals, none of which have [*sic*] the power to close off the text" (186). The concluding scene is crucial to the matter of self-definition in *Pygmalion*.

15. Northrop Frye, *A Study of English Romanticism* (New York: Random House, 1968), 111–12.

16. Geoffrey Hartman, *The Unmediated Vision: An Interpretation of Wordsworth, Hopkins, Rilke, and Valéry* (1954; reprint, New York: Harcourt Brace & World, 1966), 128.

17. Samuel Taylor Coleridge, *Biographia Literaria* (London: J. M. Dent, 1975), 169.

18. Martin Heidegger, *What Is a Thing?* trans. W. B. Barton, Jr., and Vera Deutsch (South Bend, Ind.: Regnery/Gateway, 1967), 128.

19. The Emerson references are to "The Transcendentalist," "Nature," and "Experience," in *Selected Essays*, ed. Larzer Ziff (Harmondsworth: Penguin Books, 1982), 242, 39, 305, respectively.

20. Heidegger, *What Is a Thing?* 178.

21. Immanuel Kant, *Prolegomena to Any Future Metaphysics*, trans. Paul Carus, rev. James W. Ellington (1977; reprint, Indianapolis: Hackett, 1982), 62.

22. Heidegger, *What Is a Thing?* 99.

23. René Descartes, *Meditations*, pt. 1, in *Philosophical Works of Descartes*, trans. and ed. Elizabeth S. Haldane and G. R. T. Ross, 2 vols. (1911; reprint, Cambridge: Cambridge University Press, 1975), 1:145.

24. Johann Wolfgang von Goethe, *Faust*, pt. 1, 1768–71: "Mein Busen, der vom Wissendrang geheilt ist, / Soll keinen Schmerzen künftig sich verschliessen, / Und was der ganzen Menschheit zugeteilt ist, / Will ich in meinen innern Selbst geniessen."

25. Arthur Schopenhauer, *Essays and Aphorisms*, ed. and trans. R. J. Hollingdale (1970; reprint, Harmondsworth: Penguin Books, 1978), 59 (taken from Schopenhauer's *Parerga und Paralipomena*, chap. 4: "Einige Betrachtungen über den Gegetsatz des Dinges an sich und der Erscheinung").

26. Cf. Paul Ricoeur, *Freedom and Nature: The Voluntary and the Involuntary*, trans. Erazim V. Kohák (Chicago: Northwestern University Press, 1966), 368, who discusses character as fate in Democritus, Schopenhauer, and Kant.

27. Friedrich Nietzsche, "Schopenhauer as Educator," in *Untimely Meditations*, trans. R. J. Hollingdale (Cambridge: Cambridge University Press, 1983), 135.

28. Friedrich Nietzsche, *Thus Spoke Zarathustra*, trans. R. J. Hollingdale (1961; reprint, Harmondsworth: Penguin Books, 1982), 161 ("Of Redemption").

29. Friedrich Nietzsche, *Daybreak: Thoughts on the Prejudices of Morality*, trans. R. J. Hollingdale (Cambridge: Cambridge University Press, 1982), 3.

30. Cf. Harold Bloom's comments regarding Freud in relation to Schopenhauer: "Against the dualism of Schopenhauer, which set up the Will or thing-in-itself in opposition to the objective world, the world as representation, Freud now opts for a more drastic dualism, or at least what he must have regarded as the most thoroughgoing of dualisms. Beyond the pleasure principle lies not the world as representation, but what Milton had called the universe of death" (Bloom, *Agon: Towards a Theory of Revisionism* [New York: Oxford University Press, 1982], 130).

31. De Man, *Allegories of Reading*, 93.

32. See, for example, Stanley Rosen, *Nihilism: A Philosophical Essay* (New Haven: Yale University Press, 1969).

33. Martin Heidegger, "What Are Poets For?" in *Poetry, Language, Thought*, trans. Albert Hofstadter (New York: Harper & Row, 1971), 92.

34. Paul Valéry, "The Crisis of the Mind," in *Paul Valéry: An Anthology* (Princeton: Princeton University Press, 1976).

35. Martin Heidegger, "The Question Concerning Technology," in *The Question Concerning Technology and Other Essays*, trans. William Lovitt (New York: Harper & Row, 1977), 34.

36. Martin Heidegger, *What Is Called Thinking?*, trans. J. Glenn Gray and F. Wieck (New York: Harper & Row, 1968), 19.

37. Richard Hooker, *Of the Laws of Ecclesiastical Piety* (London, Everyman's Library, 1907), 1:157.

38. See Unger, *Passion*, passim, and especially 6.

6
From Expressivist
Aesthetics to
Expressivist Ethics

In discussing the moral qualities of the natural considered in romantic terms, rather than the more familiar moral category of the sublime, my own essay leads up to Charles Altieri's discussion of expression as an ethical term. Historically, the development of an expressivist ethic draws on idealism as much as romanticism, and idealism is already given central consideration in the concluding section of Altieri's earlier work, Act and Quality (1981); but as I hope to have suggested, and as others have pointed out, idealism and romanticism are closely related phenomena. In addition to romanticism and idealism, however, the development of an expressivist ethic shares certain interests and presuppositions with contemporary philosophers such as Stanley Cavell, Alasdair MacIntyre, Angel Medina, Robert Nozick, and Charles Taylor. While they constitute no unified school or group, their work is linked by the ways in which each sets the claims of the ethical in some degree of opposition to the claims of the moral: where the latter involves determining principles of judgment capable of establishing measures of the good to which all agents should subordinate themselves, the former requires the prior, usually neglected question of how any individual agent determines its own good, thus defining his or her stance toward those forms of thinking in which all subjects are treated under the same rubrics. I would underscore the concern for the individual and for one's particular position or stance as an ethical agent, for the specific set of choices which one does indeed make are also those that in turn define him or her as an individual.

By attending to the ethical and its claims over and above the moral, Altieri is able to say how ole might begin to go about justifying the particular choices we do in fact make, the programs of value we as individuals choose to follow in situations where no one of them would be required of us more strongly than any other. This work in ethics is of potential value to literary theory in a number of ways, as Altieri makes clear. Literature, Danto's essay has warned, is in jeopardy of being regarded as superfluous when truth-claims (which may be characterized as logical necessities) are counted as our highest goals. However, if sufficient weight is attributed to the ethical over and above the moral, and to the matter of individual "alignment" with those goods that require universal acceptance, then literature can be seen as providing a field for the realization of the ethical by providing cultural models and modes of self-representation. Our relationship to these models will of course depend on certain assumptions about *how* (and not only *what*) they themselves express. Consider Altieri's analysis of how it may be possible to express individual qualities so that they can become the basis for gaining identities from a community: "So long as we must define our categories for judgment on the basis of predicates already established as the operational vocabulary for specifying the nature of actions, our assessments will emphasize conformity or nonconformity to a norm. But suppose we can imagine acts that ask to be read as possible labels, as aligning the person with certain possible groupings of characters or of specifying qualities that warrant claiming a particular identity for oneself. If we were dealing with Hamlet, the former alternative would force us to judge his actions in relation to some determinate moral code; the latter would make sense of his desire to have Horatio tell his story. For it is within the individual story that Hamlet finds the terms at once to make sense of his actions and to take responsibility for them."

At this juncture, Altieri's concerns overlap with his earlier inquiry into the relationship between action and judgments of quality and also with his inquiry into the "performative sublime" in connection with Plato (*New Literary History*, 1985). If one is troubled by Harry Berger, Jr.'s, critique of the assumptions behind the "dramatistic" approach to Plato, then here is a theory that might recuperate the dramatic model for specifically ethical ends. Altieri's more explicit purpose is to refurbish the Kantian category of the (moral) sublime by realigning our interest in the aesthetic object along ethical lines. Kant specified certain features of sublimity which, he said, would lead to moral intuitions; in nature, for example, we would come, through the experience of the sublime, to sense the presence and design of God. Departing from this Kantian track, Altieri proposes certain similarities between ethical judgment and aesthetic taste. The kinds of investment appropriate to the ethical sphere of human action overlap with expressivist ethics in the following ways: as models of value, they define fundamental needs;

they enable us to show how humans have the requisite powers to pursue relevant values; they establish nonrational models of judgment necessary for the understanding, assessment, and modification of one another's use of those powers; and they indicate plausible grounds in cultural and historical traditions to which both actors and judges can appeal in the process of forming and evaluating the identities entailed by personal choice.

Central to the alignment of expressivist ethics and expressivist aesthetics is the reliance and modification of Wittgenstein's later work. The risk that followers of Wittgenstein inevitably incur is that ethical choices may become relegated to a sphere that is entirely "subjective," if not lacking altogether in rational self-consciousness. But if one follows Wittgenstein in the way that, for example, Stanley Cavell does, then one might come to regard criteria, which inhere in language, as providing us with a moral ground for action and evaluation, while the engagement of those criteria would set the range of ethical choices which an individual comes to make and by which he is defined. However, what remains unspoken in Wittgenstein, and only implicit in the work of Cavell, becomes fully voiced here: the model of literary or, more broadly, of aesthetic experience is shown to be central to the achievement of ethical goals because Altieri is concerned largely with specifying the features of the "how" of individual desires and with outlining the procedures by which particular values may be linked to a common and rational domain. In this respect, the crucial phrase of the present essay is a quotation from Wittgenstein: "here everything seems to turn so to speak on *how* one wants."

From Expressivist Aesthetics to Expressivist Ethics   *Charles Altieri*

I

The resurgence of antifoundational thinking has had substantial effects on the once moribund domain of analytic ethics. As Richard Eldridge describes it, philosophers as diverse as Bernard Williams, Philippa Foot, Alasdair MacIntyre, and Martha Nussbaum have each in their own way "sharply circumscribed moral authority, denied the universality of moral judgments, and rejected any accounts of practical reasoning that are cast in terms of abstract principles emphasizing fairness and equality and failing to accord over-riding conduct-relevant value to specific persons or communities or desires.[1] Only slightly different emphases would lead us to include the concern for individual ethical performances in the work of Stanley Cavell, Angel Medina, and Robert Nozick, as well as the efforts of Jean-François Lyotard to imagine models of justice appropriate for a poststructural philosophy. Each philosopher seems to be responding to the fundamental contradiction that drove Kant's moral theory round and round in a narrow pound—that the very claim of rational universality gives us no way to understand how empirical agents can possibly see the ethical life as continuous with their concrete situations and commitments. Thus rationalism purchases a third-person standard for the good at the cost of first-person predicates that capture the stakes in being ethical at all.

I do not intend to offer a survey of these shifts. Rather, I am interested in exploring their implications for our understanding of possible social roles that can be played by aesthetic experience and the reflective discourses it generates. Put baldly, one can say that the new orientation in ethics calls attention to the centrality of the first person in ethical life but has very limited resources with which to flesh out the ways in which first persons actually construct values and seek to have them assessed. At the other pole, "sophisticated" discourse about the arts now devotes itself to a variety of critical theories concentrating on the analysis of texts as aspects of the social life of their time. First-person stances then seem epiphenomena best read in third-person terms as effects of a culture's signifying practices, practices themselves intelligible only as positions within a struggle of concrete social interests.[2] My hope is that by showing how reflection on the arts helps us elaborate one basic aspect of first-person ethical life, I can also demonstrate the possibility that the fullest social uses of art have less to do with exposing the historical conditions of their genesis than with clarifying the ways in which they help us understand ourselves as value-creating agents and make possible communities who can assess those creations without relying on the categorical terms traditional to moral philosophy.

I shall assume that it is not necessary to summarize the various critiques that philosophers like Williams have made of the effort to base ethical values on universal principles. There is a substantial role to be played by universals within any ethical order because they ensure forms of reciprocity necessary for both the application of moral calculi and the elaboration of social justice. But these terms must presume an authority over individuals and a shared framework for defining responsibilities which cannot be justified within the third-person terms of rational analysis. For suppositions about moral universals impose an abstracted common domain, which in fact addresses neither the individual's actual nature nor her moral priorities. And should the proponents of such rational universals shift to a more empirically oriented model of objectivity, arguing, for example, that certain kinds of rule-following activities are in the agent's best long-term interests, they would find themselves confronting the daunting opposition of Plato's Gyges' ring. No matter what one promises about the practical advantages of seeking reciprocity, the very model of the good on which the claims rely would demand that individual agents seek their own advantage if they can ensure not being caught. Reciprocity is always best for me when others all follow the rules, leaving me free to attempt to manipulate the system.[3]

These considerations convince me that a secular morality will have to derive its third-person principles from first-person commitments (as is in fact the case with Kant's deontological version of why agents seek rationality—not because of specific reasons that rationality demonstrates, but because in being rational they align themselves with their highest nature). We accept obligations because they somehow are seen as congruent with the specific ideals we have for our personal identities. That puts a heavy burden on how ethical theory constructs these first-person commitments. And that, I submit, is why and where aesthetic experience and aesthethic theory can make significant contributions to ethical theory. For it is in that domain that the culture has most fully articulated models of expression that can connect first-person states to second-order concerns for self-reflexive public identity, concerns that tie self-interest to obligations involving a range of ideals and cultural exemplars. Therefore I shall address myself to the ways in which that theorizing about expression might help articulate aspects of first-person behavior necessary for certain aspects of ethical life but not yet elaborated within the new philosophical movement. I shall not insist that all first-person emphases in ethics must account for the full powers of expression which artworks help us attribute to human agents. But I shall try to sketch what I call an expressivist ethic, which makes it possible to employ a strong sense of the first person and to attribute to it a pursuit of values which still depend on Kantian distinctions between mere preferences and efforts to constitute ethical identities. While such claims cannot rely on any structure of arguments that might make them compelling, they do have the advantage of deriving from a set of cultural examples with substantial power to show by contrast how alternative theories appear seriously impoverished, at least in certain areas of ethical life.

I hope to show that these cultural examples provide a rich dialectic—on the one hand demonstrating the importance of those psychological traits that Kant identified with his model of aesthetic judgment, and on the other enabling us to extend those principles into the ethical realm. The psychology consists primarily in showing that it still makes sense to see human beings as demanding for themselves forms of identity and identification which cannot be reduced to the choice of immediate pleasures. For judgment can still take the form of approaching one's deeds with a concern for the ways that one's reasons will establish one as a particular agent within a community, bound by certain commitments and characterized by certain qualities of concern. And because this thickened model of judgment is aesthetic, it preserves a way of speaking about moral identity before that community which does not depend on the universal principles defined within both Kantian and utilitarian ethics. One acts with an appeal to the approval of a community, not because the deed is rational but because it carries certain qualities of intentionality which an agent can project as deserving certain evaluations from those who can be led to describe it as the agent does. Once we so redefine judgment, we have strong grounds for preserving the dramatic sense of life established by the pursuit of ideals like nobility and dignity which have become all too easy to parody. For we still have ways of responding to those like G. E. Warnock who profess to be mystified about why Western culture seems to attribute so much more to practical reason than to theoretical reason.[4] Were I to act in accord with theoretical reason, the action would only incidentally be *my* action, since the imperative is there in the methodology and the methodology is not in question. But when we make the kind of judgments that warrant speaking of a practical reason, the choice is deeply mine because my identity as a person depends on both the grounds of reasoning which I accept and the qualities that I exhibit in manifesting that acceptance. In practical reason I do not simply accept an established practice; rather, I treat the specific deed as establishing the kind of loyalties that give me distinctive claims to a public identity.

These issues are obviously too large and complex for me to claim that this one essay will establish an ethical theory. I hope only to outline the specific considerations that make such an ethic seem desirable and plausible, then to demonstrate the specific conceptual resources that aesthetic theory provides for elaborating the components of an expressivist ethics.[5] Even those chores will take several steps. First I shall try to spell out the basic components of the expressivist semantics that characterizes most romantic and postromantic models of art. Then I must construct a model of first-person behavior for which a particular kind of expressive activity becomes the basis for ethical values. That will entail teasing out ways in which certain actions can be seen as self-constituting—not quite in Kant's strong sense of the term but rather in the sense that such actions ask to be judged in terms of the states of the person they embody or reflect. Charles Taylor's seminal work on the elaboration of expressive models of selfhood will provide the necessary beginning, although I hope to make substantial revisions of his formulations. Those should provide a sufficient basis for then turning to the particular ways in which expressivist theory provides specific resources for contemporary ethics. These consist on the one hand of pointing to experiences that show how the claims one must make about human powers and concerns have a substantial basis in the experience of those responsive to the arts, on the other of showing how the theory helps one address four fundamental questions that any ethic must attempt to resolve—what needs people have for the values idealized, what powers the theory can elaborate that show how it is possible for us to satisfy those needs, what models of judgment one can rely on in assessing values, and what communal standards one can rely on when one relegates universalist concerns to a secondary role.

II

My first task is to link the forms of expression we describe in aesthetic theory to those that could provide a basis for ethical judgments. Fifteen years ago this would have seemed an absurd dream because analytic philosophy had confined the provenance of the term *expression* to specific aspects of artworks that induce us to attribute anthropomorphic properties to them. A scene can express sadness or joy, a melody express something like deep melancholy. But, as Guy Sircello showed, this view allows no way to distinguish between discrete properties of the work and those properties that one can attribute to experiencing the work as a whole. Even more important, when we so isolate expressive properties we blind ourselves to the probable reason why any deep sense of expression is anthropomorphic—it calls our attention to the inescapable fact of an intense authorial presence in the work which elicits and takes responsibility for those expressive properties.[6] Artworks are not things but products suffused with intentions that the author wants us to see embodied in the finished work. So any interpretive language adequate to art must be able to subsume properties under intentional states of an embodied authorial act, and it must be able to show that embodiment can satisfy certain plausible social motives for the labor, like the desire to produce new attitudes or models for realizing certain powers of mind.

Expression is not simply a matter of intentionality. Contemporary criticism is all too aware of the symptomatic aspects of expressions that reveal what the author would rather keep hidden. But the artistic analogue for how intentions do suffuse certain intentional objects provides fairly strong grounds for insisting that one can distinguish between expressions that reveal symptoms and those that allow the forms of responsibility that enable us to speak of deliberate choices. For example, one could employ a distinction like the one I make in *Act and Quality* between behavior one interprets as expressive despite the agent's intentions and behavior that calls attention to certain traits by manipulating possibilities for "expressive implicature" embedded in our cultural practices. Where Paul Grice's conversational implicature explains how an audience can understand the ways that contextual factors modify semantic conventions, expressive implicature locates similar principles that enable speakers to project certain qualities of their own acts as significant aspects of their message.[7] William Carlos Williams's "This Is Just to Say," for example, concentrates less on the fact that there are no plums left in the refrigerator than on the speaker's and poet's abilities to call attention to certain qualities within their specific way of handling the act of apologizing. On the mimetic level the relevant implicatures attach to the speaker's act, characterizing him as someone who asks his auditor to understand how this way of putting the case displays his sense of their relationship. But since the speech-act is within a poem, other conventions allow the author to use that mimetic structure as itself a focus of implicatures displaying his grasp of the relationship between such relationships and the just saying that is poetry. And that provides a clear distinction between expressive and mimetic models of art. As self-conscious "just saying," in all its senses, the poem cannot be seen as primarily an attempt to portray a scene of apology for its truth or falseness in relation to the ideas we might hold about human behavior. Rather, the work presents itself as the literal and figurative embodiment of specific qualities that give it a distinctive grasp of the nature of apologies. One test of the difference crucial to what will follow is our awareness that this note and this poem are not speculations about how things are but the actual taking responsibility for the agents' capacities to stage themselves as the kind of persons who can perform deeds in certain ways that establish aspects of their identity for an audience.

This semantic contrast to the mimetic has important consequences for how we envision the nature of judgment. We need to show how we can understand and assess expressions without following the standard route (at least in philosophy) of treating assertions as propositions to be tested by some measure of truth and falsity of reference. For expressions to be fully expressive of individual qualities, they must be interpretable as embodying the distinctive traits, not merely as referring to them. And the interpretation must somehow result not in a generalized statement but in a sense of how specific qualities are configured within the particular. These are not simple chores. But Nelson Goodman's work on the semantics of exemplification provides a powerful instrument for our needs. That work arises from efforts to contain the domain of labels or forms within an extensionalist nominalism, efforts that in *Act and Quality* I argue make it impossible to borrow directly from Goodman to handle phenomena as dependent on intensional properties as literary expressions. But that limitation need not prevent us from borrowing his critique of the simplistic empiricism that leads most modern philosophy to make all reference depend upon a propositional model of signs. In that model reference is successful if and only if the signs delineate a state of affairs which one can actually establish is the case under some specified conditions of observation. Goodman insists that this need not be the only route by which reference takes place. In addition to denoting states of affairs, names can be used as examples to "denote that which they are denoted by."[8] We can visualize the standard case of reference by imagining someone holding up a swatch of color to refer to the shade of a shirt someone is wearing. Exemplification occurs when instead of using the swatch as a picture of a state of affairs one proposes it as a means for sorting some set of objects in order to locate those the label might fit. In the former case we check the name against the world; in the latter we check its use in our repertoire of possible labels.

This begins to matter for ethics when we ask how it is possible to express individual qualities so that they can become the basis for gaining certain partial identities from a community. So long as we must define our categories for judgment on the basis of predicates already established as the operational vocabulary for specifying the nature of actions, our assessments will emphasize conformity or nonconformity to a norm. But suppose we can imagine acts that ask to be read as possible labels, as aligning the person with certain possible groupings of characters or of specifying qualities that warrant claiming a particular identity for oneself. If we were dealing with Hamlet, the former alternative would force us to judge his actions in relation to some determinate moral code; the latter would make sense of his desire to have Horatio tell his story. For it is within the individual story that Hamlet finds the terms at once to make sense of his actions and to take responsibility for them. Such stories then take on the role of labels within a cultural repertoire that subsequent agents can modify or elaborate as they attempt to establish or interpret expressive implicatures.

III

These models of expression become crucial for ethical theory when rational models of value seem no longer to suffice. For then we must face the apparently more fundamental question of how we align ourselves with the sets of constraints and obligations within which it makes sense to speak of the compelling force of moral reasons. And once there is reason to assume that Hamlet's story might have a role to play in our making ethical judgments about him, there is also reason to assume that the considerations that go into the reading of stories may have something to contribute to ethical theory. But clarifying the connection between expressive implicature and ethical identity will demand an intricate weaving of mutually reinforcing concepts. I shall begin with the two modern philosophers most fully aware of the role the concept of expression can play in ethical theory—Wittgenstein and Charles Taylor—but it will take considerable modification of their ideas before I can elaborate a satisfying picture of an ethical order fully responsive to human expressive energies and needs.

Wittgenstein proves so useful for my purposes because he so clearly understood both the appeal of Kant's moral rationality and the need to reformulate that position so that its deontological force as a model of self-constitution could be separated from the particular version of rational agency that Kant felt was necessary to preserve dignity and nobility. By making those shifts, Wittgenstein could provide an even stronger case than Kant's for the absolute distinction between the ethical and those models of value which might be established by empirical research:

Can there be any ethics if there is no living being but myself?

If ethics is supposed to be something fundamental, there can . . .

As the subject is not a part of the world but a presupposition of its existence, so good and evil are predicates of the subject, not properties in the world . . .

If the will did not exist, neither would there be that centre of the world, which we call the I, and which is the bearer of ethics.

What is good and evil is essentially the "I," not the world . . .

Here everything seems to turn so to speak on *how* one wants . . .

But can we conceive a being that isn't capable of Will at all, but only of Idea (of seeing for example)? In some sense this seems impossible. But if it were possible then there could also be a world without ethics . . .

Ethics does not treat of the world. Ethics must be a condition of the world, like logic.

Ethics and aesthetics are one.[9]

Ethics and aesthetics are one, I think, because both depend on a concept of expression, on the ways in which a particular subject's "how" projects its purposiveness within the objective world. Expressive subjects constitute worlds, not by entering the categorical demands of rationality, but by manipulating categories so that one's action takes responsibility for the differences it asserts. And this direct assertion also frees Wittgenstein from the psychology that attends Kant's ethics—a dream that somehow agents can reflexively determine themselves as rational and hence as able to view their preferences from an absolute third-person point of view. Kant's subject must be both the "I" of desire and the "anyone" of rational method. Wittgenstein's, on the other hand, is if anything too radically subjective, emerging not by a process of self-reflection but with the same irreducible immediacy that we can predicate of the sense of the first person embedded in our perceptions.

The best way to grasp the status of the Wittgensteinian subject is to appreciate both the transcendental and the psychological implications of his analogies to the ways in which logic too can only be expressed and not derived from other principles or read off the world by empirical descriptions. The transcendental claim equates the ethical subject with the structuring force of logical forms in order to insist that this conditioning of the world is not something evanescent but something so absolutely fundamental that all our descriptions of existing phenomena must presuppose it in order to be of any practical use. Logic cannot be described by any form of scientific explanation because the explanation itself would have to rely on the very rules of logic for which it purports to account. Thus we can only attribute our knowledge of logic to the process of exemplification by which its rules are manifest. We can see how it works; we can measure its effects and grant its power; but we can only purport to know it by the differences it makes. Logic never stands as an object—a point that Quine confirms when he tries to subsume philosophy under the operational principles of science. There are no explanations for the basic terms of our explanations; there can only be methods for assessing the "conditions" these grounding terms produce.

Ethics involves the same principles because its ultimate terms, the sense of fundamental goods and evils, can also never be determined by any analysis: "You cannot lead people to what is good; you can only lead them to some place or other. The good is outside the space of facts."[10] To restate Kant, we cannot be argued into basic attributions of good and evil, we simply define them by the same actions that constitute ourselves as subjects. That is why "what is good and evil is essentially the 'I,' not the world." But then every explanation we try to muster depends on the sense of value which shapes the result. Just as logic is always present in our efforts to make truthful descriptions, the will is always present in our efforts to account for the kind of values which lead us to talk about an individual's happiness or unhappiness. There simply are no facts of the matter not always already constructed in relation to a specific sense of happiness, so there can be no determinate calculus that can be used to decide how to assess these facts for their ethical significance.

We can speak of self-constituting acts not dependent on categorical reason. But then are we not faced with a simple relativism that essentially destroys ethics as a subject? Having replaced Kantian rationality, we are in danger of simply reinventing the bourgeois subject. I am not sure how Wittgenstein might have reacted to that charge. Whatever his sentiments, though, he was bound by his own constraints to insist that nothing more can be said about the nature of the will once it is freed from the authority of empirical description. Nonetheless, I think a great deal can be shown about it by continuing the aesthetic analogies. Kant's aesthetics might yield versions of expressive agency and of communal judgment which show how we locate the subject in his or her deed and how we go about assessing actions that cannot be accommodated to empirical or utilitarian calculi. Even though there is no universalizable criterion, there is an inescapable public theater in which we have practices of responding to the "how" of people's constitutive acts.

Aesthetic analogies make it possible to concentrate on two fundamental features of Wittgenstein's "how." First, as we shall see more fully in what follows, the "how" expresses ethical identity by eliciting a process of attention very close to that which Kant defined through his concept of the purposiveness carried by the formal dimension of artworks. Purposive form is not a reified substance but a condition of the work's action which emphasizes the intentional force of the artist's constructive activity. Form establishes a site where something can be *of* the world without being *in* it in the same way that facts are. In ethics its corollary is the necessity of connecting deeds to agents and basing one's assessment of the person as an ethical agent on some particular qualities that these actions embody. It is this embodied intentionality that then enters concrete life in ways much too fluid and manifold for rational criteria to handle, and much too intimate for the chains of deduction and generalization which rational methods require. Yet because we do focus on an embodied intentionality, we can invoke a second aspect of the "how" which establishes a public dimension for our ethical assessments. Suppose that one were to distinguish, as Wittgenstein did not, between "hows" that are nonreflective habits or immediate responses to phenomena and those in which the agent had self-conscious investments. Then it becomes possible to treat assessment in this domain of ethics in terms closely paralleling Kant's model of aesthetic judgment. There are cases in which expressions are simple matters of preference and those in which the agent seeks a certain kind of approval, at least to the degree that he or she can imagine trying to cast an action in a way that appeals for the approval of a particular community. Aesthetic experience shows that we do not need universal laws in order to maintain sharp distinctions between subjective responses and efforts to elicit forms of approval which are in principle shareable by other people. Instead, we can describe specific qualities exemplified by actions in a manner that makes it possible to appeal to the common terms of judgment basic to various aspects of public life.

If we want a fuller account of this version of judgment, we must turn from Wittgenstein's cryptic brilliance to the patient efforts of Charles Taylor devoted to recapturing in contemporary terms the force Kant's work had for his immediate successors.[11] Only then, Taylor thinks, will ethics be able to free itself of the oppositions between the rational and the empirical that otherwise cripple Kantian thought. It was Hegel who most fully recognized the need to establish a new model of agency, because those he had inherited made it impossible to escape Kant's conflicts between pure and practical reason. The authority of reason seemed inseparable from deterministic notions of a self bound to some form of universal law, be it of reason or of matter. Yet the more a rational attitude seemed to align the self with determined substance, the more the self's activity, the experiential base of our ideas of spirit, required a Cartesian dualism in which the subject wins autonomy only to the extent that subjectivity is defined in opposition to principles for offering collective judgments on actions. At best the practical reason must take the form of purely self-legislative willing, incompatible with pure reason without the magic of Kantian dialectics.

Hegel saw that the arts were creating an alternative view of the self. In Herder and Schiller a new "expressivist anthropology" posited a model of individuality based on the experience of Kantian contradictions. The self would only become self-legislating by a self-reflexive process of objectifying its interests and desires so that this knowledge became the substance in and against which spirit posited its claims to personal identity. Persons come to know and in a sense to choose selves by attempting to define and take responsibility for the specific forces that form them. Thus, as Taylor puts it, "Human life culminates in self-awareness through expression" (*Hegel*, 17). The expressive act is the simultaneous recognition of what our past allows us and the legislation of a particular form or purpose which puts the effects of that past under the sign of intentionality—the in-itself established as a for-itself (17–18).

However, Hegel's theory of expression admits no model of judgment except the tribunal of the actual course that history takes, a tribunal far too demanding to ground a practical ethics. Faced with that limitation, Taylor returns to Kant, reinterpreting in a Hegelian spirit the distinction between the empirical self, bound to practical interests or hypothetical imperatives, and the self who can legislate in categorical terms, insisting on actions directed toward establishing a particular identity. Once the expressivist framework has been articulated, distinctions like these require no metaphysics. They depend only on practical tests of whether different kinds of interests involve different cultural practices, each with its distinctive sense of human agency. Kant's empirical self operates in what Taylor calls first-order valuings, while the legislative self is manifest in those choices that clearly involve second-order reflections. We find ourselves, then, with distinctions remarkably close to the distinctions between preferences and approvals which Kant locates in aesthetic judgment.

First-order valuings are judgments that measure goods simply by virtue of the direct gratifications they seem capable of producing. Here choice is unmediated, at least in the sense that the medium for formulating the choice is not relevant to assessing it. In fact, in this domain there is a strong sense in which ethical judgment is not at stake at all. There is an important sense in which no one preference can be measured against any other, since they conform to no criteria beyond the specific desire of the chooser and some very general rules of social conduct. The only relevant constraints are practical considerations of possibilities and consequences. It becomes impossible to combine two choices only when practical conditions rule out one of the options, for example if one wanted both to save one's money and to splurge on some large purpose. Thus the "I" need not view itself in third-person terms, nor imagine the kind of identity these might afford. Second-order valuings, on the other hand, are less concerned with the goods chosen than the identity made available by "how" one disposes oneself as a chooser. Here how we choose defines who we are or what predicates about agency we earn. So it is here that first- and third-person stances enter complex interrelationships. Strong evaluations place a choice within a network of reasons, where the reasons can entitle a person to the desired self-representation if they fit the situation.

The clear sign of second-order status is the nature of the constraints encountered in such choices. If I want to consider myself courageous, there are some cowardly things I cannot do—not because it is impossible or because I will be overtly punished but because the deeds are incompatible with a set of defining terms I have chosen for my actions. Second-order choices are contrastive because they are choices of meanings, not objects. Thus, they are constrained by the network of public associations that establishes meaning. But those constraints are precisely what enables expressive activity. For a person's identity with respect to a specific decision or area of decisions is established by the specific way in which he or she takes responsibility for those constraints. Selves have public identity when they consistently maintain the contrastive schemes projected in their reasons for their actions. This need not entail conformity to social codes: because the society in question is based on grammars, not dogmas, no single contrast is definitive. The opposition of courage and cowardice can be interpreted in many ways because the interlocking contrastive frameworks are not fixed categories but malleable structures. One constitutes oneself as a person by establishing the specific meaning of the contrast and acting in accord with the implications of that meaning. (Socratic dialogues might be considered complex strong evaluations.) When we cannot see a connection between words and deeds or cannot place deeds in a contrastive context, then we simply cannot speak of ethical identity at all. A person who calls himself courageous but acts in what would normally be called cowardly terms without offering any alternative interpretation of those terms has no public identity, except, perhaps, as expressing symptoms. This person, I must add, could still have quite strong and determinate interests. What would be lacking is any process of purposiveness, any sense that the person determined his interests with a stake in being a certain kind of person.

Once we ask for more particulars about what it means to be a certain kind of person, however, I must break with Taylor. Like Robert Nozick (and, probably, Wittgenstein), he allows the self-realization aspects of expression to align him with existentialist themes—precisely in areas where a Kantian version of Wittgenstein's "how" provides a much richer alternative. Taylor emphasizes second-order valuings as a process of coming to define the person's fundamental commitments. One wants one's self-representations to match the reality of one's actions. But this way of formulating responsibility makes self-knowledge in itself a more important motive than the social relations one achieves by so embodying one's purposes. This means knowledge must ultimately be its own reward—an old saw I find hard to believe in any area of human experience. More important, ideals of self-knowledge must posit as the object to be known something like a "true self," which I am not alone in thinking is a chimera. There is no way to know a self apart from its expressions. So what matters is not whether they are true to some preexisting process but whether a person's way of making actual deeds intelligible earns the evaluative predicates one wants to attribute to them.

I prefer therefore to take second-order valuings as projections that claim an aspect of identity before a community.[12] That community may be an actual social institution or a construct based on at least some actual persons sharing a grammar for evaluating actions derived from historical sources. In either case, the value of our accounts is simply their capacity as expressions to pass a certain kind of muster. When we analyze ourselves in this vein we try to satisfy expectations we learn by viewing our actions from the third-person stances that are part of the heritage transmitted through social life. One cannot universalize these terms for judgment. But one can specify them for the specific group one wants to win identity from, and this may have to suffice for a post-Kantian age. At the least, so modifying Taylor gives the subject a plausible motive for self-scrutiny—the desire to claim certain kinds of identity—and makes it possible to show how agents need not be entirely subject to values of the specific social group they inhabit: identity is not the same thing as status. In representing ourselves we partially define the kind of audience whose judgments can confer the desired identity, and we bind ourselves to accounting for shifts we might make in our invocation of different communities. If one keeps shifting communities, one gives up the crucial identity of someone who maintains some kind of long-term loyalties. So while casuistry is a serious danger within this model, the model does have the power of demonstrating the price one thereby pays.

IV

All I can claim at this point is to have outlined a specific version of the concept of expression which enables us to understand a particular aspect of ethical life opened for reflection by contemporary concerns with the limitations of traditional emphases on rational, third-person models for evaluating actions. It remains to be seen how fully the aesthetic analogues both demonstrate the centrality of these concerns and flesh out adequate interpretations of the concrete elements that must go into the portrayal of this model of values. In order to begin that discussion I want first to summarize the range of analogies which will enter that effort. Then we shall have a full sense of the available resources as we work with particular concepts. Therefore I propose six fundamental parallels between the principles of expressivist semantics and the basic tenets one would have to rely on in order to account for an expressivist ethic.

(1) Expressivist views of art require a firm contrast to the various semantic orientations attributed to works by mimetic theorists. Instead of having responsibility to some version of actual states of affairs, the work matters for the productive conditions that it makes manifest by producing new configurations for experience or new ways of pressing out possibilities for spiritual life. (2) These configurations have their force as particulars. They present examples we contemplate rather than instances we try to subsume under some more general category. Thus the object is expressive both as a pressing out and as an

embodiment of distinctive emotional tones. (3) In order to explain how objects can be at once created and meaningful, yet not dependent on universals, expressivist aesthetics must emphasize some form of the maker's presence as a constitutive force of meaning. Thus the work has significance because it embodies an active authorial principle at work composing relations among meanings afforded by social codes. For the nineteenth century the author was a biographical concept, but in the twentieth "author" refers primarily to an intentional state constructed from the work as the necessary means of making the signs cohere as one act. (4) Because expressive acts must be judged as particulars, they require categories of understanding and use which are not congruent with those that have epistemological authority in the overall culture's discursive practices for dealing with general concepts. We must be able to speak of nondiscursive forms of communication and judgment. (5) Accounts of this nondiscursive alternative to "rational" procedures will usually involve some version of the concept of exemplification worked out by Goodman. Expressions create the possibility of particulars serving as exemplary labels that define possible meanings or values even when there is no clear discursive rationale for what they present. (6) If one tries to produce a general account of the cultural values contributed by expressive works, the answer will have to put some concept of *Bildung* in the place of appeals to truth or beauty. Texts are *Wirkungen*, establishing the idealizations and contrasts that constitute a cultural grammar or ways of world-making. Thus the fullest paradigms for expressivist *Bildung* are comprehensive syntheses among expressive states like Dante's *Commedia* or Hegel's *Phenomenology*.

It seems possible, when reflecting upon my speculations about an expressivist ethic, to suggest the following parallels, which I shall then elaborate in subsequent discussion: (1) Where expressivist aesthetics sets itself against mimetic theories, expressivist ethics depends on contrasts to any rationalist model of values—be it deontological or consequentialist. Value is not derived from a universal schema or principle but relies on how persons configure individual identities.[13] (2) The crucial expressivist act consists in calling attention to how one takes responsibility for a particular deed as one's second-order claim to earn a specific identity. Expression becomes a process of manipulating expressive implicatures so as to achieve what Angel Medina calls a process of "existential elucidation." (3) Implicatures are not the instantiation of concepts but claims to have defined the self through a particular structuring of cultural elements which must be appreciated in their particularity as an action sustaining an explanatory context. (4) Yet if the appeal is to a public conferral of an identity, the description of the act must be publically assessable. This means that we must extend to ethics the interpretive grammars allowing us to treat acts as coherent and to understand how they imply certain consequences, both for the agent who wants certain attributions and for someone who imposes judgments on them. (5) A history of expressive acts is instrumental in shaping this grammar because the acts become the examples that define fit and that elicit desires for achieving certain identities. Although exemplification is largely a cognitive matter in aesthetics, in ethics it also indicates how we come to desire the achievement of expressive identities. (6) Where Hegelian or Kantian structures for intricate paths of *Bildung* are the fullest realization of expressivist aesthetics, the ethic culminates in the productive tensional life of the city as imagined by Kant and Simmel. In the place of Hegel's expressive spirit knowing itself in its totality, we have expressive agents reveling in the world of differences, provocations, and sympathies they produce by their efforts at self-definition.

V

Now that the fundamental principles of the ethic have been posited, we must ask how useful the model will prove. Does it play conceptual roles that allow us to offer plausible and distinctive characterization of some commitments and concerns that seem basic to those behavioral domains where many of us think it is appropriate to speak about ethical values? Four questions should pose the necessary tests of both the model's descriptive adequacy and its role in positing the kind of ideal images for the ethical life which people once sought in philosophy: What needs can the ethic's values be said to address? What powers in human agents make us capable of achieving those values? What principles of judgment allow us to make the kind of evaluations the ethical model calls for? and What grounds or sources can be said to sanction the evaluative principles? Obviously the confines of this essay, among many other constraints, make it impossible for me to match my answers to the grandiosity of the questions. Instead I shall limit my response to the barest of outlines, in the hope that the overall effort will generate sufficient filaments to provide a fairly secure structural framework that can in the future be filled in.

The best way to illustrate the importance of basing one's ethic on second-order needs like those Taylor discusses is to point out the price one pays for refusing to consider them. Hobbes provides a superb example. His political theory is brilliant on the differences involved between the realm of nature and the realm of law. But his empiricist psychology will not admit any principle that would explain what people might gain from in fact submitting to the law. If our desires are based only on possessive instincts, there are only the baldest practical motives for submitting to the social order. And the story of Gyges' ring tells us how those motives are in fact likely to shape social relations when there are no second-order needs directly dependent on social relations.

The expressivist tradition, on the other hand, makes the need for having meaning for the self no less a part of material life than needs for food and warmth. Hegel's remains our best account of those needs. But now the most I can do is indicate how heirs like Lacan and Habermas spell out the ways in which these second-order needs operate. Lacan puts them within a developmental dynamic, and Habermas shows how we need not accept the alienation story Lacan generates. The symbolic order cannot restore the objects or the audience that one's fantasy life seeks, but it does provide a transpersonal means for partially satisfying the need to achieve recognition by *l'autre* and *L'Autre*. We have at the least a basis for judging how and why some displacements are more debilitating than others, some judgments more internally contradictory than others. We may never reach any single essential self, but we can come to recognize the cumulative effect of having achieved a series of partial identities within overlapping communities.

My discussion of expressive implicature should enable me to be equally brief on the subject of illustrating our powers to dramatize the "hows" that can earn for us the desired identities. We make claims to ethical identity when wish becomes will, or, to paraphrase Wittgenstein, when what only precedes the event as a hypothetical construct becomes an inseparable modifier of it (*Notebook*, 88e). And we best make sense of those claims by returning to Kant on the relation between purposiveness and genius.[14] For he shows that artworks have a claim to be read as individual constructs, rather than as instances of some category, because they embody a particular intentionality inseparable from the unfolding of the internal relations within the work. Purposiveness, then, defines states—in art and in life—when concepts of purpose are too general to capture the distinctive qualities of a "how" that remains the central focus of our attention, even after we recognize other ways to describe the action.[15] We understand *Hamlet* and Hamlet not as simple conjunctions of various structural codes but as synthetic transformations of those codes into a single purposive enactment. Even if we do not agree on the specific nature of the play or the character, we find it hard to say someone is responding to *Hamlet* or Hamlet if he does not try to interpret the configuration of historical materials (like stories about ghosts and conventions of revenge) in terms of specific intentionalities not reducible to conceptual frameworks. Hamlet, perhaps more than any other person in literature, projects the essence of purposiveness as an energy born in the struggle to align oneself with general purposes while refusing their categorical claims.

Claims about purposiveness involve us in the most perplexing and pressing issue of modern thought—how we can establish principles of judgment which enable us to acknowledge the limitations of rationalism without denying the possibility of appreciating and assessing those actions that appeal to the forms of approval required to satisfy the desire for giving one's life second-order meanings. If we determine our own audiences, or if audiences make up their own performers, there is no second-order desire that is not reducible to a disguised practical interest. But Kant's aesthetics provides two very useful ways beyond that dilemma. First, his description of judgment makes clear how flexible the "I" can be as it balances between first-person assertions or identifications and third-person recognitions of how we depend on transpersonal ideals for understanding and assessing whatever enters the symbolic order. Second, his efforts to understand the significance of this flexibility lead to an even richer account than Goodman's of the ways that individual examples can finesse some of the problems that beset the categorical judgment, which he thought essential to rational understanding.

Kant found aesthetic experience a necessary subject for philosophy because only in that domain could one account for originality and demonstrate concrete instances of subjective desire choosing to be bound by impersonal criteria. There it seemed plausible to make a distinction between the gratification of immediate interests and a "reflective" capacity to so direct personal interests that they require us to ally ourselves with what we imagine to be a plausible universal attitude. To approve a work of art (rather than simply to like it) means to treat the agent's free, legislative response as if it were in accord with "a ground of satisfaction for all men" (*Critique of Judgment*, sec. 6). This constitutes the subjective universality that in itself is not "cognizable" in categorical terms. Yet the feeling of relation to universal forms of reflection becomes a symbol of the rational universality afforded by moral judgments. For even without the transcendental force of rationality, the subject recognizes different ways in which it can take up reflective attitudes toward its preferences and thereby align itself with a shareable third-person stance. By seeking to state the terms of one's approval, one must actualize those aspects of the psyche which one can try to share with other subjects, and one must test one's own interests by the ways that they can take form within that perspective.

But how do we know what is shareable without relying on a set of universal principles, which in its turn restores an insuperable gulf between the domain where universals are possible and the empirical realm of irreducible differences among actual human interests? Facing that problem led Kant to some remarkable insights into the nature of symbolic examples capable of providing an instrument for judgment which can negotiate agreements without relying on either universals or their opposite, the raw assertion of individual power. When Kant speaks of the beautiful as "a symbol of the morally good" (sec. 59), he treats the symbolic relation as a case of *"hypotyposis"* or indirect presentation of the concept:

All intuitions which we supply to concepts a priori are . . . either schematic or symbols, of which the former contain direct, the latter indirect, presentations of the concept. The former do this demonstratively; the latter by means of an analogy (for which we avail ourselves even of empirical intuition) in which the judgment exercises a double function, first applying the concept to the object of a sensible intuition, and then applying the mere rule of the reflection made upon that intuition to a quite different object of which the first is only the symbol. Thus a monarchical state is represented by a living body if it is governed by national laws, and by a mere machine (like a hand mill) if governed by an individual absolute will; but in both cases only *symbolically*. For between a despotic state and a hand mill there is . . . no similarity; but there is a similarity in the rules according to which we reflect upon these two things and their causality.[16]

This indirect similarity can take two different forms, illustrative or exemplary. In the former case the symbol simply demonstrates the existence of what can be rendered in other, conceptual terms. But even this formulation creates the possibility of seeing symbols as in their own right presenting or demonstrating realities for which concepts themselves are inadequate. This is what art exemplifies—symbols that are a constitutive and not merely a regulative tool because the very powers they dramatize can become more significant than the abstract claims they clarify. Thus beauty is symbolic of morality because the experience of it actually demonstrates the reality of the will giving "the law to itself" in respect to objects of satisfaction:

As in a rational idea the *imagination* with its intuitions does not attain to the given concept, so in an aesthetical idea the *understanding* by its concepts never attains completely to that internal intuition which the imagination binds up with a given representation. Since, now, to reduce a representation of the imagination to concepts is the same thing as to *expound* it, the aesthetical idea may be called an *inexponible* representation of the imagination. (*Critique of Judgment*, 189)

Three properties of these inexponible representations make it possible to define a distinctive form of judgment that can appeal to shareable standards without relying on rational categories. First, the presentational aspect of the example illustrates what is involved in speaking of a noncategorical intelligibility.[17] As Goodman shows, examples possess and do not simply refer to properties, so they can themselves provide forms that judgment can use without relying on abstract understanding. Consider the way we usually teach someone to ride a bicycle simply by demonstrating how it is done; I am not sure that I could explain all the principles involved. Similar practices dominate cultural activities like using representative instances to illustrate what words mean and do, or what gestures entail.

The second property leads us from the intelligibility of meanings to the presentational strategies that, in Wordsworth's terms, actually produce "truth that is its own testimony." This claim need not force us to invoke unmediated visions. Instead, we need only concentrate on the "how," the way in which the truth is rendered or performed. An assertion becomes its own testimony to the extent that the powers it literally or figuratively possesses seem demonstrated by the mode of experience required to make sense of the example. Thus lyric poems can be said to demonstrate the value of disposing one's imagination in certain ways, for example by literally participating in the force of Wallace Stevens's intricate evasions of "as." Or other cultural exemplars like Socrates come to matter less for what they say than for the specific embodiment they give, allowing us to share a sense of what it would mean to be like Socrates. His performances survive in the culture as specific examples that invite us to identify with processes of thinking about eros or of negotiating contradictions, or even of the possibilities inherent in a particular style of teaching.

When we turn to how examples might be used, a third trait emerges, which is especially important to ethical judgment. Examples allow us a range of projective sympathies so that we come to appreciate what is involved in given choices. That is why we can maintain a grammar of second-order concepts. Courage is not simply an abstract attribute; it is a predicate we associate with a range of examples that then come to constitute the set of contexts we consult when we are confronted with a claim about courage applied in unfamiliar situations. One can make the same point perhaps more forcefully by pointing to the ways in which our using examples can undermine what seems secure on an abstract basis. Consider how much more plausible Kant's case for the categorical imperative seems before he gives his four examples (*Fundamentals*, secs. 422–34), each of which reminds us of how much more pragmatic and flexible is the set of moral concerns that prevails in the much less rigid schema that govern practical life. Indeed, it is precisely at this point that the concreteness of purposive example provides enough evidence to make the claims seem symptomatic: reason's distance from concrete causes appears more a problem than a power, and the projection of moral rationality threatens to collapse into the pietistic moralizing of Kant's family background, requiring in recompense the rhetoric of the sublime.

Judgment is a faculty for evaluating phenomena. The quality of its assessments depends on its having resources that enable it to offer capacious comprehension of both the complexity of performances and the range of traditional examples which the agent might call upon as the appropriate context for an act. (Imagine the plight of a culture reduced to the grounds for judgments that seem to prevail in the Reagan administration.)

Thus my final question requires spelling out the resources that enable judgment to confer forms of ethical identity on purposive acts that are capable of satisfying the needs I have been considering. And that will demand putting considerable pressure on the notion of community which so far I have used very loosely. Describing the role of cultural communities in ethical judgment involves two basic components—one epistemological and the other axiological. I shall here assume there is no epistemological problem in treating one's education into a culture as the learning of a grammar of exemplary acts and texts which we then can use in explaining or assessing particular actions. But we need to ask how such grammars can carry a normative force able to replace the role of rational universals without requiring a conservative fidelity to the specific values the examples encode. This means showing how cultural traditions can be preserved on the level of principles that can be abstracted from specific positivities.

Clearly, cultural grammars establish conditions for identity: Telemachus becomes truly Odysseus's son when he imitates his father's courage and cunning. But it does not take Lacan to remind us of the price we pay because we must subsume our desires under the Father's authoritative models. So *Hamlet* becomes the measure of a world unsatisfied with the ideals Telemachus served. But for a culture that had to develop expressivist principles, even these alienated heroics could no longer suffice. We require a model of community responsive to Joyce's transformation of Telemachus and Hamlet into a self-consciously adopted heritage where one's public identity lies precisely in how the agent manipulates complex structures of identity and difference. The character of Stephen Dedalus posits, reveals, and tests, something that endures in the examples of Telemachus and Hamlet, while at the same time insisting on the necessity of defining one's own difference by pursuing principles abstract enough to make received positive values and actual social affiliations seem mere positivities, the tokens that communities must rely on when they are not fully responsive to the imaginative worlds we can invoke as alternative contexts giving a richer sense of both the content and the possible significance of certain values.

Once we get this flexible and inventive, however, have we not surrendered the actual normative force of this communal background? Joyce shows that we can make the past our own, but so much so that there is no longer a coherent past to use as a measure. We can appreciate individual expressive acts, but we have no real way to confer a social status upon them. Instead of serving moral roles, expressivist aesthetics seems to destroy the very framework we need for an ethic. It leaves us with the organicist versions of autonomy idealized in the New Criticism, and it makes it clear why philosophers like Donagan and Gewirth continue to be obsessed with the Kantian pursuit of universal moral principles.

Indeed, there remains a strong need for impersonal, objectively applied standards for what I have been calling morality. But these do not help us appreciate what agents seek in their choosing of moral stances. The only proposal that will work, I think, requires a simple transformation of Kantian aesthetics. The normative ground for expression is a grammar for valuing action sustained by the specific community from which an agent seeks identity. Agents choose communities, but then they accept as a substitute for universals the principles of judgment observers construct as plausible within the community. This approach requires constant negotiation, but it satisfies in practice the basic practical concerns that drove Kant to rationalism: determinations of the good must be different from the simple pursuit of preferences, because the agent in the former case cannot be the only arbiter. There must be sufficient critical force in one's concept of community to allow it to generate three conditions for ethical actions—goals to pursue, possibilities of distinguishing purely empirical interests from principled actions, and means of standing in judgment on our own behavior as it responds to these goals and possibilities. Communities must be sufficiently determinate to provide standards and criteria, but sufficiently indeterminate to allow agents to criticize their values, form new allegiances, and change the level on which the culture's products are viewed so as to distinguish positivities from principles. If this can be described, we can claim to reconcile the Kantian polarities of actuality and ideality.

The major influence of aesthetic theory here is on how we choose to specify what holds a community together so that we internalize its role as a normative ground in our acts of judgment.[18] Obviously, relying on rules or principles simply recreates the gulf between anyone and someone, while, at the other pole, definition of communities in terms of beliefs we ground in social practices or responses to questionnaires eliminates the question of second-order ethics, save as a specific cultural formation. The "I" begins to look suspiciously like "anyone," on the basis of social rather than rational determinants. Longinus's advice to writers provides a very different example:

Accordingly it is well that we ourselves also, when elaborating anything which requires lofty expression and elevated conception, should shape some idea in our minds as to how perchance Homer would have said this very thing, or how it would have been raised to the sublime by Plato or Demosthenes or by the historian Thucydides. For those personages, presenting themselves to us and inflaming our ardor and as it were illumining our path, will carry our minds in a mysterious way to the high standards of sublimity which are imaged within us. 2. Still more effectual will it be to suggest this question to our thoughts: What sort of hearing would Homer, had he been present, or Demosthenes have given to this or that when said by me, or how would they have been affected by the other? For the ordeal is indeed a severe one, if we presuppose such a tribunal and theater for our own utterances, and imagine that we are undergoing a scrutiny of our writings before these great heroes, acting as judges and witnesses. 3. A greater incentive still will be supplied if you add the question, in what spirit will each succeeding age listen to me who have written thus?[19]

A great deal more than sublime writing is at stake in this perspective. One might even say that it provides an expressivist means for pursuing what Kant called "the moral sublime" by so describing rhetoric as to capture the human desires it can realize. First and most important is the fact that the writer's community, and, by analogy, any community that holds our affections, is established by the authority of personal exemplars, not the authority of rules or dogmas or even shared material interests. All ethical grounds must provide transitions between the empirical and the ideal. Here that conjunction takes explicit human form, allowing a direct equation between the psychological processes that constitute both ego ideals and ideal egos and the symbolic ones sustained by cultural traditions. And because we base cultural authority on the dual properties of serving as a grammar and serving as an audience, we can understand how ideals can exist on the level of principles rather than positivities. We use the past in order to make ourselves intelligible, and we construct from the past an audience capable of serving as judges of the modifications we make in what they exemplify. We cannot, of course, specify conditions for these judgments, but we can use the context provided by the model of an audience as the basis for communal discussions.

Thus, culture as a set of contents becomes culture as a shareable process of identifications and projections. Different people can read somewhat different Socrates and still use him as an exemplar they hold in common. Or they can negotiate ways of reading what he offers as the relation between positivities and principles. Or they can use the same readings of characters to explain differences on another level—by developing contrastive stories that use the models or by accounting for a range of their own emotional investments. Conversely, there is strong pressure on us to locate identities that are capacious enough to allow our different expressions to remain intelligible to one another, even to make demands on one another. We need not have only one fixed canon of saints in order to be able to define how our ideals form overlapping circles.

Instead of the one canon, we need an attitude that acknowledges what Angel Medina calls the reciprocal play of regressive and progressive moments in the process of existential elucidation ("Edwardian Couples," 67–68). The regressive features of identification entail taking responsibility for both a personal past and its relation to the exemplars that make a community articulate about its values. That becomes the basis for making public and testable the projections that construct possible future selves. If one desires these progressive moments to sustain a sense of continuous identities (not necessarily a rigid single self), one could not simply choose any community that comes to hand as a possible source of approval for one's actions. Because the projection of identity looks both backward and forward, it constrains us to be able to explain why we do or do not remain committed to the communities we have invoked on past occasions. Thus while one can in principle keep changing one's community, one cannot on this basis seek any of the forms of deep ethical identity which in our culture seem to have made the process worth pursuing in the first place.

VI

Expressivist principles cannot in themselves establish an alternative social theory. That is a domain requiring instruments capable of judging competing judgments about collective goods—those goods on which we have a claim by virtue of being "anyone." But the expressivist can try to so define the powers in past exemplars that their tribunal sits in inescapable judgment on our social visions. In regressing this way, we also make a significant progressive contribution by keeping alive ideals that, one can argue, anyone should have the right to pursue. It may even be the case that once we ask how future societies will judge us, we will feel an expressivist obligation to help give our society some claims on those judgments. At the very least, we may see that Habermas's political norm of equal access to communication is something that has a good deal more than rational claims upon us. His vision may well capture the dynamic basis for constructing in the future a city of ends based on the kinds of reciprocity expression requires. To enjoy fully the tensions of expressivist life, we must think that we engage people sufficiently free and sufficiently well educated to make judgments and to assert their own challenging self-definitions.

Expressivist theory can, though, play a large role in establishing ideals and identifications for literary critics. On the simplest level, it provides a clear ethical justification for traditional practices of mediating texts. By specifying and contextualizing those qualities that distinguish rich, purposive expressions, we establish a range of models and contrasts that help develop people's capacity for expressive acts. And we create a richer imaginative tribunal for judging the efforts that ensue. Analytic reasoning can trace the cracks in foundational thought and, as Rorty and Cavell do, propose the need for edifying or therapeutic discourses. But in a society in which therapies proliferate almost as quickly as needs, the desperate need is for practices of interpretation which can define a stage on which the therapies themselves can be judged and demanding ideals formulated. That takes reading imagina-

tive literature, and reading well takes the production of finely contoured cultural contexts that situate our imaginative heritage.

There are, of course, good ethical justifications for other models of
reading like Geoffrey Hartman's calls for making reading itself a creative performance. Imperatives of expression apply to criticism as well as
to art. But the better we articulate the tribunal literary expressions
create, the stronger will be the claim on most critics to base our expressive needs on how well we clarify exemplary acts that tend to mock our
efforts to compete with them. And accepting limits can be a powerful
expression of how one comes to terms with the givens that in large part
compose any identity.

There are also some limits that expressivist theory shows us it is
dangerous to accept. It is clearly important in our cultural traditions to
forge some kind of political identity. But given the relation literary
criticism has to the entire grammar of elements that goes into forging
identities, it seems important that we not make politics the exclusive
arbiter of our literary judgments. If we try to locate our principles of
idealization in a direct engagement with the actual political order, we
risk what I think is the inevitable despair over idealization that comes
from dwelling on political events and structures. I find it significant
that Jerome McGann and Roger Sale—two of the finest critics who
insist on reading works primarily in historical terms—end up identifying with a Byronic nihilism as the only authentic way to survive the
very history they embrace. Or one could remind oneself of how
French Marxism seems to have prepared the way for theocentrism—
Tel Quel, the paradigmatic expression of bemused contemporaneity,
becomes L'infini, and Marx gives way to Jesus. Politics may not always
be the art of despair. In our world, however, where the many pursue
dreams and tribunals that must sicken those fostered on alternative
communities, one's dreams of reforming the world always border on
nightmares of being swallowed up by it. It is far more prudent to base
one's commitments as a teacher on the effort to afford individuals
some degree of power over their lives by showing them the imaginative
possibilities their culture offers for trying out identities and for being
recognized in their efforts. Then at least one has the consolation of
identifying with all those who formed both models and tribunals out
of that deepest of struggles—not with others or with the self—but with
the actual social conditions that force us to imagine alternative communities. History may make dreamers of us all, and dreams may help
some of us make at least a private history worthy of reflection.

Notes

1. Richard Eldridge, "The Phenomenology of Moral Consciousness: Moral Relativism, Moral Rationalism, and Conrad's *Lord Jim*," a paper given at the International Association for Philosophy and Literature Conference, May 1986. I suggest the following basic texts as good examples of this shift in ethical theory: Bernard Williams, *Ethics and the Limits of Philosophy* (Cambridge: Harvard University Press, 1985); Philippa Foot, *Virtues and Vices* (Berkeley and Los Angeles: University of California Press, 1978); Alasdair MacIntyre, *After Virtue* (South Bend, Ind.: University of Notre Dame Press, 1981); and Martha Nussbaum, *The Fragility of Goodness: Luck and Ethics in Greek Tragedy and Philosophy* (Cambridge: Cambridge University Press, 1985). For the additional philosophers mentioned in the remainder of this paragraph, see Stanley Cavell, *The Claim of Reason: Wittgenstein, Skepticism, Morality, and Tragedy* (New York: Oxford University Press, 1979); Angel Medina, "Edwardian Couples: Aesthetics and Moral Experience in *The Golden Bowl*," *New Literary History* 15 (1983): 51–72; Robert Nozick, *Philosophical Explanations* (Cambridge: Harvard University Press [Belknap Press], 1981); and Jean-François Lyotard and Jean-Loup Thebaud, *Just Gaming*, trans. Wlad Godzich (Minneapolis: University of Minnesota Press, 1985).

2. I take my distinction between first- and third-person stances from Kurt Baier's equation of rationality with the point of view of "anyone" in *The Moral Point of View* (Ithaca: Cornell University Press, 1948). Obviously, that "anyone" takes radically different forms within the social analyses proposed by contemporary literary critics. But, however ironically, it is clear that an accurate analysis of social relations requires the same placement of the subject within objective practices as we find in the most abstract of scientific procedures.

3. The problematic relationship between ideality and the realm of subjective differences is perhaps clearest in the effects that occur when philosophers try to stress one pole without fully realizing the pressures imposed from the other. Thus Lyotard assumes a radically Nietzschean stance emphasizing the need for acknowledging the many incommensurable differences that characterize empirical subjects. But he has left no social bonds in any way obliging one agent to others, so in order to generate a "prescription" calling for respecting the rights of each agent but not presuming to derive from some description that can have universal ethical implications he must turn to what is most problematic and idealistic in Kant. Unable to invoke Kant the rationalist, he invokes the Kant of transcendental ideas, locating there a sense of obligation to the freedom of others based on "the whole of reasonable beings, or the preservation of the possibility of the prescriptive game" (see 59, 70–78). On this transcendental level, however, there is no difference between the tough-minded Nietzschean and the pious liberal desperately positing conditions of sociality which his analytical commitments have destroyed.

One comes, nonetheless, to appreciate both why Lyotard takes the stance he does and how difficult the task is to connect expression with judgment when one observes the duplicities that haunt the contrary case of trying to ground individual wills within some objectivist schema for determining the good. E. J. Bond, *Reason and Value* (Cambridge: Cambridge University Press, 1983), provides a very good example because he too uses an "esthetic paradigm" to establish his model of how judgment can be responsive to objective imperatives. Suppose that I think Brahms's music is a good for anyone who has the capacity of appreciating it. Then it makes sense for me to try to show someone with the relevant capacity the nature of this good, with every expectation that the experience will elicit the recognition of value and then produce a desire that had been merely potential. So we respect individual freedom but show how it can be bound to align its desires with conclusions objectively derived (35–39, 63–64).

But Bond does not recognize the enormous gap between acknowledging that this phenomenon can be valuable and actually judging that one ought to take certain steps to bring the value about. In the latter case, one must also be able to make comparisons—not simply say that Brahms is a good but that its goodness makes it imperative to give up other goods. There may be objective properties of the music or psychic states it produces that demonstrably produce fuller effects in some desired dimension than the alternative choices. But do we ever really discover that, or can we be sure that the case is so objective? The more we look, the more we are forced to return to subjective factors, so that it becomes aspects of what I shall call an expressivist ethic which provide the sense that there is a pressure on the subject deriving from some more public domain. We usually idealize certain possibilities as those "I" should pursue, not because we recognize their objective goodness, but because we admire others or desire the approval of others who pursue the ideal. We seek to claim certain identities for ourselves, and these involve identifications with actual or potential states honored by a given community that promises to confer the relevant identity. The relative value of Brahms will depend in large part on one's sense of the powers one admires in those who are devoted to Brahms, of what those powers could make available for the self, and of the definition of oneself one takes on by pursuing such taste.

On a deeper level, one "chooses" to honor what seems the rationally objective good, or to accept prescriptions about "the whole of reasonable beings," because one admires those who have maintained such ideals and wants to be able to take on the same predicates that identifying with the ideal allows. Such identifications are not merely abstract attributions or imaginary forms of status. They give consistency, direction, and focus to a life so that one becomes free to explore in experience the range of possibilities that the identifications afford. Cultivating Brahms, for example, becomes a warrant for exploring related musicians like Mahler, and it can oblige one to develop, for example, the capacity to discuss the music at a certain level.

4. G. E. Warnock, *Morality and Language* (Oxford: Basil Blackwell, 1983), 160–61, 179–91. This suspicion of practical reason affords another, somewhat ironic link between the recent directions in Anglo-American philosophy and poststructuralist thought, especially Derrida's reading of Kant in "Parergon," *La vérité en peinture* (Paris: Flammarion, 1970).

5. It is important to note that once ethics loses its connection to a distinctive medium, that of Kantian rationality or perhaps even of utilitarian calculi, and once it is connected to expression, its model of valuation will become closely aligned to other forms of value not traditionally associated with ethics. Ethical identity becomes simply one of the ways that first persons seek distinction within established practices. Maintaining a distinctive identity that takes responsibility for its own performances is clearly crucial to art or even to sports. But rather than seeing this as a weakening of the moral, I think it has the salutary effect of showing how deeply moral concerns in fact permeate the empirical order that gave Kant so much trouble.

6. Guy Sircello, *Mind and Art: An Essay on the Varieties of Expression* (Princeton: Princeton University Press, 1972).

7. In discussing Grice and, later, Nelson Goodman, I rely on my extended discussions in *Act and Quality: A Theory of Literary Meaning* (Amherst: University of Massachusetts Press, 1981). And for my specific treatments of how individual writers articulate versions of an expressivist ethic and appeal to communities, see "Plato and the Performative Sublime," *New Literary History* 16 (1985): 251–74, and "Pound's Vorticism as a Renewal of Humanism," *Boundary 2*, nos. 12/13 (1984): 439–62.

8. Goodman's clearest treatments of exemplification may be found in *Languages of Art* (Indianapolis: Bobbs-Merrill, 1968). It is worth noting that for Goodman expression is metaphorical exemplification (85–95). By that definition he hopes to capture the distinctive way that works possess certain anthropomorphic properties without relying on the intensionalist model of authorial energies which I think Sircello is correct to emphasize.

9. Ludwig Wittgenstein, *Notebooks, 1914–1916*, trans. G. E. M. Anscombe (New York: Harper Torchbooks, 1969), 79, 80, 78, 77.

10. Ludwig Wittgenstein, *Culture and Value*, trans. Peter Winch (Chicago: University of Chicago Press, 1980), 3e.

11. The following summary derives primarily from Taylor's *Hegel* (Cambridge: Cambridge University Press, 1975), and "Responsibility for Self," in *The Identities of Persons*, ed. Amelie Rorty (Berkeley and Los Angeles: University of California Press, 1976), 281–300.

12. I speak about aspects of identity to underscore the fact that this theory in no way tries to account for anything like a central self or deep self. The relative depth and centrality of the identities sought and earned will be a question of how large a part the community in question plays in one's life. Similarly, there is no assumption that the kind of identities one seeks in these public theaters will provide the degree of satisfaction imagined by romantic theorists of the self from Augustine to Lacan.

13. It is important to recognize basic differences between this approach and the ethical extension of literary models that one finds in Martha Nussbaum and, less programmatically, in Stanley Cavell. As Nussbaum's reliance on Aristotle might indicate, hers is essentially a mimetic version of both literature and ethical good. Thus "Flawed Crystals: James's *The Golden Bowl* and Literature as Moral Philosophy" and "Reply," *New Literary History* 15 (1983): 25–50, 201–8, assume that interpersonal relations constitute the basic domain for defining and testing moral identities. This leads her to concentrate exclusively on what characters learn to see that influences their relation toward other people, and it makes her norm for judgment one of responsiveness to one's situation. That in turn enables her to believe with Aristotle that there is one best choice in each situation, available to the most sensitive recording instrument.

These are not minor concerns, and Nussbaum makes a superb case for the moral importance of a sensitivity that may even have to improvise on established moral expectations if it is to handle the situation adequately. But it has the severe limitation of confining the ethical force of literary experience to what might be called its traditional novelistic and dramatic functions. In literary terms that underplays the significance of other modes like the lyric and the romantic or of other styles like experiments in the noniconic. And that has the ethical corollary of so focusing on what one knows that one ignores the ways in which literary eloquence might have consequences for how one imagines what one is. Attention to relations with others blinds her to the roles individual, constitutive acts of self-definition in relation to imagined communities may play in establishing goods or in establishing the kinds of attention we owe others.

Nussbaum's ways of reading and drawing moral analogues tie us to the activity of witnessing, assuming that our minds have as their primary obligation a fully contoured picture of the actual circumstances we confront. If, on the other hand, we take our model from Yeat's lyricist's insistence on the difference between wars with the world and wars with the self, we have an alternative paradigm for the good emphasizing the process of constructing selves and directly responding to exemplary models of behavior. Ignoring such distinctions leads Nussbaum to collapse three necessary differences—moral philosophy as a discipline specifying grounds for argument and procedures for making judgments, moral thinking as a dramatic event, and the elaboration of principles by which people bind themselves to certain moral attitudes. In addition to narrowing the range of moral analogues we can draw upon, the mimetic stance tends to dismiss those like Dostoyevsky and Kierkegaard at one pole, Wilde and Barthes at the other, who devote their lives to promoting models that provide alternatives to the whole idea of a primarily moral, interpersonal ideal of the good.

14. I have found the following materials very helpful for using Kant as I do. Most useful was Ted Cohen, "Why Beauty Is a Symbol of Morality," in Cohen and Paul Guyer, eds., *Essays in Kant's Aesthetics* (Chicago: University of

Chicago Press, 1982), 221–36, which elaborates a spatial, as opposed to a logical, model of the good will in order to explain how in aesthetics and in morality it makes sense to see the "I" taking its own state as an end (227–35). Also important to me were Hardy Jones, *Kant's Principle of Personality* (Madison: University of Wisconsin Press, 1971), on the moral theory connected to problems of what a person is; Richard E. Aquila, "A New Look at Kant's Aesthetic Judgments," in Cohen and Guyer, 87–114, on the ways that Kant's aesthetic involves intentional concerns aligning it with expressivism; and Paul Guyer, *Kant and the Claims of Taste,* (Cambridge: Harvard University Press, 1979), on the place of the third *Critique* in Kant's overall theories.

15. The best way to appreciate the force of Kant's concept is to see how it sneaks into his own ethic; see *Fundamentals of the Metaphysics of Morals*, par. 435. That passage in turn gives me the confidence to differ with Cohen on purposiveness. He takes it as something the audience brings to the work (p. 231), but I see it as our recognition that the work derives from an artist's intentions for which we cannot find adequate concepts. Guyer, who prefers the term *finality*, is very good on the ambiguity in Kant that leads to such disagreements (211–27). It is important also to recognize that purposiveness is a sliding concept in the sense that it applies to different levels of identity. Specific aspects of work or specific deeds can be purposive because they invite us to attribute expressive implicatures, but we can also treat entire works or segments of lives as phenomena for which we take a form of responsibility that involves different conditions of coherence. Finally, that flexibility requires us to recognize the possibility of different forms of expression allowing for different ways to posit identity. Most alternatives to rationalist ethics which use literary analogies (like Nussbaum's, Medina's, and MacIntyre's) emphasize narrative discourse as the only alternative to argument. But narrative tempts us to treat all appeals for identity as involving matters of who I am rather than where I am now positioned; it posits a hypothetical other—a unified self we approximate by seeking a kind of temporal causality—and it ignores forms of coherence like those explored in modernism which attempt to resist the narcissistic implications in narrative's promise to recover a whole, self-defining self. There must also be lyrical, presentational ways to assert responsibility.

16. Immanuel Kant, *Critique of Judgment*, trans. J. H. Bernard (New York: Macmillan [Hafner Press], 1968), 197–98. The ground for these exemplary presentations is not reason but the two faculties that establish a "sensus communis"—one of pleasure and pain, the other a more reflective one that makes judgments without a determinate rational base.

17. For the radically opposed poles of thinking about examples, compare Paul de Man in *Allegories of Reading* (New Haven: Yale University Press, 1984) to Catharine Elgin's marvelously concise two-page application of Goodman to moral issues (90–91) in *With Reference to Reference* (Indianapolis: Hackett, 1983). De Man refuses to allow any way of using examples so that they create shareable contexts abstracted from the will to power, but Elgin manages to take all mystery out of the power to serve as exemplar.

18. Richard Eldridge, "Philosophy and the Achievement of Community." *Metaphilosophy* 14 (April 1983): 124–25, is an instructive case because, although he is quite good on the roles examples play as a form of knowledge carried by a culture, he ignores the force of idealization which they can project. Conversely, Nozick's model of realization is very powerful on how individuals can pursue ideal states. But his atomistic sense of society makes him very thin on what it is one can realize. Without a strong sense of communal bonds he is trapped in the vaguest romantic abstractions about unity and complexity, with each of these predicates filled out largely in terms of perceptions and relations to immediate scenes rather than cultural contexts.

19. Longinus, "On the Sublime," in Hazard Adams, ed., *Critical Theory since Plato* (New York: Harcourt, Brace, 1971), sec. 14.

7
"Finely Aware and Richly Responsible": Literature and the Moral Imagination

Insofar as modern moral philosophy takes its bearings from the work of Immanuel Kant, the requirements of moral knowledge and the imaginative task of literature have proved difficult to reconcile. Kant's moral philosophy makes fully articulate the conception of moral knowledge as consisting in the ability to speak for the categorical "I," and of moral agency as consisting in the ability to follow universal rules. As Charles Altieri has pointed out in the preceding essay, however, Kant's moral philosophy meets a dilemma as soon as one considers the relationship between moral principles as universals (the Kantian "maxims," or rules) and the fact that it is the empirical "I" who must acknowledge values and be moved to action. Indeed, Kant himself was unable to resolve the anomaly of how pure reason could be practical. Literature may be thought of as providing a solution to this dilemma, by regarding its imaginative dimension as a means of moral suasion for the empirical "I." But this at best divides the imaginative nature of literature into two unrelated domains, one that meets the needs of pleasure and another that fulfills the requirements of morality. Literature may thus be seen to serve morality, but the reconciliation of morality and imagination remains unachieved. Altieri avoids this dilemma, and the pitfalls of Kantian morality more generally, by developing an approach to morality which is grounded in Kantian aesthetics. Here it is revealed that noncategorical judgments can indeed command assent and motivate action by virtue of their force of reference to the entire symbolic order of a culture.

An alternative approach to these problems is the one that Martha Nussbaum proposes here. Rather than begin from the Kantian premise that moral knowledge and agency are grounded in the intuition of and obedience to universal rules, Nussbaum implicitly rejects the conception of reason on which Kantian morality rests. By drawing on the notion of morality as a form of practical reason, or *phronēsis*, as formulated by Aristotle in the *Nicomachean Ethics*, Nussbaum is able to circumvent the anomaly of Kantian moral philosophy mentioned above, viz., of how to make pure reason practical. She is able in addition to demonstrate the centrality of literature as an imaginative enterprise to the task of moral philosophy. Considered as a form of practical reason, moral knowledge stands closer to insight or imagination, and to those modes of knowledge conventionally transmitted through fabulation or myth, than to "pure," or "formal," reason. A related position has been argued by Alasdair MacIntyre, who in *After Virtue* (1981) provides a lengthy discussion of the role of epic literature in the transmission of moral knowledge in "classical," or "heroic," societies. Rather than concentrate, as does MacIntyre, on the category of the virtues, however, Nussbaum is concerned to demonstrate that the appropriate language of moral philosophy is the vocabulary of attention. Here she draws explicitly on the work of Iris Murdoch, who in *The Sovereignty of Good* (1970) argues for a conception of morality based on the paradigm of attentive seeing.

According to the arguments presented in this essay, moral knowledge may by its very nature be made available, and also educated, through what Henry James would call the articulate "rendering" of experience. And because this conception of morality demands attention to particulars rather than a grasp of formal rules, the specificity of that rendering (another word for which might be "expression") is in all respects crucial. Because the moral life is rich in particulars, it is resistant to formulation in rules and to theoretical abstraction in much the same way that literature is resistant to paraphrase. The implications of this argument are thus that literature, in the fullness of qualities which it (re)presents, is itself a form of moral imagination, and that the imaginative dimension of literature is an essential component of the moral life. As Nussbaum says, Henry James often stressed the fact that the work of moral imagination in some manner resembles the novelist's creative task, but her claims are more powerful ones: first, that a conception of the moral life as sustained by attention and vision finds in the novel its most appropriate realization; and second, that the novel is itself a moral achievement. If these claims can be granted, then it can also be shown that no charge of "aestheticism" can soundly be leveled against the proposition that the moral life is like a literary work of art, for the well-lived life will be seen to depend on just those qualities of lucidity, attention, and insight on which the creative imagination draws.

In the preface to *The Golden Bowl*, Henry James argues that "to 'put' things is very exactly and responsibly and interminably to do them." The two prongs of this claim may be taken as indicative of the twin claims advanced in this essay. First, that the artist fulfills a moral task in the imaginative dimension of his or her work, responsibly attending to the world through efforts to discover the descriptive words and nuanced tones appropriate for its rendering. Second, that this is an example of moral conduct, and an example of practical reason as well; for the work of expression, which relies on a fine sense of the particular qualities of the world, is itself a form of action.

"Finely Aware and Richly Responsible": Literature and the Moral Imagination

Martha Craven Nussbaum

"The effort really to see and really to represent is no idle business in face of the constant force that makes for muddlement."[1] So Henry James on the task of the moral imagination. We live amid bewildering complexities. Obtuseness and refusal of vision are our besetting vices. Responsible lucidity can be wrested from that darkness only by painful, vigilant effort, the intense scrutiny of particulars. Our highest and hardest task is to make ourselves people "on whom nothing is lost."[2]

This is a claim about our ethical task, as people who are trying to live well. In its context it is at the same time a claim about the task of the literary artist. James often stresses this analogy: the work of the moral imagination is in some manner like the work of the creative imagination, especially that of the novelist. I want to study this analogy and to see how it is more than analogy: why this conception of moral attention and moral vision finds in novels its most appropriate articulation. More: why, according to this conception, the novel is itself a moral achievement, and the well-lived life is a work of literary art.

Although the moral conception according to which James's novels have this value will be elicited here from James's work, my aim is to commend it as of more than parochial interest—as, in fact, the best account I know of these matters. But if I succeed only in establishing the weaker claim that it is a major candidate for truth, deserving of our most serious scrutiny when we do moral philosophy, this will be reason enough to include inside moral philosophy those texts in which it receives its most appropriate presentation. I shall argue that James's novels are such texts. So I shall provide further support for my contention that certain novels are, irreplaceably, works of moral philosophy. But I shall go further. I shall try to articulate and define the claim that the novel can be a paradigm of moral activity. I confine myself to *The Golden Bowl*,[3] so as to build on my previous interpretation.[4]

I begin by examining the nature of moral attention and insight in one episode, in which two people perform acts of altruism without reliance upon rules of duty, improvising what is required. This leads to some reflection about the interaction of rules and perceptions in moral judging and learning: about the value of "plainness," about the "mystic lake" of perceptual bewilderment, about "getting the tip" and finding a "basis." Finally I probe James's analogy (and more) between moral attention and our attention to works of art, between moral achievement and the creation of a work of art. In short: I begin assessing the moral contribution of texts that narrate the experiences of beings committed to value, using that "immense array of terms, perceptional and expressional, that . . . in sentence, passage and page, simply looked over the heads of the standing terms—or perhaps rather, like alert winged creatures, perched on those diminished summits and aspired to a clearer air" (GB, pref., 17–18).

I

How can we hope to confront these characters and their predicament, if not in these words and sentences, whose very ellipses and circumnavigations rightly convey the lucidity of their bewilderment, the precision of their indefiniteness? Any pretense that we could paraphrase this scene without losing its moral quality would belie the argument that I am about to make. I presuppose, then, the quotation of chapter 37 of *The Golden Bowl*. Indeed, honoring its "chains of relation and responsibility," I presuppose the quotation of the entire novel. What follows is a commentary.

This daughter and this father must give one another up. Before this "they had, after all, whatever happened, always and ever each other . . . to do exactly what they would with: a provision full of possibilities" (GB, 471). But not all possibilities are, in fact, compatible with this provision. He must let her go, loving her, so that she can live with her husband as a real wife; loving him, she must discover a way to let him go as a "great and high" man and not a failure, his dignity intact. In the "golden air" of these "massed Kentish woods" (472) they "beat against the wind" and "cross the bar" (478): they reach, through a mutual and sustained moral effort, a resolution and an end. It is, moreover (in this Tennysonian image), their confrontation with death: her acceptance of the death of her own childhood and an all-enveloping love (her movement out of Eden into the place of birth and death); his acceptance of a life that will be from now on, without her, a place of death. She, bearing the guilt that her birth as a woman has killed him; he, "offering himself, pressing himself upon her as a sacrifice—he had read his way so into her best possibility" (481). It is a reasonable place for us to begin our investigation; for the acts to be recorded can be said to be paradigmatic of the moral: his sacrifice, her preservation of his dignity, his recognition of her separate and autonomous life.

The scene begins with evasion, a flight from dilemma into the lost innocence of childhood. For "it was wonderfully like their having got together into some boat and paddled off from the shore where husbands and wives, luxuriant complications, made the air more tropical" (471). They "slope" off together as "of old" (470); they rest "on their old bench," far from the "strain long felt but never named" (471), the conflicts imposed by other relations. They might have been again the only man and woman in the garden. They immerse themselves in "the inward felicity of their being once more, perhaps, only for half an hour, simply daughter and father." Their task will be to depart from this felicity without altogether defiling its beauty.

The difficulty is real enough. Could it be anything but a matter of the most serious pain and guilt for her to give up, even for a man whom she loves passionately, this father who has raised her, protected her, loved her, enveloped her, who really does love only her and who depends on her for help of future happiness? In these circumstances she cannot love her husband except by banishing her father. But if she banishes her father he will live unhappy and die alone. (And won't she, as well, have to see him as a failure, his life as debased, as well as empty?) It is no wonder, then, that Maggie finds herself wishing "to keep him with her for remounting the stream of time and dipping again, for the softness of the water, into the contracted basin of the past" (473–74). To dare to be and do what she passionately desires appears, and is, too monstrous, a cruel refusal of loyalty. And what has her whole world been built on, if not on loyalty and the keen image of his greatness? It is no wonder that the feeling of desire for her husband is, in this crisis, felt as a numbing chill, and she accuses it: "I'm at this very moment . . . frozen still with selfishness" (478).

This is moral anguish, not simply girlish fear. Keeping down her old childish sense of his omnipotence exacerbates and does not remove her problem: for seeing him as limited and merely human (as Adam, not the creator) she sees, too, all the things he cannot have without her. And in her anguish she has serious thought of regression and return: "Why . . . couldn't they always live, so far as they lived together, in a boat?" (471) In pursuit of that idea she calls upon her ability to speak in universal terms, about what "one must always do." The narrator says of this "sententious[ness]" that it "was doubtless too often even now her danger" (473)—linking the propensity for abstractness and the use of "standing terms" with her past and present refusals to confront the unique and conflict-engendering nature of her own particular context.

I say this to show the moral difficulty of what is going on here, the remarkable moral achievement, therefore, in his act of sacrifice which resolves it. The general sacrificial idea—that he will go off to America with Charlotte—is in itself no solution. For it to become a solution it has to be offered in the right way at the right time in the right tone, in such a way that she can take it; offered without pressing any of the hidden springs of guilt and loyalty in her that he knows so clearly how to press; offered so that he gives her up with greatness, with beauty, in a way that she can love and find wonderful. To give her up he must, then, really give her up; he must wholeheartedly *wish* to give her up, so that she sees that he *has* "so read himself into her best possibility."

Maggie has spoken of her passion for Amerigo, saying that when you love in the deepest way you are beyond jealousy—"You're beyond everything, and nothing can pull you down" (476). What happens next is that her father perceives her in a certain way:

The mere fine pulse of passion in it, the suggestion as of a creature consciously floating and shining in a warm summer sea, some element of dazzling sapphire and silver, a creature cradled upon depths, buoyant among dangers, in which fear or folly, or sinking otherwise than in play, was impossible—something of all this might have been making once more present to him, with his discreet, his half shy assent to it, her probable enjoyment of a rapture that he, in his day, had presumably convinced no great number of persons either of his giving or of his receiving. He sat awhile as if he knew himself hushed, almost admonished, and not for the first time; yet it was an effect that might have brought before him rather what she had gained than what he had missed . . .

It could pass, further, for knowing—for knowing that without him nothing might have been; which would have been missing least of all. "I guess I've never been jealous," he finally remarked.

And she takes it:

"Oh it's you, father, who are what I call beyond everything. Nothing can pull you down." (477)

This passage records a moral achievement of deep significance. Adam acknowledges, in an image of delicate beauty and lyricism, his daughter's sexuality and free maturity. More: he wishes that she be free, that the suggestion of passion in her voice be translated into, fulfilled in a life of sparkling playfulness. He assents to her pleasure and wishes to be its approving spectator, not its impediment. He renounces, at the same time, his own personal gain—renounces even the putting of the question as to what he might or might not gain. (For even the presence of a jealous or anxious question would produce a sinking otherwise than in play.) The significance of his image resonates the more for us if we recall that he used to see Maggie (and wish her to be) "like some slight, slim draped 'antique' of Vatican or Capitoline hills, late and refined, rare as a note and immortal as a link, . . . keeping still the quality, the perfect felicity of the statue" (153–54). That image denied (with her evident collusion) her active womanliness; it also denied her status as a separate, autonomous center of choice. It expressed the wish to collect and keep her always, keep her far from the dangers so often expressed, in the thought of these characters, by the imagery of water and its motion. Now he wishes her moving and alive, swimming freely in the sea—not even confined to his boat, or to the past's "contracted basin." Not "frozen stiff" with guilt, either.

We can say several things about the moral significance of this picture. First, that, as a picture, it *is* significant—not only in its causal relation to his subsequent speeches and acts, but as a moral achievement in its own right. It is, of course, of enormous causal significance; his speeches and acts, here and later, flow forth from it and take from it the rightness of their tone. But suppose that we rewrote the scene so as to give him the same speeches and acts (even, *per impossibile*, their exact tonal rightness), with a different image—perhaps one expressing conflict, or a wish to swim alongside her, or even a wish for her drowning—in any of these cases, our assessment of him would be altered.[5] Furthermore, the picture has a pivotal role in his moral activity here that would not be captured by regarding it as a mere precondition for action. We want to say, *here* is where his sacrifice, his essential moral choice, takes place. Here, in his ability to picture her as a sea creature, is the act of renunciation that moves us to pain and admiration. "He had read his way so into her best possibility"—here James tells us that sacrifice *is* an act of imaginative interpretation; it is a perception of her situation as that of a free woman who is not bound by his wish. As such it is of a piece with the character of his overt speech, which succeeds as it does because of his rare power to take the sense and nuance of her speeches and "read himself into" them in the highest way.

The image is, then, morally salient. I need to say more about what is salient in it. What strikes us about it first is its sheer gleaming beauty. Adam sees his daughter's sexuality in a way that can be captured linguistically only in language of lyrical splendor. This tells us a great deal about the quality of his moral imagination—that it is subtle and high rather than simple and coarse; precise rather than gross; richly colored rather than monochromatic; exuberant rather than reluctant; generous rather than stingy; suffused with loving emotion rather than mired in depression. To this moral assessment the full specificity of the image is relevant. If we had read, "He thought of her as an autonomous being," or "He acknowledged his daughter's mature sexuality," or even "He thought of his daughter as a sea creature dipping in the sea," we would miss the sense of lucidity, expressive feeling, and generous lyricism that so move us here. It is relevant that his image was not a flat thing but a fine work of art; that it had all the detail, tone, and color that James captures in these words. It could not be captured in any paraphrase that was not itself a work of art.

The passage suggests something further. "It could pass, further, for knowing—for knowing that without him nothing might have been." To perceive her as a sea creature, in just this way, is precisely, to know her, to know their situation, not to miss anything in it—to be, in short, "a person on whom nothing is lost." Moral knowledge, James suggests, is not simply intellectual grasp of propositions; it is not even simply intellectual grasp of particular facts; it is perception.[6] It is seeing a complex, concrete reality in a highly lucid and richly responsive way; it is taking in what is there, with imagination and feeling. To know Maggie is to see and feel her separateness, her felicity; to recognize all this is to miss least of all. If he had grasped the same general facts without these responses and these images, in all their specificity, he would not really have known her.

Her moral achievement, later, is parallel to his. She holds herself in a terrible tension, close to the complexities of his need, anxiously protecting the "thin wall" (480) of silence that stands between them both and the words of explicit disclosure that would have destroyed his dignity and blocked their "best possibility." Her vigilance, her silent attention, the intensity of her regard, are put before us as moral acts: "She might have been for the time, in all her conscious person, the very form of the equilibrium they were, in their different ways, equally trying to save" (480). She measures her moral adequacy by the fullness and richness of her imaginings: "So much was crowded into so short a space that she knew already she was keeping her head" (480). And her imagination, like his, achieves its moral goal in the finding of the right way of seeing. Like an artist whose labor produces, at last, a wonderful achieved form, she finds, "as the result, for the present occasion, of an admirable traceable effort" (484), a thought of her father "that placed him in her eyes as no precious work of art probably had ever been placed in his own" (484). To see Adam as a being more precious than his precious works of art becomes, for her, after a moment, to see him as "a great and deep and high little man" (484)—as great *in*, not in spite of, his difficulty and his limitation and his effort, great because he is Adam, a little man, and not the omnipotent father. In short, it is to see that "loving him with tenderness was not to be distinguished, one whit, from loving him with pride" (484). Pride in, belief in the dignity of, another human being is not opposed to tenderness toward human limits. By finding a way to perceive him, to imagine him not as father and law and world but as a finite human being whose dignity is in and not opposed to his finitude, Maggie achieves an adult love for him and a basis of equality. "His strength was her strength, her pride was his, and they were decent and competent together" (485). Her perceptions are necessary to her effort to give him up and to preserve his dignity. They are also moral achievements in their own right: expressions of love, protections of the loved, creations of a new and richer bond between them.

Moral communication, too, both here and later in the scene, is not simply a matter of the uttering and receiving of general propositional judgments. Nor is it any sort of purely intellectual activity. It partakes both of the specificity and of the emotional and imaginative richness of their individual moral effort. We see them drawing close in understanding by seeing where they come to share the same pictures. When we hear of "the act of their crossing the bar" and their "having had to beat against the wind" (478), we discover all at once that we cannot say whose image for their situation this is. We can only say that it belongs to both of them: each inhabits, from his or her own point of view, the world of the same picture. "It was as if she had gotten over first and were pausing for her consort to follow." The paragraph melds their two consciousnesses and two viewpoints—not by confounding their separateness, for they see each other, within the picture, as distinct individuals, but by showing the extent to which fine attention to another can make two separate people inhabit the same created world—until, at the end, they even share descriptive language: "At the end of another minute, he found their word." And: "she helped him out with it." Together they give birth, in love and pain, to a lucid description of the moral reality before them. Father and mother both, he carries and nurtures it; she assists in the delivery. The true judgment is the child of their responsive interaction. In the chapter's final moments we hear talk of "their transmitted union" (485)—as if to say that moral like-mindedness is neither, on the one hand, merely a shared relation to something external (a rule, a proposition), nor, on the other, something internal in such a way that awareness is fused and separateness lost. It is the delicate communication of alert beings who always stand separated as by "an exquisite tissue" (480), through which they alertly hear each other breathing.

The final moment of the scene describes the act that is the fruit of this communicating. I have said that these picturings, describings, feelings, and communications—actions in their own right—have a moral value that is not reducible to that of the overt acts they engender.[7] I have begun, on this basis, to build a case for saying that the morally valuable aspects of this exchange could not be captured in a summary or paraphrase. Now I shall begin to close the gap between action and description from the other side, showing that a responsible action, as James conceives it, is a highly context-specific and nuanced and responsive thing whose rightness could not be captured in a description that fell short of the artistic. Again, I quote the passage:

"I believe in you more than anyone."
"Than anyone at all?"
She hesitated, for all it might mean; but there was—oh a thousand times—no doubt of it. "Than anyone at all." She kept nothing of it back now, met his eyes over it, let him have the whole of it; after which she went on: "And that's the way, I think, you believe in me."
He looked at her a minute longer, but his tone at last was right. "About the way—yes."
"Well then—?" She spoke as for the end and for other matters—for anything, everything else there might be. They would never return to it.

"Well then—!" His hands came out, and while her own took them he drew her to his breast and held her. He held her hard and kept her long, and she let herself go; but it was an embrace that august and almost stern, produced, for its intimacy, no revulsion and broke into no inconsequence of tears. (485)

We know, again, that the overt items, the speeches and the embrace, are not the only morally relevant exchange. There are, we are told, thoughts and responses behind her "Well then"—thoughts of ending, feelings of immeasurable love, without which the brief utterance would be empty of moral meaning. But we can now also see that even where the overt items are concerned, nuance and fine detail of tone are everything. "His tone at last was right": that is, if he had said the same words in a different tone of voice, less controlled, more stricken, less accepting, the whole rightness of the act, of his entire pattern of action here, would have been undone. He would not have loved her as well had he not spoken so well, with these words at this time and in this tone of voice. (His very tentativeness and his silences are a part of his achievement.) Again, what makes their embrace a wonderful achievement of love and mutual altruism is not the bare fact that it is an embrace; it is the precise tonality and quality of that embrace: that it is hard and long, expressive of deep passion on his side, yielding acceptance of that love on hers; yet dignified and austere, refusing the easy yielding to tears that might have cheapened it.

We can say, first, that no description less specific than this could convey the rightness of this action; second, that any change in the description, even at the same level of specificity, seems to risk producing a different act—or at least requires us to question the sameness of the act. (For example, my substitution of "austere" for "august" arguably changes things for the worse, suggesting inhibition of deep feeling rather than fullness of dignity.) Furthermore, a paraphrase such as the one I have produced, even when reasonably accurate, does not ever succeed in displacing the original prose; for it is, not being a high work of literary art, devoid of a richness of feeling and a rightness of tone and rhythm that characterize the original, whose cadences stamp themselves inexorably on the heart. A good action is not flat and toneless and lifeless like my paraphrase—whose use of the "standing terms" of moral discourse, words like "mutual sacrifice," makes it too blunt for the highest value. It is an "alert winged creature," soaring above these terms in flexibility and lucidity of vision. The only way to paraphrase this passage without loss of value would be to write another work of art.

II

In all their fine-tuned perceiving, these two are responsible to standing obligations, some particular and some general. Perceptions "perch on the heads of" the standing terms: they do not displace them. This needs to be emphasized, since it can easily be thought that the morality of these hypersensitive beings is an artwork embroidered for its own intrinsic aesthetic character, without regard to principle and commitment.[8] James, indeed, sees this as its besetting danger; in the characters of Bob and Fanny Assingham, he shows us how perception without responsibility is dangerously free-floating, even as duty without perception is blunt and blind. The right "basis" for action is found in the loving dialogue of the two. Here, Maggie's standing obligations to Adam (and also those of a daughter in general to fathers in general) pull her (in thought and feeling both) toward the right perception, helping to articulate the scene, constraining the responses she can make. Her sense of a profound obligation to respect his dignity is crucial in causing her to reject other possible images and to search until she finds the image of the work of art with which she ends (484). Adam's image of the sea creature, too, satisfies, is right, in part because it fulfills his sense of what a father owes an adult daughter.

So, if we think of the perception as a created work of art, we must at the same time remember that artists, as James sees it, are not free simply to create anything they like. Their obligation is to render reality, precisely and faithfully; in this task they are very much assisted by general principles and by the habits and attachments that are their internalization. (In this sense the image of a perception as a child is better, showing that you can have the right sort of creativity only within the constraints of natural reality.) If their sense of the occasion is, as often in James, one of improvisation, if Maggie sees herself as an actress improvising her role, we must remember, too, that the actress who improvises well is *not* free to do anything at all. She must at every moment—far more than one who goes by an external script—be responsively alive and committed to the other actors, to the evolving narrative, to the laws and constraints of the genre and its history. Consider the analogous contrast between the symphony player and the jazz musician. For the former, all commitments and continuities are external; they come from the score and from the conductor. The player reads them off like anyone else. The jazz player, actively forging continuity, must choose in full awareness of and responsibility to the historical traditions of the form, and must actively honor at every moment his commitments to his fellow musicians, whom he had better know as well as possible as unique individuals. He will be more responsible than the score reader, and not less, to the unfolding continuities and structures of the work. These two cases indicate to us that a perceiver who improvises is doubly responsible: responsible to the history of commitment and to the ongoing structures that go to constitute her context; and especially responsible to these, in that her commitments are internalized, assimilated, perceived, rather than read off from an external script or score.

Furthermore, the case of moral improvisation shows an even deeper role for obligation and rule than do these artistic cases. For a jazz musician, to depart from tradition in a sudden and radical way can be disconcerting, sometimes self-indulgent or irresponsible; but it can equally well be a creative breakthrough before which the sense of obligation to the past simply vanishes. In Jamesian morality this is not, I think, the case. There will be times when a confrontation with a new situation may lead the perceiver to revise her standing conception of value, deciding that certain prima facie obligations are not really binding here. But this never takes the form of leaping above or simply sailing around the standing commitments. And if the perceiver, examining these commitments, decides that they do in fact bind her, then no free departures will be permitted, and the effort of perception will be an effort of fidelity to all elements of the situation, a tense and labored effort not to let anyone down. It is not open to Maggie, as perceiver, to turn her back upon her father, not open to him to depart from her. The task of "the whole process of their mutual vigilance" (480) is to know "that their thin wall might be pierced by the lightest wrong touch" (480); good improvisation preserves, and does not rend, that "exquisite tissue."

How, then, are concrete perceptions prior? (In what sense are the descriptions of the novelist higher, more alert, than the standing terms?) We can see, first, that without the ability to respond to and resourcefully interpret the concrete particulars of their context, Maggie and Adam could not begin to figure out which rules and standing commitments are operative here. Situations are all highly concrete, and they do not present themselves with duty labels on them. Without the abilities of perception, duty is blind and therefore powerless. (Bob Assingham has no connection with the moral realities about him until he seeks the help of his wife's too fanciful but indispensable eyes.)

Second, a person armed only with the standing terms—armed only with general principles and rules—would, even if she managed to apply them to the concrete case, be insufficiently equipped by them to act rightly in it. It is not just that the standing terms need to be rendered more precise in their application to a concrete context. It is that, all by themselves, they might get it all wrong; they do not suffice to make the difference between right and wrong. Here, to sacrifice in the wrong words with the wrong tone of voice at the wrong time would be worse, perhaps, than not sacrificing at all. And I do not mean wrong as judged by some fortuitous and unforeseeable consequences for which we could not hold Adam responsible. I mean wrong in itself, wrong of him. He is responsible here for getting the detail of his context for the context it is, for making sure that nothing is lost on him, for feeling fully, for getting the tone right. Obtuseness is a moral failing; its opposite can be cultivated. By themselves, trusted for and in themselves, the standing terms are a recipe for obtuseness. To respond "at the right times, with reference to the right objects, towards the right people, with the right aim, and in the right way, is what is appropriate and best, and this is characteristic of excellence" (Aristotle *EN*, 1106b21–23).

Finally, there are elements in their good action that cannot even in principle be captured in antecedent "standing" formulations, however right and precise—either because they are surprising and new, or because they are irreducibly particular. The fine Jamesian perceiver employs general terms and conceptions in an open-ended, evolving way, prepared to see and respond to any new feature that the scene brings forward. Maggie sees the way Adam is transforming their relationship and responds to it as the heroic piece of moral creation it is—like an improvising actress taking what the other actor gives and going with it. All this she could not have done had she viewed the new situation simply as the scene for the application of antecedent rules. Nor can we omit the fact that the particularity of this pair and their history enter into their thought as of the highest moral relevance. We could not rewrite the scene, omitting the particularity of Maggie and Adam, without finding ourselves (appropriately) at sea as to who should do what. Again, to confine ourselves to the universal is a recipe for obtuseness. (Even the good use of rules themselves cannot be seen in isolation from their relation to perceptions.)

If this view of morality is taken seriously and if we wish to have texts that represent it at its best (in order to anticipate or supplement experience or to assess this norm against others), it seems difficult not to conclude that we will need to turn to texts no less elaborate, no less linguistically fine-tuned, concrete, and intensely focused, no less metaphorically resourceful, than this novel.[9]

III

The dialogue between perception and rule is evidently a subject to which James devoted much thought in designing *The Golden Bowl*. For he places between us and "the deeply involved and immersed and more or less bleeding participants" (GB, pref., 8) two characters who perform the function, more or less, of a Greek tragic chorus. "Participants by fond attention" just as we are (Fanny alone of all the characters is referred to as "our friend"), they perform, together, an activity of attending and judging and interpreting that is parallel to ours, if even more deeply immersed and implicated. James has selected for his "chorus" neither a large group nor a solitary consciousness but a married couple, profoundly different in their approaches to ethical problems but joined by affection into a common effort of vision. In his depiction of their effort to see truly, he allows us to see more deeply into the relationship between the fine-tuned perception of particulars and a rule-governed concern for general obligations: how each, taken by itself, is insufficient for moral accuracy; how (and why) the particular, if insufficient, is nonetheless prior; and how a dialogue between the two, prepared by love, can find a common "basis" for moral judgment.

Bob Assingham is a man devoted to rules and to general conceptions. He permits himself neither surprise nor bewilderment—in large part because he does not permit himself to see particularity:

His wife accused him of a want, alike, of moral and intellectual reaction, or rather indeed of a complete incapacity for either . . . The infirmities, the predicaments of men neither surprised nor shocked him, and indeed—which was perhaps his only real loss in a thrifty career—scarce even amused; he took them for granted without horror, classifying them after their kind and calculating results and chances. (72)

Because he allows himself to see only what can be classified beforehand under a universal, he cannot have any moral responses—including amusement—that require recognition of nuance and idiosyncrasy. (By presenting him for *our* amusement, as a character idiosyncratic and unique, James reminds us of the difference between the novelist's sense of life and his.)

Fanny, on the other hand, takes fine-tuned perception to a dangerously rootless extreme. She refuses to such an extent the guidance of general rules that she is able to regard the complicated people and predicaments of her world with an aestheticizing love, as "her finest flower-beds"—across which he is, to her displeasure, always taking "short cuts" (274). She delights in the complexity of these particulars for its own sake, without sufficiently feeling the pull of a moral obligation to any. And because she denies herself the general classifications that are the whole of his vision, she lacks his straight guidance from the past. Her imagination too freely strays, embroiders, embellishes. By showing us these two characters and the different inadequacies of their attempts to see and judge what stands before them, James asks hard questions about his own idea of fine awareness. He shows how, pressed in the wrong way, it can lead to self-indulgent fantasy; he acknowledges, in Bob, "the truth of his plain vision, the very plainness of which was its value" (217). So he suggests to us (what we also see in his protagonists, though less distinctly) that perception is not a self-sufficient form of practical reasoning, set above others by its style alone. Its moral value is not independent of its content, which should accurately connect itself with the moral traditions of the community. This content is frequently well preserved, at least in general outline, in the plain man's attachment to common sense moral values, which will often thus give reasonable guidance as to where we might start looking for the right particular choice.

And in a scene of confrontation between Bob and Fanny, James shows us how a shared moral "basis," a responsible vision, can be constructed through the dialogue of perception and rule. Fanny has been led to the edge of the realization that she has been willfully blind to the real relationship between Charlotte and the Prince. In this chapter (23) she and her husband will acknowledge together what has happened and accept responsibility for nourishing the intrigue by their blindness. Their preparation for real dialogue is announced by the contiguity of the metaphors in which they represent themselves to themselves. She, brooding, becomes a "speechless Sphinx"; he is "some old pilgrim of the desert camping at the foot of that monument" (273). As he stands waiting before her, we begin to sense "a suspension of their old custom of divergent discussion, that intercourse by misunderstanding which had grown so clumsy now" (273). She begins to perceive in him a "finer sense" of her moral pain (273); and this very sense of her trouble is, on his side, fostered by his old characteristic sense of his duty. He imagines her as dangerously voyaging in a fragile boat; and he responds to this picture, true to his plain, blunt sense of an old soldier's requirement, with the thought that he must then wait for her "on the shore of the mystic lake; he had . . . stationed himself where she could signal to him at need" (274).

As the scene progresses, this very sense of duty brings him to a gradual acknowledgment of her risk and her trouble—and these elements of his old moral view combine with anxious love of her to keep him on the scene of her moral effort, working at a richer and more concrete attention. His sternness, on the other hand, prevents her from finding an evasive or self-deceptive reading of the situation, an easy exit; his questions keep her perceptions honest. Bob, while becoming more "finely aware," never ceases to be himself. Still the duty-bound plain man, but loving his wife concretely and therefore perceiving one particular troubled spot in the moral landscape, he begins to attend more lucidly to all of it; for only in this way (only by being willing to see the surprising and the new) can he love and help her: "He had spoken before in the light of a plain man's vision, but he must be something more than plain man now" (280). Something *more*, and not something *other*: for it is also true that he can help her in *her* effort to perceive well only by remaining true to the plainness of his vision. Because he sees himself as on the shore to help her, she cannot evade her presentiment of moral danger. He keeps her before the general issues, and thus before her own responsibility.

As they move thus toward each other, they begin to share each other's sentences, to fill, by an effort of imagination, each other's gaps (275). And they move from contiguity in images to the inhabiting of a shared picture that expresses a mutual involvement in moral confrontation and improvisation: they are now "worldly adventurers, driven for relief, under sudden stress, to some grim midnight reckoning in an odd corner" (277). A short time later she presents him with a picture and he "enters into" it (279). At the climactic moment, Fanny feels (as the result of *his* effort) a sharp pain of realized guilt; and Bob, responding with tenderness to her pain, opens himself fully to her moral adventure, to the concrete perception of their shared situation. She cries, and he embraces her,

all with a patience that presently stilled her. Yet the effect of this small crisis, oddly enough, was not to close their colloquy, with the natural result of sending them to bed: what was between them had opened out further, had somehow, through the sharp show of her feeling, taken a positive stride, had entered, as it were, without more words, the region of the understood, shutting the door after it and bringing them so still more nearly face to face. They remained for some minutes looking at it through the dim window which opened upon the world of human trouble in general and which let the vague light play here and there upon gilt and crystal and colour, the florid features, looming dimly, of Fanny's drawing-room. And the beauty of what thus passed between them, passed with her cry of pain, with her burst of tears, with his wonderment and his kindness and his comfort, with the moments of their silence, above all, which might have represented their sinking together, hand in hand, for a time, into the mystic lake where he had begun, as we have hinted, by seeing her paddle alone—the beauty of it was that they now could really talk better than before, because the basis had at last, once for all, defined itself . . . He conveyed to her now, at all events, by refusing her no gentleness, that he had sufficiently got the tip, and that the tip was all he had wanted. (282)

Both plainness and perception, both sternness and bewilderment, contribute to the found "basis." Perception is still, however, prior. They are, at the end, in the "mystic lake" together, not upon the dry shore. To bring himself to her he has had to immerse himself, to feel the mystery of the particular, leaving off his antecedent "classifying" and "editing." The "basis" itself is not a rule but a concrete way of seeing a concrete case. He could see nothing in this case until he learned her abilities; and he was able to learn them only because there was already something in him that went beyond the universal, namely, a loving, and therefore particular, vision of her. The dialogue between his rules and her perceptions is motivated and sustained by a love that is itself in the sphere of perception, that antecedes any moral agreement. James suggests that if, as members of moral communities, we are to achieve shared perceptions of the actual, we had better love one another first, in all our disagreements and our qualitative differences. Like Aristotle, he seems to say that civic love comes before, and nourishes, civic justice. And he reminds us, too, of Aristotle's idea that a child who is going to develop into a person capable of perception must begin life with a loving perception of its individual parents, and by receiving their highly individualized love. Perception seems to be prior even in time; it motivates and sustains the whole enterprise of living by a shared general picture.

Finally, James's talk (or Bob's talk) of "getting the tip" shows us what moral exchange and moral learning can be, inside a morality based on perception. Progress comes not from the teaching of an abstract law but by leading the friend, or child, or loved one—by a word, by a story, by an image—to see some new aspect of the concrete case at hand, to see it as this or that. Giving a "tip" is to give a gentle hint about how one might see. The "tip," here, is given not in words at all but in a sudden show of feeling. It is concrete, and it prompts the recognition of the concrete.[10]

I have already argued that Jamesian perceiving and correct acting require James's artful prose for their expression. Now I can go further, claiming that the moral role of rules themselves, in this conception, can only be shown inside a story that situates rules in their appropriate place vis-à-vis perceptions. If we are to assess the claim that correct judgment is the outcome of a dialogue between antecedent principle and new vision, we need to see the view embodied in prose that does not take away the very complexity and indeterminacy of choice that gives substance to the view. The moral work involved in giving and getting "the tip" could hardly be shown us in a work of formal decision theory; it could not be shown in any abstract philosophical prose, since it is so much a matter of learning the right sort of vision of the concrete. It could not be shown well even in a philosopher's example, inasmuch as an example would lack the full specificity, and also the indeterminacy, of the literary case, its rich metaphors and pictures, its ways of telling us how characters come to see one another as this or that and come to attend to new aspects of their situation. In the preface to this novel, James speaks of the "duty" of "responsible prose" to be, "while placed before us, good enough, interesting enough and, if the question be of picture, pictorial enough, above all *in itself*" (GB, pref., 11). The prose of *The Golden Bowl* fulfills this duty.

I say that this prose itself displays a view of moral attention. It is natural, then, to inquire about the status of my commentary, which supplements the text and claims to say why the text is philosophically important. Could I, in fact, have stopped with the quotation of these chapters, or the whole novel, dropping my commentary on it? Or: is there any room left here for a philosophical criticism of literature?

The text itself displays, and is, a high kind of moral activity. But, I think, it does not itself, self-sufficiently, set itself beside other conceptions of moral attention and explain its differences from them, explaining, for example, why a course in "moral reasoning" that relied only on abstract or technical materials, omitting texts like this one, would be missing a great part of our moral adventure. The philosophical explanation acts, here, as the ally of the literary text, sketching out its relation to other texts, exposing the deficiencies of other forms of moral writing. I find that the critical and distinction-making skills usually associated (not inaccurately) with philosophy do have a substantial role to play here—if they are willing to assume a posture of sufficient humility. As Aristotle tells us, a philosophical account that gives such importance to concrete particulars must be humble about itself, claiming only to offer an "outline" or a "sketch" that directs us to salient features of our moral life. The real content of that life is not found in that outline, except insofar as it quotes from or attentively reconstructs the literary text. And even to be the ally of literature—not to negate the very view of the moral life for which it is arguing—the philosopher's prose may have to diverge from some traditional philosophical styles, toward greater suggestiveness. And yet, so long as the temptation to avoid the insights of *The Golden Bowl* is with us—and it will, no doubt, be with us so long as we long for an end to surprise and bewilderment, for a life that is safer and simpler than life is—we will, I think, need to have such "outlines," which, by their greater explicitness, return us to our wonder before the complexities of the novel, and before our own active sense of life.[11]

IV

We must now investigate more closely James's analogy between morality and art and its further implications for the moral status of this text. I speak first of the relationship between moral attention and attention to a work of art; then of the relationship between artistic creation and moral achievement.

Maggie begins, as I argued elsewhere, by viewing people as fine art objects in a way that distances her conveniently from their human and frequently conflicting demands. As she matures, however, she makes a more mature use of analogy; she does not drop it.[12] At the novel's end, her ability to view the other people as composing a kind of living, breathing painting, her attention to them as a response to this work (cf. 459), expresses her commitment to several features of James's moral ideal which are by now familiar to us: a respect for the irreducibly particular character of a concrete moral context and the agents who are its components; a determination to scrutinize all aspects of this particular with intensely focused perception; a determination to care for it as a whole. We see, too, her determination to be guided by the tender and gentle emotions, rather than the blinding, blunt, and coarse—by impartial love for them all and not be "the vulgar heat of her wrong" (459).

But this conception of moral attention implies that the moral/aesthetic analogy is also more than analogy. For (as James frequently reminds us by his use of the author/reader "we") our own attention to his characters will itself, if we read well, be a high case of moral attention. "Participants by a fond attention" (*AN*, 62) in the lives and dilemmas of his participants, we engage with them in a loving scrutiny of appearances. We actively care for their particularity, and we strain to be people on whom none of their subtleties are lost, in intellect and feeling. So if James is right about what moral attention is, then he can fairly claim that a novel such as this one not only shows it better than an abstract treatise, it also elicits it. It calls forth our "active sense of life," which is our moral faculty. The characters' "emotions, their stirred intelligence, their moral consciousness, become thus, by sufficiently charmed perusal, our own very adventure" (AN, 70). By identifying with them and allowing ourselves to be surprised (an attitude of mind that story-telling fosters and develops), we become more responsive to our own life's adventure, more willing to see and to be touched by life.

But surely, we object, a person who is obtuse in life will also be an obtuse reader of James's text. How can literature show us or train us in anything, when, as we have said, the very moral abilities that make for good reading are the ones that are allegedly in need of development? James's artistic analogy has already, I think, shown us an answer to this question. When we examine our own lives, we have so many obstacles to correct vision, so many motives to blindness and stupidity. The "vulgar heat" of jealousy and personal interest comes between us and the loving perception of each particular. A novel, just because it is not our life, places us in a moral position that is favorable for perception and it shows us what it would be like to take up that position in life. We find here love without possessiveness, attention without bias, involvement without panic. Our moral abilities must be developed to a certain degree, certainly, before we can approach this novel at all and see anything in it. But it does not seem far-fetched to claim that most of us can read James better than we can read ourselves.

The creation side of the analogy is succinctly expressed in James's claim that "to 'put' things is very exactly and responsibly and interminably to do them" (GB, pref., 25). The claim has, in turn, two aspects. First, it is a claim about the moral responsibility of the novelist, who is bound, drawing on his sense of life, to render the world of value with lucidity, alert and winged. To "put" things is to do an assessible action. The author's conduct is *like* moral conduct at its best, as we have begun to see. But it is more than like it. The artist's task *is* a moral task. By so much as the world is rendered well by some such artist, by so much do we "get the best there is of it, and by so much as it falls within the scope of a denser and duller, a more vulgar and more shallow capacity, do we get a picture dim and meagre" (AN, 67).[13] The whole moral content of the work expresses the artist's sense of life; and for the excellence of this the novelist is, in James's view, rightly held (morally) accountable:

The question comes back thus, obviously, to the kind and the degree of the artist's prime sensibility, which is the soil out of which his subject springs. The quality and capacity of that soil, its ability to "grow" with due freshness and straightness any vision of life, represents, strongly or weakly, the projected morality. (*AN*, 45)

On the other side, the most exact and responsible way of doing is, in fact, a "putting": an achievement of the precisely right description, the correct nuance of tone. Moral experience is an interpretation of the seen, "our apprehension and our measure of what happens to us as social creatures" (*AN*, 64–65). Good moral experience is a lucid apprehension. Like the imaginings and doings of Maggie and Adam, it has precision rather than flatness, sharpness rather than vagueness. It is "the union of whatever fulness with whatever clearness" (*AN*, 240). Not that indeterminacy and mystery are not also there, when the context presents them, as so often in human life it does. But then the thing is to respond to that with the right "*quality* of bewilderment" (*AN*, 66), intense and striving.

Again we can see that there is more than analogy here. Our whole moral task, whether it issues in the words of *The Golden Bowl* or in Maisie's less verbally articulated but no less responsive and intense imaginings, is to make a fine artistic creation. James does not give linguistic representation pride of place: he insists that there is something fine that Maisie's imagination creatively does, which is rightly rendered in his words, even though Maisie herself could not have found those words. Perceptions need not be verbal (*AN*, 145). But he does insist that our whole conduct is *some* form of artistic "putting" and that its assessible virtues are also those for which we look to the novelist.

Two clarifications are in order. First, this is not an aestheticization of the moral; for the creative artist's task is, for James, above all moral, "the expression, the literal squeezing out of value" (*AN*, 312). Second, to call conduct a creation in no way points toward a rootless relativism. For James's idea of creation (like Aristotle's idea of improvisation) is that it is thoroughly committed to the real. "Art deals with what we see . . . it plucks its material in the garden of life" (*AN*, 312). The Jamesian artist does not feel free to create just anything at all: he imagines himself as straining to get it right, not to miss anything, to be keen rather than obtuse. He approaches the material of life armed with the moral and expressive skills that will allow him to "squeeze out" the value that is there.

This ideal makes room, then, for a norm or norms of rightness and for a substantial account of ethical objectivity. The objectivity in question is "internal" and human. It does not even attempt to approach the world as it might be in itself, uninterpreted, unhumanized. Its raw material is the history of human social experience, which is already an interpretation and a measure. But it is objectivity all the same. And this is what makes the person who does the artist's task well so important for others. In the war against moral obtuseness, the artist is our fellow fighter, frequently our guide. We can develop, here, the analogy with our sensory powers that the term *perception* already suggests. In seeing and hearing we are, I believe, seeing not the world as it is in itself, apart from human beings and human conceptual schemes, but a world already interpreted and humanized by our faculties and our concepts. And yet, who could deny that there are some among us whose visual or auditory acuity is greater than that of others; some who have developed their faculties more finely, who can make discriminations of color and shape (of pitch and timbre) that are unavailable to the rest of us? Who miss less, therefore, of what is to be heard or seen in a landscape, a symphony, a painting? Jamesian moral perception is, I think, like this: a fine development of our human capabilities to see and feel and judge; an ability to miss less, to be responsible to more.[14]

V

Is this norm practical? Is there any sense to claiming that the consciousness of a Maggie Verver or a Strether can be paradigmatic of our own responsible conduct? In short (James reports a critic's question), "Where on earth, where roundabout us at this hour," has he found such "supersubtle fry" (*AN*, 221)? And if they are not found, but "squeezed out" from coarser matter by the pressure of the artist's hand, how can they be exemplary for us? James's answer is complex. He grants, first, that he cannot easily cite such examples from daily life (*AN*, 222). He insists, on the other hand, that these characters do not go so far beyond actual life that their lucidity makes them "spoiled for us," "knowing too much and feeling too much . . . for their remaining 'natural' and typical, for their having the needful communities with our own precious liability to fall into traps and be bewildered" (*AN*, 63). Like Aristotle's tragic heroes,[15] they are high but possible and available, so much so that they can be said to be "in *essence* an observed reality" (*AN*, 223). And: if the life around us today does not show us an abundance of such examples, "then so much the worse for that life" (222).

Here the opponent responds that it surely seems odd and oddly arrogant to suggest that the entire nation is dense and dull and that only

Henry James and his characters are finely sensible enough to show us the way. Surely patterns for public life must be nearer to home, straightforwardly descriptive of something that is readily found. James has moved too far away; his sense of life has lost its connection with real life. James's answer is that there is no better way to show one's commitment to the fine possibilities of the actual than (in protest "against the rule of the cheap and easy") to create, in imagination, their actualization:

to *create* the record, in default of any other enjoyment of it: to imagine, in a word, the honourable, the producible case. What better example than this of the high and the helpful public and, as it were, civic use of the imagination? . . . Where is the work of the intelligent painter of life if not precisely in some such aid given to true meanings to be born? He must bear up as he can if it be in consequence laid to him that the flat grows salient and the tangled clear, the common—worst of all!—even amusingly rare, by passing through his hands. (AN, 223–24)

If he has done this—and I think he has—then these alert winged books are not just irreplaceably fine representations of moral achievement, they are moral achievements on behalf of our community. Like Adam Verver's sacrifice: altruism in the right way at the right time in the right images and the right tone, with the right precision of bewilderment.[16]

Notes

1. Henry James, *The Art of the Novel* (New York: Scribner, 1934), 149. For reasons of space, individual preface titles will not be given. The title quotation is from AN, 62.

2. Henry James, *The Princess Casamassima* (New York: Penguin Books, 1977), 133.

3. All page references to *The Golden Bowl* (GB) are to the Penguin Modern Classics edition (New York, 1966).

4. "Flawed Crystals: James's *The Golden Bowl* and Literature as Moral Philosophy," *New Literary History* 15, no. 4 (1983): 25–50. The issue also contains replies to this paper by Richard Wollheim, Patrick Gardiner, and Hilary Putnam, and my reply to them.

5. See Iris Murdoch, *The Sovereignty of Good* (Boston: Routledge & Kegan Paul, 1970).

6. On Aristotle's similar view, see Nussbaum, *The Fragility of Goodness: Luck and Ethics in Greek Tragedy and Philosophy* (Cambridge: Cambridge University Press, 1986), chap. 10; and also Nussbaum, "The Discernment of Per-

ception: An Aristotelian Model for Private and Public Morality," in *Proceedings of the Boston Area Colloquium in Ancient Philosophy*, 1 (1985): 151–200.

7. See also *AN*, 65, where James attacks "the unreality of sharp distinction . . . between doing and feeling . . . I then see their 'doing' . . . as, immensely, their feeling, their feeling as their doing."

8. For the objection, see Putnam's reply in *New Literary History*. For my reply, see also "The Discernment," where I develop the point about improvisation, with reference to Aristotle.

9. For related arguments, see "Flawed Crystals"; *Fragility*, chaps. 1, 2, 6, 10; and "The Discernment."

10. Compare Ludwig Wittgenstein, *Philosophical Investigations*, trans. G. E. M. Anscombe (New York: Macmillan, 1968) pt. 2, sec. 11, 227e:

Correcter prognoses will generally issue from the judgments of those with better knowledge of mankind.

Can one learn from this knowledge? Yes; some can. Not, however, by taking a course in it, but through *"experience."* —Can someone else be a man's teacher in this? Certainly. From time to time he gives him the right *tip.* —This is what "learning" and "teaching" are like here.— What one acquires here is not a technique; one learns correct judgments. There are also rules, but they do not form a system, and only experienced people can apply them right. Unlike calculating-rules.

What is most difficult here is to put this indefiniteness, correctly and unfalsified, into words.

11. I develop this point further in "Love's Knowledge," in *Self-Deception*, ed. Amelie O. Rorty and Brian McLaughlin (Berkeley and Los Angeles: University of California Press, 1987).

12. For development of this point, see Gardiner's reply to "Flawed Crystals," and mine to him.

13. This claim, in context, is actually about the novel's hero or heroine, but it is applied elsewhere to the author: see "Flawed Crystals."

14. This view has strong similarities with the view developed in Nelson Goodman's *Ways of Worldmaking* (Indianapolis: Hackett, 1978). I am grateful to Goodman for helpful comments on an earlier version.

15. On the Aristotelian hero, see *Fragility*, Interlude 2.

16. A shorter version of this article was published under the title "Finely Aware and Richly Responsible: Moral Attention and the Moral Task of Literature," in *Journal of Philosophy* 82 (1985): 516–29, and presented in an American Philosophical Association Symposium on Morality in Literature, 29 December 1985. On that occasion my commentator was Cora Diamond, whose excellent paper (entitled "Missing the Adventure") has contributed in several ways to the development of my views in this present version.

8
Why Intentionalism
Won't Go Away

Within the domain of literary theory, and of aesthetics more generally, idealism may be thought to govern that view according to which the work of art is regarded as the product of human action; idealist criticism accordingly is the attempt to locate the proper categories for the description of action in, or in relation to, the work of art. While idealism in its Hegelian form has come under serious attack from a number of angles, there has more recently been an effort among literary theorists to purify, through critique, those insights of idealism central to the humanistic idea of literature. Charles Altieri's exploration of the concept of expression in the present volume is one such case, as is the essay by Martha Nussbaum, in which Henry James's capacity for the articulate "rendering" of the world is taken as exemplary of the moral task of imaginative literature. We shall again see an engagement with generally idealist notions in the work of Alexander Nehamas, who begins from a discussion of Foucault and proceeds toward a reformulation of the concepts of "writer," "text," "work," and "author."

The present essay on the concept of intentionalism may be regarded as part of the purification of the idealist tradition mentioned above, in among other ways by extending its consideration to include the judgments, evaluations, and cognitive determinations of the literary-critical act. Denis Dutton in essence completes Nussbaum's insights into the qualitative differences between literature and criticism with a series of arguments that demonstrate the continuity of these two forms of writing: the concept of literature as human action which is central to idealism is largely determined by what it makes sense to say, by way of criticism, about a particular text. Contrary to the arguments of Wimsatt and Beardsley, who may be regarded as pillars of the traditional humanistic approach to literature (largely through its manifestation in the form of the New Criticism), Dutton proposes that the concept of intention is ineradicable from any approach to literary theory. Its centrality is indeed suggested by its resilience in the face of attacks not only by the New Criticism but by structuralism and deconstruction as well.

Beginning from certain romantic postulates, Dutton nevertheless finds that the concept of intention at work in existing literary theory needs substantial revision. These are especially the notions that romanticism shares with philosophical idealism, and which would hold that the artist enjoys a privilege of access to the meaning of his or her work and that this meaning may be identified with an "inner state" of the artist's mind. At the same time, Dutton considers several lines of attack against the notion of intention *tout court*: the ordinary-language philosophy of Wittgenstein, developed with respect to the concept of intention by G. E. M. Anscombe, and the deconstruction of intention by Derrida.

Drawing on the notion of "categorial frameworks," Dutton constructs a position that he characterizes as intermediate between romantic intentionalism and the various "deconstructions" of intention named above. Only once a categorial framework for understanding has been established (and the framework would of necessity have to reflect an awareness of intention) can criticism using nonintentionalist criteria be undertaken. This is a position akin to, but not identical with, standard conventionalism. According to that view, the first task of criticism would be to make plain the rules within which the artwork must be understood; yet, Dutton argues, the "purely conventionalist view cannot be the whole story, for there may be cases in which there is simply no recourse in identifying the 'proper' conventions other than to appeal to intentionalist evidence. In literature, this . . . may . . . require a determination of what an actual historical author meant to do in creating a text. For conventions are, after all, *used* by authors and artists."

The notion of intentionalism outlined by Dutton thus also allows for a clarification of some of the difficulties faced by hermeneutic theories of meaning. Dutton's claim is that the concept of intention, or of something very much like it, is necessary in criticism precisely because of the circularity of the hermeneutic circle: there is nothing within the circle itself capable of indicating whether a given interpretation is within the bounds set by the work-as-act; indeed, the most striking examples of misinterpretation (e.g., missed or mistaken ironies, anachronism) may be characterized as "stepping into the wrong [hermeneutic] circle." And, as Dutton goes on to say, "once you have stepped into the wrong hermeneutic circle, there may come to light no obvious evidence to help you overcome your mistake. In such situations, reliance on external evidence, including evidence of intentions, is inevitable." In this way, the concept of intention, not unlike that of the author, may be regarded as irreducibly relevant for the concept of criticism, guiding us in determining what it might make sense to say about a given work of art.

Why Intentionalism Won't Go Away   *Denis Dutton*

Considering the philosophic intelligence that has set out to discredit it, intentionalism in critical interpretation has shown an uncanny resilience. Beginning perhaps most explicitly with the New Criticism, continuing through the analytic tradition in philosophy, and culminating most recently in deconstructionism, philosophers and literary theorists have kept under sustained attack the notion that authorial intention can provide a guide to interpretation, a criterion of textual meaning, or a standard for the validation of criticism. Yet intentionalist criticism still has avid theoretical defenders and plenty of informal practitioners. The essay that follows, while an exercise in neither such defense nor practice, nevertheless attempts to demonstrate why intentional questions can be expected to be of permanent concern to criticism.

The intentionalism Wimsatt and Beardsley objected to in their famous paper, "The Intentional Fallacy," had its roots in romanticism.[1] In many versions, this view has it that the artist is essentially a communicator, one who speaks. His work of art, moreover, possesses a meaning that he alone gives it—indeed, which he alone may truly know. Thus the work of art is a bridge to the mind of the artist, and finding out what it means requires finding out what it means or meant to its creator. The work of art unlocks, as it were, the secrets of the artist's inner life, and since the artist may be a woman or man of genius, those secrets may be well worth knowing.

Romantic intentionalism embodies several different ideas that, for diverse reasons, have come under periodic scrutiny in the history of philosophy. First, and perhaps most fundamentally, it presupposes that the artist has some clear idea of the meaning of his or her work. However imperfectly the work may have been executed, however wanting in clarity or craft, on this view the artist at least is in the best possible position to understand what it truly means. Again, this original meaning—or originary meaning—can be identified as some sort of *inner state* of the artistic mind: an intention, a purpose, a project. Perhaps it will additionally include associated images, forms, narrative elements, personalities of characters, emotion, and other imaginative paraphernalia the artist employs. To all of this, the artist is supposed to possess privileged access.

Characterized in this way, romantic intentionalism may seem a bit faded and tattered, but it should not be forgotten that aspects of it have exercised a strong hold on important philosophers of art. Goethe insisted that one cannot know what an artist has achieved without first knowing what he intended to do. Tolstoy accepted it, though he allowed that through a lack of what he termed *clarity* artistic ideas often fail to be communicated, and for him expressive communication was fundamental to the experience of art. And most recently, in championing the cause, E. D. Hirsch, Jr., has provided a target for old New Critics, reborn New Critics, deconstructionists, and other modern anti-intentionalists.[2]

Hirsch's intentionalism stands apart from that of someone like Tolstoy because it is not so much a particular conception of art which motivates him to adopt it as it is a strongly held view of criticism. For Hirsch, unless we have a standard of interpretive correctness, criticism loses its status as a *cognitive* discipline. Without a notion of the author's meaning as a guide—almost a regulative ideal, it would seem—criticism would be unable to decide between competing interpretations of works of literature (or art). The result, for Hirsch, would be chaos: anybody's interpretation as good as anybody else's. Hirsch does not deny, of course, that works of art may mean different things to critics or to audiences in different historical epochs. This is in fact how it is that works of art can have different *significances* to people. But the meaning of a text is always one and the same thing: it is a meaning that the work had for its maker, the artist or writer.

Detractors of Hirsch's brand of intentionalism have not always criticized it with the aim of trying to subvert the cognitive status of criticism. Monroe Beardsley is a good example, and he carried on the attack against intentionalism in his later years, particularly in his provocative little book, *The Possibility of Criticism*.[3] He provides in that volume three principal arguments against the idea that the meaning of a literary text must be understood as the meaning that it had to its author. First, that we can read and understand texts that have meaning independent of authorial intention is shown by the fact that computer-generated texts are meaningful, and that texts with significant or interesting typographical errors are meaningful (consider the so-called newsbreaks the *New Yorker* uses to fill an odd column). As he puts it, these texts have meaning, "but nothing was meant by anyone" (19). In the second place, the meaning of a text can change after the author has died (or, by implication, we may suppose, an hour after he or she wrote it). To quote Beardsley again, "And if today's textual meaning [of a line of poetry] cannot be identified with any authorial meaning, it follows that textual meanings are not the same thing as authorial meanings" (20). Finally, Beardsley argues that because a text can have meanings an author was not aware of, it again follows that textual meanings are not identical with authorial meanings.

Before examining some implications of these arguments, I should note why Beardsley wishes to adduce them in the first place. That authors have intentions, and that those intentions are found embodied in texts, is something he does not seriously question. In this respect, his attitude remains unchanged from "The Intentional Fallacy," where he and Wimsatt wrote that "the design or intention of the author is neither available nor desirable as a standard for judging the success of a work of literary art." In fact, they define "intention" straightforwardly as "design or plan in the author's mind." The terms *availability* and *desirability* suggest two conventional lines of argument which have been brought to bear against intentionalism. Authorial intentions are not desirable as a "standard" or "criterion" for assessing a literary text because the text itself will always speak with greater authority than any suppositions or speculations about the author's purposes. After all, rewarding criticism can in many cases be carried out even when we have little or no idea of an author's intentions (the interpretation of classical texts, for example); the author's intended meaning often strikes us as crazy, or at least eccentric (part of the point insisted upon by Socrates in the *Ion*); and we know that in any event authors are forever changing, adjusting, and altering their plans and designs as they create—authorial intention is not just one coherent thing from beginning to end of the creative process.[4]

Yet this last observation I take to be different from the previous points. The previous considerations are essentially *epistemic*: they are concerned with what we can ever know about such things as authorial intentions. In many cases we can know with certainty little or nothing. Moreover, often what we think we know comes in direct conflict with the evidence for meaning which is directly and publicly provided by the text itself and is therefore dispensable. It seems to me that within analytic philosophy, assaults on intentionalist criticism have tended to have this epistemic origin; they are based on the realization that often there is little that we can reliably know about intentions of authors, and in any event such knowledge could never match in weight our immediate and determinate knowledge of the text at hand.

But the assertion that authorial intention is not a stable, identifiable mental state that can be appealed to in interpretation suggests another line of argument different from this epistemic consideration of the uncertainties about intentions. This is the *metaphysical* attack on intentionalism. It is the line of argument which holds that it is the very concept of an intention itself, some purposing or designing mental state, which is in doubt. This form of attack is most associated with Derrida's general debunking of the concept of presence, though it has clear analogies in the analytic tradition. In particular, the Wittgensteinian treatment, one might say deconstruction, of "understanding" as a mental state, along with, for example, G. E. M. Anscombe's and Jack Meiland's thorough explications of intention, belongs to this tradition.[5] I term this form of attack metaphysical, not because it is necessarily tied to some grand philosophic system, but because it is directed to the ontological status of the intentional state itself. The analytic (usually epistemic) school says to intentionalist criticism that we cannot ever know with certainty what authorial intentions are or were; the deconstructionist (usually metaphysical) school says not to worry, there is nothing to be known. (This is part of what is implied by the slogan that there is nothing outside the text.)

Again, on both sides of the English Channel both lines of attack have been put to use. Derrida has mounted epistemic arguments, and Wittgensteinian influence has made metaphysical arguments familiar to writers in the analytic tradition. So, given the widespread acceptance of either or both of these forms of assault on intentionalism, why doesn't it simply die? Why isn't it given up as irrelevant to criticism, in the same way that, for example, the intuitive feeling of certainty has long been discarded as a criterion for the validity of empirical knowledge claims?

We can begin to understand why by considering an example. Some years ago I came across the following passage in Robert Redfield's *Primitive World and Its Transformations*: "Ruth Bunzel, studying Pueblo potters, found that the Indian woman who was *in fact copying* the designs of other potters with only the smallest variations was *unaware that she copied*, condemned copying as wrong, and had a strong conviction that she was in fact inventive and creative."[6] That there was something wrong with this report seemed certain, and subsequent research confirmed this initial reaction. In fact, Bunzel's interpretation of Hopi pottery decorating practices, which leads her to the astounding conclusion that Hopi potters are suffering from some sort of mass delusion with regard to their own view of their originality, may be based on an instructive misunderstanding of what Indians are up to in decorating pots. Bunzel claims to have noticed that the Indian women *copy* one another, though they themselves vehemently deny this. She tells us that they suffer from a "sterility of imagination," that the whole matter is a "very simple and rather amusing" failure to align their ideals of creativity with their actual practices of plagiarism.[7] But is this the case? Suppose a Hopi anthropologist were to travel to New York to study the art of piano playing as carried on by some of the more famous practitioners of keyboard performance. He goes to Carnegie Hall one night and hears Ashkenazy play a Schubert sonata; the next night he returns to hear Pollini, who as luck would have it, happens to be performing the very same Schubert work. As he exits the hall, our Hopi social scientist exclaims that despite the enormous claims that are made for the artistic creativity of Mr. Pollini, it is clear that he merely "copied," with "only the smallest variations," Ashkenazy's piano playing of the night before.

In fact, there is considerable evidence to bear out the view that Ruth Bunzel misunderstands Hopi pottery decoration practices in a way that is very close to our fictional Hopi anthropologist. It may well be that inventing entirely new designs is simply not what counts as "being original" in painting pots, but rather the inventive use of designs and motifs already in, as it were, the established decorative repertoire. In this sense, painting a pot may be more like performing from a score than it is like composing a new work, either in music or in pottery decoration.

Now if I am right with regard to this example, take note of what it *does not* illustrate: it is not as though Bunzel has failed, for example, to understand the meaning of some particular symbol in pottery design; nor is it as though she has mistaken, perhaps, a pot used in one sort of ceremony for a pot used in another. Rather, it is that she has at some deeper level misunderstood the whole point of pot decoration, by failing to grasp what counts as originality. And if she misunderstands in this fundamental way what the Hopi are engaged in, misunderstands their purposes in trying to achieve originality in decorating pots, then careful attention to the details of their behavior will, far from tending to show how they are being misinterpreted, show only how closely they "really are" copying one another. (Just as tape recordings of Ashkenazy and Pollini would only have served to confirm to the Hopi social scientist that Pollini "really was" copying the other pianist.)

What kind of mistake did she make? Apparently she misconstrued the practice in question at so primitive a level that continuing research based on the mistake could not work to overturn it. To the contrary, it could only work further to confirm it. By misconstruing in this way something taken for granted by the potters, she has miscategorized their activity. And it is this assignment of the practice to the wrong category of activity which poses the most interesting questions in connection with artistic or authorial intention.

In every respect, Beardsley has seemed to want to exclude appeals to intention as relevant to criticism as it ought to be conducted. Equally insistent have been theorists such as Hirsch or Betti in claiming that authorial intentions are the central criterion for interpretive validity. But the case of the Pueblo potters suggests a third, perhaps intermediate position. For once a categorial framework for understanding has been established (using intentionalist criteria), it might be argued that only then can criticism be undertaken (using nonintentionalist criteria). Some theorists might claim that this would be less a matter of granting a privileged status to the intentions of artists and more one of understanding the proper conventions within which the art object must be understood. Yet such a purely conventionalist view cannot be the whole story, for there may be cases in which there is simply no recourse in identifying the "proper" conventions other than to appeal to intentionalist evidence. In literature, this is not just a question of voice, of persona, of fictional narrator or implied author: it may also require a determination of what an actual historical author meant to do in creating a text. For conventions are, after all, *used* by authors and artists.

Anthropological examples, such as those provided by Bunzel's discussion of Hopi potters, are particularly illuminating because in ethnographic contexts we are much less tempted to apply ready-made conventions than we are in, say, reading nineteenth-century novels. Such contexts deny us the comfort of relying on a standard repertoire of familiar genres. We are more likely to be forced to ask in such situations, What are these people up to? Having grasped that, we may come to understand a convention well enough to dispense with intentional appeals in ordinary interpretive moments; but this does not entail the irrelevance of intentions—it is only by virtue of having established so much familiarity with intentions that we can afford to disregard them and talk only of conventions. Intentions are thus not ignored by appeals to conventions; such appeals presuppose them.

Irony is revealing in this connection because here again intentions appear to constitute a bedrock without which valid interpretation is impossible. Consider Strauss's only work for piano and orchestra, his *Berleske*, written in 1885. The innocent listener who supposes the piece to be a straight attempt to compose a one-movement piano concerto will no doubt find it in many ways attractive and rewarding. But the meaning, for example, of Strauss's mad double-octave passages, which evaporate at the top of the keyboard (rather than leading into big cadences), or the long runs that go nowhere, will elude such a listener. In this instance the composer has helpfully provided a title that gives a hint that the work is intended as a sendup of the romantic virtuoso piano concerto. But authors are not always so helpful; and in any event, whether they are is immaterial so far as the purely conceptual question is concerned.

In this dispute between Beardsley and various intentionalist theorists, I have long felt Beardsley's arguments to be the more persuasive. But they do not address the crucial question of assignment of a work to its genre. Certainly once a categorial framework for critical understanding has been established, then, *pace* Hirsch, the artist's own view cannot be taken as privileged, but I would persist that intentions cannot be irrelevant to establishing that framework. Beardsley denies this with specific reference to irony: he says that if a poem is to be taken as ironic, then the "alleged irony" must be supported by analysis of the text. But in understanding a piece of ironic writing, it is not always enough simply to attend to the text, as though it can always be relied upon to supply internal clues to its ironic status. On the contrary, it may presuppose an understanding between author and reader which is excluded from the text precisely in being taken for granted, presupposed by both sides.

The phenomenon I am describing can be explained in terms of the hermeneutic circle. Accounts of the hermeneutic circle usually have it that one comes to understand a text by an increasing grasp of the reciprocal relation between parts and whole. One develops, or maybe just guesses at, a conception of the whole meaning and then proceeds to interpret individual elements of it in line with this hypothesis about the nature of the whole. This procedure need not be viewed as vacuous or trivially self-validating, because one can revise or correct a misapprehension about either a part of the text or the whole of the text in light of the ways that it fails to cohere with the rest of one's interpretation. However, the point to note is that there is no guarantee that some false hypothesis about the nature of the whole, once formed, will be overturned by an examination of the parts. To the contrary, the hypothesis may entail an intepretation of the meaning of the parts which continues indefinitely to support the hypothesis. Thus with examples of misinterpretation I have so far mentioned—supposing that the point of Pueblo pottery decoration is the creation of new designs or imagining Strauss's *Berleske* to be a serious attempt to add to the literature of the romantic piano concerto—we are faced with a situation that can be characterized as stepping into the wrong circle. The lesson here for the theory of interpretation is that once you have stepped into the wrong hermeneutic circle, there may come to light no obvious evidence to help you overcome your mistake. In such situations, reliance on external evidence, including evidence of intentions, is inevitable.

Conventionalism is usually presented as the required alternative to the view being presented here. It holds that it is not knowledge of intentions which makes possible ironic readings of texts, but familiarity with literary conventions, including those used in irony. And skillful ironists do indeed often supply their readers with conventional clues to their ironic intent. But the ways of the ironist are many and varied, and there is no guarantee that any particular text will contain suitable clues that will let the reader in. Exclusion, in fact, may be part of the author's design. David Kaufer has discussed irony in terms of "audience bifurcation," a strategy with which an ironist divides his potential audience into *confederates* with whom he shares his irony and *victims* against whom he uses it.[8] This useful distinction suggests that there may be instances in which an author shares irony with his confederates while leaving his victims innocent. Many ironists, from Swift to Art Buchwald, have laced their texts with cues indicating how they are to be taken, but it is also possible for the ironist to refrain from doing this in order not to let his victims in on the joke. In such cases, irony is a particular use of conventions, rather than the use of particular (i.e., ironic) conventions.

Victims may include members of the author's audience, another author, or, implicitly, another author's audience. Wayne Booth has provided a delicious example of such victimization in David Hume's account of Charles I awaiting execution: "While everything around him bore a hostile aspect, he reposed himself with confidence in the arms of that Being, who penetrates and sustains all nature, and whose severities, if received with piety and resignation, he regarded as the surest pledge of unexhausted favour."[9] How do we know that this sentence is heavily ironic? Not by any cues, hints, or conventions, nor by anything in the context of its appearance. Rather, it is against the background of Hume's whole life and philosophy that we understand it. Enjoyment of it can only be derived by treating it as an intentional act of the historical David Hume.

The idea of an author victimizing a reader, of leading a reader down the garden path, inviting him to step into the wrong hermeneutic circle, as much necessitates that there be a real historical author as it requires a real historical reader to step into it. Some eighteenth-century readers would have heaved a sigh at Hume's description of Charles I: they are his intended victims, and those who enjoy the thought are his confederates. But the relish that might be received from the passage depends on its having been written by an actual historical figure, David Hume.

In this connection, some recent treatments of the question of intentionality in literary interpretation have in my view fallen short of the mark. Alexander Nehamas and Roger Scruton have both written essays that to all appearances set out to find some legitimate place for intentionalist criticism. And both end by almost, but not quite, embracing the notion that reference to a historical author is necessary to criticism. Nehamas allow that texts must be understood as the products of human agents, but then takes back what he seems to have granted when he says that "just as the author is not identical with a text's fictional narrator, so he is also distinct from its historical writer. The author is postulated as the agent whose actions account for the text's features; he is a character, a hypothesis which is accepted provisionally, guides interpretation, and is in turn modified in its light. The author, unlike the writer, is not a text's efficient cause but, so to speak, its formal cause, manifested in though not identical with it."[10]

This is a case of wanting to have the methodological advantages conferred by affirming the critical relevance of authorship without incurring the problems, epistemic but probably also metaphysical, of having to identify actual historical authors and their intentions. A similar strategy can be detected in Scruton's essay, "Public Text and Common Reader." Scruton is opposed to currents in contemporary philosophy which would advance the idea that "anything goes" in aesthetic interpretation. He distinguishes the meaning of a text from the fortuitous associations it may have for a reader or critic—the former in the text, the latter not—and then goes on to say that "part of what enables us to make this distinction lies in a 'sense of intention' with which every work of art is imbued."[11] Scruton does not take this as implying that a work of art must mean what the author intended, though he does think that any meaning imputed to the work must be one that the author might have entertained. And his point, consistent as it is with Kant's dictum of the work of art as possessing purposiveness without purpose, is well taken. But it does not cover every case, for it is not merely a felt sense of intention which is at issue in some instances of irony, but rather the recognition that the reader, text, and (actual, historical) author stand in a particular relation. Especially in cases that victimize some individual or group, a postulated, fictive, or implied author is insufficient to provide anything more than a postulated, fictive, or implied irony. Yet real irony of this sort exists and is found in literature.

Implied author theories of criticism tend to accompany psychologized theories of literary response, theories that try to sidestep difficulties of the reference of the literary work, the existence of the historical author, and the relation of the work to its traditions by concentrating attention on the reader's response. Even Gadamerian hermeneutics is not immune from milder forms of such subjectivist tendencies in stressing that the best or most adequate interpretation of a work of art is the one according to which the work is seen as the richest, the most rewarding, the most profound. This is a tempting view, and if it could be demonstrated with finality it would place in doubt the kind of intentionalism I have been arguing for here. A version of the argument (one not necessarily derived from Gadamer) is found in Laurent Stern's article "On Interpreting." According to Stern, "If there is agreement on the canonical status of a text [i.e., if it can be agreed upon that a text is a work of art], then among two competing interpretations that may equally fit the text, the one which assigns greater value and significance to the text will be preferred."[12] Stern makes this claim in the context of a discussion of irony, a discussion that attempts to discredit the idea that ironic works are decisive in supporting the need for appeals to authorial intentions in textual interpretation. Thus Stern tells us that Defoe's *Shortest Way with the Dissenters* admits of two interpretations, literal and ironic, but it is much better understood as a piece of irony, even without any external evidence. Similarly, *A Modest Pro-*

posal ought to be considered ironic because it is a more valuable text read in that way and would be difficult to understand at all taken literally.

I have nothing to disagree with in Stern's account of these two examples; but the question remains whether they can be marshaled in support of a *general* rejection of the need for intentional reference in identifying cases of irony. That they do not support this form of anti-intentionalism, and that therefore it is not the case that the best interpretation is inevitably the one under which the work of art is seen to possess the greatest significance or value, can be shown by considering cases of bad art, something like Richard Bach's *Jonathan Livingston Seagull*. There is no doubt that Bach intended this little book (one may think of it as a very long greeting card) to be a serious work of literature with important messages for the human spirit. But in fact it would have had greater value and significance had he meant it as a sendup of inspirational literature. It would have been better as a lampoon: one could laugh with it, instead of at it. Yet even if it is seen in the best light and taken as ironic, we cannot do so if we have sufficient evidence that Bach did not intend it to be so taken. The closest Stern comes to considering this question is to remark that *The Shortest Way* would be merely "a historical document of some marginal interest" were we to take it literally. But if it were meant to be taken straight, we could not take it ironically and thus endow the work with an illusory significance and value.

It is not up to interpreters arbitrarily to impose conventions in order to produce an interpretation according to which the work seems best: this would be to stretch charity beyond the limit. In considering the poetic achievements of such notables as William McGonagall (sometimes called "The World's Worst Poet") and Julia A. Moore (more affectionately known as the "Sweet Singer of Michigan"), Stephen Leacock coined the term *supercomic*. Merely comic poets, such as Ogden Nash, produce work that belongs to an entirely different category of expression from the supercomic. To attain the status of the supercomic a poet must write stunningly bad verse and do so with great earnestness. It is a category that depends for its very existence on an author's having intentions of a certain sort, specifically *not* ironic. As it is, there are no conventions at all peculiar to supercomic verse: seriousness of purpose and sublime ineptitude are its only requirements.

Like the previously discussed cases of stepping into the wrong hermeneutic circle, whether a text can be taken as ironic entails questions about what it makes sense to say about a work of literary art. And there remains at least one more area where there is a relevance to authorial intention with respect to the limits of critical sense: anachronism. In his defense of "the authority of the text," Beardsley cites some lines written in the eighteenth century: "Yet, by immense benignity inclin'd/To spread about him that primeval job/Which fill'd himself, he rais'd his plastic arm." "Plastic" has not completely lost the meaning it had for the poet, Mark Akenside, in 1744, but it has gained an additional meaning since then. "Consequently," Beardsley says, "the line in which it occurs has . . . acquired a new meaning . . . . Of course, we can inquire into both meanings, if we will; but these are two distinct inquiries. And if today's textual meaning of the line cannot be identified with any authorial meaning, it follows that textual meanings are not the same thing as authorial meaning."[13]

Yet, how many readers would have any interest whatever in an interpretation of the poem which took "plastic" in this case to refer to that polymer material found everywhere these days? It is not that such an anachronistic interpretation is out of line with Akenside's intentions so much as it does not accord with *any possible intention* he might have had. An article by Jack Meiland presents the intentionalism question in a way that is useful in understanding this issue. In his own defense of the anti-intentionalist position, Meiland argues that criticism ought to concern itself with the possible meanings of texts, rather than with authorial intentions. He cites remarks by Gerald Graff opposed to this view saying that actuality is more important and more interesting than possibility, hence we ought to focus critical attention on the actual meanings of a text for its author, rather than the text's merely possible meanings. Between these two positions it is fairly obvious that there is a third, which has been overlooked. Meiland may be right in making possible meanings more significant to criticism than actual (authorial) meanings, but he is wrong to suggest that criticism might concern itself purely with possible textual meanings ("word-sequence" meanings, he calls them), while completely ignoring authorial intention. The reason is that such a program would allow outrageously anachronistic readings of texts. Meiland says that "in the case of a word sequence there *cannot* be a privileged meaning."[14] But even a criticism that refused to make privileged the author's intention as determining textual meaning would nevertheless leave something privileged: not a single authorial meaning, but rather all the possible meanings the author could have had. In this way, criticism maintains a link to authorial intention—not necessarily to any actual intention but as a minimum qualification to possible authorial intentions. This has the negative effect of ruling out interpretations that, though possible according to one set of conventions or another, would have been nonsensical or otherwise unintelligible to the author.

This consideration adequately accounts for Akenside's use of "plastic" and can be made clearer by applying it to another, more famous example. In the "Jerusalem" lyric of *Milton*, William Blake asks, "And was Jerusalem builded here/Among these dark Satanic mills?" and critics have since in their turn asked, What does "mills" mean? Harold Bloom, among others, tells us that contrary to appearances these mills have "nothing to do with industrialism";[15] perhaps they refer in some way to the wheels of Newtonian science. I would not wish to settle the issue, except to this extent: even if biographical scholarship tells us that Blake did not mean to refer to industrial mills, we must still ask if that was something he could have meant, or if such an interpretation would be anachronistic or otherwise unintelligible to Blake. A trip to the *OED* does reveal in this case that Blake could indeed have intended a reference to industrial mills, so Bloom is perhaps a bit hasty in writing the meaning off. But the principle that links the text to its author still holds: we will allow in court only the meanings that the words might possibly have had for Blake, not the meanings they might possibly have for anybody, anytime. (This is not, of course, to say that the lines cannot make significant commentary on modern conditions Blake could not know about; but the application of a poem to later conditions is not anachronistic in the sense being discussed.)

Again, the predictable challenge will come from conventionalists claiming that it is enough to know the conventions of the time which were available to an author, the purely personal or psychological aspects of the words for the author being generally beyond the interests of criticism, though not of biography. But I do not think it will ever be possible to separate criticism and biography in so tidy a manner as is required by conventionalism and its textualist variants—the intricacies of Blake interpretation demonstrate this as clearly as any example. Granted, to be sure, that the meanings of texts are hardly exhausted by what they meant to their authors, it remains nevertheless that, since words and texts are used by authors for myriad purposes, their intentions will never be found generally irrelevant to some of the interesting and legitimate things that critics may sometimes wish to say about some texts.

Note well that this does not amount to trying to legislate some permanent and predetermined place for authorial intention in the edifice of criticism. For it seems to me that progress on this question has been blocked by just that attitude. Criticism is no more an edifice than literature is a multinational corporation. The contexts of critical practice are as varied as those of literature itself, and I do not foresee the day when the place of authorial intention within it (or without it) will be determined once and for all. This is the essential fault of such works as Hirsch's *Validity in Interpretation* and Peter Juhl's *Interpretation: An Essay in the Philosophy of Literary Criticism*,[16] and from the other side of the dispute it shows itself in Roland Barthes's programmatic essay "The Death of the Author." Barthes says, "It is language which speaks, not the author," an interest in whom is "the epitome and culmination of capitalist ideology" and, even perhaps more unforgivably, "positivism." Writing is the "destruction of every voice, of every point of origin," and once the author is out of the way, criticism's "claim to decipher a text becomes quite futile." "We know now that a text is not a line of words releasing a single 'theological' meaning (the 'message' of the Author-God) but a multi-dimensional space in which a variety of writings, none of them original, blend and clash." The image of the author as God, with the critic presumably as priest, "suits criticism very well, the latter then allotting itself the important task of discovering the Author . . . beneath the work: when the author has been found, the text is 'explained'—victory to the critic."[17]

By presenting such a wildly overdrawn caricature of "criticism," Barthes ipso facto provides a caricature of his own version of textualism. "Criticism" is not the methodologically unified pattern of practice that Barthes describes (any more than "philosophy" is the coherent body of received opinion, something like Catholicism, that Derrida habitually talks about). Barthes does share, despite himself, at least one thing in common with the positivism he so detests: a yearning for some final, determinate place for the concept of the author in—or banished from—criticism.

My own recommendations are rather less grandiose. We must recognize that sometimes part of our interest in literary texts may be in how they have been made and used by authors in the historical traditions and contexts of their genesis. To acknowledge this would not be to deify the author or to refuse to see the extent to which traditions, and indeed language itself, help to "make" texts. It would not be to identify a putative sole meaning of a text with an author's intention; even less should it imagine that texts could ever have single, determinate meanings. But it might, contra Beardsley, find a legitimate place for authorial intention in criticism, and it might, contra Barthes, set some limits on what we find worthwhile talking about in criticism. Not that these limits should be feared as oppressive, since they will doubtless turn out to be the ones already tacitly followed: I know of no critic yet ready to recommend unself-conscious anachronism in the reading of seventeenth-century poetry. Whimsy, *jeu* if you wish, might occasionally enable an amusing or illuminating remark about Akenside's use of "plastic" in relation to the modern sense of the word as "polymer." But simply and ignorantly to read his "plastic" as our "polymer" doesn't go: and if it doesn't, then there never was a textualism in which "anything goes."

The other limits involved in what criticism allows that it make sense to say—assigning a work to a category, most conspicuously with regard to its possibly ironic aspects—will also observe boundaries in place. A systematic treatment of these limits would have to take full cognizance of the epistemic constraints on intentionalism stressed by the analytic philosophical tradition, as well as the metaphysical attack on authorial presence mounted by deconstructionism. But just as Hume's critique of causality did not prevent him from playing billiards, and Derrida's deconstruction of presence does not keep him from being absent from, present at, or sleeping through seminars, so I think criticism will find itself better informed but not radically altered by the incorporation of these insights. Despite the many uncertainties, such a New Intentionalism would ask that we take into account—to the extent that we find it intelligent or enlightening—the author's view of her or his own work, including how that stands against the rest of literary or human history. In a remarkable passage calling for a typology of forms of iteration used in performative utterances, Derrida strikes an uncharacteristically reasonable chord: "In this typology, the category of intention will not disappear; it will have its place, but from this place it will no longer be able to govern the entire scene and the entire system of utterances."[18] Not even in Austin was it ever able to govern the entire system—but that is another matter. It is time for a systematic examination and restoration of the concept of intention in criticism.[19]

Notes

1. William K. Wimsatt and Monroe C. Beardsley, "The Intentional Fallacy," *Sewanee Review* 54 (1946): 568–88.

2. E. D. Hirsch, Jr., *Validity in Interpretation* (New Haven: Yale University Press, 1967), and *The Aims of Interpretation* (Chicago: University of Chicago Press, 1976).

3. Monroe C. Beardsley, *The Possibility of Criticism* (Detroit: Wayne State University Press, 1970), esp. chap. 1.

4. A good summary of the objections to intentionalism can be found in William R. Schroeder, "A Teachable Theory of Interpretation," in *Theory in the Classroom*, ed. Cary Nelson (Champaign: University of Illinois Press, 1986), 9–44.

5. G. E. M. Anscombe, *Intention* (Oxford: Basil Blackwell, 1957); Jack Meiland, *The Nature of Intention* (London: Methuen, 1970).

6. Robert Redfield, *The Primitive World and Its Transformations* (Ithaca: Cornell University Press, 1953), 15 (emphasis added). I am indebted to Jenifer Onstott Ring for having first brought this book to my attention.

7. Ruth Bunzel, *The Pueblo Potter: A Study of the Creative Imagination in Primitive Art* (New York: Columbia University Press, 1929), 51–54. I have discussed this and other aspects of Bunzel's monograph in "To Understand It on Its Own Terms," *Philosophy and Phenomenological Research* 35 (1974): 246–56, and esp. in "Art, Behavior, and the Anthropologists," *Current Anthropology* 18 (1977): 387–407.

8. David Kaufer, "Irony and Rhetorical Strategy," *Philosophy and Rhetoric* 10 (1977): 90–110. Kaufer refuses fully to endorse the confederate/victim distinction because the reader may understand irony without considering herself or himself either.

9. Wayne C. Booth, *A Rhetoric of Irony* (Chicago: University of Chicago Press, 1974), 3–4. The quotation is from the *History of England*. Booth's book has become a standard treatment of the topic of irony.

10. Alexander Nehamas, "The Postulated Author: Critical Monism as a Regulative Ideal," *Critical Inquiry* 8 (1981): 133–49. The quotation, given correctly here from Nehamas's typescript, was published erroneously (145) with "thought" instead of "though" in the last clause.

11. Roger Scruton, "Public Text and Common Reader," in *The Aesthetic Understanding* (London: Methuen, 1983), 30.

12. Laurent Stern, "On Interpreting," *Journal of Aesthetics and Art Criticism*, 39 (1980): 124.

13. *Possibility of Criticism*, 19–20.

14. Jack W. Meiland, "The Meanings of a Text," *British Journal of Aesthetics* 21 (1981): 199 (emphasis in original).

15. Harold Bloom, *Blake's Apocalypse* (Garden City, N.Y.: Anchor Books, 1963), 335.

16. P. D. Juhl, *Interpretation: An Essay in the Philosophy of Literary Criticism* (Princeton: Princeton University Press, 1980). Martin Warner has written a most insightful review of this book for *Philosophy and Literature* 6 (1982): 172–79.

17. Roland Barthes, "The Death of the Author," in *Image/Music/Text*, trans. Stephen Heath (New York: Hill & Wang, 1977), 142–48.

18. Jacques Derrida, "Signature Event Context," in *Margins of Philosophy*, trans. Alan Bass (Chicago: University of Chicago Press, 1983), 326.

19. My thoughts on these issues have been enriched by discussions with Neil Flax, Jack Meiland, David Novitz, Edward Sayles, and Denis Walker.

9
The Limits of
Interpretation

Current interest in the relationship between philosophy and literature may in part be traced to the desire among literary theorists to find an adequate theory of interpretation. In some of its more sophisticated manifestations, literary theory has looked to philosophical hermeneutics for guidance in this task. In the following essay, which questions whether a theory of interpretation may be possible at all, Stanley Rosen characterizes this apparent increase in sophistication as showing a narrowing of range and a loss of creative impetus in which literature deteriorates into criticism (in *Allegories of Reading*, Paul de Man insisted that the difference between them was a "delusion"). The contemporary crisis of interpretation, about which we are, in Rosen's view, symptomatically reticent to speak, is marked by all the features of a decline; indeed, the age of hermeneutics might be described as the age of decadence. The difference between where we now stand and where Schleiermacher and Dilthey once stood (which some would call the "postmodern" difference) is that the reading of theory and criticism has now become problematic as well: "The necessity of metahermeneutics has led to the paradoxical proliferation of popular accounts or academic introductions to the esoteric documents of hermeneutics. . . . The difficulty is analogous to that posed by Hegel and Wittgenstein in their respective attempts to make an absolute entrance into the absolute."

It would be easy to read Rosen's opening remarks as signaling a rejection of theory or of the need for sound methods of reading. As he goes on to explain, however, his purpose is to suggest that a theory of interpretation is impossible—given certain assumptions about what in fact constitutes a theory (e.g., completeness) and about what its proper objects should be (objects of human culture). Rather than repudiate Gadamer or Derrida, Rosen seeks to show that their suggestions are valuable "despite the incoherence of their theoretical substructure. There is no theoretical substructure of reading *or* of writing; there is only the infrastructure of the reader and the writer." Read in a different light than may be intended here, such a statement might be taken as a warrant for the postmodern pragmatism that Berel Lang describes. But this need not be so. One might also proceed from the fact that reading and writing possess an infrastructure but no substructure to a formulation of the ethical demands that reading makes, a point that is germane to what both Nussbaum and Altieri have to say. Rosen's purpose is somewhat different. His concern is to show how the failure of theory follows from certain facts about human nature which the temptation to theory may have led us to forget: "Reading and writing are confirmations of Nietzsche's epigram that man is the unfinished animal. But this is precisely human nature: to be unfinished, and hence, to exist partially as the thinking or theorizing animal, the animal who is looking for completeness." This sets possible limits on the scope of literary theory, but cannot be taken as a warrant against the theoretical project.

Rosen regards the advent of the decadent, hermeneutic age as following historically the displacement of *phronēsis*, the pretheoretical domain of common sense, by theoretical construction. Perhaps since Bacon, probably since Descartes and Vico, and certainly since the time of Kant, our conception of theory has been dissociated from its ancient etymology and sense; in its ancient form, theory was not restricted to the vision of pure forms but also embraced human nature and deeds. Here Rosen provides additional background on the historical process by which nature, including human nature, became an object of (theoretical) knowledge, as I say in my essay on romantic responses to Kant. The problem that ensued as theory gained increasing ground at the expense of *phronēsis* was the self-vitiating expansion and multiplication of theory, which was itself a consequence of the need to find ways to judge among proliferating theories that generated their own presuppositions.

Readers familiar with the work of Heidegger will be relatively unsurprised by Rosen's introduction of the question of ontology at this point in his argument. Heidegger's ontology in *Being and Time* is not only a phenomenology of being but a hermeneutic of the world. This confirms Rosen's earlier suggestion that, in the hermeneutic age, ontology and interpretation are one and the same. Derrida, glossing Heidegger, might say that Being is a text; one might argue along the same lines, as theorists of reading and subjectivity have done, that the self is a text. I can imagine that one might rally to Heidegger's defense by proposing a reading of *Being and Time* as a novelistic text, but Rosen could anticipate this strategic move and claim that its limitations are shown up by Heidegger himself: "If the world is a text, then we who read it are nothing more than characters in its antiplot. It is no longer meaningful to speak of 'understanding' or 'interpreting,' and the ostensible freedom from the domination of classical metaphysics becomes simply another version of *amor fati*."

In the context of postontological deconstruction, Heidegger appears as a surprisingly traditional rationalist who confirms the distinction between mathematical reason and poetry. This does not, of course, keep Rosen from recognizing the unorthodox and esoteric strains in Derrida's thought, but Derridean deconstruction, he says, stands to ontological hermeneutics as does negative to positive theology. Ontological hermeneutics may be said to be similar to contemporary mathematical theory (and hence representative of a more general crisis of theory in our time) in two discernable ways. The mathematical cast of hermeneutics makes itself evident in that (1) one theory (a local theory of the text as "intentional artifact") is given a presumably grounding interpretation within another, more general theory; and that (2) the ontological theory is itself a "system of judgments rather than of propositions, because what the ontologist means by 'theory' is precisely 'interpretation.'" This latter fact might be taken as a cardinal hermeneutic rule.

If Rosen's arguments can indeed be granted, then a theory of interpretation is impossible, given the operating assumptions of contemporary theoreticians of interpretation. And yet this incoherence may serve to show us something about the objects of interpretation which had previously gone unremarked. Rosen's conclusion formulates technically what may well be the only sound reason for any possible resistance to theory at all, that is, the need to recognize the "pretheoretical talent of natural reason (sometimes called *phronēsis*), or . . . the domain upon which the talent may be exercised." I would formulate this as the need to recognize the proper place of insight in our relationship to literary texts, both in their making and in their reading, a place that may precede the claims that will be required by any theory of interpretation.

The Limits of
Interpretation

Stanley Rosen

I

Decadence may be understood as an exacerbation of the nervous sensibility. Experience does not merely transpire; it accumulates. The result, as Nietzsche showed in such brilliant detail, is both intensification of perception and a concomitant deadening of the critical faculty. As the artist becomes more refined and penetrates to a deeper level of psychological analysis, this increase in self-reflection leads also to a dissatisfaction with the traditional languages and forms of art. The ensuing creation of new forms becomes indistinguishable, not merely from a rejection of the old, but from the dissolution of what is at first called the "traditional concept of form" and, eventually, of form itself. What looks initially like an extraordinary release of creative energy begins soon to deteriorate into what may be called experimental mannerism, or the unmistakable rictus of energy deflected into the attempt to find a lost bearing. Writing becomes initially more exquisite, and the increased subtlety of language stimulates a corresponding increase in the subtlety of reading. By a gradual process of what looks like an increase in sophistication, but is in fact a narrowing of range and loss of creative impetus, writing itself comes to be more and more like reading: art deteriorates into criticism.[1] The scene is set for the advent of the age of hermeneutics.

One does not like to speak about "the contemporary crisis"; at the same time, this reticence must be understood as itself a mark of decadence. Reading is for us today no longer a pleasure or an illumination; it is a problem, an ontological exercise, a laborious act of deconstruction. To be sure, the characteristic eros of the twentieth century is technophilia; we seem no longer able to perform any fundamental activity without the assistance of a technical manual. But this observation leaves unanswered the question of how we are to read our manuals. The necessity of metahermeneutics has led to the paradoxical proliferation of popular accounts or academic introductions to the esoteric documents of hermeneutics. However, these introductions are, as it were, "precritical," or constructed in the very language that requires deconstruction. The difficulty is analogous to that posed by Hegel and Wittgenstein in their respective attempts to make an absolute entrance into the absolute. It is all very well to speak of "discarding the ladder" once one has gained the heights, but how can we identify the appropriate ladder in the first place? If the entrance into the absolute is itself absolute, then so too must be the ladder.

One need not go to the absurd extreme of rejecting methodology outright in order to observe that the obsession with method is a sublimated form of the desire for the absolute. Descartes's attempt to construct a universal method on the model of mathematics was intended, not simply as a rejection of, but as a replacement for metaphysics. The metaphysical absolute (not, of course, a Cartesian expression) is replaced by the absolute certainty of effective solutions to practical problems. In our own century, the mathematical formalism of Hilbert is the outstanding example of the attempt to capture the absolute in a methodological net. The problem here is not with method but rather with our attitude toward method. One cannot perform the simplest acts of everyday life without method, but it does not follow from this that everyday life requires the absolute grounding of a metaphysics of methodology. The metaphysics of methodology is the attempt to replace the judicious selection of methods with a comprehensive method of selection. In the case of hermeneutics, it is the attempt to replace or to fortify the judgment of the reader with a methodology for the selection of methods of reading.[2] Whether in art, mathematics, or hermeneutical philosophy, decadence manifests itself as a loss of confidence in what Husserl called "the natural attitude." But the desire to re- or deconstruct the natural attitude in accordance with sound methodology is like the desire to climb to the absolute by means of an absolute ladder. When nature is replaced by history, and history is transformed into a methodological artifact, there is no criterion by which to select the correct artifact other than taste, or, as in fact happens, than by chance, disguised as the will to power.

The remarks to follow will be misunderstood if they are taken as a rejection of the need for sound methods of reading. By the same token, they are not intended as the deconstructive propaedeutic to a correct theory of interpretation. Their purpose is to lend support to the thesis that a theory of interpretation is impossible. Again, this is very far from the charge that everything said by hermeneutical thinkers is worthless. Stated in another way, as Nietzsche has also taught us, it is already a mark of decadence to be a resolute enemy of decadence. What one may hope to show is that the refined perceptions of a Gadamer or a Derrida are valuable not because of, but despite, the incoherence of their theoretical substructure. There is no theoretical substructure of reading *or* of writing; there is only the infrastructure of the reader and the writer. Reading and writing are confirmations of Nietzsche's epigram that man is the unfinished animal. But this is precisely human nature: to be unfinished, and hence, to exist partially as the thinking or theorizing animal, the animal who is looking for completeness. If we replace human nature with an ontological theory, or what comes to the same thing, deconstruct it, we thereby obliterate the sense of reading and writing. Being is not a text, nor does it provide us with the sense of a text. Unfortunately, however, neither do the canons of sound philology. I shall now restate these generalities in greater detail.

II

If there is no human nature that remains constant within historical change, and so that defines the perspectives of individual readers as perspectives on a common humanity, then reading is impossible. Whether one's primary orientation is ontological or philological, interpretation depends upon the initial accessibility of the sense of the text as independent of clarification and deepening by the subsequent application of theories, methods, and canons. This point is at least implicitly recognized by those representatives of philological hermeneutics who formulate maxims recommending *subtilitas legendi* or *Verstehen*. We do not become subtle through the study of philology; on the contrary, only those who are subtle by nature will make an appropriate use of their philological training. And there are neither philological canons nor ontological definitions of subtlety.

I have suggested that hermeneutical theories are the consequence of two closely related processes of deterioration. The first is a progressive separation of our understanding of the obvious from an intensifying conviction that nature, and so human nature, is a historical myth that must be replaced by a scientific construction. Just as the intuitive comes to be stigmatized as the source of logical contradictions, so the obvious is relegated to the category of superstition. In fact, we continue to rely upon our intuitions and to take our bearings from the obvious; but in attempting to protect ourselves against the defects, real and imagined, of these beginnings, we obstruct their true nature by ever more complex methodologies. The second is a product of the refined sensibility of historical old age: subtlety decays into ingenuity, and the speculative imagination, unrestrained by the standard of nature, or by "the given," which is now unmasked as an epistemological error, slips into the dream world of fantasy.

One way in which to render more specific this process of double deterioration is by viewing it as the gradual disappearance of the distinction between theory and interpretation. The stages of this disappearance can be documented with considerable precision. At least since the time of Bacon and his two great successors, Descartes and Vico, but most dramatically since Kant, we find that the term *theory* has been used in ways having little if anything to do with its etymology. The Greek word *theoria* designates a contemplative gazing upon divine phenomena, and by extension a purely intellectual apprehension or vision of the natural order. At least until the time of Aristotle's tripartition of the sciences into the theoretical, practical, and productive, *theoria* was not restricted to the vision of pure forms, but could also refer to the understanding of human nature, and especially of human deeds. For Aristotle, *episteme theoretike* is discursive knowledge which is founded in sensuous and intellectual perception of natural beings as well as the forms of species and genera. Nature, in the sense of the "essences" or "substances" of things, is neither produced nor modified (although it is "actualized") by the processes of cognition, whether intuitive or discursive.

In Plato, as well as in Aristotle, it is far from clear how the intellectual perception of the natural order is related to, and remains pure from modification by, what may fairly be called the constructive procedures of language, which are indispensable to the acquisition of scientific knowledge. In other words, the silence associated with the metaphor of vision is compatible with a passive reception of the natural order. But talking is already *making*, or what we today call concept construction. With Plato and Aristotle, we may describe this as the constructive activity of technical linguistic devices, by means of which we attempt to state what we have seen. If I may modify a thesis of Derrida, there is in speech as much as in writing an absence of the purely visible, and a substitution of a verbal construction for the absent being.

It is for this reason that there can be no suppression of intellectual intuition in favor of discursive intelligence, contrary to some current interpretations of Aristotle. Discursivity is the necessary supplement to the intuitive perception of form. If the purely visible were entirely absent, then to know would be to construct discursively. Substitution, supplementation, and surplus would at once become creation *ex nihilo*. It is therefore a fundamental error to regard the "supplementary" role assigned by classical theory to writing as in principle different from the same role assigned to speech. Supplementation is neither orientating nor superfluous. It stands to the direct perception of phenomena (formal as well as sensuous) as does art to nature: art completes nature, but there must be a nature to complete if art is to be distinguished from fantasy. The ostensible rigor of discursive artifacts is thus compromised by the fact that judgment is also a discursive artifact. The modern axiom that we know only what we make carries with it the corollary that we make what we know. Knowledge is then poetry; to judge is thus to interpret.

One finds at the beginning of modern philosophy the intention of regulating discourse, or of preserving the distinction between theory and interpretation, by appeal to a natural standard of desire or passion. Whether this standard was conceived in physiological or voluntative terms, however, it was soon aborted by the steady triumph of the doctrine of historicity, or the view that even desire is a concealed discursive interpretation, a product of historical circumstances and perspectives. Nature is no longer completed but is rather produced by art. The historical perspective, also known as the linguistic horizon, by the irony if not the cunning of history, thus replaced in effect the parousia of the discredited invisible essence of classical metaphysics.

It is important to emphasize that Aristotle's tripartition of the sciences into the theoretical, practical, and productive was not intended as an artificial conceptual schematism to bring order out of indeterminate beginnings. It corresponds to distinguishable but related aspects of nature. Thus theory is distinguished from the exercise of practical intelligence, and is assigned a higher status in the order of excellence; but in a fundamental sense, theory is regulated by practice. From the standpoint of political life, it is up to the exercise of *phronēsis* to determine who are the theoretical experts, and what role they play in the public economy. Even the sage must tend to the needs of the body before he is free to cultivate the soul; conversely, a soul that is politically cultivated is thereby qualified to establish those conditions that are essential prerequisites for the development of the sage. Perhaps the main point is this: whereas the man of *phronēsis* may not always, or even often, be a man of *theoria*, there is a natural harmony between these faculties, independent of political distinctions, including those of distinct city-states as well as of historical periods.

The judgments of practical intelligence are directed toward the here and now, or toward particular, and hence at least partially contingent, events. But these judgments are not themselves radically contingent, because they are grounded in a perception of human nature which could be restated in theoretical terms. If the contingent is intelligible, which is to say here, if it is amenable to judgment, then the basis of intelligibility or judgment cannot itself be contingent. It is true that the wise decision under present circumstances may be foolish under other circumstances. But the wisdom of the decision under present circumstances is not arbitrary. To judge is to understand, not to create *ex nihilo*. This point should be related to the previously cited Aristotelian maxim that art completes nature. One oversimplifies and misunderstands the Greeks by attributing to them the view that "life in accordance with nature" is validated by nature as an unvarying, perfect, and always benevolent standard. This oversimplification is impossible to sustain in the face of Greek myth and tragedy, which expresses vividly the profound discontinuities in human nature, as well as the senses in which the natural cosmos is hostile or indifferent to human life. Judgments in accordance with nature are those that *complete* nature. But the possibility of judgment, confirmed by success as well as by failure, means that there is a nature to complete. To repeat an earlier observation, if this were not so, it would be meaningless to speak of man as the incomplete animal.

By way of transition from classical to modern thought, we may say that, for the Greeks, the distinction between theory and interpretation was rooted in the distinction between seeing and making. Whereas we must state what we have seen, it is equally necessary to see what one is talking about. This distinction is not only not incompatible with the modern project to master nature, it is indispensable to the rationality of the distinction between masters and slaves. If that distinction is discursive or "merely verbal," then it may be obliterated by an additional statement. What is a master from one historical or linguistic perspective is a slave from another. This state of affairs is guaranteed by the transformation of nature into a historical concept. The sense of power is erased by excessive garrulity; "analytical clarification" decays into infinite technical progress, and progress is indistinguishable from chaos.

The critical moments of the modern epoch are all visible in the mathematical, scientific, and philosophical writings of Descartes. Practice is first reunited with production, as in Plato, and then the distinction between theory and practice is dissolved. In order to transform human beings from natural slaves into masters of nature, one must reconstitute nature itself. Geometrical intuition, the Cartesian analogue to the Aristotelian intuition of essences, is an initial step in this process. The analysis of practical problems or physical bodies into geometrical schemata amounts to a "geometricizing" of the world. These schemata are then themselves replaced by equations consisting of ratios of the known and unknown magnitudes of the line segments in the figures. And the entire analysis proceeds in accordance with the intention of the investigator. Man's desire to solve problems and to achieve mastery regulates the method, by which the natural world is prepared for what can without exaggeration be called "the will to power." Descartes's scientific writings thus confirm the traditional interpretation of the *Meditations*, according to which the *ego cogitans* is the direct ancestor of the Absolute Ego or principle of the production of the empirical world. And the primary importance assigned to the intention of the investigator is reconfirmed by the *Passions of the Soul*, which requires citation. In article 142 of part 3, Descartes says, "I notice in us but one thing which might give us good reason to esteem ourselves, and that is the use of our free will . . . it renders us in a way like God, by making us masters of ourselves." In article 143, Descartes defines *"generosité"* as the attribute by which we legitimately esteem ourselves, provided that we carry out all affairs that we deem best.

Moral virtue is the carrying out of *"grandes choses"* (3: 156) through the exercise of *"generosité."* If we take this text in conjunction with the scientific writings as well as with the *Discourse on Method*, it is reasonable to perceive in Descartes the paradigm of the Englightenment view of the identity of virtue and scientific knowledge. This amounts to an unself-conscious identification of theory and interpretation, or the confidence in the self-evident truth of one overriding interpretation, namely, of the intrinsic or ultimate (and hence historical) virtuousness of the will to power. This self-confidence was attacked in complementary ways by Hume and Rousseau. If memory cannot be distinguished from imagination except by liveliness of sensation, and if causality and necessary connections are the result of habit or custom, then theories are not merely interpretations but *fantasies*. Hume's so-called empiricism would be better named "surrealism"; its role in the prehistory of romanticism, existentialism, and contemporary historicist hermeneutics has not yet been properly appreciated. In Rousseau, the analogous development, a consequence of his denial of the identity between knowledge and virtue, was the subordination of reason to sensibility. Rousseau gives an ambiguous account of the implications of sensibility, an account in which traditional morality is compromised by an unmistakable penchant for the aesthetic fantasies of the solitary promenader. In principle, the net effect of the joint doctrines of Hume and

Rousseau was not the natural law teaching of the former or the classical republicanism of the latter, but incipient nihilism. The world is an interpretation.

This sets the scene for Kant. Kant attempted to rescue scientific knowledge from the radical skepticism of Hume and to construct a rational foundation for Rousseau's moral sensibility by his doctrine of the transcendental ego, according to which rational order is constituted by a set of logical conditions that are binding for all sentient creatures who employ sense perception together with conceptual thinking. According to Kant, we know only what we make, but the "made" world-order is not a historical artifact; with respect to its categorial determinations, it is a transcendentally constituted structure. In this specific and fundamental sense, it is, as it were, an *eternal essence,* not a contingent or perspectival consequence of an empirical interpretation of the world. At the same time, it would be difficult if not impossible to say that the doctrine of the transcendental ego is "theoretical." It is rather the case that theories are consequences of transcendental conditions. But the empirical content of a scientific theory is indeed contingent and historical. Whereas the conditions, and so the categorial structure, of a theory cannot be subject to interpretation, this in itself shapes, but is not the same as, knowledge of experience. We do not need to explore the status of scientific laws and mathematical truths in Kant, because for our purposes what is of importance is that Kant's immediate successors regarded as unsatisfactory the dualism between the transcendental and the empirical. This dualism established a cognitively inaccessible domain of noumena which includes not merely things-in-themselves but also the human soul and God. The noumenal domain is thus the locus of the significance for human life of scientific theories. In an attempt to render this domain accessible to reason *(Vernunft),* the German Idealists transformed the transcendental ego from a set of logical conditions into a living absolute spirit, from which emanates (or is projected) the empirical world, but also the soul and, at least in the case of Schelling, God as well. In producing the world, the absolute becomes accessible to human reason as the productive activity itself. This productive activity was inevitably historicized in the course of the nineteenth century and purified of its extrahuman character by Feuerbach, Marx, and Nietzsche. So, like Aristotle's "invisible essence" before it, Kant's transcendental ego was assimilated into the insubstantial blend of human or historical production. Mathematical reason was explained by dialectico-speculative logic, and this in turn was identified with the historical process. The next step was the dissolution of the ostensibly absolute nature of that process.

In the ensuing age of "theory construction," understanding a theory as a formal structure did not alter its artifactual status, since forms were taken to be, not "actualized," but literally created by human cognitive activity. The attack, whether Platonic or Kantian, against psychologism, led at first by Frege and Husserl, and then by Russell and the early Wittgenstein, has been effectively negated by historicist doctrines of linguistic activity. Not even Husserl's conception of transcendental subjectivity has proven immune to temporal and historical dissolution. As a result, the phenomenological *Wesensschau* has become a kind of optical illusion in which the discursive *Sinn* is the genuine, and genuinely historical, "essence" of visual appearances. Owing in part to the influence of the later Wittgenstein, but also to a variety of other factors, the same situation obtains in the mathematically or "analytically" oriented branches of the philosophy of science. Science as a linguistic process has triumphed over the pre-Darwinian, pre-Einsteinian sense of science as theoretical understanding of the immutable laws of nature. And thanks to alternative algebras, non-Euclidean geometries, the shipwreck of formalism, and the apparent infinity of possible axiom systems, exactly the same is true of mathematics. We now see that at the decisive level, theory has been transformed into interpretation: *doxa* is the successor to *episteme*, and poetry has triumphed in its ancient quarrel with philosophy.

III

I am now in a position to assert the striking fact that as the scope of theory has expanded, the difference between theory and interpretation has narrowed. In general terms, the natural basis of theory, whether understood as the domain of *phronēsis* or as the pretheoretical domain of common sense, has been replaced by theoretical construction. Theories have multiplied, while at the same time they have both confirmed and invalidated themselves by producing their own presuppositions. To make the same point in more up-to-date terminology, the validity of each theory is relative to an indeterminate number of antecedent and coordinate "background" theories (just as a mathematical proof for the consistency of one branch of mathematics is relative to another mathematical theory). The cosmos of *theoria* is replaced by the multiple and multiply fractured worlds of competing or successive theories, with the result that unity is a question of interpretation. As we have now seen, the condescension expressed by many contemporary "rationalists" of a scientific or analytical bent toward the new popularity of hermeneutics is entirely unwarranted. It is a case of the pot calling the kettle black.

My next step will be to illustrate briefly the self-vitiating consequences of the expansion and multiplication of theory, or its transformation into theory construction, by way of the example of hermeneutics. The science of hermeneutics originated as a philological attempt to fix the boundaries of the correct reading of Holy Scripture. Whereas the initial impetus was dogmatic, it was not long before the intrinsic relativism of philology, as well as the ostensible impartiality of science toward theological conflicts, produced both a multiplicity of philologically certified "correct" accounts of Scripture and a radically impious, because quite "positivistic," scientific restatement of the hermeneutical problem. In Spinoza's *Tractatus Theologico-Politicus*, we see an influential example of the combination of these two tendencies. One could say that for Spinoza, there was a theoretical continuity between the attempt to read the "book of nature" and the attempt to read the "book of God." In principle, Spinoza had opened the horizon of a universal hermeneutic, which is on the one hand scientific, or which embodies the sound methodology of the adaptation of scientific reasoning to the needs of philology, but which on the other hand allows a distinction between method and content. It would seem that a rigorous application of this method would lead to a repudiation of all claims to dogmatic certainty concerning Holy Writ. We see here the paradigm for the later definition of philological hermeneutics as a "regulative" discipline that establishes canons, not laws, and that recommends or guides us among the multiplicity of possible interpretations, rather than certifying one or another as *the* correct interpretation. Differently stated, the regulative function of modern hermeneutics is a consequence of the failure of Biblical hermeneutics.

In any case, the scientific sense of the theoretical function of hermeneutics was dropped in favor of the philological sense when hermeneutics was extended by Schleiermacher and Boeckh to encompass first the ancient humanistic texts, and then more generally the domain of the philological sciences. Thus Boeckh's major work on hermeneutics bears the title *Enzyklopädie und Methodenlehre der philologischen Wissenschaften.* This shift from a natural-scientific to a philological paradigm brought with it the decisive entrance of history, which had not yet infected the experimental and mathematical sciences, into hermeneutics. The historical sciences cannot be mathematicized. In reading the hermeneutical aphorisms of Schleiermacher dating between 1805 and 1809, in which he speaks of the infinite task of *Verstehen* as *subtilitas legendi* (31), and then emphasizes *Gefühl* rather than methodical rules (61), one thinks of Pascal's *esprit de finesse* and Rosseau's *sensibilité*. The same theme leads in the 1819 manuscripts to the linking of hermeneutics with rhetoric and dialectic (80) and in the 1829 manuscripts to the equation of *Verstehen* with *Auslegen*, or linguistic interpretation (124).[3] It is scarcely necessary to insist upon the importance of these notions for the development of the hermeneutical theories of Dilthey, Heidegger, and Gadamer. What we need to notice is that Schleiermacher's maxims or "canons" are quasi-mathematical in the sense that they are empty of content.[4] At the same time, they are considerably weaker than mathematics, not to say platitudinous, when considered as regulative maxims. It is useful to be reminded of Plato's distinction between the measures of arithmetic and of the suitable, or of Pascal's distinction between the *esprit géométrique* and the *esprit de finesse*. But is this the basis for a theory of interpretation?

In his book on philological method, Boeckh emphasizes the historical as opposed to the purely conceptual nature of hermeneutics (18, 31), as well as its own "productive" or "constructive" function in the reproduction of historical knowledge (14, 17). In the natural sciences, in other words, to conceive is to grasp things as they are. In the *Geisteswissenchaften*, thanks to the historical nature of *Geist*, to "grasp" is already to transform or to interpret. The scientific nature of the methodological aspects of philology is thus external to the historical or perspectival nature of the content or subject matter of philology. In an important passage, Boeckh defines the essence of *hermeneia* as "what the Romans call *elocutio*, that is, not understanding but making understandable" (80). This last distinction embodies what we may call the "classical" conception of hermeneutics: one can make understandable only that which contains a potential sense. But the act of fulfilling this potency is entrusted to *elocutio*, not to mathematical reason. As in oratory or rhetoric, the selection of terms by the "eloquent" speaker is regulated both by his subjective capacities and by his assessment of the specific capacities of his audience. In order to be "made understandable," the material must be "made" or reshaped, that is, interpreted. For Boeckh, the potency of sense inheres neither in the text nor in the interpreter alone, but in their interaction. This is the philological basis for Gadamer's later doctrine of *Horizontverschmelzung* (fusion of horizons).

Boeckh's distinction between understanding and making under-standable is rooted in the same considerations that led Schleiermacher to associate hermeneutics with rhetoric and dialectic. These consider-ations issue in the enunciation of the hermeneutical circle: interpreta-tion presupposes a knowledge that is derivable only from an under-standing of the material to be interpreted (84). The knowledge to which Boeckh refers is not an understanding of the detailed content of the text before having read it but a self-knowledge that allows us to understand the thoughts of other human beings. As we shall see, this point was given an ontological formulation by Heidegger. Heidegger apart, the philological conception of interpretation is plainly rooted in the thesis of a common human nature, and one that remains stable within history. It is this common human nature, not, of course, uni-form but qualified in endless ways, that is the content of our preunder-standing and that enables us to employ our philological tools in a man-ner not merely "valid" or "technically sound" but *subtle*. At the same time, Boeckh's acceptance of the modern doctrine of the historicity of the human spirit contradicts his efforts to ground understanding in self-knowledge. Boeckh echoes Schleiermacher's observation on the infinite nature of hermeneutical interpretation by citing the *Peri Physeos* by the orator Gorgias. The listener (or reader) never under-stands words in the same sense as the speaker (*oudeis heteros hetero tauto ennoei*). Boeckh comments, "Since therefore the alien individuality can never be completely understood, the task of hermeneutics can only be fulfilled through unending *approximation*, that is, through a gradual approach that proceeds point by point but is never completed" (86). *Verstehen* rests finally upon a natural capacity of tact (*der richtige Takt* [87]).[5] Boeckh does not notice that the infinity of the journey compro-mises the "correctness" of tact. There is in hermeneutics no equivalent to the limit of an infinite series in mathematics.

The shift from the paradigm of natural science to that of historical philology was deepened by Dilthey and Nietzsche, who extended her-meneutics to the study of human history, and in Nietzsche's case, still more radically to the interpretation of the world as a series of historical perspectives. Nietzsche resolved, or attempted to resolve, Boeckh's problem by transforming infinity into the closed circle of the eternal return of the same. He failed to notice, incidentally, that in so doing, he was adapting to his own purposes the central intuition of Hegel. However, Nietzsche left the evidence of circularity or totality to the vision of the individual interpreter. Dialectico-speculative logic was thus replaced by aesthetic perspectivalism; the absolute was rendered logically incoherent in its new identity as the will to power. So too Nietzsche celebrated Spinoza's *amor fati* as an anticipation of his own teaching. But in substituting enthusiasm (in the literal sense) for the deductive structure of fate, Nietzsche transformed pantheism into solipsism and fate into chance. There is no cosmological basis to support the assertion that the world is a work of art, and so that art is worth more than the truth. The concept of being "worth more" depends upon a hierarchy of values, as does Nietzsche's fundamental distinction between noble and base nihilism. But the self-assertion of value by the "self," who is merely a phenomenal manifestation of the will to power, amounts to the equation of interpretation with the fluxions of chaos.

Heidegger attempted to rescue Nietzsche's main themes from chaos by incorporating them in an ontological structure that also rescued the hermeneutical circle of philology from inconclusiveness. He combined the radical individualism of Nietzsche's aesthetic perspectives and Kierkegaard's notion of genuineness in a transcendental structure at once Kantian and Hegelian. The finite world of man *(Dasein)* is organized by his categorial (existential) structure, which projects in advance the "formal" basis for individual interpretations of the content of the world. The "meaning" or "sense" of the world is "secreted" by man in a way that is intended to express the general structure as the individual decision or interpretation of the unique individual. But the structure is itself understood as temporal or historical, to be sure in the "ontological" sense of these terms. This is the Hegelian element in Heidegger's ontology. But the Hegelian element does not blend with the Kantian element of a transcendental structure of onto-logical categories (to borrow a Heideggerean hyphen). Having banished the absolute to the transtemporal and transhistorical domain of the (in effect) *Jenseits* of classical Christian Neoplatonism, Heidegger was never able to explain discursively (and *Sein und Zeit* is a discursive or "academic" work of ontology) the ground of his existential categories. He was unable to progress beyond the level of Nietzsche.

In a word, Heidegger's early ontology is not a phenomenological description of the world but an interpretation. What are for the student of hermeneutics the crucial paragraphs 31 and 32 of *Sein und Zeit* thus inadvertently reveal the crucial shortcoming of the work as a whole. In these paragraphs, Heidegger explains how *Dasein* produces "in advance" the sense or meaning *(Sinn)* of all concrete interpretations of everyday life, itself the womb of all subsequent theorizing. It does this by means of the existential (i.e., ontological or categorial) faculties

of *Verstehen* and *Auslegung* ("understanding" and "interpreting"), together with the "vision," or "transparency" *(Durchsicht)*, that corresponds very approximately to a historicized *phronēsis*. *Sinn* is thus for
Heidegger itself an existential of *Dasein* and not a property of things
(Seienden). This is the basis for the doctrine that the world is a text.[6]
Accordingly, ontology is transformed into hermeneutics. But the relativism intrinsic to philology, the chaos that marks Nietzsche's will to
power, and Heidegger's inability to negotiate discursively the separation of the ontological from the ontic are all fragments of traditional
rationalism by comparison with postontological deconstruction, as
Derrida himself insists. If the world is a text, then we who read it are
nothing more than characters in its antiplot. It is no longer meaningful
to speak of "understanding" or "interpreting," and the ostensible freedom from the domination of classical metaphysics becomes simply another version of *amor fati*.

In this context, to repeat, Heidegger is a traditional rationalist. But
by in effect making the world a text, and ontology into hermeneutics,
Heidgegger showed that he accepted the modern distinction between
reason as fundamentally mathematics, and poetry. The quasi-mathematical character of a discursively accessible categorial ontology is dissolved by the poetic character of the unique perspectivism of what the
Germans call *Decisionismus*. I give meaning to my world by choosing
authentically. "Only *Dasein* can therefore be meaningful *(sinnvoll)* or
meaningless *(sinnlos)*" [sec. 32, p. 151]. Heidegger, of course, insists that
the existential structure of *Dasein*, by which its decisions are structured, gives stability and sense to the "authenticity" of the individual
choice. However, these structures are at best empty transcendental
categories that make possible, not stability, but the human expression
of the transience of its lived world. And at worst (as well as in fact), the
structures are, as we have seen, themselves historical interpretations.
Heidegger's analysis of ontological preunderstanding, or of the hermeneutical circle, was thus not successful. He followed what amounts to
Boeckh's standard philological thesis that all interpretation depends
upon our having already understood (implicitly) what is to be interpreted. According to Heidegger, the circle is not vicious, but the expression of the fact that *Dasein* provides from within its most general
structure the categories and illumination upon which any interpretation rests (sec. 32, pp. 152–53).[7] In one sense, Heidegger went beyond
the philological position, as well as the dualism of Kant, by attempting
to derive his categories from human existence, rather than from scien-

tific method or formal logic. However, this advance was negated by the analysis of "existence" as temporal *ekstasis*.

The Heideggerean "ecstasy" did not take human being "beyond" the contingency of the temporal process but attempted to stabilize this process via its own pattern of change. The tenses—future, present, and past—replaced Kant's table of categories. The hermeneutical circle is thus Nietzsche's eternal return, not with respect to the content of life, but with respect to the circularity of the temporal patterning of intentional activity. We can therefore see that the initial brilliance of Heidegger's technical mastery was in the end a *reductio ad absurdum*. Both the shaping categories and the shaped content of existence were derived from the temporalization process, which consequently erases that to which it gives birth, in the very act of genesis. Whereas *Dasein* secretes time, time secretes *Dasein*. This is a circle, but not a hermeneutical circle. In the last analysis, to interpret, or to give sense to the world, is to do nothing significant, nothing that signifies beyond its own expression. *The sign signifies nothing.* This is because Heidegger rejected both the classical doctrine of nature and the modern doctrine of the absolute. There is neither an initial nor a concluding foundation to theory, and so, no basis for distinguishing between a theory and an interpretation.

After Heidegger, what? In the usual interpretation of logic, everything follows from a contradiction. When the agent of contradiction is a great and difficult thinker, the consequences of the contradiction obey a hermeneutical law of their own: philosophy is succeeded by professorial adaptation and commentary, which in turn give rise in the following generation to the attempt to progress by taking up one or another of the premises that led to the self-contradiction in the late master's thought. However, whether because of the comprehensive force of Heidegger's thought or because in some sense Hegel was correct and history, or at least the history of philosophy, is completed, there has been no advance beyond Heidegger's *reductio ad absurdum*. We live in a generation of epigones. This is, of course, not to suggest that the epigones are all Heideggereans, but to make the point that the master of hermeneutics in the late twentieth century is historicism, whether lightly concealed by appeals to philological responsibility or painted in the gaudy colors of structuralism and poststructuralist "deconstruction." Linguistic horizons, deviant logics, the arbitrariness of axiom-sets, all drink from the same waters as do the motley band of Marxist, Nietzschean, Freudian, Heideggerean, pragmatist, phenomenological, and even quasi-Kantian hermeneuticists of our academic community. Amid the plethora of hermeneutical theories, what it means to be a theory is a matter of interpretation.

I conclude this survey of the history of hermeneutics with the following remark. The initial purpose of hermeneutics was to explain the word of God. This purpose was eventually expanded into the attempt to regulate the process of explaining the word of man. In the nineteenth century, we learned, first from Hegel and then, more effectively, from Nietzsche, that God is dead. In the twentieth century, Foucault informed us that man is dead, thereby opening the gates into the abyss of postanthropological deconstruction.[8] As the scope of hermeneutics has expanded, then, the two original sources of hermeneutical meaning, God and man, have vanished, taking with them the cosmos or world, and leaving us with nothing but our own garrulity, which we choose to call the philosophy of language, linguistic philosophy, or one of their synonyms. If nothing is real, the real is nothing; there is no difference between the written lines of a text and the blank spaces between them.

IV

What is today called "hermeneutics" traces its proximate origins to philology on the one hand and ontology on the other. It is, however, important to remember that the actual beginning of hermeneutics lies in the impasse that marked the atempt to establish Biblical doctrine by the authority of the prophetic tradition, whether in the written word of God or by way of subsequent revelations. We should not be misled by the numerous contemporary references to pagan rhetoric, dialectic, and jurisprudence into supposing that, in the Greco-Roman world, there was a hermeneutical problem analogous to the one that perplexes the heirs to the Judaeo-Christian tradition. Ambiguous statements attributed to the pagan gods were explained by the events of everyday life. Philosophers, although certainly aware that (in Heraclitus's words) "nature loves to hide," were convinced that she would also reveal herself to the ministrations of reason. Classical skepticism is the apparent exception that proves the rule. As Hegel pointed out, the ancient skeptics did not distrust reason but insisted upon man's ability to demonstrate by rational argumentation the impossibility of knowledge of the world. Even the Greek Sophists, unlike their contemporary admirers, believed in human nature, as is obvious, for example, from the principle of Protagoras that the good is the pleasant.

One need not accept Heidegger's oversimplification of the history of metaphysics as "Onto-theo-logik" in order to see that, as a characterization of post-Scriptural speculation, the term has merit. To summarize a complex process in a brief phrase, the failure of Scriptural philology led to the bifurcation of hermeneutics into humanistic philology on the one hand and ontotheology on the other. It is true that, in the course of time, ontotheology underwent an apparent ellipsis, transforming itself into ontology, with theology relegated largely to the role of denominational substitutes for ontology. But one may detect even within ontology the concealed presence of the hidden God (a phrase that is only apparently pleonastic). At the risk of pressing the metaphor too far, I suggest that history becomes the surrogate within modern ontology for the hidden God. By another strange irony of history, when Heidegger cites Hölderlin to the effect that "the gods have flown away from this parlous epoch," he is speaking neither as a pagan nor as a Christian but as a Jew. Heidegger's "Hebraic" tendencies could be further documented by a detailed study of his preference for listening and hearing to seeing, and of his coordinate substitution of the voice of an invisible Being for the parousia of eternal form.

The Jews are the chosen people; with them, history in the proper sense begins. History, or the story of the Jews, is the quest for the hidden God, or at least for the Messiah. For those of little faith, history is thus virtually indistinguishable from nihilism. As to the Christian, the arrival of the day of judgment, or the fulfillment within eternity of his temporally conditioned faith, is postponed indefinitely by the (to him) barely comprehensible tenacity of the Jews. The historical people prefer the hope of the future to the blessing of presence. This obstinacy condemns the Christian to a continuation of historical existence, and the cleft opened within eternity by history casts a shadow of ambiguity over Holy Writ. *Theoria* is postponed indefinitely, to be represented for the time being (a curiously resonant idiom) by interpretation. In the absence of God and nature, the world is fractured into a multiplicity of "world views," a misleading expression in which the echo of vision is in fact a camouflaged reference to discourse. The divine logos becomes human language. The sign is detached from its referent; between them, in place of the hidden God, stands the concept, artifact of historicity.

So much for the theological substructure of the present division (not, of course, absolute) between philological and ontological hermeneutics. It is this substructure, as articulated by the developments summarized in the preceding two sections of this essay, that explains the historicism common to both schools of thought. The fundamental difference between these two schools corresponds to the difference between history and historicity. Philological hermeneutics takes its bearings from the text as an "objective" artifact, the product of an intentional consciousness whose meaning can be deciphered with the assistance of the techniques and methods of the *Geisteswissenschaften*. The regulative function of hermeneutics is thus the humanistic counterpart to the scientific experiment as explained by Karl Popper. In both cases, hypotheses are refutable, but may never be confirmed by the application of sound methodology. In both cases, the genuinely scientific or secure component is the method together with its negative results. The true or positive meaning of the content remains within the domain of belief or opinion: of *doxa* rather than of *episteme*. Needless to say, the contingency of our grasp of the content affects the techniques of the method, which is subject to progressive revision as technical knowledge grows. But it is precisely *technical* knowledge that grows, external to the enduringly doxic status of the content of the hermeneutical experiment.

The legitimacy of *technē* in scientific methodology is certified by practical results, even in those cases in which our understanding of the "theoretical" situation is uncertain or a matter of interpretation. A good example is the success of physicists in employing wave or matrix mechanics to derive successful explanations of natural phenomena from the theoretically disputable or ambiguous concepts of quantum physics. But the practical results of a philological interpretation of a humanistic text certify nothing other than the power of that interpretation. The practical results are produced by the interpretation. If the measure of validity in interpretation is the power to persuade, then philological hermeneutics is a testimonial, not to objective methods, but to the will to power. In fact, even as a methodologist, the philological hermeneuticist turns to history in the attempt to distinguish legitimate from illegitimate interpretations. As a result, his interpretations illustrate with depressing frequency the fundamental defect of history as the standard of legitimacy. The thesis that every text must be understood within the context of its historical period, and so that the intentions and results of the author are a function of his historical perspective (political, social, economic, psychological, scientific, and so on), that even the senses of words undergo change through historical transformation, that there is no enduring stratum of human nature, and consequently no problem, let alone solution, apart from a given historical formulation, leads inexorably to the conclusion that there is no meaning of the text to be grasped by the reader who belongs to a different historical perspective.

In a way much more extravagant, and hence more paradoxical, than obtains within quantum physics, the hermeneutical attempt to understand a text by using the techniques of historical philology interferes with the meaning of that text. On the one hand, the philologist speaks of objectivity; on the other, he renders objectivity in principle impossible. The common assumption that everything must be understood historically leads to the consequence that nothing can be understood, not even the validity of one's methods, let alone their significance. Or else it leads to the consequences that all understanding is self-understanding. To interpret a text is then in fact to produce one's own text. But does not our historicity lead us to produce differing interpretations of the same text at different periods of our life, so that the "sameness" of the text disappears? There is then no real difference on this point between the two leading contemporary schools of hermeneutics as represented by Hans-Georg Gadamer and Emilio Betti.

Betti's Kantian orientation is an empty formalist gesture that does not conceal his failure to think through the consequences of his substantive historicism. Gadamer is entirely superior to Betti in the quality of his interpretations. Furthermore, there is considerable merit in his critique of the attempt to establish methods of interpretation and in his recommendation of classical *prudentia* or *subtilitas legendi*. Yet after devoting more than half of *Wahrheit und Methode* to what is certainly intended as an objective or sound exposition of the thought of the founders of hermeneutics, Gadamer, without any visible recognition of the contradiction, cancels the validity of his own expositions by promulgating a doctrine according to which objective interpretation is impossible. Instead, Gadamer holds that an interpretation is a *Horizontverschmelzung*, a fusion of one's own historical perspective with that of the author (357–59). The inner historicity of experience (329) guarantees the uniqueness of each standpoint or perspective. When Gadamer formulates the Heideggerean thesis that "Being that can be understood is language" (450),[9] he implicitly equates the understandability of Being with its production by the speaker. To read, and so to understand, is to create works of art.

Gadamer is surely no less aware than Betti of the need for philological competence. He is undoubtedly correct to hold that there are no canons that serve as an equivalent to *subtilitas legendi*, or that philology does not engender *prudentia*. However, he is surely mistaken, and, despite his greater subtlety, he is mistaken in the same way as the philologists, when he attempts to apply classical *phronēsis* to a modern historicist view of human nature. At his best, namely, in presenting his textual analyses, Gadamer demonstrates that the gift of understanding is indeed superior to method, and even, thanks to his own *phronēsis* or *prudentia*, to an internally incoherent theoretical foundation. When Gadamer is illuminating about Plato, Dilthey, or Heidegger, it is because the doctrine of *Horizontverschmelzung* is erroneous, just as its philological equivalent, the relativity of historical perspectives, is erroneous. Both fall short of the ontological complexity of history, which is intelligible despite its multiplicity of perspectives. Ontology to one side, the student of Heidegger and the descendant of Boeckh share a common and vitiating historicism. But Gadamer rises above this in the best of his readings, and this is a sign that Boeckh was in fact right to invoke *"der richtige Takt."* Ontology and philology are both helpless in the face of the work of genius. It is as absurd to reduce an extraordinary production to the "prevailing views," "established tropes," and "customary usage of terms" of philology as it is to dissolve it in our own effort to appropriate it. In both cases we are left grasping at air.

The philologist is correct in his assertion that a lack of sound methods leads to the obliteration of the distinction between subtlety and madness. But even if he understands that subtlety is prior to, or independent of, and must itself regulate, all philological methods, he has no way qua philologist to distinguish between subtlety and mediocrity. Since there are no canons for the exercise of subtlety, the philologist is in practice all too often driven to the desperate expedient of equating subtlety with the exercise of sound methodology. The usual result is to define subtlety in terms of historical consensus, that is to say, in terms of the doctrines that characterize the school to which the individual philologist belongs. For there is no such thing as a philosophically neutral philology, except in the sense of the establishment of linguistic procedures to be employed by someone who is not neutral, whether for good or for bad, in the exposition and evaluation of texts. To repeat, this consensus is itself a kind of *Horizontverschmelzung* or fusion of two historical constructions. The given community of scholars, whether Marxist, Freudian, positivist, or Heideggerean, "fuses" with the historical community of the text. But the text is itself by-passed and invisible. Homer, Vergil, Descartes, Goethe, all are situated within "the context of their time." But this is to place them within the precise dimension from which their genius was employed to detach them. The discontinuity between genius and mediocrity is covered over with a porous mesh of self-dissolving historical platitudes. And the result is to encourage, indeed, to justify, the "madness" of ontological or postontological hermeneutics. If truth is a platitude, or if there is no truth but only art, then why should there not be extraordinary art? Why should we be bored to death by historical soundness, if soundness is itself without objective value? *Only disconnect*: thus one might restate E. M. Forster's famous maxim. The tragedy of philological hermeneutics is its often honorable lack of awareness that it is the secret cause of deconstruction.

Deconstruction stands to ontological hermeneutics as does negative to positive theology. As Derrida himself insists, deconstruction necessarily occurs within metaphysical thinking. The fact is, however, that Derrida and his disciples take their bearings neither from metaphysics nor from postmetaphysics. We cannot begin with what has not yet been written, which in any case, once it appears, must itself undergo deconstruction. Instead, we begin with a religious longing for the "not yet," the *deus absconditus* understood as the "never." Derridean hermeneutics is in a way like the Kantian critique, in the sense that it hovers "above" rather than inside or outside of metaphysics, and states the conditions for the possibility of deconstruction. It is religious to the extent that the "beyond" is a *Jenseits*, but at a more immediate level the discursive articulation of the desirability of deconstruction is an expression of the fashionable post-Hegelian inversion of the ideology of Enlightenment. The modern celebration of freedom (which, as Fichte asserted, is higher than Being), given a Marxist tincture as well as an anarchic nostalgia, is detached from the sobering spread of illumination and linked to the maddening plunge into darkness.

Despite the "Hebraic" ancestry of Derrida's thought, already plain in Heidegger, there is no question here of orthodoxy. Like the assimilated Reformed Jew, Derrida is thoroughly "up to date." It is therefore misleading to speak of Derrida's textual exegeses as Talmudic. The esoteric wisdom of the Talmud is a prudentially disguised version of a positive teaching, whereas Derridean deconstruction is the intemperate revelation of what Hegel called the terrible labor of negativity, except of course that for Derrida there is no negation of the negation, no *Aufhebung*. Nevertheless, there is an introductory or predeconstructive justification that serves as a positive doctrine, which is parasitic upon ontology.

I shall therefore disregard the distinction between construction and deconstruction and shall refer to ontological hermeneutics as the principal contemporary alternative to philological hermeneutics. In so doing, I do not imply that every ontological doctrine is itself a theory of interpretation (although, for reasons given in the second section of this essay, many theories are themselves interpretations without knowing it). And some theories of interpretation that look vaguely like ontologies are neither that nor legitimate forms of interpretation. To take the outstanding example, all talk of "phenomenological hermeneutics" that attempts to derive its justification from Husserl rather than Heidegger is surely incoherent. Once we discard academic jargon, what, for example, does it mean to speak of "a phenomenological reading of *The Wings of the Dove*"? Husserlian phenomenology is a descriptive method, not an ontological doctrine and certainly not an interpretation. An exact description of *The Wings of the Dove* would be at best an error-free reproduction of the text of the novel, and at worst a restatement of the text in Husserlian terminology. To give one more example of a Kantian as well as Husserlian flavor, what light is cast upon the novel in question when we are correctly informed about the structure of the transcendental ego of which not only Henry James, but every failed novelist, is an exemplification?

A hermeneutical ontology is one that treats the text, whether a philosophical essay, a work of art, or a dream, as a sign, not of its own sense, but of some comprehensive theory of human existence, even of Being. An example is Freud's doctrine of the interpretation of dreams. The analyst does not treat the dream as a conscious product of human intentionality, in which the author constructs, for an end known to himself, both the explicit and the concealed elements as parts of an integral whole. Instead, the analyst "deconstructs" the dream as dreamed in accordance with a general dictionary of signs, in order to arrive at the decoded message from its actual author, the unconscious (an ancestor of Derridean "difference"). The message is taken to be an expression in local or contingent terms of the Freudian ontology of the soul. If we exaggerate slightly and regard the explicit or presented meaning of the dream as an interpretation of experience in its own right, we may say that one theory is interpreted within another, presumably more general theory. This is in principle the scientific procedure that is formalized in the axiomatic method. The "consistency" of the dream is thus demonstrated within the "logic" of the theory of the interpretation of dreams. For reasons that do not require spelling out, few if any would quarrel with the attempt to provide an explanation of dreams from the waking domain of theory. This is because it is intuitively persuasive to us that the sense of the dream is at best unclear in its own terms, that dreams are insubstantial. But the application of ontological hermeneutics to humanistic texts is itself an unconscious affirmation of the Shakespearean metaphor: "We are such stuff as dreams are made on, and our little lives are rounded with a sleep."

Ontological hermeneutics treats the text as indirect evidence of a general doctrine of Being, or in other words, as data to be transformed, and hence replaced by a theoretical artifact. The deeper affiliation between the apparently distinct schools of ontological and philological hermeneutics is evident from the fact that in both cases, one perspective is replaced by, or fused into, another. But there are two preliminary questions that need to be answered. First, can we actually see a "perspective" in its own terms, as it is seen, or seen through, by its genuine residents, *before* we assimilate it into our own theory? Second, is the value of conflicting perspectives itself perspectival, or can we interchange perspectives for the better? If the answers to these two questions are negative, then hermeneutics, or theorizing in general, becomes pointless pseudointerpretation, that is to say, dreaming.

It is worth noting that perspective hermeneutics has its logical counterpart, and in a way its source, in the Kantian thesis that discursive thinking is judgmental, not propositional in the alternative idiom. Without misrepresenting Kant, we may say that every judgment is an "interpretation" in the following sense. To say that S is p is not to perform an analysis upon a preexisting structure but to constitute or synthesize that structure by subsuming one item under a determinate category. In Kant, of course, these subsumptions or interpretations are transcendental, and in no sense either subjective or historically contingent. However, they become so when the transcendental ego is either historicized or suppressed outright. The categorial structure of judgment is then transformed into a linguistic horizon. Recourse to logic or mathematics changes nothing, since even formal languages are expressions, via their axioms or presuppositions, of a contingent linguistic act of the will.

Ontological hermeneutics is similar to contemporary mathematical theory in two senses. First, one theory (the local theory of the text as intentional artifact) is interpreted within another, presumably more general or fundamental theory. Second, the ontological theory is itself a system of judgments rather than of propositions, because what the ontologist means by "theory" is precisely "interpretation." That this point holds true of contemporary axiomatic mathematics is plain from the Löwenheim-Skolem theorems, the general purport of which is that an axiom set cannot uniquely specify a system of mathematical objects. In other words, axiomatics cannot fulfill the precise purpose for which it was devised. The question of which system of objects is intended thus becomes a matter of the judgment, intuition, or common sense of the model-theoretician, in other words, of judgment modified by conventional agreement.[10] Axioms are thus interpretations in the double sense that one set must be validated via the authority of another set and that the model-theoretic function of the axiom set is not categorical: the theorist must exercise *"der richtige Takt."*

Given this hermeneutical similarity between ontology and mathematics, it is useful to consider the one case in contemporary thought in which there seems to be a precise distinction between a theory and an interpretation, namely, the study of the foundations of mathematics. I have already suggested that the distinction here too is ambiguous if not spurious. But an example will also illustrate the practical disadvantages of using a general theory in which to interpret less general theories, of which one subspecies is the humanistic text. The abstract or formal nature of the analogy between ontological and mathematical hermeneutics permits me to employ this example without running the risk of blurring the numerous specific differences between the two enterprises.

There is a wide range of specific mathematical theories of geometrical form, algebraic equations, real numbers, and so on. There is also a specific theory, set theory, which may be called "general" in the sense that it purports to be a theory of all mathematics. The peculiar status of set theory arises from the apparent fact that any mathematical object can be defined as a set. (The hermeneutical analogue here with respect to texts would be to define any text as equivalent to a theoretical entity within a general ontology.) It therefore seems possible to interpret (in a sense about to be explained) all parts of mathematics within set theory. What one does is to add the special axioms of the branch of mathematics at issue to the axioms of set theory. Let us suppose that we do this with the axioms of geometry. The variables in the axioms of set theory can be interpreted as designating geometrical objects, and the predicates or relations of these axioms can be defined as geometrical predicates or relations. We can now do two things. First, we are in a position to prove metatheorems about the theory of geometry. For example, if we can prove within set theory that the special axioms of geometry are tautologies of set theory, we have proved that if set theory is consistent, so is geometry. Second, we can prove additional theorems in geometry by proving their logically equivalent theorems in set theory.

There are obvious advantages that accrue from the interpretation of some other mathematical theory within set theory. It is not so obvious that analogous advantages accrue from the interpretation of, say, a novel or a philosophical treatise within a general theory of interpretation of texts as texts. For example, it might very well be a rule of that part of our theory dealing with interpretations that a legitimate interpretation must be consistent. There seem to be two ways in which one could show consistency. The first way is formal. We would then have to agree upon a method by which to formalize the interpretation (and presumably the text as well). In so doing, however, we would have shifted from general hermeneutics to mathematics. Even assuming success here, the specific interpretation would be assimilated to a general form of interpretation. This might be interesting in its own right, but it would add nothing to the specific interpretation, which was achieved, and could only be achieved, by nonmathematical means. We note further that the theory of interpretation, at least with respect to the rule of consistency, would itself be interpreted within set theory and first-order predicate logic.

We can safely agree that the hypothetical procedure just sketched would be of technical interest to mathematical, but not to humanistic hermeneuticists. The second way of showing consistency, appropriate to informal or humanistic texts, is by explaining the text in some natural language and leaving it to the audience to see, by their own act of reading, that the interpretation is comprehensive and coherent. In other words, using "hermeneutics" now in its narrow sense, if we formalize, then we are no longer doing hermeneutics but concerning ourselves with a new theoretical artifact: a formal abstraction. But if we do not formalize, we are merely stating our interpretation. If we and our audience accept the rule of consistency in hermeneutics, there are no further rules by which to show that we have achieved it. There is, incidentally, a serious difficulty attached to the employment of the rule of consistency in humanistic hermeneutics. Ironical texts like *Gargantua and Pantagruel*, dialectical texts like Plato's dialogues, and witty texts like Molière's plays are examples of texts that present a consistent teaching or interpretation as concealed by a surface that is inconsistent or absurd when taken literally. No rule can explain to us how to penetrate the masks, which, as Nietzsche assures us, are loved by whatever is profound. And what, in any case, does "consistency" mean in the case of works of art?

To come back to the general example, there are also disadvantages that accrue from the interpretation of a mathematical theory within set theory. And analogies to these disadvantages are plainly visible

The Limits of Interpretation / 237

within a general theory of ontological or humanistic interpretation. To continue with the case of geometry, we gain no insight into what is significant or profound in geometry by translating it into set theory. These distinctions normally arise from geometrical intuition, which cannot function if it is deprived of its proper objects. Contemporary formalizations of Euclidean geometry thus typically assume from the outset what would be for Euclid and his contemporaries wrong if not dubious: the logical equivalence of geometry and algebra. Even granting that geometry can be algebraicized with no logical problems, we leave the domain of the intuition or direct reflection upon objects of unique types for the domain of equivalences. But the reflection upon equivalences will not reveal to the geometrician, as reflection upon geometrical objects can do, problems worth exploring. It will not protect the geometrician from the mechanical labor of proving trivial theorems. The creative imagination of the geometer, in order to be directed to its proper task, must do geometry, not set theory. And there is a parallel to all of this in ontological hermeneutics. The generalized restatement of a definite text, in order to be of value in its own right, must be based upon a proper understanding of the text itself. If we read a poem as an example of an ontological theory of human being, then we are not paying attention to the poem as poem. Furthermore, we are deprived of our poetic intuition, which is replaced by ontological speculation, just as geometrical intuition is replaced by algebra or logical analysis. This is not an objection to a general theory of poetry. But such a theory is valid if and only if it understands what poems are, and there is no apparent way in which to arrive at such an understanding except by the close study of actual poems.

The point made above about equivalences needs to be expanded. The statements of set theory are statements about sets and not about geometrical objects. Even though a statement about sets may be shown to be logically equivalent to a statement about a geometrical object, the former statement depends upon the latter statement (or upon the independent existence of geometry). A logical equivalence is a relation. The shift from geometry to set theory in my example is representative of the deeply held modern conviction that mathematics, and finally, all rational knowledge, consists in the relations of intrinsically unknowable things rather than in the natures of things. But the interpretation of a humanistic text is based upon the assumption that the text is intelligible in itself, not as a member of a logical equivalence to something else, say a theoretical element in a general ontology. If we are genuinely interpreters of the text itself, then we cannot in that guise be fundamental ontologists. Furthermore, an ontology of art-works (say) is not itself a set of relations or logical equivalences but once more a specific account in some natural language of the artworks as artworks. A completely general ontology is validated by its success in casting light upon entities of all kinds, including works of art or humanistic texts. But these must first be understood in some sense that is prior to the general ontology. Otherwise, we can never say that the general ontology succeeds in explaining or in applying to such particular artworks.

If it is true that set theory is a general interpretation of mathematics, it is not the case that set theory does something analogous to what a general theory of humanist interpretation is supposed to do. Set theory does not tell us what it means to be a mathematical object. It tells us only that mathematical objects may be represented by sets. It would be meaningless to claim that mathematical objects are "ultimately" sets. Second, set theory does not tell us what it means to be a mathematical theory. It tells us things about the formal structures of theories, but it can do this if and only if we know that what we are studying is in fact a mathematical theory. Third, set theory is useless in the task of giving an informal interpretation of a mathematical theory or of mathematics in general, as for example of the philosophical, artistic, or even political significance of mathematics.

As it turns out, however, a general theory of interpretation also does not do what such a theory is supposed to do. First, it does not tell us what it is to be a text of *this* kind, but rather (ostensibly) what it means to be a text of any kind. However, it is fair to suggest that properties holding good for texts of all kinds will also hold good of things other than texts, and perhaps of everything. It does not, incidentally, follow from this that everything is a text. Second, a general theory of interpretation does not tell us what it means to be a theory, but (at best) only what it means to be an interpretation, that is, provided we accept certain presuppositions or historical perspectives. Third, if a general theory of interpretation offers a general distinction between legitimate and illegitimate interpretations, such a distinction will be both too general and too clumsy to distinguish between relevant and irrelevant, or profound and trivial, interpretations.

My mathematical example casts light upon two general contentions of this essay. The first is that, even at the most abstract level, contemporary attempts to distinguish between theories and interpretations are failures. This is mainly because these thinkers reject the pre-theoretical talent of natural reason (sometimes called *phronēsis*), or else the domain upon which the talent may be exercised, or finally the "absolute" termination and fulfillment of the historical process of interpretation. The second is that, even within mathematics, one pays a price for the shift from one theory into another, a price that in the case of ontological hermeneutics is not accompanied by any balancing advantages. In conclusion, a theory of interpretation is impossible upon the premises of contemporary theoreticians of interpretation. What remains is philology or madness, each in unconscious pursuit of phronēsis.

Notes

1. Cf. Paul de Man, *Allegories of Reading* (New Haven: Yale University Press, 1979), 17 ("A literary text simultaneously asserts and denies the authority of its own rhetorical mode") and 58 ("But if reading is truly problematic, if a non-convergence between the stated meaning and its understanding may be suspected . . .").

2. This point is clearly recognized by E. D. Hirsch, Jr., with respect to the understanding of the meaning of a text; cf. *Validity in Interpretation* (New Haven: Yale University Press, 1967), 170, 203. Hirsch makes a very sensible criticism of theories claiming to account for the understanding of meanings, and thus too of Schleiermacher's canons. But his own theory of validation of interpretations amounts to the methodological defense of one meaning as more probable than another. And this in turn rests upon the assumption that meanings of texts are at least "probably" objective. What Hirsch understands by this is evident from his first statement of the goal of his method, namely, "to reach a consensus, on the basis of what is known, that correct understanding has *probably* been achieved" (17). This is not "Platonism," as Hirsch's position is sometimes described, but, at least practically, conventionalism or, in other words, traditionalism of the same sort that Hirsch objects to in the case of Gadamer (250). Hirsch does not explain what he means by a consensus. He takes it for granted that the objectivity of the meaning of a text is the same as its public accessibility by means of methodological devices. In the case of interpretations of humanistic texts (and especially of "eminent" texts or works of genius), a consensus is either worthless or worth no more than the persons who constitute it. And what method validates superior judgment?

3. Page references for Schleiermacher refer to Fr. D. E. Schleiermacher, *Hermeneutik*, ed. Heinz Kimmerle (Heidelberg: Carl Winter Universitätsverlag, 1959).

4. This has been correctly appreciated by Hirsch; see note 2 above.

5. Page references for Boeckh refer to August Boeckh, *Enzyklopädie und Methodenlehre der philologischen Wissenschaften*, ed. Ernst Bratuschek (Stuttgart: Teubner, 1966).

6. That is, it is the ontological basis that ostensibly justifies a subsequent widespread misinterpretation of Saussure's correct doctrine of the arbitrariness of the signifier. Simply stated, it does not follow from the arbitrariness of names that they possess arbitrary meanings apart from those that have conventionally been assigned to them.

7. Page references for Heidegger refer to Martin Heidegger, *Sein und Zeit* (Tübingen: Max Niemeyer Verlag, 1977).

8. It should be noted that Alexandre Kojève announced the death of man a generation before Foucault (or Lévi-Strauss), but in the sense of the transformation of human beings into gods. For an interesting discussion of Kojève's influence on his successors in France, see Vincent Descombes, *Modern French Philosophy* (Cambridge: Cambridge University Press, 1980).

9. Page references for Gadamer refer to Hans-Georg Gadamer, *Wahrheit und Methode* (Tübingen: J. C. B. Mohr/Paul Siebeck, 1960).

10. This point emerged from a conversation with David R. Lachterman, whose criticism of an earlier version of this paper was very helpful.

10

Endowment, Enablement, Entitlement: Toward a Theory of Constitution

In the course of remarks about Cartesian subjectivity made in connection with an inquiry into the nature of the "thing" at Freiburg in 1935–36, Martin Heidegger said that in Descartes, philosophy was first brought to the insight that it must begin with reflection on the possibility of knowledge before it could proceed with any other matter. This is one account of Descartes's establishment of a philosophical system, and it is most famously shown by the role of Cartesian doubt and its place at the beginning of philosophical inquiry (at the conclusion of his essay on postmodernism in philosophy, Berel Lang proposes one way in which this modernist suspicion might be overcome). Epistemology has come to provide the foundation for modern philosophy, and, according to Heidegger, it is central to the constitution of all philosophy since Descartes and Kant. As a consequence of the epistemological revolution, our relationship to the world is so determined that, as I said in my essay on romantic responses to Kant, it becomes principally a function of our knowledge of it; the world in turn becomes a representation to us. In Heidegger's words, this means that from Descartes onward, "a theory of knowledge had to be erected before a theory of the world."

In some of his later work, Heidegger undertook to specify the ways in which our relationship to the world might resist this reduction to representation. Similarly, Heidegger sought in such essays as "The Origin of the Work of Art" to provide a theory of the world as prior to a theory of our knowledge of it. As the title of that essay makes clear, this effort draws on certain conceptions of art (and especially of poetry) at crucial junctures. David Halliburton, who has written elsewhere on Heidegger's later phase, continues this project here in an essay subtitled "Toward a Theory of Constitution." As he says at the outset, a theory of constitution is a theory of the world.

The principal functions entailed by this theory are endowment, enablement, and entitlement. Endowment is, in Halliburton's account, analogous to a founding relationship such as occurs, for example, in logic, where X may be said to be the necessary condition of Y (and Halliburton depends on the fact that endowment names a necessary—though not necessarily causal—relation). It is a function that appears in Plato, for instance, whose theory of the constitution of the world "is such that there must be, as the necessary condition of the . . . ordinary world, another world beyond it. The latter thus enjoys the same relation to the ordinary world as the phenomenal basis enjoyed in relation to the idea as aspect." The theory of endowment offered here derives, furthermore, from the relational terms Firstness, Secondness, and Thirdness, proposed by Charles Sanders Peirce. Of Peirce's terms, Thirds may be of greatest interest, for they provide for efficient relations, for the function of signs and representations, and thus for the possibility of aesthetic experience; this is in part because the judgment of taste does not address the existence of the aesthetic object but deals only with one's representation of it. Finally, Halliburton turns to Heidegger, who provides a theory of endowment in two descriptions of the ontological "fourfold": one in the relations between artist, art, artwork, and audience, and another in the relations of earth, heavens, divinities, and mortals. Given Heidegger's interest in poetry and his particular devotion to Hölderlin's romantic verse, one is not surprised to find close connections between the aesthetic-poetic and the cosmological series, and one may take it as evidence of Heidegger's belated romanticism that he should seek to relate the two.

The functions of enablement and entitlement may be viewed as resting on this theory of endowment. If endowment is a function that capacitates or makes possible, then enablement may be seen as corresponding to the possibility of perfection. ("Creatural endowment," which Halliburton says would be solely earthly if it were not enabled, "is nothing if the condition of the endowed being is not satisfactory".) Finally, endowment makes possible or enables certain further communal and social functions, which are functions of entitlement: "Endowment makes possible such enabling as is necessary to realize the further entitlement of having a language, or a voice, and participating in a community."

Halliburton concludes with a reading of Hobbes's *Leviathan* which attempts to show that the functions of endowment, enablement, and entitlement are interwoven throughout that text. This is an original understanding of the *Leviathan* in two ways. First, it provides a confirming example of the ways in which these relational terms provide a theory of the political world, and not only the natural world, which makes no prior appeal to the theory of knowledge. And second, it challenges the more conventional view of the *Leviathan* (with its scientific bias and its efforts to inaugurate the theory of natural right) within the same episteme as the *Meditations* and the *Discourse on Method* of Descartes. Through Heidegger, Halliburton succeeds in dissociating Hobbes from what critics such as Timothy J. Reiss have called the "discourse of modernism" (see Reiss's 1982 book of that title) and from the analytical-referential thinking on which that modern discourse depends.

Endowment, Enablement,   *David Halliburton*
Entitlement: Toward a
Theory of Constitution

A theory of constitution is a theory of the world. It articulates principles according to which worldly beings and their environment, in the broadest sense of the term, are composed. (The "toward" in my title concedes that this particular attempt at such a theory remains tentative and incomplete.)

In the course of his investigations into logic, Husserl hit upon a type of relation that does not correspond with familiar conceptual models. It is not causal; neither of its members exists because the other brings it about. It is not serial; neither member antedates the other. It is not spatial, there being no fixed locus that either member must occupy. Nor is it organic, there being no parturition nor any development. Founding occurs when the being of an X is the necessary condition of the being of a Y. In such a relation there can be no Y without X. Therefore Y is said to be founded by X; or, X founds Y.

A similar phenomenon appears outside of logic as such. This will be called *endowment* for two reasons: first, because endowment and foundation may be associated by analogy but are by no means identical; second, because endowment, like enablement and entitlement, is best thought of as a function. This is to say that each has the bearing of the office it fulfills, which is performative and connective. *Bearing* here echoes an old sense of the term, prominent in *Hamlet*, indicating the manner in which one carries oneself (*OED*, s.v. "function" 2).

The function of endowment appears, for example, in Plato and in commentaries on Plato. The ordinary world as we know it could not be without that other, higher one, the realm of the Ideas, which transcends it, and which it, imperfectly, reflects. The former endows the latter; the latter is endowed by the former. In "The Question Concerning Technology" Heidegger tries another, related angle. The issue is a reversal Plato makes in the basic concept of the idea.

We, late born, are no longer in a position to appreciate the significance of Plato's daring to use the word *eidos* for that which in everything and in each particular thing endures as present. For *eidos*, in the common speech, meant the outward aspect (*Ansicht*) that a visible thing offers to the naked eye. Plato exacts of this word, however, something utterly extraordinary: that it name what precisely is not and never will be perceivable with physical eyes. But even this is by no means the full extent of what is extraordinary here. For *idea* names not only the nonsensuous aspect of what is physically visible. Aspect (*idea*) names and is, also, that which constitutes the essence in the audible, the tasteable, the tactile, in everything that is in any way accessible.[1]

The concept of idea in the received sense depends as much as Plato's recension does upon endowment. There must be something in the phenomenon on the basis of which we cognize any aspect. Because the orange is constituted as it is, we can have an idea, in the early sense, of its rondure; we could experience no such aspect were it not so endowed. Structurally, the Platonic transformation of the concept is, then, quite simple. Plato merely turns it around. His theory of the constitution is such that there must be, as the necessary condition of the orange and the rest of the ordinary world, another world beyond it. The latter thus enjoys the same relation to the ordinary world as the phenomenal basis enjoyed in relation to idea as aspect.

In his own logical investigations Peirce too discovered important relations generally overlooked by philosophers, with the partial exception of Kant and Hegel, though what he discovered extends, as in the case of Husserl, much further. The key relations are those that connect the ideas of Firstness, Secondness, and Thirdness. Firstness is the mode of being that is what it is without regard to any other. Secondness is the mode of being that is what it is with regard to another but not to a third. Thirdness is the mode of being that is what it is by virtue of relating a Second to a First. Illustrations may help.

"The typical ideas of firstness are qualities of feeling, or mere appearances. The scarlet of your royal liveries, the quality itself, independently of its being perceived or remembered, is an example . . . It is simply a peculiar positive possibility regardless of anything else." As a phenomenon of pure immediacy, firstness is noncognitive, hence incapable of being explicitly articulated.

"The type of an idea of Secondness is the experience of effort, prescinded from the idea of a purpose . . . The experience of effort cannot exist without the experience of resistance [*sic*]." The example that follows points out the difference, in a concrete situation, between a Second and a First.

Imagine yourself to be seated alone at night in the basket of a balloon, far above earth, calmly enjoying the absolute calm and stillness. Suddenly the piercing shriek of a steam-whistle breaks upon you, and continues for a good while. The impression of stillness was an idea of Firstness, a quality of feeling. The piercing whistle does not allow you to think or do anything but suffer. So that too is absolutely simple. Another Firstness. But the breaking of the silence by the noise was an experience.[2]

The sphere of the Second is that of "brute action," of "the brutal sheriff" whose strong arm gives effect to law; but the law as such is a Third. Now, Thirds are peculiarly powerful. To think of Thirdness is to think of Secondness, Peirce suggests, without mentioning Firstness and without saying why he does not. He does not, one may surmise, because he is, in Michael Polanyi's distinction, attending-from it rather than attending-to it. That is, he assumes the relation of First to Second in such a way that thinking about the latter entails the former. In any case, Thirdness has the power of lawfulness, of the general, which is the power of giving sense to the particular. This can be seen in its signifying capacity, which needs brute action in order to have something to explain, just as brute action needs some wherewithal with which to act. But Thirdness, the court, determines meaning. Drop a pencil on the floor and there will be brute action, resistance, Secondness: the friction of the body against the air as it descends, the striking, bouncing, settling of the body on the surface of the floor. But the law of gravity determines the falling, and law is Thirdness. That is why any sign may be thought of as a kind of law, for it brings about a relation whose lawfulness, habit, or general rule comes to be only in the bringing of that relation.

Peirce offers, in effect, a theory of endowment. Thirds are endowed by Seconds, Seconds by Firsts; for each entails the other, if mediately: that is, a Third cannot relate to a First without a Second. The theory does not offer, in other words, a thoroughgoing reciprocity of equally matched constituents, as does the threefold theory I am sketching here. Peirce admitted with reluctance that he was working out a version of the stages of thought in Hegel, and his theory follows similar teleological lines. For there is a sense in which Thirds are stronger than Seconds and Seconds than Firsts. Thirdness has a temporal function in a way that Firstness and Secondness do not, though Peirce does not achieve a great deal of clarity on the subject. Without the intervention of Thirdness, Firstness and Secondness would be static, unable to connect, which is another way of saying, as he does at one point, that their relations would be inefficient. It is the office of Thirdness, by bringing them into relation with one another, to make the relations efficient. Since only efficient relations can do anything, and since doing necessarily goes beyond any present state of affairs, Thirdness futurizes. Peirce's commitment to perfectibility, and more specifically to certain modes of evolution, necessitates a very large measure of predictability. The truth is what reasonable persons can and will agree on, given enough time, which is cumulative and progressive. Inasmuch as a sign functions in time, bringing a Second into the same relation to a First in which it, as Third, stands to the First, it inaugurates more being: "a sign is something by knowing which we know more."[3] The same may be said of logic and empirical science, which thrive on signs and lawfulness generally. Hence the modality of the future cannot be distinguished from the modality of rational inquiry, through which past predictions come to fruition. The future

has the kind of compulsiveness that belongs to inductive reasoning, or experimental inquiry, really the most mighty cogency there is. For experimental inquiry sets out with a hypothesis, upon which it bases predictions as to the issue of experiments, and it is left to the future experiment to bring forth the conclusion from the womb of the future.[4]

The commitment to evolution and scientific progress helps to explain the hierarchical aspect of the dynamic, with Firsts having enough power to provide wherewithal to Seconds, which can traffic in reactions, resistances, and the like, but no more, leaving it to Thirds to determine ultimately the meaning of the very relation that only a Third can effect.

This theory improves considerably upon the notion of a direct casuality that has endured as a residue of the *causa efficiens*, the latter being itself the only one of the four ancient causes to survive into the modern world. The theory does not get worked out in as much detail as one might wish, and certain obscurities remain. The chief of these is the extent to which it is cofoundational, that is, the extent to which the threefold is an approximation, with respect to the relative significance of its constituents, to the fourfold of Heidegger, to which I turn below. A genuine cofounding privileges no component, and there is no leading up from one to another as in the movement from Firsts to Seconds to Thirds. To complicate the matter, there is at least one area of consideration, the aesthetic, in which the First and Third are privileged and the Second is not. Peirce wants to know what to call the quality it is that appears under such linguistic guises as *beau*, "beautiful," or *ta kalon*. The term must be a sufficiently general sign to represent the lawfulness of its being applicable to a plurality of instances. All over the United States one can find statues, aesthetically undistinguished, that yet possess meaning for the inhabitants of the town in which they stand; and what they mean is the death and destruction of the Civil War:

The very fact of their vulgarity, which the statue proclaims above all else, makes this universal self-sacrifice on the altar of abstraction which we call the "general government" pathetically sublime. To each such family, that very realistic statue is one piece of granite . . . Yet it is what we call a "general" sign, meaning that it is *applicable* to many singulars. It is not *itself* General; it is its Object which is taken to be general. (8:357)

The quality essential to the aesthetic phenomenon therefore has Thirdness, else it would not possess the requisite generality and lawfulness. Since quality is by definition a First, the phenomenon must be both a First and a Third but not a Second. In the aesthetic phenomenon the agonistic tension, the brute action or reaction of Secondness, is absent. Peirce does not clarify his reason for exempting the aesthetic from the threefold rule of law that claims universality. It may be supposed that his long study of Kant has something to do with it. Kant, too, eliminates effort from the aesthetic experience. The pure judgment of taste does not concern itself with the existence of the aesthetic object but with one's representation of it. Kant imagines that the palace he has been using as an illustration could be wished into being through scant effort.

Suppose, finally, that I found myself on an uninhabited island, without hope of ever again coming among men and could build myself such a palace by sheer wish and magic. I can quite easily convince myself that I should still not trouble to exert even this little effort so long as I had a hut that was comfortable enough for me. That may all be conceded and approved; only it is not to the point. All one wants to know is whether the mere representation of the object is accompanied in me by pleasure, no matter how indifferent. In order to say of an object that it is *beautiful* and to prove I have taste, the important thing, as can easily be seen, is not my dependence on the object's existence but what I make of its representation in myself.[5]

In his reflections on language, the Hegel of the Philosophy of Spirit goes further. To arrive at that height of intellectual power which is true freedom, one transcends, in stages one's obligation to the "external" world. Closest to the external world are words that function iconically, as Peirce would say. An icon resembles or exhibits directly what it signifies, in the manner of a photograph or diagram. Hence Hegel's preference for pure signs rather than hieroglyphics. A subsequent stage witnesses the internalization of the word. In this stage the word has the flexibility associated with the world of inner experience, together with the definiteness associated with the outer world. After this, one discontinues the effort to make sense of the words and simply manipulates them mechanically. The effort to mean dissolves; sense is no longer what words must be made to have but that which they already are.

With both Kant and Hegel, Peirce stressed the representative function, though his aesthetic theory aims at a balance between the representer and the thing represented. In the aesthetic sphere may be found "a sort of intellectual sympathy, a sense that here is a Feeling that one can comprehend, a reasonable Feeling. I do not succeed in saying exactly *what* it is, but it is a consciousness belonging to the category of Representation, though representing something in the Category of Quality of Feeling" (5:113).

If regarding the aesthetic phenomenon as a First that is also a Third left Seconds out, the approach of Seconds to Thirds provides a remedy. Now Seconds come into play by association with Thirds, in whose direction they move, so that the First that is also a Third is a Second too, as it must be if the trichotomy is to be as thoroughgoing as it is supposed to be. Peirce simply did not attend to the matter closely enough to see how the prescinding could be overcome. Another reason for the shortfall is that he is doing two things at once, as suggested by the distinction between "would" and "does." The latter reflects the actual and processual—the datable, locatable event. It belongs to what might be called the phenomenological phase of the trichotomy. The former, "would," designates the structural and the necessary—what must be the case irrespective of particulars—and belongs to what might be called the ontological phase. Looking back at the passage on aesthetic enjoyment, we can discern, retrospectively, the tendency to move from the one to the other. The collaboration of the first person singular and plural occurs in a state (aesthetic enjoyment) and proffers an act (attending to). It is an attempt to render phenomenologically processes that commonly occur. But by the conclusion the ontological comes into prominence. A dip into the waters of experience is followed, in other words, by speculation on the high ground of the structural and the necessary. The indefinite approach of the dynamical to the final interpretant draws the aesthetic away from its purely qualitative toward its lawful phase, and tends to assimilate its peculiar excellence to the excellence of sound logic and proper conduct.

No such interpretative exertion is necessary for a theory of constitution worked out by Heidegger in several versions. In "The Origin of the Work of Art," the relation of artist, art, artwork, and audience forms the constitutive matrix. The artist produces the particular entity, the work, in relation to norms and expectations governing what will count as such a work; this is what we call art, which consists also of the virtual ensemble of all particular works. The work as finished product is experienced by an audience, which plays, however, a more active role than audiences in some other theories. For those who experience the work thereby preserve it, the preservation being no less crucial to the continuity of art than are the artist and the work. When the art is literary, the counterparts of work, art, artist, and audience become, respectively, poem, poetry, poet, and people.

Of the two later versions of the fourfold, the one spelled out in "The Question Concerning Technology" is the closer to the early conception. At issue is the fourfold casuality of the Western philosophical tradition, the *causa materialis, formalis, finalis, efficiens,* which alters beyond recognition the Greek *aition* from which it derives. For *aition* means, not causing or bringing about, but responsibility. The silver of which a chalice is made, the *hyle,* or material, is said to be coresponsible for the chalice. To the silver the chalice is indebted for its appearing as this particular configuration and not some other other, such as a ring: "Thus the sacrificial vessel is at the same time indebted to the aspect (*eidos*) of chaliceness." Here *eidos* signifies aspect in the traditional sense that Plato, as noted above, reversed. What accounts for the sacrificial character of the chalice is neither the stuff it is made of nor the aspect singly, nor even their relation. What accounts for this character is the debt of that relation to the governing *telos,* as what determines the boundary of the thing. The stuff would not emerge in the aspect of chalice were it not for this responsible guiding. There remains the being analogous to the poet in the earlier conception.

The silversmith considers carefully and gathers together the three aforementioned ways of being responsible and indebted. To consider carefully [*überlegen*] is in Greek *legein, logos. Legein* is rooted in *apophainesthai*, to bring forward into appearance. The silversmith is co-responsible as that from whence the sacrificial vessel's bringing forth and resting-in-itself take and retain their first appearance. (*Question Concerning Technology*, 8)

Of the two versions of the fourfold worked out in the 1950s, the one described in "The Thing" is probably the more familiar. Its members are the earth, the sky or the heavens, the divinities, and the mortals. "Earth is the building bearer, nourishing with its fruits, tending water and rock, plant and animal."[6] Here the earth does not wear quite the same guise as in the earlier writings. There it was counterpoised against the world, the sphere of human beings in all manner of historical, social, political, economic, religious, public, and private manifestations. Earth was a nourisher, but also a stubborn thing inaccessible to the kind of interpretation that discloses ontological structures in the ontic plenitude.

In the later mythopoeia, the thinking gaze moves upward. "The sky (*Himmel*) is the sun's path, the course of the moon, the glitter of the stars, the year's seasons, the light and dusk of day, the gloom and glow of night, the clemency and inclemency of the weather, the drifting clouds and blue depth of the ether" (ibid). Like the earth, this sky is very benign, with only the gloom of night and the inclement weather providing a negative note. *Himmel*, which also means "heaven," of course, prepares for the divinities, traditionally associated with higher realms. The association is not made explicit, but the proximity, in the exposition, between the heavens and the divine beings may suggest it. The previous reference to the ether, an ancient phenomenon with a rich cultural history and prominent in Hölderlin, Heidegger's favorite poet, inclines in the same general direction.

The divinities are the beckoning messengers of the godhead. Out of the hidden sway of the divinities the god emerges as what he is, which removes him from any comparison with beings that are present. (Ibid.)

These beings are not to be taken for members of some pantheon. It is not even supposed that they have come into being. They are beings of the future tense; hence their communicative office, which is that of giving advance notice to the remaining realm of the fourfold, the realm of the mortals.

The mortals are human beings. They are called mortals because they can die. To die means to be capable of death as death. Only man dies. The animal perishes [*verendet*]. It has death neither ahead of itself nor behind it. Death is the shrine of Nothing, that is, of that which in every respect is never something that merely exists, but which nevertheless presences, even as the mystery of being itself. (Ibid.)

Having thus briefly described the theories, let us examine them more closely. All address the problem of regions and regional ontologies.

Region is just the highest and most inclusive generic unity belonging to a concretum, that is, the essential unitary connexion of the summa genera which belong to the lowest differences within the concretum.[7]

To each region there corresponds a regional Ontology with a series of self-limited regional sciences, which eventually rest on one another and correspond to the highest genera which have their unity in the region.[8]

As an account of relations in the strictly aesthetic sphere, the regional ontology of the first fourfold (art, artist, artwork, audience; or poetry, poet, poem, people) meets the criterion of parsimony: it does not provide more constituents than are necessary. Art guides the artist into the work, the poet into the poem; the audience, or people, preserves, and preservation is a long-range function that can succeed only if assimilations, adjustments, and adjudications keep occurring. This is an extremely complex responsibility. What is more, in Heidegger's theory, each age opens itself to a different epochal interpretation precisely because each differs in certain ways from every other. The question is whether the concept of audience or people, as it stands, is sufficient, or whether some further differentiation is in order. To suggest that this is the case amounts to nothing more, perhaps, than affirming the sense, to which many subscribe, that the Heideggerean theory could be augmented by recourse to social, political, and economic history. The work of Hannah Arendt is, among other things, an attempt to achieve that aim.

The second ontological fourfold concerns a different but closely related region, that of the artifact. The problems that arise because of its religious character cannot be considered within the compass of this essay. As in the previous case, the account answers the criterion of parsimony, but one constituent appears to be "overdetermined." *Hyle* is responsible for the unworked stuff that *eidos* is responsible for guiding into a concrete aspect, while the coresponsibility of the craftsman consists in so relating to the other constituents as to enable their mutality. It is *telos* that opens the door, being "a third that is above all responsible for the sacrificial vessel." This is because *telos* bounds the vessel into consecration and bestowal. Putting the matter that way avoids the appearance of a merely purposive process, one aiming, that is, at the realization of a goal that would be the correlate of an effect deriving from a cause. Putting the matter that way also implies that the application or use of the thing in question possesses particular significance, for there would be no occasion for any of the cognizant relations if there were to be no consecration or bestowal. In this sense *telos* is more responsible. Such a view does not alter the basic cofoundational character of *telos*, however. Something that endows functions *ab ovo*, as indicated by the Latin phrase, which points to a radical beginning such as birth. *Telos*, by contrast, proceeds by drawing its correlates along with it, so to speak. That is one difference. Another is that *telos* does not meet the criterion of endowing. To do so, one would have to say that *hyle*, *eidos*, and craftsman could not be if *telos* were not; and that is clearly not the case. There can be silver without *telos*, or a chalice aspect, or a craftsman. So *telos* cannot endow. But without the prospect of application in consecration there could be no chalice; neither could there be a chalice without *hyle*, *eidos*, and craftsman, which means that *telos* is reciprocal in relation to the three others. It also suggests the scope of differentiae.

In the fourfold of earth, sky, divinities, and mortals, reciprocity and partnership reign, which is why Heidegger says that each of the four mirrors the others, and that they dance and play together, constituting the world.

This appropriating mirror-play of the simple onefold of earth and sky, divinities and mortals, we call the world. The world presences by worlding. That means: the world's worlding cannot be explained by anything else nor can it be fathomed through anything else. This impossibility does not lie in the inability of our human thinking to explain and fathom in this way. Rather, the inexplicable and unfathomable character of the world's worlding lies in this, that causes and grounds remain unsuitable for the world's worlding . . . The human will to explain just does not reach to the simpleness of the simple onefold of worlding. The united four are already strangled in their essential nature when we think of them only as separate realities, which are to be grounded in and explained by one another.[9]

One difficulty lies in the fact that "the world, while constituted by four coequal regions, depends for much of its force on the least-secular region, that of the gods. It is also the most problematic region, as Heidegger himself suggests by the word 'also': 'But the jug's gift is at times also given for consecration.' "[10] In contrast to the chalice, which is made to serve in consecration, the jug described in "The Thing" performs that function sometimes. In any case, the acknowledgment of the problematic status of the realm of the gods, if tacit, connects with the office of the holy. Traditionally, the holy names the *mysterium tremendum*, the numinous, and the spontaneously or institutionally sacred, and as such belongs to the already—to those phenomena that one experiences as preceding one in being. The holy in Heidegger is, by comparison, an openness. It has not happened, and may not; it is the possibility of making a cultural decision about the sacred. This concept of the holy, in other words, is a contemporary and contingent attitude toward the traditional one.

But the more important difficulty consists in the relation of earth and sky to the rest of the fourfold insofar as they already relate to its elemental background. This background, for lack of a better term, is that of the cosmos. One is tempted to call it nature, but, if Oskar Becker is right, that would be wrong. *Being and Time* finds in nature "a limited case of the being of possible entities in the world" and suggests that human being, *Dasein*, can know nature within the world only in a certain, presumably limited way (*Sein und Zeit*, sec. 65). Becker replies that this tallies with the way nature appears within the world but leaves in the dark what is peculiar about nature, its own being, or *Eigenwesen*.

In truth, however, nature belongs to the cosmos, representing the form of its totality. Cosmos in the sense intended here is not world but stands in polar opposition to it. As world belongs to Dasein, cosmos belongs to Dawesen . . . The relation of daseienden (historical) human being to the world . . . is entirely different from the relation of dawesenden human beings to the cosmos . . . The daseiende human being stands in the center of the world-sphere—the analysis of worldly spatiality, which Heidegger has offered, proves it; the dawesende, however, isomorphically represents the "micromos" as "microcosmos."[11]

Dasein embraces the human and worldly, *Dawesen* the creatural and cosmic. "Cosmos" is more than the vaguely astronomical concept to which the term is often restricted. Any entity on earth is part of the cosmos, and even the world—the environing sphere of human activities—has cosmic dimensions. Cosmos includes everything from stellar motions to Dylan Thomas's "force that through the green fuse drives the flower," to the sun igniting the force, to the insects on the leaves around the bloom and the gardener who tends the plant. As transcendence and possibility belong to the worldly human, immanence and necessity belong to the cosmically creatural. The creatural model is the mode of life, of organic vitality, biological function, birth, growth, decay. Its counterpart is existence, the phenomenon of worldliness, which embraces the making of practical things and instruments, the establishing and preserving of institutions, the acts of speaking, acting, reflecting, and all that characterizes what we call human being.

Succinctly: cosmos endows earth as earth endows world. This is the case because earth could not be without cosmos, but the converse does not hold; and because world could not be without earth, but the converse does not hold. This account reflects the need to delineate ontic regions and to provide regional ontologies for them, a need that Husserl, as seen above, made explicit and that Heidegger continued to recognize. It also aims at another Husserlian goal, the delineation of functions.

Yet the greatest problems of all are the *functional problems,* or those of the *"constituting of the objective field of consciousness."* They concern the way in which, for instance, in respect of Nature, noeses, animating the material, and weaving themselves into unitary manifolds, into continuous syntheses, so bring into being the consciousness of something, that in and through it the objective unity of the field of objects (*Gegenständlichkeit*) may permit of being consistently "declared," "shown forth," and "rationally" determined.[12]

My concern here is not so much with consciousness, which is only one constituting function in the world, as with the facilitating or enabling that goes on, and that Husserl rightly regards as problematic: animating, weaving, bringing into being. These functions are seen in relation to the cosmos, which Husserl calls nature, because that relation throws into relief the active role of human beings, who perform the important role of enabling the cosmic, enabling it, that is, for operation in the world. The cosmic as such, as pure endowment, is what it is, and the earth, as such, as pure endowment, is what it is. Each is responsible but not coresponsible: the cosmos cannot be indebted to earth as earth is to cosmos any more than earth can be indebted to world as world is indebted to earth. The line or direction of the function, so to speak, is unilateral.

Not so enabling, which is precisely what animating, weaving, bringing-to-be are all about. Endowing capacitates: it makes something, for the world, of what earth endows it with. To be born on earth is, for human beings, the most basic of endowments. It is because it is so basic to the human condition, and to its mortality, that Arendt, at least partly in answer to Heidegger's being-toward-death, insists upon the paradigmatic significance of what she calls natality. But endowment would remain an earthly function, and nothing more, if it were not enabled. Other human beings, previously endowed and enabled, must draw the newborn into the world, bringing its creatural nature along with it. The newborn is entitled to this, which is one thing we mean when we speak of birthright. This right means also, and centrally, that the endowed creature is entitled to well-being, and, together with this, the right to have a voice and the right to participate in a community (to be considered below). Well-being, the state of a satisfactory, healthy condition, is so taken for granted that it rarely figures in Western thought. That it does figure in Sir Thomas More's *Utopia* suggests that by the close of the Middle Ages there was a need to revitalize its normative role—ironically, by presenting what was once normal as an imagined ideal:

Their second type of physical pleasure arises from the calm and regular functioning of the body—that is, from a state of health undisturbed by any minor ailments. In the absence of mental discomfort, this gives one a good feeling, even without the help of external pleasures. Of course, it's less ostentatious, and forces itself less violently on one's attention than the crudest delights of eating and drinking, but even so it's often considered the greatest pleasure in life. Practically everyone in Utopia would agree that it's a very important one, because it's the basis of all the others.[13]

Creatural endowment is nothing if the condition of the endowed being is not satisfactory. It is precisely because the condition of well-being is normative that we have developed, on the one hand, notions of illness, dysfunction, abnormality, and the like, and, on the other, procedures to enable the return of the normal state. As if to underscore the centrality of well-being, several overlapping senses of the term *perfection* have come down to us over the centuries. A perfect peach is not the finest peach that ever was but a peach that, having come into its own as the kind of entity it is, is just fine. Lack of deficiency became a benchmark for perfection because well-being already was.

Endowment makes possible such enabling as is necessary to realize the further entitlement of having a language, or a voice, and participating in a community. Stating the issue this way verges on tautology. Unless Wittgenstein and all the major linguistic theorists are mistaken, there can be no truly private language. Language does not exist without a community any more than a community exists without language. This does not make language a mere tool at the service of communal interests. Through the paradigmatic architecture of *langue* and the syntagmatic protocols of *parole*, language keeps its own house in order. If language can nonetheless be put to a variety of communal purposes—if it can be instrumental, say, in establishing a political state or overthrowing one—it is because the same words in a different situation are not the same words. Situations enable matrices, which is why Sartre has spent so much energy describing them.

We still do not know very much about language. "Language is obscure in terms of its function, which is to render everything else clear. It cannot be observed or grasped directly; it can only be exercised."[14] There is something to be said for the pragmatic view that the meaning of language is the consequence of its exercise in a situation. Kenneth Burke's insistence on the entelechial motive in rhetorical strategies moves in the same general direction. There is something to be said, too, for the view that, since language is no more or no less than its capacity of realization through exercise, training is of the essence. Wittgenstein, perhaps the only modern philosopher to teach grammar school, did not hesitate to speak of training rather than education. What the community trains in its members is a capacity to which all are entitled as a constituent of their well-being. Training is a way to enable the entitlement.

The situation can also work the other way around. A language learner who turns into a writer can become an enabler in turn, training the community up, as it were, to a new level of realization:

Language [*langage*] has a function analogous to the language [*langue*] of a new writer who, at first, is not understood, but who little by little becomes understandable by teaching people to understand him. His gestures seem to point in non-existent directions; then, little by little, some notions begin to find for themselves a potential [*virtuel*] home in these gestures.[15]

So to function is to enlarge the range of entitlement and, at the same time, to enable its realization. Enlarging and enabling entitlement in such a manner alters taste, the importance of which was recognized by Gracián.[16] His *gusto* is, in my terminology, a component of creatural endowment. *Gusto* indicates the innate capacity to distinguish one flavor from another, to discriminate between this bouquet and that one, and so on. The function of training, which he calls by the traditional name of education, is to enlarge the range of entitlements: to establish new experiences as susceptible of positive judgment, as meeting criteria of correctness and good upbringing; training at the same time enables all this by teaching the individual, or the learning cohort, how to make proper distinctions and discriminations, thus transforming the creatural endowment into a worldly one.

Endowment, enablement, and entitlement weave in and out of Hobbes's *Leviathan* as well. The artificial animal who is man is a trope for the one kind of entity, body, and the one kind of function, motion, to which the Hobbesian bears witness. Body capable of motion is the central creatural endowment. But so long as bodies and their motions remain at their original stage, which Hobbes calls nature, they keep moving in their own interest, there being no other. In this stage to be is to be more; to have is to have more; everyone has the same right to have everything: these are variations on the universal theme of bodies moving. The state of eternal war that this amounts to is justified by the First Law of Nature, "*That every man, ought to endeavour Peace, so farre as he has hope of obtaining it; and when he cannot obtain it, that he may seek, and use, all helps, and advantages of Warre.*"[17] The proposition stresses, as propositions in political philosophy have a way of doing, entitlement: Hobbes's philosophy, no less than all the others, is an exercise in self-justification (even if it enables itself, as it certainly does in Hobbes, by the steady application of rhetorical muscle). The conception of the first law potentiates the obligation Hobbes wants to invoke. Parties are entitled to war only on the condition that peace is unobtainable. This is an important qualification. If the philosopher can devise a theory to enable entitlement to peace, no party can claim entitlement to war. Hobbes's theory will manage, of course, to do just that. But first, a closer look at the first law of nature.

The deontological "ought" entitles every actor to do what he can to obtain peace, such doing being precisely the enabling acts that could effect peace. The vague "hope" evidently embraces the range of these possible acts, the anticipation of their result, and the situation or situations in which they are performed. By recognizing that some people have more help and advantages than others, Hobbes, in effect, proposes a kind of secondary endowment modeled on the creatural. For just as the creatural gives one such and such capacities primordially, so may such and such capacities be conferred at a later stage. This is no invention of Hobbes's. Hobbes is simply attending to a phenomenon that many other thinkers had long attended to. But the function of modeling marks a significant difference. The stored-up capacities, whether inherited or acquired, and whatever they may be, resemble creatural endowment but do not come to the same thing. The secondary phenomenon is something to which one is entitled because one has been enabled to possess it, and not because it manifested itself primordially as a necessary condition of earthly and worldly being. This is to say that the phenomenon in question is, for all practical purposes, a worldly endowment.

Contract, or covenant, enables the entitlement called price. Transcendence of the warring state and supersession of the civil occurs when equals agree to mutually binding political obligations, such as the delegating of authority from many persons to one person. Delegation of authority to a sovereign, as a worldly endowment, is marked by reciprocity, in contrast to the unilateral endowment of the creatural. Here reciprocity takes the form of a contractual limit, a qualification unthinkable in creatural endowment:

And because the Multitude naturally is not One, but Many; they cannot be understood for one; but many Authors, of every thing their Representative saith, or doth in their name; Every man giving their common Representer, Authority from himself in particular; and owning all the actions the Representer doth, in case they gave him Authority without stint: Otherwise, when they limit him in what, and how farre he shall represent them, none of them owneth more, than they gave him commission to Act. (*Leviathan*, 220–21)

In giving up their natural right to act only in their own interest, for the aggrandizement of their own power and glory, those who covenant realize their entitlement to "propriety"—the "ownness" of a thing, including the right to alienate it for a price; in a word, property. The highest name for entitlement in this system, which defines what is right as that which is contracted for, is justice. Taking rare recourse to the Schools, Hobbes borrows the definition of justice as *"the constant Will of giving to every man his own.* And therefore where there is no *Own,* that is, no *Propriety,* there is no *Injustice;* and where there is no coercive *Power* erected, that is, where there is no *Common-wealth,* there is no *Propriety;* all men having *Right* to all things" (202).

The Leviathan state enables the entitlement of well-being, language, and community. The communal resides in the commonwealth as such, which guarantees that the wealth shall be common, the mode of guarantee being the contract, which relies on words. Now words work, in the Hobbesian theory, by forming chains of reasoning that lead to consequences; meaning is that which names add up to, or can be reduced to by subtraction. Hence the ease with which Hobbes turns reason into reckoning. Geometry being the equivalent for Hobbes of what music is in Pater's hierarchy of the arts, Hobbes strives to approximate, in his reasoning, the rigor of mathematical argument. Yet he holds to the primacy of language: "So that without words, there is no possibility of reckoning of Numbers, much lesse of Magnitudes, of Swiftnesse, of Force, and other things, the reckonings whereof are necessary to the being, or well-being of man-kind" (104). This makes linguistic capacity as such a creatural endowment, on the basis of which words, then numbers, are learned.

Language and community make common cause with that well-being which Hobbes, in a telling association with reckoning, equates with the very being of mankind. For if the essence of justice is the individual possession of property, the contract must at some point express itself in numerical terms. It must bind with words, in chains of consequence, at the same time that it stipulates the numbers that the property, as valued entity, amounts to. Hence, "The Value, or WORTH of a man, is as of all other things, his Price; that is to say, so much as would be given for the use of his Power: and therefore is not absolute; but a thing dependant [sic] on the need and judgment of another" (151–52). Well-being is not price per se, for this varies from situation to situation. Well-being is the enabled entitlement of full participation in the price-structure system. It is the very being of the individual as possessor of entities, including himself, whose ultimate communal expression is price.

That versions of endowment, enablement, and entitlement appear in a major work of political philosophy is far from accidental. The theory of constitution I am describing is palpably political, taking that term in a broad sense. By way of further demonstration, each function of the manifold corresponds to the functions of government sketchily drawn by Montesquieu in his discussion of democracy as an ideal type and implemented in the Constitution of the United States. Through the Constitution and the other laws it passes, the legislature confers a worldly endowment; for without such legislation no constitutional democracy would exist. Enablement, for its part, falls to the executive branch. Through administrative procedures and enforcement, laws are put into effect and regulations are written to carry out in greater details the general legislative intent. Finally, the office of entitlement is assigned to the judiciary. The endowment having been enabled, courts must adjudicate, deciding which parties to adversarial proceedings have the more just claim. This organization of functions is roughly parallel, incidentally, to the functions of Peirce's Firsts, Seconds, and Thirds.

For a political discourse in which threefold constitution may be seen, consider the declaration beginning, "We hold these truths to be self-evident, *that all men are endowed by their creator with certain inalienable rights*" (emphasis added). Not all the functions are set forth with equal clarity, there being a chiasmus between what might be called the expository structure and the interest structure (employing the latter as Habermas does in *Knowledge and Human Interests*). The expository structure is the sequence of words as it unfolds. The interest structure is the case the authors of the expository structure want to plead successfully, that is, the public vindication of their revolutionary act. As the interest structure proceeds from assumptions, the expository structure proceeds toward suasion.

The expository structure leads with endowment. Rights come from a creator whose discursive presence, in so prominent a rhetorical site, lends tacit support to the process of assertion. Enablement consists not so much in the rights that are specified as in the *possession* of the rights, which is couched in negative terms. The privative adjective reflects the assumption that it is right to possess them because we possess them, as a consequence of which—entitled to them as we are—they cannot be alienated. This meets a criterion of effort, in that it takes less effort to deny to others what we possess than to justify the fact that we possess it. "Rights" appears at the end of the clause as the culminating entitlement that is the ultimate aim, in this discursive situation, of the authors' interests.

The interest structure begins where the clause ends, with entitlement. Now the aim is to elevate rights to primacy without appearing to do so, which means that the clause reinforces the general drift of the document: above all, the claim of entitled independence must be argued convincingly; otherwise the authors are lawbreakers and their actions are politically illegitimate. How do we come by the entitlement? By endowment, the source of which is God. Had the authors made the expository and the interest structures coincide, the statement would not lead, as it presently does, with its strong suit, which is divine endowment. Leading with entitlement would put entitlement up for immediate scrutiny, following which the claim of endowment could seem gratuitous.

Having examined a political philosophy, a method of constituting government, and a piece of political discourse, I conclude with a poetic text, Frost's "The Gift Outright," in which threefold constitution is busily at work.

The land was ours before we were the land's.
She was our land more than a hundred years
Before we were her people . . .
. . . .
Something we were withholding made us weak
Until we found out that it was ourselves
We were witholding from our land of living,
And forthwith found salvation in surrender.

The poem takes up the complex challenge of entitling the enablement of endowment by enabling that entitlement. The endowment is the land, an indefinite *Dawesen* that a definite *Dasein* owns by virtue of occupation. Other entitlements and enablements could have been mentioned, including French ownership of territory west of the colonies, or the Louisiana Purchase, or the elimination of Mexican interest in the Southwest and Far West. But these do not suit the ideology of the poem, which is a kind of natural imperialism.

The story of the poem temporizes essence, to borrow Kenneth Burke's idea. *The Social Contract* of Rousseau is a locus classicus: "Man was born free, and everywhere he is in chains." Rousseau belies that the essence of being human is freedom. But the belief cannot be stated in that form—the interest would beam right through. Moreover, the present-tense definition raises a problem of authority: Who is he to tell us what an essence is? Hence Rousseau's recourse to story, which has its own authority. "Once upon a time" does not argue, it narrates, and narratives are a lot better at winning assent than argumentation. Story tells the way it was, not the way that someone thinks it ought to be.

Frost's story of enablement is pure magic.

Such as we were we gave ourselves outright
(The deed of gift was many deeds of war)
To the land vaguely realizing westward,
But still unstoried, artless, unenhanced,
Such as she was, such as she would become.

The enablement, by which the citizenry finally came into full possession of the continental United States, is almost everything that concrete history is not. It is autonomous, immanent, passive, gratuitous, and natural. Autonomous: the people do not respond to events or to other peoples, nor do they interact, nor do they assert themselves. Possession simply comes about. Immanent: the discovery that the present and future are predetermined, and that we are the transmitters of what will be, just dawns on us, as the cogito is supposed to have dawned on

Descartes. Passive: the people have only to surrender. Gratuitous: the entire process is a gift, ourselves being the given. Natural: it is not a people's history that is realizing, but the land's, and this process too is autonomous. Concrete history leaves a deposit of sorts in the parenthetic line, which reveals an interesting assumption. Besides the gift there is the deed of the gift, as though the deed were the fallen form of a pure idea. In fact, there is more to the hierarchy, for the deed functions as an essence capable of various instantiations: The deed of gift, plural, is deeds of war, plural. The gift outright, to borrow again from Burke, is a god term, through which endowment, enablement, and entitlement merge, much as they do in Manifest Destiny (which would have been an appropriate alternate, if too obvious, title).

As entitlement the poem assumes the justice of that possessive giving which makes the collective destiny manifest. In sum:

Endowment inaugurates.

Enablement facilitates.

Entitlement adjudicates.

Notes

1. Martin Heidegger, *The Question Concerning Technology and Other Essays*, trans. William Lovitt (New York: Harper & Row, 1977), 20.

2. *Semiotic and Significs: The Correspondence between Charles S. Peirce and Lady Victoria Welby*, ed. Charles S. Hardwick (Bloomington: Indiana University Press, 1977), 26.

3. *Semiotic and Significs*, 31–32.

4. *Collected Papers of Charles Sanders Peirce*, ed. Arthur W. Burks (Cambridge: Harvard University Press, 1966), 7:666. Quotations from Peirce will hereafter appear parenthetically according to the convention of volume and paragraph number.

5. Immanuel Kant, *Analytic of the Beautiful*, trans. Walter Cerf (Indianapolis: Bobbs-Merrill, 1963), 5.

6. Quotations from "The Thing," in Martin Heidegger, *Poetry, Language, Thought*, trans. Albert Hofstadter (New York: Harper & Row, 1971), 178.

7. Edmund Husserl, *Ideas: General Introduction to Pure Phenomenology*, trans. W. R. Boyce Gibson (New York: Macmillan [Collier], 1962), 69.

8. *Ideas*, 186.

9. *Poetry, Language, Thought*, 179–80.

10. David Halliburton, *Poetic Thinking: An Approach to Heidegger* (Chicago: University of Chicago Press, 1982), 174. Comments in the present section draw on discussions in this book.

11. Oskar Becker, *Dasein und Dawesen: Gesammelte philosophische Aufsätze* (Pfullingen: Neske, 1963), 85–86.

12. Edmund Husserl, *Ideas: General Introduction to Pure Phenomenology*, trans. W. R. Boyce Gibson (1931; reprint, New York: Macmillan-Collier, 1962), 230–31.

13. Thomas More, *Utopia*, trans. Paul Turner (Harmondsworth: Penguin Books, 1965), 96.

14. Maurice Merleau-Ponty, *Consciousness and the Acquisition of Language*, trans. Hugh J. Silverman (Evanston: Northwestern University Press, 1973), 6.

15. *Consciousness and the Acquisition of Language*, 29.

16. These remarks draw on Hans-Georg Gadamer, *Truth and Method*, ed. Garrett Burden and John Cumming from second-edition translation (New York: Seabury, 1975), 34.

17. Thomas Hobbes, *Leviathan*, ed. C. B. Macpherson (Harmondsworth: Penguin Books, 1968), 190. Further quotations from *Leviathan* appear by page number in parentheses.

11

Writer, Text,
Work, Author

Alexander Nehamas begins his essay roughly where David Halliburton leaves off, which is to say with Hobbes's *Leviathan*, and specifically with its proposed relationship between authors and ownership. Seen from the angle of Halliburton's essay, the Nehamas piece might be viewed as an investigation into the function of "entitlement" as determined by the relationship between authors and texts. According to Hobbes, authors may be said to own their words and actions, so that, as Nehamas points out, the writings of literary authors may be said to be their property. So seen, the authorial relation sets in motion fields of related concern in ethics, morals, and social and legal history. As soon as one begins to regard writers as author-owners of their words and implies that the words are their property, then one introduces questions of responsibility in a way that casts new light upon the central assumptions of modern literary theory and criticism. As Nehamas demonstrates in this essay, these are in need of serious reconsideration. By framing the problem of authorship in relation to property, it is possible to open up the social and historical dimensions of the problem which have been closed off both by the New Criticism and by the speech-act theory dispute between Searle and Derrida. To this extent, Nehamas is willing to accept the historicist assumptions of Michel Foucault. Yet to the extent that Foucault's historicism is also found lacking, Nehamas proposes a theory of authorship along hermeneutic lines: the notion of authorship (and, implicitly, the concepts of writer, text, and work) is determined only as a function of interpretation and criticism.

In this essay, Nehamas first takes his bearings from Roland Barthes, who in "The Death of the Author" said that the author function is a peculiarly modern one, "emerging from the Middle Ages with English Empiricism, French Rationalism and the personal faith of the Reformation." From Barthes he turns quickly to Foucault, who has studied the emergence of the author in connection with one specific aspect of the problem of ownership, that is, the development of a certain type of penal system. According to Foucault, authorial-type ownership "has always been subsequent to what one might call penal appropriation. Texts, books, and discourses really began to have authors . . . to the extent that authors became subject to punishment." Authorship is, in other words, historically linked to repression.

Granting that the author function is a determinable historical phenomenon (even if, as Nehamas suggests, it is not a function of exactly the history that Foucault tells), it is possible to ask whether the author function might be "overcome." This would mean assimilating the historicist notion of authorship to a theoretical critique of authorship as a logical concept, as Nehamas seeks to do. If we agree that the author is a function or role, while the writer is a person—a difference that might also be stated in terms of Hobbes's contrast of the "person artificial" and the writer as a historical person; it might be easy to move from the "artificiality" of the author to the view that the author is one more fictional character. This is especially so if one is willing to accept J. Hillis Miller's proposition that the author is an *effect* of the text. Nehamas argues that this is a reductive view, and accordingly he draws out some of the more complex relations that obtain between authors and their texts.

If the author is indeed some function of the text, then that function is bound to be determined by the ways we regard texts. It is possible to do various things with texts—read them, draw instruction from them, disagree with them, like or dislike them, understand them, and so on. But not all kinds of texts admit the same set of possible treatments. In particular, it is not necessary to deal with texts by interpreting them; this is the case only with authored texts. Accordingly, an understanding of what it means to be an author entails an understanding of what it means to "interpret" a text. Nehamas resists any view of interpretation as an effort to uncover meaning or to produce a paraphraseable content, but instead regards interpretation according to the more general model by which we attempt to locate or place actions in a contextual web. This substantiates the suggestion, made earlier, that a theory of authorship requires a corresponding theory of human action. As Nehamas explains, the author is the agent postulated in order to account for the construal of a text as the product of an action.

If the author (and, as Nehamas says, the work as well) is a construct "situated toward the notional end of interpretation and not at its actual beginning," then one faces the risk that the author may be seriously arbitrary. In his concluding section, Nehamas proposes that we might regard the author as a "plausible historical variant" of the writer or, if one believes that all identities are in some fashion shaped like texts, then as "a character the writer could have been." Regarding the writer as a historical person and the author as an artificial person does not remove the author from history, if one has an appropriate conception of history. History might be seen as those conditions or possibilities within which writer and author achieve their various identities; or the concepts of writer and author might somehow be regarded as different realizations, and history as the set of possible functions within which these are determined.

By beginning the sustained portion of his argument from Foucault, Nehamas suggests a way in which we may reconcile the notion of the literary text as significant human action with a vision of human action as inextricable from its historical context. The work of interpretation as suggested by such a program might be thought of as one of adequation rather than recovery. Its success or failure would be measured according to standards of breadth and richness, which go considerably beyond mere correspondence to the (historical) facts.

Writer, Text, Work, Author   *Alexander Nehamas*

Of persons artificial, some have their words and actions *owned* by those whom they represent. And then the person is the *actor*: and he that owneth his words and actions, is the Author: in which case the actor acteth by authority. For that which in speaking of goods and possessions, is called an *owner*, and in Latin *dominus*, in Greek κύριος; speaking of actions, is called author. And as the right of possession, is called dominion; so the right of doing any action, is called AUTHORITY.

This passage from the *Leviathan* (bk. 1, chap. 16) concerns social roles, "persons artificial," in general. But though it does not specifically mention literature, it is easy to see that it can apply to the case of the literary author as well. It expresses, with the disarming straightforwardness so characteristic of Hobbes, his view of the relationship between all authors and what he takes to be their products. Authors, according to Hobbes, own their words and actions. The writings of literary authors, therefore, are also their own, their possession and property.[1]

This conception of the author as owner and of authority as possession constitutes the specific background against which we must read Roland Barthes's view that the author is "a modern figure, a product of our society insofar as, emerging from the Middle Ages with English Empiricism, French Rationalism and the personal faith of the Reformation, it discovered the prestige of the individual, of, as it is more nobly put, the 'human person.'"[2] Hobbes's possessive conception supplies at least part of the motivation for Barthes's negative attitude toward the author.

Ownership involves the right to dispose of one's property as one wishes. In addition to the institutions surrounding the ideas of intellectual property and copyright, and from which we must try to keep it distinct, disposition in the literary case emerges as interpretation, to which the author is often assumed to bear a special relationship. But any such right or privilege can be exercised only within the law, and it therefore entails responsibility for one's actions and for what is subsequently made of them. Hobbes makes it clear that from his view "it followeth that when an actor makes a covenant by authority, he bindeth the author, no less than if he had made it himself; and no less subjecteth him to all the consequences of the same" (*Leviathan*, bk. 1, chap. 16).

This connection between ownership and responsibility, in turn, constitutes the background against which we must read another attack against the author closely related to that of Barthes. This is the view of Michel Foucault, who begins from the thesis that "this type of ownership has always been subsequent to what one might call penal appropriation. Texts, books, and discourses really began to have authors . . . to the extent that authors became subject to punishment."[3]

Such an approach seems almost calculated to shock and to startle. Since, as we shall see, it faces some deep difficulties, it should be defended against some obvious misunderstandings. First, we must notice that the conception of the author as a historical phenomenon is not by itself intended to, and cannot, undermine the author's reality. To argue that this figure emerged at a particular time for particular reasons is only to argue that our notion of the author is part of our history. And being a part of history is not an alternative to reality: it is one of its modes. Yet, though historicity does not undermine reality, it does undermine necessity. If something has a history, if, that is, it has a beginning, then it may also have an end. If the world did not contain authors at some time, then perhaps someday it can be without them again.

Second, the historicist conception of the author is not the view that one day we made the empirical discovery (as if we had not known this before) that certain texts were composed by individuals. Rather, this conception asks why these texts began to be treated in certain specific ways at some time, what purposes such treatment served, what values such purposes promoted. In proclaiming the author "dead," writers like Barthes and Foucault do not claim, as William Cain has correctly pointed out, "that authors don't exist at all or that texts (as if by magic) write themselves."[4] Their argument, particularly Foucault's, which will mainly occupy me in what follows, is more subtle and more complicated.

Schematically and in abstract terms, this argument consists of two stages. Beginning with the idea that the notion of the author is a historical phenomenon and that the way of reading texts associated with it has a definite temporal beginning, the first stage concludes that this notion *can* come to an end. The second stage then produces what it considers as good reasons for actually bringing this possible end about. The argument finally concludes that both the notion of the author and the treatment of texts it underwrites, that is to say, literary interpretation, *must* come to an end.

The second part of this argument, in my opinion, is more important than the first. Nevertheless, Foucault's historical claims raise some serious questions. He writes, for example, that the author emerged, that literature ceased being "authorless," only during the seventeenth and eighteenth centuries (149).[5] Yet, though perhaps Foucault is right in claiming that literature was accepted simply on the grounds of its "ancientness" during the Middle Ages, this clearly represented a radical departure from the practices of late antiquity. A complicated author figure, though of course one quite different from present-day notions, is implicit in Diogenes Laertius's *Lives of the Philosophers*, in the scholia to the tragic poets, or in the complex discussions of Homer's allegorical interpreters. Foucault also believes that the figure of the literary author that was established during the Enlightenment represents a direct transposition of the scientific author of earlier times. Now it may be true that scientific texts "were accepted in the Middle Ages, and accepted as 'true,' only when marked with the name of their author" (149). But this transposition, if such it was, was anything but direct. The role of the scientific author, who was supposed to guarantee the truth of a treatise, is very different from that of the literary author, the truth of whose texts has not been the central concern of modern criticism. In addition, the literary texts of antiquity did actually make claims to truth, though such claims were more often based on divine inspiration than on the author's identity. Plato's attacks on poetry in the *Republic* (bk. 10) and in the *Ion* show that the relationships between literature, science, and philosophy are immensely more complicated than Foucault's admittedly schematic discussion suggests. Finally, Foucault's view that in St. Jerome's *De viris illustribus* we can find, in naive and primitive form, all the criteria by means of which we attribute and evaluate texts today, is questionable (150–51). Jerome seems to me to rely exclusively on only two of Foucault's four criteria of authorship, that is, only on linguistic and stylistic features of texts.[6] In short, though the figure of the modern literary author may well be, not surprisingly, a modern phenomenon, the figure of the author in general has a much longer and more complex history than Foucault allows.[7]

Nevertheless, simply to dispute such historical claims and to rest content with pointing out that their truth is far from certain is to avoid facing the serious challenge Foucault's discussion presents to current literary practice. This challenge consists, first, in showing that whenever and however the author emerged in modern times, it is not so much a person as a figure or a function or a role—to use Hobbes's term again, though not only in its legal sense, a "person artificial."[8] This absolutely crucial distinction, which, I will argue below, Foucault himself sometimes overlooks, will occupy much of the discussion that follows. Though all texts have writers, not all texts have authors: "A private letter," Foucault writes in a passage to which we shall have to return, "may have a signer—it does not have an author; a contract may well have a guarantor—it does not have an author. An anonymous text posted on a wall probably has a writer—but not an author" (148). To consider that a text has an author, therefore, is not to make a discovery about its history. It is to take a particular attitude toward that text, to be willing to ask certain questions of it, and to expect certain types of answers from it. Texts that have authors are for Foucault texts that since the Enlightenment have been construed in a particular manner.

This particular manner of construing texts is reflected, according to Foucault, in the "aspects of an individual which we designate as making him an author" and which "are only a projection, in more or less psychological terms, of the operations that we force texts to undergo, the connections that we make, the traits that we establish as pertinent, the continuities that we recognize, or the exclusions that we practice" (150). And since the author, "at least in appearance, is outside . . . and precedes" the text (141), we come to think of literary texts as the products of an independent conscious agent, important for what they show us about that agent, and study them "only in terms of their expressive value or formal transformations" (158).

The second constituent of Foucault's challenge, and the real target of his attack, is just this particular manner in which, since the Enlightenment, authored (as opposed to merely written) texts have been construed: the expectations we have had and the questions we have asked of texts to which, as in the case of literature, we assign authors. The historical part of Foucault's argument aims to show that this manner of construing texts is not inevitable and that it can be abandoned. The second part argues that current critical practice must in fact be abandoned.

According to Foucault, our critical practice is centrally characterized by an effort to show that the texts of an author are continuous and not inconsistent, internally or with one another. This practice, he believes, is motivated by the hope that in this manner we may capture what the author really meant and that thus we may recapture the unique mental state, meaning, or message, which we assume all authored texts to express and communicate. But this vain hope directs us to the wrong enterprise. In thinking of the author as the preexisting seat of the single and coherent meaning which every text is assumed to possess, we tend to impose such a meaning on every text and we therefore actually use the author as a repressive "principle of thrift in the proliferation of meaning" (153).

According to this view, the figure of the author is the concrete expression of the idea that the purpose of criticism is to provide definitive interpretations of texts, revelations of their meaning. As such, the essential function of criticism is to exclude possible but "implausible" uses of literature, suggestive but "inaccurate" interpretations. The author is at the center of construing criticism as an activity that aims to describe literature and that is thus located on a different level from the object it describes, much as natural science is thought to be radically distinct from the reality it represents. The author, for Foucault, prevents us from thinking of criticism as an extension and elaboration of literature, as an activity essentially continuous with its object, aiming to produce new meanings and not to describe old ones. It prevents us from thinking of criticism as literature whose subject, unlike the case of other genres, is explicitly literature. Foucault's attack on the author is nothing less than an attack on this descriptive and interpretive conception of criticism as a whole.

This is the heart of Foucault's view. In order to come to terms with it, we must immediately press the distinction between writer and author. A writer is a historical person, firmly situated within a specific context, the efficient cause of a text's production. Writers often misunderstand their own texts, and they commonly utter little more than vague platitudes about them. They are no more knowledgeable about them than most of us are about the sense and significance, and sometimes the very nature, of our most complex and opaque actions. Writers (but not, as we shall see, authors) exist outside their texts and precede them in truth, not in appearance only. And precisely for this reason, writers are not in a position of interpretive authority over their writings, even if these are, by law, their property. We must keep the legal version of ownership, with which we began, clearly apart from what we might well call its "hermeneutical" aspect.

Writers are extrinsically related to their texts. This is reflected in the possibility that Henri Beyle, for example, never wrote the works that are commonly attributed to him. Perhaps throughout his life he was an ardent admirer of the *ancien régime* who, through some curious mixup, came to be thought of as Stendhal. It is, so to speak, not necessary for Henri Beyle to have written Stendhal's works, to have been Stendhal. But notice how we must construe the expression "to have been Stendhal" in this context: it simply specifies the feature of having been the author of Stendhal's works, and nothing more; it is not, despite appearances, a reference to an actual person. This, in turn, reflects the essential connection between Stendhal and the texts of which, necessarily, he is the author. Stendhal is whoever can be understood as the author of these texts; it is these texts that point us to him, and it is in this sense that he precedes them only in appearance. Stendhal, and every author so construed, is to a great extent the product and not the producer of the text, its property and not its owner.

This line of thought might seem to suggest that the author is completely constituted by properties of the text. As J. Hillis Miller has written, "There is not any 'Shakespeare himself.' 'Shakespeare' is an effect of the text . . . The same can be said of the texts published under the name of any author."[9] If this is so, it may now appear that the author cannot readily be distinguished from the very characters of fiction, since fictional characters, too, emerge out of texts in such a manner. Charlus does just what Proust's text says he does; he *is* just what the

text says he does—there is no more to him than that. One of the purposes of literary interpretation is, precisely, to establish just what it is
that Charlus is said to do in the text and so, in a literal sense, to determine who he is. And just as everything we understand Charlus to have
done (itself, of course, a matter of continuing debate) is essential to his
being the character he is, so, we might think, is the case with his author, Proust himself. Proust, and the author in general, seems to be
whoever can be understood to have produced the text as we have construed it. According to this reasoning, the author is one more fictional
character, totally immanent, like all fictional characters, in the text
out of which he emerges.

   This is a conclusion I would like to resist. Though we have generally
identified the author of each text with its writer too quickly and too
easily, it is no less quick and easy to infer from this that the author is
therefore nothing over and above the text, a pure and total product of
the peculiar language of fiction. The relation between authors and
texts is much more complex than the relation between texts and fictional characters. The first cannot be reduced to the second; it is not,
in particular, an immanent relation. Though an author, too, is a character, it is a character manifested or exemplified in a text and not depicted or described in it. The distinction is significant. "The author,"
John Sturrock as written, "can never finally appear in the text as subject. The representation of a subject is, inevitably, an object, requiring
a further, invisible subject as its representer."[10] The relation between
author and text can be called, not simply because a better word is lacking, "transcendental." Unlike fictional characters, authors are not simply parts of texts; unlike actual writers, they are not straightforwardly
outside them.

   In order to understand this equivocal relationship, we must distinguish the author figure from the notion that Wayne Booth has introduced by means of the term "implied author." The main differences
are three. First, as Booth's very term suggests, the implied author is the
product of the text and the creature of the writer. In this respect, at
least, the implied author is very close to a fictional character. Second,
the implied author is immanent in the text in the further sense that
even if several texts have been composed by a single writer, their implied authors are held to be distinct. A writer's different works, Booth
writes, "will imply different versions, different ideal combinations of
norms . . . the writer sets himself out with a different air depending on
the needs of particular works."[11] Third, though Booth emphasizes the
distinction between implied and actual author, he sometimes suggests

that the distinction is a practical matter. In discussing *Emma,* for example, he refers to the "'author himself'—*not necessarily* the real Jane Austen but an implied author, represented in this book by a reliable narrator" (256, emphasis added). This statement leaves open the possibility that actual and implied author may coincide—if, for example, the views expressed by the narrator and Jane Austen's actual views turn out to be the same. "A great work," according to Booth, "establishes the 'sincerity' of its implied author regardless of how grossly the man who created that author may belie in his other forms of conduct the values embodied in his work. For all we know, the only sincere moments of his life may have been lived as he wrote his novel" (75). This shows that if a writer did actually accept whatever propositions are expressed in a text, then no logical reason compels us to distinguish a real from an implied author.

Booth originally introduced the implied author in order to account for the relationship between the general views, propositions, and norms expressed in a literary text and the views, propositions, and norms accepted by the writer of that text, since these need not be the same. The author figure, with which we are now concerned, is broader in two interconnected respects. First, in contrast to the implied author, this figure is not correlated only with individual works. On the contrary, the author is a figure that emerges from a whole *oeuvre.* It in fact constitutes the very principle that allows us to group certain individual works together and to consider them as parts of such an internally related collection. Since the author, as we have seen, is never depicted, but only exemplified, in a text, this figure is transcendental in relation to its whole *oeuvre* as well as to the individual texts of which that *oeuvre* consists. This, in turn, leads naturally to the second main difference between these notions. The author figure is relevant not only to the attribution of general views to particular texts but also, as we shall see, to every question of interpretation. Both the implied author and the author figure are interpretive constructs. But the latter plays a broader, more directive, and more regulative role in interpretation.

I now want to articulate and defend this transcendental conception of the author and to argue that it is very important for our understanding of literary interpretation. The distinction between writer and author, on which this conception depends, owes a great deal to Foucault's discussion, though, as I shall claim, Foucault, ironically, seems to collapse the two into each other after he has opened a gap between them. And it is, I shall also claim, just this collapse that prompts him to take so negative an attitude toward interpretation that he ends his essay with a call for its abolition. My own view is that just as the author must be consistently distinguished from the writer, so interpretation must be separated from the search for meanings concealed within the text and located in the writer's intention or experience.

We have already seen that to say that a text has an author is to say that it is subject to literary interpretation. If this is true, then it is plausible to claim that though all texts are written, since not all are given literary readings, not all texts are authored. Could we perhaps give a general account of the texts that belong to this class? Interestingly, this is just what is implied in Foucault's statement that private letters, contracts, and anonymously posted texts lack authors (148). This is not, of course, a general theory, but it suggests that some texts are essentially incapable of having authors, and therefore of being interpreted.

Yet private letters do sometimes offer themselves to interpretation. Often, of course, these are the letters of established authors. But the extraordinarily personal and private letters of Madame de Sévigné show that this is not necessarily the case, since it is just these letters that constitute her as an author: apart from them she makes no claim to our attention. And though it does seem unlikely that many anonymously posted texts will have authors, I still cannot think of any general argument that shows that none ever can.

Whether a particular text has an author depends, then, not only on its genre but also on some additional factors, which seem extremely difficult to characterize both generally and informatively. Fictional texts are likely to generate author figures, but not all of them need to. Broadly speaking, texts that, either by imitating or by explicitly flouting literary convention, invite their readers to consider them as literary works make such claims. But, again, the connection does not appear necessary unless we trivialize it by simply defining literary works as authored texts. Much of the literature sold under the heading of "Popular Fiction" in bookstores, for example, may well be authorless.

The reason for this is not that such writings are subliterary or of poor quality but that there is a distinction to be made between understanding in general and interpretation in particular. The view I am developing implies that we can read texts, learn from them, disagree with them, perhaps even like or dislike them, without necessarily interpreting them. The difference, actually, is one of degree. Understanding does involve interpretation, but it appeals only to obvious, generally shared, and uncontroversial conventions or background assumptions.

All such conventions, of course, must be learned, and not all of them are shared by everyone. Each person belongs to a number of different interpretive communities,[12] and each community accepts some of its own basic conventions. Such conventions are always in the background, and they constitute the various contexts with which, necessarily, we engage in the effort to interpret and to understand. Since all understanding presupposes some such conventions, it is always to that extent interpretive. But in many such cases only the most basic conventions of a particular context are involved, and interpretation can be so automatic that it constitutes a limiting, null case. Depending on who one is, this can apply to a sign warning hikers that a cliff is dangerous, to an article on genetic programming, or even to a fictional account of an Elizabethan Englishman shipwrecked on the shores of Japan. Cases like these can often require no special assumptions, no idiosyncratic hypotheses on our part; and this is why we speak of understanding without interpretation. The difficulties begin when we try to specify which cases require understanding that is genuinely interpretive.

It is often said (and more often believed) that interpretation is required when a particular text conceals an implicit and, ideally, profound meaning differing from the meaning that text appears to have. Literary texts in particular demand to be interpreted because these surface meanings differ from their real significance, because, as Susan Horton has written, "a text means beyond itself . . . a railroad is more than a railroad."[13] Such views hold that interpretation is needed when the meaning of a text is somehow "beyond" or "behind" it. But this distinction, which is subject to all the difficulties that face any distinction between what merely appears and what really is the case, has been the reason why so much recent criticism has attacked the very notion of interpretation. If interpretation does in fact presuppose this distinction, of which there is good reason to be suspicious, then perhaps there also is good reason to be suspicious of interpretation itself.

I believe, however, that interpretation does not depend on such metaphors of depth and concealment and that it does not involve a radical distinction between the apparent and the real meaning of a text. I would like to articulate an alternative account of interpretation which is connected to the transcendental conception of the author I have been discussing. If such a view is acceptable, interpretation need not be seen as the revelation of a text's hidden meaning. And if this is so, perhaps we can see that much of the suspiciousness with which interpretation has recently been regarded is not really justified.

On the account I propose, interpretation is the activity by means of which we try to construe movements and objects in the world around us as actions and their products. The movement of an arm may, though it need not, be a greeting; the accidental forgetting of a name may, though it need not, be an unconscious aggressive gesture; a long written text may, though it need not, be a novel. But to construe something as an action is not to discover a meaning distinct from its apparent one, a meaning that underlies its seeming sense. Rather, it is to take that movement, or object, or text to be susceptible to a certain sort of question and to a certain sort of account and explanation. It is to want to ask "Why?" of it and to expect an answer that refers to an agent, to intention and to rationality. In most cases, this activity is automatic: we appeal only to general assumptions and classify our object as an action of an obvious, general, and not idiosyncratic sort. When my friend waves her arm at the station as my train is beginning to move, the waving is a farewell. My understanding is not interpretive in the strict sense. But in interpretation strictly conceived we account for the features of an object by appealing to the features of an unusual, original agent whose action we take it to be and who is manifested in it. We take the action, by means of an explicit and often complex process, as an unusual, original event—an event characteristic of its agent, to be sure, but not of many (or any) others. And even in those cases where we say that an action or a text means something other than what it appears to mean, we do not have two meanings, one real and one apparent. All we have, even in the case of psychoanalytic or Marxist interpretation, is a series of progressively more complicated, detailed, and sophisticated hypotheses aimed at construing a text as an action, at trying to find the meaning it does have in its relationship to its agent and to that agent's other actions, or texts. To identify the results of an automatic, early, rough, and general guess at the significance of something with its "surface," as opposed to its "real," meaning is like arguing that when we think that a square tower, seen at a distance, seems round, there is such a thing in the world as a round appearance in addition to the tower's square reality. Both reifications are equally unjustified.

Interpretation can and must be separated from the metaphors of depth and uncovering, which create this metaphysical difficulty. If we think of it instead in terms of breadth and expansion, we may be able to resist attacks that, like Foucault's, are motivated by the rejection of the distinction between appearance and reality. And by connecting this view of interpretation to the figure of the author, we may also be able to resist Foucault's attack against a naively psychological conception of this latter notion.

Of this proposal, to take a text or one of its parts as the product of an action is to undertake to relate it to other actions and their products, to account for its features by appealing to theirs and for their features by appealing to its own. We become interested in whoever it is who can be said to have produced that text and to be manifested in its characteristics. We assume that the text's characteristics, unusual as they may be, are as they are because the agent who emerges through them is as he is. Interpretation so construed is not an effort to take a stretch of language which means one thing and to show that it means something else instead. There are no surface meanings, just as there are no appearances—except in the trivial sense that we can be wrong about what texts mean, just as we can be wrong about what things are.

Interpretation, therefore, must be pictured not as an effort to place a text with a continually deepening context but as an attempt to place it within a perpetually broadening one. Nietzsche's comment is perfectly appropriate: "The most recent history of an action is related to this action; but further back lies a pre-history that covers a wider field: the individual action is at the same time a part of a much more extensive, later fact. The briefer and the more extensive processes are not separated."[14] The more extensive process of which an action can be seen as a part can in turn generate a different interpretation of at least part of the original action. This, again, can indicate that a new, more extensive process, perhaps containing at least part of the original one as its own part, must now be invoked. Such a process of continual adjustment has no end. Interpretation ends when interest wanes, not when certainty is reached. Nietzsche's comment, "one acquires degrees of Being, one loses that which *has* Being," is at least as apt when applied to meaning instead.[15]

One of the most striking examples of this understanding of interpretation is provided by the practice of the narrator of Proust's *Remembrance of Things Past*. As a child and later as an adolescent, the narrator is obsessed with the idea that not only books but all objects, natural as well as artificial, conceal messages of various sorts. He is convinced that happiness no less than literary success depends on the ability to decipher these messages. But the messages always remain elusively inaccessible. His fascination and frustration with the hawthorns along Swann's way is a famous case in point:

But it was in vain that I lingered beside the hawthorns—inhaling, trying to fix in my mind (which did not know what to do with it), losing and recapturing their invisible and unchanging colour, absorbing myself in the rhythm which disposed their flowers here and there with the lightheartedness of youth and at intervals as unexpected as certain intervals in music—they went on offering me the same charm in inexhaustible profusion, but without letting me delve any more deeply, like those melodies which one can play a hundred times in succession without coming any nearer to their secrets . . . in vain did I make a screen with my hands, the better to concentrate upon the flowers, the feeling they aroused in me remained obscure and vague, struggling and failing to free itself, to float across and become one with them. They themselves offered me no enlightenment.[16]

As long as the narrator searches for such hidden messages, he fails to find them and, of course, to write about them. Only when (much later in life) he succeeds in writing about the flowers' very silence and in seeing his experience of that silence as part of the process that finally enables him to become an author, that is, only when he takes this experience of "incomplete" understanding itself and gives it a place with the complete account of his life and his effort to become able to write, does his writing begin.

We should not, I suggest, accept the child narrator's point of view and try to decipher the underlying meaning of the perceptions of the young author-to-be. This is nowhere more obvious than in the well-known episode of the steeples of Martinville and Vieuxvicq.[17] Once again the narrator recalls the intimation of a message:

In noticing and registering the shape of their spires, their shifting lines, the sunny warmth of their surfaces, I felt that I was not penetrating to the core of my impression, that something more lay behind that mobility, that luminosity, something which they seemed at once to contain and to conceal. (196)

But all of a sudden the message seems to become clear; without warning,

their outlines and their sunlit surfaces, as though they had been a sort of rind, peeled away; something of what they had concealed from me became apparent; a thought came into my mind which had not existed for me a moment earlier, forming itself in words in my head . . . I could no longer think of anything else. (197)

Here, if anywhere in this book, we should expect to find at least an intimation of what such messages are like. This is especially true because the narrator tells us that he decided to write that thought down then and there and, once in this whole work, he reproduces his early prose for his readers to read. The passage that follows is therefore the earliest part of the book that he composed (198). But the fragment that is reproduced is stunning in that it nowhere contains the slightest mention of any such meaning. The narrator describes the three steeples as "three flowers painted upon the sky" and likens them to "three maidens in a legend, abandoned in a solitary place over which night has begun to fall" (ibid.). But these similes do not constitute the underlying secret, the covert meaning for which this text keeps urging us to search, always in vain.

What, then, is the thought that comes into the narrator's mind as he is looking at the three steeples? What is the thought that was not in his mind before but is there now? Proust's text dictates one answer to that question, and that answer does not in any way involve a message behind the steeples' changing appearance. The thought that the narrator now has is simply the thought contained in the passage that he goes on to compose and that he reproduces for us here. The thought is just the ability, and the exercise of the ability, to write about the steeples. It is the description of their surfaces and of their appearance, their incorporation, incomplete as they seem both to him and to us, into the narrative. The message hidden in the steeples, a message that is not obvious to the young narrator even as he writes his account but that becomes apparent once the account is embodied in the completed text, is that nothing really hides behind appearance. It is "appearance" *itself* that is difficult to understand: the very distinction between obvious appearance and obscure reality may therefore be untenable. The narrator's thought is simply the articulate account of the steeples which he is able to write down. The steeples are neither flowers nor maidens, nor is that what they have been trying to intimate. In calling such images to mind, they allow themselves to become part of the narrative in which we are engaged. Their significance, their meaning, does not consist in the message, the search for which constantly leaves Proust's narrator not only frustrated and unhappy but also literally unable to write. Their significance is their very ability to become part of this text, their susceptibility to description, even if this description is exhausted by their surface. For the text is nothing over and above the juxtaposition of many such surfaces, the meaning of which is to be found in their interrelations. The steeples' meaning for the narrator is their ultimate contribution to his completed text, their inclusion in it. The meaning of the episode within the narrative itself is that the meaning of such phenomena is nothing over and above the material they provide this narrator, and narrators in general, for constructing a work that is ultimately at least partly about them. Coherence, unity, and meaning are generated through the proliferation of surfaces, not through the discovery of a single principle that underlies them. The steeples are important, significant, or meaningful because they are being written about, not because writing reveals something about or behind them.

How is this different picture of interpretation connected to the author figure with which my discussion began? The author now emerges as the agent postulated in order to account for construing a text as the product of an action. In Neitzsche's terms, the author is the ultimate "more extensive process," which contains the original text as its part— which is not to say, of course, that this process can ever be finally captured and displayed. In construing a text as an action, we necessarily see it as the partial expression or manifestation of a character: the author is that character. Different parts of a text may generate different or even inconsistent agents or characters. Different texts by the same writer may also do the same. But interpretation proceeds upon the principle that a more consistent narrative of these (perhaps inconsistent) actions can always be devised.[18] Consistency is achieved, not by finding a single meaning underlying all the differences and changes in a work, but by constructing a consistent account of such changes.

We are thus confronted with the following sequence. Writers produce texts. Some texts are subject to interpretation: understanding them involves seeing them as the products of idiosyncratic agents. Interpretation construes texts as works. Works generate the figure of the author, a character manifested, though not represented in them. We cannot know in advance whether a particular text is or is not suited for interpretation. And, as is always the case with character and action, the relationship between author and work involves them in a process of mutual adjustment which cannot, in the nature of the case, ever end.

Both work and author, therefore, are constructs. Both are situated toward the notional end of interpretation and not at its actual beginning. The most we can assume in interpreting a text is that it constitutes a work, not that we know what that work is: to establish that is the very goal of interpretation. And it is a defeasible goal; in actual fact, we often fail to generate a work out of a particular text.

Foucault, we must notice, doubts seriously that the notion of a work can be given a general and useful articulation (143-44). He sees very clearly that the concepts of work and author are deeply interrelated. He sees that once the author was banished, the work emerged instead as a means of justifying the practice of traditional criticism. That is, given the close connection between the two, the unity the author had been intended to represent now came to be attributed to the work itself. But, Foucault argues, such an appeal is bound to fail. Though "intended to replace the privileged position of the author," the work, he claims, cannot possibly fulfill that role (143). Foucault gives two reasons for being suspicious of this notion. First, he wonders whether we are at all entitled to speak of an individual's work if that individual is not an author. Second, he writes that even when an author is in fact involved, we have no general principle for deciding whether something that author wrote does or does not form part of his work: "How can one define a work among the millions of traces left by someone after his death? A theory of the work does not exist." Therefore, "it is not enough to declare that we should do without the writer and study the work itself. The word 'work' and the unity that it designates are probably as problematic as the status of the author's individuality" (144).

It seems to me undeniable that a general "theory of the work" does not exist. Such a theory would have to be a universal account of everything that is (and isn't) relevant to interpretation. It would have to specify in general terms exactly which features are responsible for a text being construed as a work. Is the fact that we lack such a theory unfortunate? More specifically, does this lack prevent us from being able to engage in interpretation and to construe particular texts as works of authors?

It is ironic that Foucault's view exhibits the form of argument a whole generation of scholars put in Socrates' mouth in his fruitless search for the nature of virtue in Plato's early dialogues. The argument is that we can never recognize, say, a particular instance of courage if we don't already know what courage is, if we lack its definition. But since what we are looking for in the first place is the very definition of courage, the search is bound to fail: it cannot even begin. This argument has been named "the Socratic Fallacy." And though it is a fallacy, Socrates never committed it.[19] But the argument that constitutes it is not very different from the claim that we cannot decide whether a particular text is or is not a work unless we already possess a general theory, a definition of what a work is.

Interpretation does not seem to me to require any such theory or definition. It is not, as its proponents often grant its opponents, a two-step process. It does not begin with a clear idea of what the work is that is to be interpreted and conclude when it has established its meaning. On the contrary, a text's status as a work and its meaning are essentially interconnected. To take a text as a work in the first place is already to have construed it, at least partly, as the product of a particular action: this is just to have formulated at least a partial interpretation of it. Just as we lack a general theory explaining which of the indefinitely many movements in which we engage constitute the actions we perform, so we lack a general account articulating which of the many texts with which we are confronted constitute the literary works we produce. And just as we construe as actions those movements of the significance of which we have at least a rudimentary intentional account, so we construe as works those texts of which we have at least minimal interpretations.

This is also why there is no theoretical account that distinguishes authored texts from texts that are merely written. Some texts explicitly place themselves within the literary tradition; one way of doing this, as we have seen, is to display obvious obedience or disobedience to acknowledged convention. Such texts demand to be interpreted, but there is no guarantee that their demand will be met, that their writers will turn out to be authors. Criticism can be defined, if one is interested in such definitions, only in uninformative terms: texts that are subject to criticism are texts that can be interpreted, that is, texts that have authors. The circle is small. It is a fruitless task, which some might call "metaphysical" in a pejorative sense, to try to determine the nature of a discipline independently of its actual practice and in the hope that this nature will itself determine the practice. We can tell that a particular text is a work only when we can actually criticize it: which texts are works will depend on what counts as criticism, and what counts as criticism will depend on which texts have been considered as works. Is "the notation of a meeting, or of an address, or a laundry list" found among Nietzsche's papers, Foucault asks, part of his work? But how could we answer this question just on such information? There is, and there can be, no a priori answer. Such texts may turn out to be parts of Nietzsche's work if, for example, they can be suitably connected to other texts of his, if they can be used to support or contradict them, to illuminate them or make them more obscure than before: if, that is, in conjunction with those other texts they can generate a different "extensive process," a slightly different author. Should notations of meetings, addresses, or laundry lists, Foucault asks, be included in editions of Nietzsche's works? The question is urgent, but it can be given no general answer. The editors of Nietzsche, like all editors, will have to answer each specific question as it arises for each particular text.

Texts, then, are works if they generate an author; the author is therefore the product of interpretation, not an object that exists independently in the world. But if this is true, it may now appear that the figure of the author is seriously arbitrary. If this figure refers to whatever character is manifested in a text when it is construed as a work, and if each text can be interpreted, as it is often claimed, in different and even incompatible ways, then the author appears to collapse into fragments. Each interpretation generates its own author, and each text can give rise to many different and even inconsistent authors.

No part of the argument of this essay prevents a critic from following out the implications of this objection. I can think of no logical reason that shows that the innovation with which Borges ironically credits Pierre Menard cannot be adopted as a conscious policy. This, of course, is the "technique . . . of the deliberate anachronism and the erroneous attribution. This technique . . . prompts us to go through the *Odyssey* as if it were posterior to the *Aeneid* and the Book *Le Jardin du Centaure* of Madame Henri Bachelier as if it were by Madame Henri Bachelier . . . to attribute the *Imitatio Christi* to Louis Ferdinand Céline or to James Joyce."[20] If the author is our product, why not produce anyone we like out of any particular text?

We could, indeed, try to read the *Imitatio Christi* as if it were by James Joyce and not by Thomas à Kempis. But James Joyce is, among many other things, the Irish Catholic author of *Ulysses*. In reading the *Imitatio Christi* as Joyce's work we would have to read it as the work of the Irish Catholic author of *Ulysses*. We would have no choice about it: this is just what it is to read this as the work of Joyce. In doing so, we would have to bring the *Imitatio* into some sort of relationship with *Ulysses* and therefore change in many ways our interpretation of both works. We would thus begin to fit them into a new, more extensive process. This would now involve not only their reinterpretation but also a new reading of *A Portrait of the Artist as a Young Man*, which would in turn reflect on our interpretation of the first two works. We would also have to read anew Joyce's other works and letters, and probably some of Pound's poems and some of Beckett's early work as well, and much else (that is, everything) besides. Whether, of course, we actually did this or not does not affect the logical point: we would remain committed to this extreme revisionist approach. No argument can show that we would be wrong to try to revise the history of literature. But in order to show that the author is an arbitrary figure, we would actually have to produce such a revision, as well as a number of others, involving different but equally plausible rearrangements of the canon and even new canons. To say that this can always be done is very different from doing it. And only this latter, if it is successful and convincing, can show that the author is arbitrary.[21]

In general, the author is to be construed as a plausible historical variant of the writer, as a character the writer could have been.[22] The author actually means what the writer could have meant, even if the writer never did. In producing texts, writers are immersed in a system with an independent life of its own. Many of its institutional or linguistic features, many of its values or connections to other systems, are beyond the most unconscious grasp of any writer. For all we know, many texts would have been radically different had their writers been aware of some of those features. But the author, who is the joint product of writer and text, of critic and interpretation, who is not a person but a character, is everything the work shows it to be and what it is can in turn determine what the text shows. The author has no depth.

The objection may now be raised that the very principle that the author be a writer's plausible historical variant is itself arbitrary. And so it is, if we take everything that is supported by less than demonstrative argument as arbitrary. But this is not a useful conception of the arbitrary. To show that a well-established practice is arbitrary entails showing that at least one alternative practice, truly distinct from it, actually exists and makes a claim to being followed. Yet the critics who do not commit themselves to the author as construed here, whether they pursue their new technique in jest (as Borges does) or not, seem to me to confine themselves to partial interpretations of parts of texts. Such readings often are interesting and important. But, once again, saying that such anachronistic readings can be produced is very different from actually producing them. Only a consistent effort to read an entire text in a thoroughly anachronistic manner, an effort that would involve nothing less than reading the entire history of the literary tradition in this manner, would show that the figure of the author is arbitrary in an important or harmful sense. The mere possibility of alternatives never shows that actuality is dispensable.

The figure of the author, in contrast to that of the writer, allows us, however, to avoid the view that to understand a text is to re-create or replicate a state of mind which someone else has already undergone, and which, if I understand him correctly, is Foucault's ultimate target. Such states of mind, whatever their relation to the meaning of a text, belong to writers but not to authors. Though instrumentally important, perhaps, they have of themselves no critical significance. Authors, not being persons, do not have psychological states that might determine in advance what a text means. We can thus even accept E. D. Hirsch's view that a "determinate verbal meaning requires a determining will . . . since unless one particular complex of meaning is *willed* (no matter how 'rich' and 'various' it might be) there would be no distinction between what an author does mean by a word sequence and what he could mean by it," and turn it around.[23] It is only the latter and not, as Hirsch's argument is intended to show, the former that is the object of critical attention. We can therefore also refuse to accept the view, expressed by Erwin Panofsky but influential far beyond the disciplinary limits of art history, that "the humanist has . . . mentally to re-enact the actions and to re-create the creations of the past . . . meaning can only be apprehended by re-producing, and thereby, quite literally, 'realizing,' the thoughts that one finds expressed in . . . books and in the artistic conceptions that manifest themselves" in artworks.[24] There is nothing there, if my view is correct, for us to *re*-create.

Being a construct, the author is not a historical person whose states of mind we can ever hope, or even want, to recapture. In interpreting a text, we form a hypothesis about the character manifested in it. We thus come—always tentatively, of course—to understand that character better. But this is not to re-create and make our own someone else's experiences and thoughts. We do not need to become a character (we don't, that is, need to assume it) in order to understand it. After all, having a certain character is sometimes the most crucial obstacle to understanding it.

In a passage of *The Archaeology of Knowledge* Foucault writes:

If a proposition, a group of signs, can be called "statement" [*sic*], it is not . . . because, one day someone happened to speak them or to put them in some concrete form of writing: it is because the position of the subject can be assigned. To describe a formulation *qua* statement does not consist in analyzing the relations between the author [i.e., in our terms, the writer] and what he says (or wanted to say, or said without wanting to) but in determining what position can and must be occupied by any individual if he is to be the subject of it.[25]

In interpreting a text, in construing it as an action, we want to know what *any* individual who can be its subject must be like. We want to know, that is, what sort of person, what character, is manifested in it.

And to know this is simply to know what other actions that character can engage in, what relations it bears to other texts and to the characters manifested in them. To interpret a text, on this model, is not to go underneath it, into a meaning covert within it, but to connect it to other texts and to their authors, to see what texts have made is possible and what texts it, in turn, has made possible itself. This is the literal analogue of the metaphors of breadth and spreading to which I appealed earlier. Interpretation is an activity that relates texts, or their parts, to one another. But to do this, we must construe those texts as works, and to construe them as works we must see them as actions exemplifying a certain character. Again, to understand a character is not to become identical with it, though nothing prevents us as readers from trying, in addition, to make that character at least part of our own. Nevertheless, to understand the character manifested in *Remembrance of Things Past*, to the extent that this is something (as it is not) that can be fully accomplished, is not to become identified with Marcel Proust, even for a moment. Rather, it is to formulate a series of hypotheses about the actions which we must attribute to the author Proust in order to account for the features of this work. It is, to return to the origin of our circle, to offer an interpretation of the text.

If this is so, then the figure of the author does not constitute the repressive principle with which both Barthes and Foucault identify it. The unity the author represents, in the view I have offered, is not a unity that must be assumed to be there at first but a unity that may be possibly captured at last. The charge of repressiveness is much more appropriate against the use of the historical writer as an independent principle by means of which any interpretation of a text is to be judged. Yet Foucault, though he himself makes this distinction, does not attack the writer. On the contrary, he writes that it is the *author* who provides the means

by which one impedes the free circulation, the free manipulation, the free composition, decomposition and recomposition of fiction. In fact, if we are accustomed to presenting the author as a genius, as a perpetual surging of invention, it is because, in reality, we make him function in exactly the opposite function. One can say that the author is an ideological product, since we represent him as the opposite of his historically real function. ("What Is an Author?," 159)

It could be that Foucault believes that we wrongly confuse writer with author, and that we therefore fail to realize the greater freedom the author figure allows us. Yet he does not attack this identification; instead, he attacks the figure of the author itself. He considers as "pure romanticism" the hope that doing away with the author, as he urges us to do, will enable us to treat fiction without any constraints whatever (160). He cannot, of course, predict what those constraints will be, but he thinks that they will have to be preferable to those provided by the author, whom he sees as the sign under which a psychological construal of reading and interpretation has been victorious.[26]

Foucault's essay ends with an echo of Beckett: "What difference does it make who is speaking?" I have been arguing that the question asked about the author is not, Who *is* speaking?, but, Who *can be* speaking? Even the free circulation, manipulation, composition, decomposition, and recomposition of fiction is committed to asking this second question. Even partial, anachronistic, or consciously perverse readings of texts generate an author for them. Such readings generate a character to whom these texts, construed (partially, anachronistically, or perversely) as works, can be assigned. A text, though it usually has one writer, need never have (that is, generate) a single author. But not every author is as acceptable as any other, and the mere possibility of having many authors does not show that the author is dispensable.

My own view is that Foucault himself has fallen prey to the illegitimate identification of author with writer against which he so elegantly warns. We have seen that he believes that the author emerged only during the Enlightenment, and that there are reasons to doubt this claim. I have suggested that the history of the author is longer and more complex than Foucault believes. What may have occurred during the Enlightenment is the identification of the role of the author, which has appeared through history in many guises, with the actual historical agent who is causally and legally responsible for the text. But this has been only a moment—though important and long—in this history. Foucault identifies this moment with the history of which it is only a part.

What leads us to believe that a complex conscious or unconscious mental state, an intention or experience, lies at the origin of every text, constituting the text's meaning, and that to understand a text is to recapture that mental state, is the view that to understand a text is to understand its writer. But the ownership with which my discussion began changes radically as we move from writer to author. Foucault's joint attack on these two notions depends, I think, on overlooking that difference. Writers own their texts as one owns one's property. Though legally their own (*eigen*), texts can be taken away from their writers and still leave them who they are. Authors, by contrast, own their works as one owns one's actions. Their works are authentically their own (*eigentlich*). They cannot be taken away (that is, reinterpreted) without changing their authors, without making the characters manifested in them different or even unrecognizable. Authors cannot be taken apart from their works.

Precisely because of this, because both author and work emerge through the interpretation of a text, neither stands at the text's origin, imparting a preexisting significance to it. The author is therefore not an independent constraint, forbidding in an a priori manner desired but unlawful interpretations or extensions. Construing the author as I have done here puts the very distinction between interpretation and extension, understanding and use, into question. In "Prison Talk," Foucault accepts this distinction when he claims that he wants to "utilize" the writers he likes. "The only valid tribute to thought such as Nietzsche's," he writes, "is precisely to use it, to deform it, to make it groan and protest."[27] Bue can we use Nietzsche's thought without understanding it? Can one remain engaged with an author, make that author's thought groan and protest without, at the very same time, being in the process of interpreting it? Isn't this just what I have been doing with Foucault himself, trying to take some of his own views but using them against him, connecting them with other views, his own, and those of Barthes and Booth, and mine? Haven't I been interpreting and at the same time using him? There is, in my opinion, no clear line between these two. But to insist that criticism must engage only in interpretation and to claim that it must abandon interpretation altogether in favor of extension is to believe that such a line can be drawn. And this belief, in turn, presupposes that the author is identical with the writer and therefore also with the writer's own self-understanding. This identification, which ultimately also identifies the foes and the defenders of pure interpretation, has been the subject of my attack.

In writing to Malcolm Cowley, Faulkner once remarked:

It is my ambition to be as an individual abolished and voided from history, leaving it markless, no refuse except the printed books . . . It is my aim and every effort bent, that the sum and history of my life, which in the same sentence is my obit and epitaph too, shall be then both: He wrote the books and he died.[28]

There is irony in the fact that this passage was quoted in a review of one of Faulkner's numerous biographies. But there may be even more irony in the fact that whatever we know about Faulkner's books is also something we know about their author. And though we may not ever know what Faulkner, the writer, really was, we may come close to knowing who he could have been. Having no private property, authors also have no privacy to protect.[29]

Notes

1. Brian Silverman and David Torode, *The Material Word* (London: Routledge & Kegan Paul, 1980), 227–44, argue that a similar view can be found in John Locke's "Of Property."

2. Roland Barthes, "The Death of the Author," in *Image, Music, Text*, trans. Stephen Heath (New York: Hill & Wang, 1977), 142–43.

3. Michel Foucault, "What Is an Author?," in Josué V. Harari, ed., *Textual Strategies* (Ithaca: Cornell University Press, 1979), 149. Parenthetical page references to Foucault in the main text will all be to this essay.

4. William Cain, "Authors and Authority in Interpretation," *Georgia Review* 34 (1980): 819.

5. This view can also be found in Foucault's "Discourse on Language," in *The Archaeology of Knowledge*, trans. A. M. Sheridan (New York: Harper & Row, 1972), 222–23.

6. Foucault also makes this point in "The Discourse on Language," 223. St. Jerome discusses authorship in these sections, among others: I. 7. 9–11, V. 12. I–3, XXV. 26. 15–17, XXXIV. 86. 24–25, XLII. 90. 13–17, LXVI. 98. 24–27. The first of these passages actually suggests that attributions of authorship were already common by Jerome's time: "Scripsit Simon Petrus duas epistulas, quae catholicae nominantur; quandum secunda *plerisque* eius negatur propter stili cum priore dissonantiam" (emphasis added).

7. Part of this history, in connection with modern literature, is given by Patrick Crutwell in "Makers and Persons," *Hudson Review* 12 (1959–60): 486–507.

8. An important though sketchy discussion of social roles can be found in Alasdair MacIntyre's *After Virtue* (South Bend, Ind.: University of Notre Dame Press, 1981). MacIntyre believes that every age conceives of itself in terms of certain privileged social roles, which he calls "characters."

9. J. Hillis Miller, "Ariadne's Broken Woof," *Georgia Review* 31 (1977): 59.

10. John Sturrock, *Paper Tigers: The Ideal Fictions of Jorge Luis Borges* (Oxford: Oxford University Press, 1977), 183.

11. Wayne Booth, *The Rhetoric of Fiction* (Chicago: University of Chicago Press, 1961), 71.

12. Though this expression is intended to allude to the views Stanley Fish expresses in *Is There a Text in This Class?* (Cambridge: Harvard University Press, 1980), I also want to emphasize the multiplicity of the communities to which each person belongs. It is precisely this fact that makes it possible to criticize the conventions accepted by each community and to provide rational alternatives to them.

13. Susan Horton, *Interpreting Interpreting: Interpreting Dickens's "Dombey"* (Baltimore: Johns Hopkins University Press, 1979), 7.

14. Friedrich Nietzsche, *The Will to Power*, trans. Walter Kaufmann and R. J. Hollingdale (New York: Random House, 1968), sec. 672.

15. *Will to Power*, sec. 485.

16. Marcel Proust, *Remembrance of Things Past*, trans. C. K. Scott Moncrieff and Terence Kilmartin (New York: Random House, 1982), 1:138–39.

17. Representative of the extensive literature on this passage is George Poulet, "L'espace proustien," *Entretiens sur Marcel Proust*, ed. George Cattaui and Philip Kolb (Paris: Mouton, 1966), 75–94.

18. I discuss the problem of interpretation in general, and apply this discussion to one particular figure, in *Nietzsche: Life as Literature* (Cambridge: Harvard University Press, 1985).

19. This term was first used by Peter Geach in "Plato's *Euthyphro*: An Analysis and Commentary," *Monist* 50 (1966): 369–82. I have disputed Geach's claim in "Confusing Universals and Particulars in Plato's Early Dialogues," *Review of Metaphysics* 29 (1975): 287–306, and discuss the issue more fully in "Socratic Intellectualism," forthcoming in *Proceedings of the Boston Area Colloquium for Ancient Philosophy* 2 (1986).

20. Jorge Luis Borges, "Pierre Menard, Author of the *Quixote*," in *Labyrinths*, trans. and ed. Donald A. Yates and James E. Irby (New York: New Directions, 1962), 36–44.

21. This argument is made in detail in *Nietzsche: Life as Literature*, 62–73.

22. I have discussed this view in detail in "The Postulated Author: Critical Monism as a Regulative Ideal," *Critical Inquiry* 8 (1981): 131–49.

23. E. D. Hirsch, *Validity in Interpretation* (New Haven: Yale University Press, 1967), 46–47.

24. Erwin Panofsky, "Art History as a Humanistic Discipline," in *Meaning in the Visual Arts* (New York: Doubleday, 1955), 14. Despite his insistence on a "transcendental" author, George Poulet still believes that successful reading involves such a meeting of two minds: "What is this mind who all alone by himself occupies my consciousness?," "The Phenomenology of Reading," *New Literary History* 1 (1969): 57. It is for this reason that I do not try to align my position with his.

25. Foucault, *Archaeology of Knowledge*, 95–96.

26. Barthes also rejects the author as a constraint on interpretation and instead appeals to a "reader . . . without history, biography, psychology . . . simply that *someone* who holds together in a single field all the traces by which a written work is constituted" ("Death of the Author," 148). But can there be such a "someone"? And what single field can such a someone occupy?

27. Foucault, "Prison Talk," in *Power/Knowledge*, ed. Colin Gordon (New York: Pantheon Books, 1980), 93–94.

28. Quoted in the *New York Times Book Review*, 22 Feb. 1981, 9.

29. I am grateful to W. J. T. Mitchell for his comments on an earlier version of this essay.

12
Rewriting the Self: Barthes and the Utopias of Language

In a much-quoted remark, Nietzsche said that in order to get rid of God we would first have to get rid of grammar. In a related sense, one could say that if we want to free ourselves from the Aristotelian, Cartesian, and eighteenth-century notions of the self, we would have to free ourselves from language. If Mary Wiseman's arguments in the following essay on Roland Barthes are convincing, however, this process may already have begun. Only it takes the shape, not of a repudiation of language, but of an experimental strategy designed to use language in such a way as to speak against the weight of grammars and gods which has accumulated in it. Regarding the work of Roland Barthes as "experimental" in just this sense, Wiseman suggests that Barthesian texts like *Camera Lucida* both propose and demonstrate the will to inhabit the "utopian" space in which such a language might be elaborated.

Wiseman invokes the proposition, put forward by Barthes, that in our modernity utopias are for the first time conceived in language. One may well locate in the will to self-revision an element of modernity which reaches back to Descartes, but that this should be carried out utopically, and also in language, is something characteristic of the present age. Thus it is not surprising that the typology of Barthes's utopias reveals a conception of the human subject vastly different from that which preceded it. Indeed, the moment of the self as subject is, for Barthes, clearly a moment of the past; it is, as Barthes said in his inaugural lecture at the Collège de France, one of those "old and lovely things, whose signified is abstract, out of date." The classical "modern" self, as imaged in the Cartesian subject, is characteristically transparent and untheatricalized, and denies the opacity of its own performance. If the postmodern self bears any resemblance to its Cartesian forebear, this is only in the postmodern or revisionist readings of Descartes such as those of Jean-Luc Nancy (*Ego Sum*, 1979), in which the Cartesian subject is itself revealed to be a function of the same kind of makeup and masks that Wiseman sees in Barthes here.

The utopian function of language may be said to be theatrical in a number of ways. It is especially evident in the effort to use language and at the same time to disengage from its assertive function. Since actors quintessentially utter sentences without asserting them, writers who use language nonreferentially may be said to be like actors. To write is to act (to "act signs"), so that at the point where language attempts to speak without asserting, we find that language is itself a mask.

Such a conception of language is directed against the more traditional beliefs about language and the self which hold that language is primarily a vehicle for the expression of the desires, beliefs, and intentions of the speaker; these views also assume that words mean what they say. As children of Marx and Freud, however, we know that the self, which is posited "behind" such a language, is not a transparent thing. By this legacy we know also that the desires of the self cannot be constructed solely by the immaterial will. The self is opaque, furthermore, in that it is embodied. Thus any theory of desire in language will, in part at least, have to be a materialist one. As Wiseman demonstrates in her essay, this conception of the materiality of desire is compatible with its textualization, as seen exemplarily in the writings of Barthes. Since the body has its own (material) laws, it is only to be expected that the imposition of any direction on it in the form of an intention will bear the impress of an authorized language, that is, of a certain power, from which the body will want also to clear free. As this takes place in an endless chain, "the erotic body may be either what does the desiring or what is desired, subject or object of desire. The body that causes the writer to move through language as he does is his desiring body, the objects of whose desire are figured in the path he makes through the network of signifiers, and this text-figured desire may in turn become the desire of another."

The discovery of utopias in language, which corresponds to a shift in our understanding of those factors that constitutively define the subject and the self, is reflected in literature in privileged ways. There is, for example, a "materialization" of language in literature, as may be seen in the work of Mallarmé and in the poststructuralist critique of the transparency of the sign. This materialization might be thought of as a consequence of what Barthes calls one of the two desires of language, namely the desire for an adequacy to the real. It begins in a movement from text to materiality: "Modern writing is textual, the text is a tissue of signifiers, and signifiers are irreducibly material in that they must be inscribed." The adequacy of language to the real could thus be achieved by demonstrating that language is material and matter textual. And yet the materialization of language (even granting the textualization of the world) proves insufficient to the task of adequation, and the conception of language as material demonstrated in modern literature proves unable to satisfy the utopian desire of language. A more encompassing description of literature might, however, be entertained, and if one is willing to include photography within the literary domain, then one need not regard the history of language, literature, and the self as suspended with Mallarmé. Photography involves a conception of light-patterning, image-casting matter as textual, and so may be justifiably called a form of writing; and the mechanically recordable world may be said to be a text (a "utopian" text) because it is neither centered nor closed. And as the redescription of the world made possible by photography itself shows, it is in fact necessary to include photography within the bounds of literature. For the photographic redescription of the world is "part of a utopic reconception of the real that allows the orders of language and the real to coincide; it will breach the opposition between them, thereby satisfying literature's impossible desire. In this utopia of language, literature's desire annihilates itself, and since this desire is its project, its goal, its point, absent these, literature annihilates itself."

Not unexpectedly, objects seen in such a system are seen in an impossible representation, a utopian one, which sees as if from no point of view. Photography thus provides an image of what literature might be once representations have been outplayed. To phrase this in different terms, it suggests what it might mean to overcome theatricality while remaining within theater itself; a similar feat is contemplated by Shakespeare's Prospero, who vows to lay aside magic, but not until his representation is done. It suggests that the postmodern passage beyond representations is a passage not only beyond but through subjectivity as well.

Rewriting the Self: *Mary Bittner Wiseman*
Barthes and the Utopias
of Language

Roland Barthes, a critic of culture stunningly reminiscent of Socrates in his insistence that one can never with justice stop examining what is given nor with justice take anything to go without saying, faces the question in the work of his last years of how to evaluate tradition when all critical languages labor under tradition's weight. How can one critically examine received opinion when, as he supposes, the languages of criticism are inevitably co-opted by the powers in place, official acceptance investing them with a value they would not otherwise have, thus beclouding the issue of their own value? Barthes answers this question by tracing paths from received opinion to what he calls *utopias of language*, whose description shows both what it is desirable to change within the status quo and what reconceptions are possible. The strategy turns on discovering within the set of traditional beliefs the means for their criticism and using the discovered possibilities to escape, evade, or "cheat" the tradition. He correctly supposes that one cannot simply disavow received beliefs, for they have shaped one's thought. At best one can work through them, and one way of working through is to perform an experiment in imagination whose description is a utopia.

The experimental nature of the work of Barthes's last decade has not, I think, been properly understood. For example, Yves Bonnefoy, Barthes's successor to the chair in literature at the Collège de France, joins the number of critics who hold that in his last years Barthes was overcoming "the contemporary reluctance to raise the question of the self" in that he was resurrecting a conception that had gotten buried under the notion of a material subject determined by language and by history.[1] It might be objected that if Barthes was invoking the concept of the self it was only to bury its ghost and to exorcise once and for all the spell that it and certain of the concepts clustering around it have cast over us. This, however, is only half the story. Barthes was neither returning the self to its high seat in the scheme of our concepts nor trying to get rid of it once and for all: he was returning it marked "out of date" but as nonetheless necessary to support a new scheme. This is to say that there is no adequate theory of the material subject, and the work of Barthes's last five years in particular may well be read as instructions for the construction of such a theory.

The failure to read Barthes's work as experimental has led to two ways of interpreting the whole of it that severely inhibit the release of energies produced by his invitation in *The Pleasure of the Text* to "imagine someone . . . who abolishes within himself all barriers, all classes, all exclusions, not by syncretism but by simple disregard of that old specter: *logical contradiction,* who mixes every language, even those said to be incompatible."[2] One way is to suppose with Bonnefoy that Barthes has betrayed the revolution working itself out through structuralism and poststructuralism, rejecting structuralism's fragmented, decentered human subject and returning to a humanistic conception of a unified, centered, and centering self: Frank Kermode, for one, refers to Barthes as "a reconstituted humanist," "an old-fashioned man of letters." The other way to look at the course of his work is to see in it no break at all but rather an increasingly nihilistic subjective relativism. Each of these interpretations sees a difference between Barthes's earlier and later work: in the one case the difference is the result of a break; in the other, of a development.

There is a third way that locates difference within Barthes's texts themselves, not between stages of an alleged development. It is to find within the late texts a reconstituted humanism raising again the question of the self, with this difference, which is all the difference: it is a humanism that is at the same time a structuralism. This way of reading liberates the treasures Barthes's texts are enriching; for it mixes "every language, even those *said to be* incompatible" (emphasis added), where it is precisely what is said to be that Barthes calls into question. In particular, he questions the incompatibility of languages said to be incompatible by tracing paths from one to the other, showing the one, utopically, to satisfy impossible desires harbored in the other.

Barthes has betrayed no revolution nor become a subjectivist in any familiar sense of "subject." The revolution began with structuralism's attack on certain tenets of humanism and historicism: that literature, for example, embodies an author's act of mind and that its style is determined by its place in the continuous development that is literature's history. This attack on modernism's twin commitments is mounted on the back of the Saussurian definition of the sign as the indissoluble union of sound-image and concept whose signifying power comes from its place in a network of negative relations. Embodiment of a concept or an act of mind in some material medium implies a separability denied by the indissolubility of the sign's sense and sound. If, therefore, literature is held to speak an author's mind, it cannot be regarded as a sign, and many of the strategies of reading devised by contemporary criticism are denied it. Moreover, if significance is a function of systematic relationships irrespective of the temporal relations of the system-related units, then reading is limited only by the possibilities of language, not by the location in literary history of what is being read, and the way is open for the juxtaposition of temporally remote styles, concepts, and theories. Barthes furthers this revolution, for his experiments in imagination involve the juxtaposition of what logic and language, as well as time, have declared to be separate. The theme is sounded in the invitation to imagine someone who abolishes the specter of logical contradiction and who mixes languages.

Critics who lack a structural imagination are blind to what is most to be valued in Barthes's later work: an experimental rewriting of concepts surrounding the notion of the human subject and, in particular, a rewriting of the concept of the subject which is radical in its insight and implications. The concept shadowed forth in the work of the 1970s is arguably Barthes's most important and least appreciated contribution to contemporary criticism: most important because there is not yet a satisfactory account of the (constitution of) the structured and structuring subject; and least appreciated because, battle lines having been drawn between humanism and structuralism, it has been assumed that no work in the latter camp is worth mining for insight about the human subject.

The lineaments of Barthes's reworked concept of the human subject, as well as his strategy for reworking in general, are to be discovered in the notion of a *utopia of language*. In the 1977 lecture to the Collège de France Barthes said:

Human language has no exterior: there is no exit. We can get out of it only at the price of the impossible: by mystical singularity . . . But for those of us who are neither knights of faith nor superman the only remaining alternative is . . . to cheat with speech, to cheat speech. This salutary trickery, this evasion, this grand imposture which allows us to understand speech *outside the bounds of power*, in the splendor of a permanent revolution of language, I for one call *literature*.

I mean by *literature* . . . the complex graph of a practice, the practice of writing. It is essentially the text with which I am concerned—the fabric of signifiers which constitute the work. For the text is the outcropping of speech, and it is within speech that speech must be fought, led astray . . . by the play of words of which it is the theater. Thus I can say without differentiation: literature, writing, text. The forces of freedom that are in literature depend on . . . the labor of displacement the writer brings to bear upon language.[3]

Language has no outside, no boundaries, no limits, but it does have utopias, places where desires impossible within a given conceptual scheme may be satisfied. Their satisfaction requires conceptual displacements, massive rereadings and rewritings that we must do, tediously and laboriously, and since we cannot now describe the details of the places to which the labors of language will lead, in one sense we cannot describe the topologies of the utopias. But we can name the desires impossible of realization that are nonetheless unrealistically entertained in this place where we are.

Barthes speaks of two desires of language: that no language have power over any other and that literature represent the real. These each generate utopias, where utopias are always relative to the conceptual schemes within which the impossible desires are held in suspension. The conceptual changes sufficient to accommodate the otherwise impossible desired objects can be specified; what cannot be known before the displacements are made, however, is their effect on the whole scheme of our concepts. One cannot desire what one already has; at most, one can desire the continued possession of it—that is, a desire and its realized object cannot coexist. The satisfaction of a desire is its annihilation. Clearly, a desire that cannot be satisfied cannot be destroyed by being satisfied, and the law of inertia for desire is that in the absence of any reason for its being given up, or for its self-destruction, it will stay in place. Since impossible desires are entertained in the face of, sometimes because of, the fact that they cannot be realized, this fact does not count as a reason for their being given up. They are irrational. But deep within the very fact of them is to be descried the lineaments of the utopia in which they may be satisfied, and the prophecy and promise of these desires is that something different may be read in them from what has so far been read. This reading anew is a rewriting of the concepts in play in the desires' descriptions, and the rewritten descriptions stand at oblique angles to the topoi within which the desires are impossible.

Barthes has said that our modernity may be defined by the fact that for the first time utopias of language are conceived in it. The topology of his utopias reveals a modern conception of the human subject, whose connection with traditional conceptions is so tenuous and tortuous as hardly to be a connection at all and, some may say, as hardly to be a conception of a human subject. This new subject, displaced by a labor of language from its familiar terrain, is, as all displacements are, a trick, an evasion, a grand imposture—in the eyes of those who look from home ground. We all perforce stand on home ground, but we need not look directly at the subject rewritten in the utopias of language, even though we want to know what remains of the familiar subject. For this rewritten subject is a decoy and a lure and is best surprised by looking away from it to what it tracks in the two utopias where no language has power over any other and there is, therefore, no effect of truth; and where literature represents the real, but what is real are copies and imprints. The topology of the first utopia is that of the theater with its makeup and masks, the topology of the second that of the writing machines, the camera, and the chromosome.

Utopia One: The Theatricalization of Writing

One power of language is the power to say what is true and in saying what is true to enjoin belief. Barthes says of speech that it "is immediately assertive: negation, doubt, possibility, the suspension of judgment require special mechanisms which are themselves caught up in the play of linguistic masks: what linguists call modality is only the supplement of speech by which I try . . . to sway its implacable power of verification."[4] The power of assertion is harnessed by social institutions that sanction both the ways of conceiving embedded in the languages and the truth-claims the languages are used to make. The different powers of language and of institutions reinforce each other so that a subset of all that is sayable in a given language is supposed by dint of repetition and institutional custom to be true. If one performs a Humean demystification of the effects of custom and repetition, however, and concludes that what is called natural and necessary are fictions created by the institutions in power, then one may wish neither to use nor to be used by the languages in place, which are, nonetheless, all the languages there are. Since the roster of institutions includes universities, academies, scholarly societies, publishing houses—in short, all the means of the dissemination of ideas, the question becomes one of how to speak against or outside of an intellectual tradition whose language one cannot help but speak. For to speak tradition's language is a fortiori to accept its way of parsing the world, and to reparse the world is to start to speak a new language.

Although the power of language cannot be destroyed, it can, Barthes holds, be masked or supplemented or evaded. From the time of his first book, *Writing Degree Zero* (1953), Barthes thought that modern literature could, utopically, annul the power of one language over another. Literature is modern when its writing is conscious of itself as a productive activity of language, that is, as a text and not as an instru-

ment for expressing or representing a reality already made to be con-
sumed by the reader. Modern literature, it had seemed, could fulfill
this function because its sentences do not claim to be assertions, and
since it does not presume to refer to what is signified by the languages
contemporary with it, it is not in competition with them. By the time
of the 1977 lecture to the Collège de France, however, Barthes was convinced that modern literature is unavoidably co-opted by contemporary languages, if only by being made to refer to "modern literature";
and when it is, it can no longer fulfill the utopic function of refusing
language's referential and other semantic functions. What must modern literature become in order to refuse these functions? How must
concepts related to it change in order to enable this refusal?

The effort simultaneously to use language and to disengage it from
its assertive function involves acting: "On the impossible horizon of
linguistic anarchy—at the point where language attempts to escape its
own power, its own servility—we find something which relates to theater."[5] The discovery that the utopia of no-power is related to theater
is not remarkable: actors quintessentially utter sentences without asserting them, and writers who use language nonreferentially are, so far
forth, like actors. What is remarkable are the pirouettes Barthes's texts
make from this point: they do not argue, they perform. If writing is
theatrical, texts are performances. I will follow two of the indefinitely
many paths through the space between received beliefs about language
and linguistic performance and the utopia of linguistic anarchy. One
path leads to the masks actors wore in primitive theater and continues
on to the face in the photograph, revealed and immobilized by light.
The other leads from the fact that actors not only use language nonreferentially but also use their bodies essentially (that is, actors are bodies
that give voice to words already written), on to an interweave of the
materiality and movement of desire with the materiality and movement of the signifier. Because the paths are indefinitely many, no one
the text actually takes can have been predicted, but because they are
paths they can be followed—no matter how they wind.

Path One: Representation

Consider the difference between representation and figuration, names
for the paths before us. There will be representation, Barthes says, so
long as a "subject casts his *gaze* toward a horizon on which he cuts out
the base of a triangle, his eye (or mind) forming the apex."[6] This principle underlies perspective painting, tableaux vivant, and the theatrical

scene, which Diderot, in an aesthetics that fractures Aristotle's unities of the theater, identifies with the pictorial tableau, calling the perfect play a succession of pictorial tableaux. Barthes, Diderotian in *Camera Lucida: Reflections on Photography* (1980), associates tableaux, primitive theater, and photography through a constellation of signifiers clustering around masks and death:

If Photography seems to be closer to Theater (than to Painting), it is by way of a singular intermediary (and perhaps I am the only one who sees it): by way of Death. We know of the original relation of the theater to the cult of the Dead: the first actors separated themselves from the community by playing the role of the Dead: to make oneself up was to designate oneself as a body simultaneously living and dead: the whitened bust of the totemic theater, the man with the painted face in the Chinese theater, the rice-paste makeup of the Indian Katha-Kali, the Japanese No masks . . . Now it is this same relation which I find in the Photograph: . . . Photography is a kind of primitive theater, a kind of Tableau Vivant, a figuration of the motionless and made-up face beneath which we see the dead.[7]

A line drawn between the rice-painted face on stage and the light-made face in the photograph doubles back on itself: the photographed face is absent but revealed through its light-written traces; the masked face, present but concealed. This is just to say that in the utopia where languages do not assert and writers act signs, in the still, theatrical scene that presents itself to the eye of the audience, the familiar oppositions between presence and absence, revelation and concealment, are undone. Presence has been understood as a shining forth of what is present: for example, the presence of the form of the Good, that most real thing, was, like the dazzle of the sun, blinding to the Republican philosophers who stood before it. The actors on stage, however, are masked or made up, and there is no revelation through rice-paste makeup. Yet presence may as well, or instead, be understood as location in space and time, and this sense forces itself upon us to account for the body there on the stage. The actor is located, but nothing is revealed. "The implacable power of verification has been swayed by the play of masks," where the linguistic function of the mask is to put itself in place of what it masks, not to present but to conceal it.

To say, as Barthes does, that "to make oneself up was to designate oneself as a body simultaneously living and dead" is to say that primitive actor and modern writer alike are present in the sense of being bodies brutely, densely there, but absent in not being light (or self or soul) that shines through bodies. As the actor speaks, so the writer writes, words that are not hers. The writers' words, like the actors' bodies, are dense and opaque: nothing shows through. To say that an actor is a body simultaneously living and dead is to say also that the emblematic mask is incorporated *as a mask* and as such is and is not part of the body of the actor, just as what is written against the tradition is and is not part of the tradition. The dilemma that what is part of the tradition cannot be *against* it and what is not part of it cannot be *about* it persists so long as the possibility of incorporating the rejection of the tradition into its body is denied. If this possibility is allowed, another logic than that of identity is unleashed. So far as what had been outside—the tradition's denial—is now supposed within it, the identity of the tradition with itself is fractured and its difference from itself opens up within it.

To say that the actor incorporates his mask is not to say that under the mask is no single, still thing, because the mask, like a variable in a mathematical function, can assume any value whatsoever so long as it satisfies the functional relation, which in the case of the actor is the play's words; that is, anyone who says the words can wear the mask. In the utopia where language abdicates its power to say what is true, all speakers are masked, unable to assert either themselves or their words. But this does not warrant the conclusion that there are only masks: the concept of mask requires that of a reality behind it for "mask" to make sense. This opposition is undone in the utopia in which language surrenders its power to say what is real in surrendering the power to say what is true. For insofar as the actor incorporates his mask, we cannot talk about the body and the mask as distinct, since what had been outside the body—the mask—is now within it, and the integrity of each, body and mask, is shattered by the presence within of what had been defined as outside. The result is that we cannot say that because the mask is part of the body there is nothing under it without at the same time saying that because it is a mask there is something under it. We must say both or neither, and if we say both we are committed to there being an infinite number of bodies and masks.[8] The conceptual boundaries are broken, and the concepts are running away. The description of this delicate and ephemeral moment in the history of a concept when its familiar meaning still attaches to it even though its grounding opposition has been breached, the moment just before the displacement or shift in the economy of our concepts that results from removing the paradigmatic slash between two opposing terms, is a matter of the greatest difficulty. When we are in the midst of a deconstruction of the familiar and have not yet gotten to where the deconstruction leads, we cannot read the topography of the new land: we are in an atopia.

Insofar as actor and modern writer compose a tableau vivant, they mimic a model, they represent something to someone and require the gaze of an observer to carve out the space in which they represent and in which by the force of their logic they must stay. "This is what representation is: when nothing emerges, when nothing leaps out of the frame: of the picture, the book, the screen."[9] Barthes likens the photograph to the tableau; the space of each is defined by a point outside itself, but there is the crucial difference that the point outside the photograph is that from which the camera shoots, not from which a subject gazes. This is a fact important for the decentering of the physical, the photographable world, which decentering is, in turn, a key step on the way to the utopic textualization of the world which occurs in the utopia in which language represents the real.

Path Two: Figuration

Consider now, not the tableau cut out from the succession of scenes that constitute a play, but the succession itself. It mimes the movements of both desire and textual production in such a way as to generate the idea of a utopia in which the topoi of theater, desire, and signification intertwine. Representation is exemplified by the tableau, figuration by the theater; and the salient difference between them for us who want to see what remains of the human subject in the utopias of language is that the subject is *active* in the figured text and stands outside and *gazes* at the representational one. In short, what is figured in the former is the desire of the writer; the text presents the form of his desire just as the stage presents the form of the actor. Stage and text present the body of the actor and the desire of the writer themselves, not representations of them. What must be shown is how textual production figures desire and how the movement of the writer's desire is not a matter of the writer's revealing herself through her words, of her speaking or writing words that are hers.

Imagine language as a vast network of intersecting vertical and horizontal lines; silent and invisible, the network defines a field across which textual activity occurs. To the question "Why does a writer enter the network here and exit there, follow now this path and now that?" there is a series of answers that begins with "Because of his time and his place" and ends with "Because of his personal history." The answers do point to the choices open to a given writer, but it is precisely the limitations of culturally determined possibilities of language and thought that the utopia of no-power is designed to avoid. It might seem that the answer must come from some place beyond language and the institutionalization of language's power of assertion, but there is no such place. The writer can only cheat, trick, evade the power of language and the languages of power. One strategy for doing this, performing signs as an actor does, invites the question "Why perform them in just this way?"

When, utopically, the writer is an actor, she not only utters sentences without asserting them but uses her body to perform. Part of the legacy of Marx and Freud is that any adequate theory of desire will be a materialist one, constructing desire out of the organism's needs and characterizing desire's objects in terms of the organism's interactions with the world. The impossible desire satisfied in the utopia in which one writes her desires in the texts she produces is the desire that there be no gap between what one is and what one writes (reads, says). A well-entrenched tenet of traditional theories of language is that language expresses the beliefs, desires, and intentions of the language user and that in general words mean what the user means by them. The desire that language should perfectly express the self is impossible just because neither self nor language is so transparent that the speaker always knows all that her utterances mean and that language means all and only what the speaker wants it to mean. Both language and the human mind have their dark places and shadows that fall between speaker and speech, writer and writing. The concepts of speaker and speech, writer and writing, are reworked in the utopia where writing is theatricalized in such a way that language users and their products are irrecoverable from the performance of the activities of speaking and reading and writing.

The reworking of the concept of what the writer or speaker is begins from the theoretical fact that desire works from and through the body. Since it does, the question "Why perform signs in *this* way?" becomes "Why use this body of yours in the way that you do?" and brings the answer "It acts as it does, and this body of mine that goes its own way is what I call the body of my desire." The writer has double reason for not trying to choreograph her movements through language: first, one's control is limited at best, for the body has laws of its own, laws now being discovered by, for example, neurophysiology. Second, any direction imposed upon the body in the form of an intention will bear the press of the authorized languages whose power is to be evaded. The erotic body may be either what does the desiring or what is desired, subject or object of desire. The body that causes the writer to move through language as he does is his desiring body, the objects of whose desire are figured in the path he makes through the network of signifiers, and this text-figured desire may in turn become the desire of another.

Figuration is the way in which the erotic body appears . . . in the profile of the text . . . [T]he text itself, a diagrammatic and not an imitative structure, can reveal itself in the form of a body, split into fetish objects, into erotic sites . . .

Representation, on the other hand, is *embarrassed figuration*, encumbered with other meanings than that of desire: a space of alibis (reality, likelihood, readibility, truth, etc.).[10]

The text reveals itself in the form of a body split into pieces, and the text can figure the desired body only because the text itself is language in pieces, language divided within itself by all the oppositions and differences without which it could not signify.[11] Signification occurs along the axes of the network of signifiers, one relation of difference leading on to others, each of which leads on to others, and so on. Institutions construct meanings from the pieces of language, and the meanings constructed, the meaning-constructions, stop the movement of signification. But in utopia there are no constructions, only pieces and places: vertical lists of signifiers (paradigms) and horizontal strings of sites which members of the paradigms may occupy. Since the movement of signification, like the movement of desire, is endless, the text and the erotic body it figures are not complete, whole, final. Rather, the objects of desire and signifiers are necessarily incomplete, for no single object, no single signifier, can by itself satisfy desiring body or signifying text. A site in a signifying chain can take a given signifier as a value only if it can take other values, that is, only if the signifier is exchangeable with others. It is this circulation of signifiers that culture would stop by privileging certain assignments of value, just as fantasy would stop the circulation of objects of desire. Text and erotic body are like mathematical functions: the first is the site of the play of signification, the second the site of the restless movement of desire.

Utopia Two: The Textualization of the Body

The erotic body is *material*, occupying the space through which light travels and interrupting light in its course, reflecting it in patterns that cast images on reflecting surfaces, and *living*, occupying the time through which generations pass and interrupting this passage too, giving itself up to the genetic messages that write themselves on it. Certain similarities between genes and signifiers, between genealogical trees and networks of signifiers, and between biological individuals and texts lead to a reconstruction of the identity over time of the human subject in what is a further step in the utopic textualization of the body. Since the rewritten concept of the human being is that of a body that writes, and since writing is *the* textual activity, the body's becoming a text is the human being's becoming a text. Its matter, its stuff, is what most resists being textualized, and it is to this that Barthes turns in *Camera Lucida*. This effort is part of a larger strategy that the very notion of a utopia serves: to see what revisions can be made of, and what paths traced out of, familiar topoi. For what is made or traced out of the familiar shows us the limits of its possibility, its recesses. Again, two paths are marked.

Path One: Figuration

The textualization of the living body is suggested in this comparison between work and text: the work "refers to the image of an *organism* that grows by vital expansion . . . the metaphor of the text is that of a network; if the Text extends itself, it is as a result of a combinatory systematic (an image, moreover, close to current biological conceptions of the living being)."[12] The chromosomes of germ cells and signifiers alike are not seeds but units that couple systematically to produce indefinitely branching genealogical trees and galaxies of signifiers, neither of which has fixed beginnings or endings. Nor can the genetic or the signifying network be plotted by one point or line: meaning is produced differentially and mammals bisexually. Since signification and reproduction require at least two signifiers and genetic contributors, respectively, what is signified and what is reproduced are what they are by virtue of the relation between their contributors, each of which is itself the result of a relation. Signification and genetic transfer occur in systems. Moreover, they are systems without centers, for their units are exchangeable among themselves: what is said or reproduced is not unique. Other signifiers than those used would have done to figure or delineate what was delineated, for what language points to are constellations of signifiers, and any signifiers in the constellation will point as well as any others to the cluster. Similarly, the genetic makeup of an individual could have made up another individual. Identical twins, for example, are genetically the same, and it is possible with the techniques of genetic engineering for separately-egged individuals to have the same set of chromosomes. To say that signification and reproduction occur in systems without centers is to say that they are *"like language . . . structured but off-centered, without closure* (note, in reply to the contemptuous suspicion of the 'fashionable' sometimes directed at structuralism, that the epistemological privilege currently accorded to language stems precisely from the discovery there of a paradoxical idea of structure: *a system with neither close nor center)*" (emphasis added).[13] The genealogical tree, the tree of life, is, then, like language and is, so far forth, textual.

The body instructed by genes is textual as well. It is what it is by virtue of its place on the genealogical tree, and this in a double way: the individual body has the chromosomes it has because of the gene pool available at the time of its issue, and it has the features it has because of its chromosomes. An individual's features are simply the printout of its genetically encoded instruction: the individual is gene-written, and the connection between the individual and her stock may be illustrated by what appears in a photograph. For the photograph is "like old age: even in its splendor, it disincarnates the face, manifests its genetic essence."[14] So far as the individual is identified by its lines of descent, it is a site through which such lines pass—stopping to inform the raw material that is all that the individual contributes to himself— and is exchangeable with others on the same line. Instructed by Barthes's saying that "lineage reveals an identity stronger, more interesting, than legal status," one may construe the identity over time of a human subject to be the whole of the genealogical network, one temporal segment of which is the subject's legal identity, a fiction bounded by certificates of birth and death.

This conception of the subject's identity plays havoc with the post–eighteenth-century notion that the individual is unique; for here it is regarded as the instantiation of one of the many possible combinations and permutations of genes and, further, as an instantiation that is in principle repeatable. It plays havoc, too, with the Aristotelean notion that the individual, differentiated from other members of its species only by its matter, cannot be known, whereas Barthes posits a utopia of knowledge where there can be a *mathesis singularis,* a science of the individual.[15]

The reidentification of the individual with his genealogical tree is precisely a matter of playing havoc with received notions, for it is part of the topography of a utopia in which the body is textualized. Utopias may overlap, and the utopia in which writing is theatricalized shows the erotic body to be like language in being the place where desires occur, particular desires being values in a system that is organized by desire. In that utopia, figuration was the operation of a writer on language, undertaken in the service of desire, which yields a writing that lasts as long as the performance lasts. The particular writing was the instantiation of a possible combination of signifiers. In the utopia in which the living body is shown to be like language, figuration is the operation of gene-carrying chromosomes on matter, undertaken in the service of life. It yields a biological individual that is the instantiation of a possible combination of genes. The erotic body and the living body are, of course, both material, and it might be thought that so far as they are desiring and living they are textual, but so far as they are material they are not: for matter is brute and dumb, a remainder, intractably real, itself actual and not textual.

Path Two: Representation

Another fast-held tenet of traditional theories of language is that language is adequate to the real or, better, that such adequation is the ideal limit to which languages approach more or less closely. This could be taken to imply that it is possible actually to reach the limit or to approach it to within a distance as small as you will. On the contrary, it could be thought that such a belief is utopian and the desire that language represent the real impossible.

From ancient times to the efforts of our avant-garde, literature has been concerned to represent something. What? I will put it crudely: the real. The real is not representable, and it is because men ceaselessly try to represent it by words that there is a history of literature. Though there is no parallelism between language and the real, men will not take sides, and it is this refusal . . . which produces, in an incessant commotion, literature. We can imagine a history of . . . productions of language, which would be the history of certain (often aberrant) verbal expedients we have used to reduce, tame, deny, or, on the contrary, to assume what is *always* a delirium, i.e., the fundamental inadequation of language and the real.[16]

The concepts of language and the real may be reconstructed so that they will be adequate to each other in the utopia where literature's impossible desire is satisfied. They will be adequate so far as language is material and matter textual. (It is here supposed that matter is the aspect of the real most difficult to treat as textual.) The materialization of language is one effect of the modern conception of writing that began with Mallarmé and was furthered by the poststructural rejection of the nonlinguistic signified. Modern writing is textual, the text is a tissue of signifiers, and signifiers are irreducibly material in that they must be inscribed somewhere or other: written on wind by waves of sound, written in ink, encoded electronically or genetically, written by light on paper or eye. Even so, it might be worried that inscriptions are not material enough, they lack bruteness, they do not cast shadows, they do not pattern light. Moreover, even though language may be material, is this sufficient to show that language is adequate to the real?

There is in *Camera Lucida* a conception of raw, light-patterning, image-casting matter as textual. It turns on Barthes's reversing the traditional direction of the relation between perception and photography, according to which a photograph is a record of what someone has seen and is a stand-in for perception, that is, were one to have direct perceptual access to the photographed object, one would not be inclined to bother with its photograph. Photography is commonly thought of as mechanical perception, and perception is thought to be prior to it both in nature and in epistemological function. That is, the perception of X counts as prima facie evidence for X's presence, whereas the photograph is evidence of its object only when the photograph itself is perceived. The reversal of this priority is prompted by several considerations, the first of which is that some material object had to have been before a camera for a photograph to have been taken: cameras cannot hallucinate. The photograph is a record of the object's presence to the camera, a record, moreover, free from the distortions made by a perceiving subject. The photograph, therefore, bears perfect witness to the reality of its object, where "reality" is construed as presence. What Barthes calls a *scandal* is that the photograph can testify only to the object's past reality: the scandal is that past existence of objects can be proved by a technique of writing, light-writing, that makes impossible the proof of present existence and that, therefore, the photograph transgresses the customary association of the real with the present. The photograph is the trace of the configuration of the rays of light emanating from the object at the moment its photograph was taken, and that moment is always past.

Even though photographs are in principle free from subjective distortion, and though they store and publicize light-written traces recorded long ago, photography may still seem second to perception until a further consideration is advanced: perception is precisely the same as photography so far as the pastness of their objects goes. Light takes time to travel, and although we treat as negligible the time it takes for light to move from object to eye, time elapses, and the object perceived is the object as it was at the time that it configured the light imprinted on the perceiver's retina. Images on the lenses of camera and eye alike are two-dimensional, and when the object perceived is a long-dead distant star, it is with the retinal image just as it is with the photographic image whose original no longer exists. The only difference is that camera image lasts longer and is public, whereas eye image stays but for a moment and only for its perceiver. But in each case what is recorded are traces of past objects. Perception of the world as it is at time t will come at time $t + n$, with the result that perception of the present world is always deferred to the future. And what occurs in the future is, of course, perception of what is then past. The world is never seen as it is at the moment of seeing, nor is it camera-recorded as it was at the moment it configured the light imprinted on lens and then reprinted on paper. The presence of the world is endlessly deferred, and the system of ordered relations among light, material objects, and recording mechanism lacks closure.

It is at best misleading to reduce the material world to the perceptible; for this implies a perceiving subject, which is, then, the center of the world it perceives, and the material world is taken to be a construction out of subject-centered perceived worlds. The description of the world as never present turns on its being such as to be recorded on some surface, and this requires only a recording mechanism, not a sensing subject. The camera is a magic writing pad, magic in that it records light-traced images of the world directly without the mediation of a subject. The material, mechanically recordable world is, then, part of a system without a center. Lacking closure and center, it is a text, a utopian text, utopian in that it depends on a description of the world incompatible with our ordinary ways of thinking about perception, and yet which is such that we know more or less what sorts of conceptual changes would have to occur for the description to be apt. This description is part of a utopic reconception of the real that allows the orders of language and the real to coincide; it will breach the opposition between them, thereby satisfying literature's impossible desire. In this utopia of language, literature's desire annihilates itself; and since this desire is its project, its goal, its point, absent these, literature annihilates itself. It needed its difference from the real to be what it was, and once language and the real are so conceived as to inhabit the same logical space, the difference disappears. In its utopian reconception literature includes photography—as it includes whatever is like language in being a system with neither close nor center.

In the utopia where writers are actors, representation is exemplified by the tableau cut out by the gaze of a subject toward a horizon on which he cuts out the base of a triangle, his eye forming the apex. In the utopia where material objects are part of a languagelike system, representation is exemplified by the photograph, which represents its object from no point of view: the apex of the triangle cut out along the horizon is the point from which the camera shoots. The camera's eye is like the eye of a dead man. "In Dreyer's *Vampyr*, . . . the camera moves from house to cemetery recording what the dead man sees: such is the extreme limit at which representation is outplayed: the spectator can no longer take up any position, for he cannot identify his eye with the closed eye of the dead man: the tableau has no point of departure, no support, it gapes open."[17] We have come full circle from the mask of the dead to the eye of the dead. Rice-paste painted face speaks words that are not hers, modern writer writes words not hers. Body of the actor, face wearing paint, pattern light—that is what matter is, what patterns light. The patterned rays trace themselves on the camera's lens, and some of the objects that configure light are themselves configured by messages encoded within the very stuff of them.

What writes? In the utopia where the material-real—the living and the light-configuring—is textual, genes and light write through the information storage and transmission systems of the chromosome and the camera. In the utopia where the language user is masked and acting, desire writes. But in neither utopia does any one write, as "one" has traditionally been conceived.

Because such utopias can be imagined, the powers and the boundaries of the self need not be taken to go without saying. For in the utopia where the uses of language are theatricalized, language usurps the originating, authorizing power of the self. And in the one where the human body is textualized, its temporal boundary is lineal, not legal, and its spatial boundary is "the skin of light," not what mind can causally affect.[18]

Barthes wrote in his last five years about the discourse of lovers, personal diaries, and personal photographs, as well as an autobiography. He does, there, speak the language of the self, but always with a cataclysmic difference: he speaks it *out of context*. Of a piece with the view that words mean what a language user means by them is the view that the context of the linguistic performance contributes to the meaning of the words used. Indeed, it, together with the language used, determines what the performer can mean. Barthes's using words out of the context of their traditional conceptual frame marks his rejection of this view, which is replaced by the structuralist model of language, and it points to an answer to the question of how to speak against or outside of the prevailing languages and the meanings constructed by the institutions in power. If neither the prevailing languages nor the tradition that spawned them is natural or necessary, then one can fail to privilege both the associations of meaning made by contemporary institutions and the continuity of the tradition. One can speak out of context and, by describing utopias of language—places where neither speaker's intention nor society's ideology holds sway—recontextualize what has in its history gone by the names "soul," "self," and "subject." If one can conceive the juxtaposition of traditional humanism, on the one hand, and structuralism, on the other, putting the concepts of one into the context of the other, then one can appreciate the daring of Barthes's experiment in imagination, which will have succeeded when the reader, midwifelike, delivers the child of this unholy marriage.

Notes

1. Yves Bonnefoy, "*Image and Presence*: Yves Bonnefoy's Inaugural Address at the Collège de France," trans. John T. Naughton, *New Literary History* 15 (1984): 439.

2. Roland Barthes, *Le plaisir du texte* (Paris: Seuil, 1973). *The Pleasure of the Text*, trans. Richard Miller (New York: Hill & Wang, 1979), 3.

3. Roland Barthes, *Leçon: Leçon inaugurale de la chaire de sémiologie littéraire du Collège de France, prononcé le 7 janvier 1977* (Paris: Seuil, 1978). "Lecture in Inauguration of the Chair of Literary Semiology, Collège de France," trans. Richard Howard, *October* 8 (1979): 6.

4. Barthes, "Lecture," 5.

5. Ibid., 10.

6. Roland Barthes, "Diderot, Brecht, Eisenstein," in *Image-Music-Text*, trans. Stephen Heath (New York: Hill & Wang, 1977), 69.

7. Roland Barthes, *La chambre claire: Note sur la photographie* (Paris: Gallimard & Seuil, 1980). *Camera Lucida: Reflections on Photography*, trans. Richard Howard (New York: Hill & Wang, 1981), 31–32.

8. There is something under $mask_1$ by virtue of its being a mask, but this something cannot be $body_1$, of which it is a part; it must be $body_2$. But so far as $mask_1$ is a mask of $body_2$ it is part of $body_2$ and, as such, is itself $mask_2$. There must, then, be $body_3$, which is under $mask_2$ and incorporates it, thereby making it $mask_3$; and so on.

9. Barthes, *Pleasure*, 57.

10. Ibid., 55–56.

11. "Freud made the discovery that the object of desire need not in any sense be complete. Quite simply, there is such a thing as the 'object' of desire . . . Desire does not seek out the subject, for which it cares nothing. Rather, it seeks out the object. This object is necessarily incomplete, a tiny, minuscule thing—'the little thing,' Freud called it." Catherine Clement, *The Lives and*

Legends of Jacques Lacan, trans. Arthur Goldhammer (New York: Columbia University Press, 1983), 98.

12. Roland Barthes, "From Work to Text," in *Image-Music-Text*, 161.

13. Ibid., 159.

14. Barthes, *Camera Lucida*, 105.

15. Discussion of this utopia exceeds the reach of this essay, but the utopia is marginally here in that the utopia of language in which writers are actors, masked and writing through their bodies, requires a strong concept of performance. Texts and erotic bodies are mathematically functional sites of the performance of language and desire, where performances are values, actualizations of certain of many possibilities, the acts of choosing linguistic values, the occurrences of desire. The introduction of the strong concept of performance makes it impossible to think, and impossible to think away, questions about the identity of individuals. For performance requires a performer, and yet the performer is dissolved or annihilated at the moment of the performance. One utopic solution is to rewrite the concept of performance so that it does not entail that of performer; another is to reconceive the notion of an individual so that an individual does not have temporal extension and is a momentary existent. Criteria of identity, and criteria for the identification of performances and momentary existents, have to be decided, but whatever the decision, a group of our concepts is skewed, including the concept of knowledge, one of whose laws is that the individual cannot be known.

16. Barthes, "Lecture," 8.

17. Barthes, "Diderot, Brecht, Eisenstein," 77.

18. "A sort of umbilical cord links the body of the photographed thing to my gaze: light, though impalable, is here a carnal medium, a skin I share with anyone who has been photographed." Barthes, *Camera Lucida*, 81.

13
Postmodernism in Philosophy: Nostalgia for the Future, Waiting for the Past

In an essay entitled "The Age of the World Picture" (Die Zeit des Welt-bildes), Heidegger advanced the twofold thesis that the modern age (*der Neuzeit*) is the result of the transformation of the world into a representation or picture, and that this transformation marks a fundamental break with the medieval and ancient worlds. Indeed, it should be impossible to speak properly of a medieval or ancient "world picture": "The expressions 'world picture of the modern age' and 'modern world picture' both mean the same thing and both assume something that never could have been before, namely, a medieval and an ancient world picture. The world picture does not change from an earlier medieval one into a modern one, but rather the fact that the world becomes picture at all is what distinguishes the essence of the modern age." The establishment of the new in this case depends on the rejection of the old; the traditional concept of form is replaced by the notion of form-as-representation, which, as Heidegger says in his study of Nietzsche, is a function of the willfulness of the modern subject. In the estimation of Stanley Rosen, the extraordinary release of "creative" energy which thus accompanies the modern "begins soon to deteriorate into what may be called experimental mannerism, or the unmistakable rictus of energy deflected into the attempt to find a lost bearing." As an unsympathetic critic might charge of Roland Barthes, "Writing becomes initially more exquisite, and the increased subtlety of language stimulates a corresponding increase in the subtlety of reading."

In the present study, Berel Lang takes a more sanguine approach to the problem of postmodernism (and to the question of modernism which it implies). He in fact begins from the premise that the present age is one of extreme permissiveness. But knowing that the permissiveness of the age—its indulgence of such "experimental" writings and readings as those of Barthes—is possible only because of its boundless skepticism, this is a fact that might equally give cause for hope as for despair. Indeed, one might take the interrelations of philosophy and literature presented in this volume as tangible evidence of this permissiveness. One might take this as cause for despair if one were troubled by the fact that we no longer seem able to tell philosophy and literature apart; but one might also see this as a sign of hope, insofar as literature and philosophy are thereby both freed from the very constraints that "modernity" has imposed upon them.

The story of the displacement of literature and philosophy by each other is, however, part of the larger story which Berel Lang constructs here. As recounted by Heidegger, Rorty, and Derrida, modern philosophy sees the displacement of the apparent world by a second world, which claims priority over and seeks to subordinate the first. This is, as Berel Lang says, revisionist history based on a pattern of hierarchical displacement, and it is "just this suspicion—that it is the will to displacement, the desire for a center and then for a representation of that center, which has motivated the history of philosophy" since at least Descartes. However, once we recognize the consistent pattern of this displacement and the repetitious nature of this complaint, and once we see that there may be equal reason for hope or for despair, then the question becomes the one that Lang raises explicitly in this essay, namely "Where do we go from here?"

We might begin by dispelling the illusion that the postmodern moment involves a decisive rupture with the past. In so claiming, postmodern thinkers only reaffirm their bonds with the past, and in so saying they prove themselves incoherent, insofar as they also deny a historical past. For this reason, postmodernism might be regarded as an attempt to overcome history. Since Berel Lang begins by accepting the permissiveness of the postmodern age, he begins in sympathy with much of what the postmoderns have to say. However, he relieves their incoherence because he regards all claims about "radical breaks," "paradigm shifts," and "overcoming history" as strategies of one or another sort. Thus he can accept, for instance, that there is a "metaphysics of presence" in Plato, Descartes, and Kant, and go on to say that this commitment to presence only becomes apparent in light of the strategic ends taken up at a later time, by advocates and critics alike. And he can also then say that "the postmodernist critique is itself also a tactic in the tradition of those other tactics, not a strategy to end all strategies, as has often . . . been represented." This would nullify the suggestion, made above, that postmodernism is an attempt to clear free from history; it seeks only to clear free of an idea of philosophical history as Hegel, for example, conceived it.

In cases in which one is dealing with "tactics," the only possible response is tactical. In a recent essay on Derrida and deconstruction, Richard Rorty suggested that such a tactic might be called "circumvention." If I invoke Rorty's name in introducing Berel Lang's essay, this is in part because Lang himself mentions Rorty (in particular, Rorty's idea of the history of philosophy as a "conversation," introduced in *Philosophy and the Mirror of Nature* [1979]) and because Rorty has most thoroughly explored the pragmatic possibilities that Lang investigates here. The pragmatism these two thinkers share offers hope for human endeavor without supposing that those endeavors will have any teleological end. It is a pragmatism that does not deny history (in which case it could be indicted for proposing yet another epochal break) but that makes its investment in what Lang calls the history of the present. Pragmatism may thus avoid the degeneration of its own tactics into strategies with teleological ends. It may be impossible to avoid privileging the present over the past, which means that we are eternally condemned to a modernism of a certain sort; "but looking at the recent present also as a past, we may also see something omitted there, something that philosophers in the tradition were more candid about, even if they could not, any more than the philosophers of suspicion, do anything about it: that philosophy may begin not in suspicion but in the quite different phenomenon of wonder." If deconstruction and hermeneutics are, as Stanley Rosen says, the philosophies of a decadent age, then the pragmatic model that Berel Lang proposes here might provide one way for philosophy to move forward out of that decline. Lang suggests that if philosophy can be sustained by wonder at the newness of the present, then it might transform its habitual suspiciousness into a source of hope.

Postmodernism in
Philosophy: Nostalgia
for the Future, Waiting
for the Past

Berel Lang

> I do *believe in beginnings, middles, and*
> *ends—but not necessarily in that order.*
> —Godard

"Everything *is* permitted," we tell ourselves now, knowing, as Dostoyevsky could only anticipate, that God has indeed been found dead; confident, where Nietzsche could only speculate, that language itself no longer constrains us. ("I fear we are not yet rid of God," Nietzsche would write apprehensively, "because we still believe in grammar.") We may inhabit the first period in history that has suspected everything that *can* be suspected. We are heirs of the nineteenth-century pioneers, those by now classical philosophers of suspicion, who were so convincing in their descriptions of life underground that other stories—about life on the surface—now seem to us no less distant in their charm than the Greek myths or the experiments of medieval alchemy.

It is not just skepticism that has come to hold us, certainly not the tendentious skepticism of Descartes, who, like Job, in the end found all his worldly connections restored, not even of the Pyrrhonists or even of Gorgias, who would commit no more of himself to life or logic than the wiggle of a finger. The transformational grammars—of the psyche, of economics, of language itself—were yet to be construed, and only with those revisions do we begin to understand how difficult the labor of suspicion is: not a simple, two-termed relation in which reality finds itself displaced as appearance, but one in which the concept of reality and the techniques of displacement are *themselves* doubted. The institutions of the human world (art, political structures, science, social relations) are first disclosed as appearances move by other forces (psychological, economic, literary). Then the following examples of stratification: superstructure driven by base, sublimation by libido, historical representation by imagination, are in their own turn suspected, no longer turned upside down as Marx had prescribed for Hegel but sideways, where there could be no privileged origins or conclusions. So the forces that Marx and Freud still, for all their revolutionary zeal, took as fundamental and stable turn out themselves to be contingent features of experience, themselves requiring explanation, with the concept of explanation itself also altered. Philosophers would no longer hope for inclusive laws or models but would spin new, individual narrative threads, flattening even causality into a virtual and noncausal present.

At the edge of postmodernism, then, no idea or theory or word or even feeling is above suspicion, and whatever postmodernism does or says seems to take that fact, perhaps *only* that fact, as given.[1] This starting point turns out to be more demanding than that of the oracle or the soothsayer. All they have to do is to predict a future woven of the same fabric used in the past—a continuity that offers both comfort and a means: with only a modest reliance on Delphic ambiguity, most of us could do reasonably well as prophets. Postmodernism, however, not only has to predict but to constitute, since when nothing is given, when everything is possible (and more than that, equally possible), then prediction cannot fall back on analogy or any other logical or literary figure, all of which presuppose versions of continuity; it is obliged to spin of whole cloth. How would Joyce (or anyone who was not Joyce) have predicted *Finnegans Wake?* In a sense, however, Joyce *did* make the prediction when he wrote it. At that point, all the speculation that had preceded his writing about an impending revolution in consciousness, the possibility or impossibility of a contemporary epic, and so on, appeared suddenly in a different light. *Finnegans Wake* itself—his prediction realized, the performance—was there, available to sight and touch and even, in some loose way, since it must have been shaken up by the performance, to the mind.

We have, then, only an *apparent* choice in trying to anticipate the directions of postmodernism (whether in philosophical discourse or some other) in terms similar to those we would apply to other plans for the future. We might, on the one hand, speak about that future, extrapolating from the present (somehow overriding the postmodernist claim of a sharp gap between past and present, the *disanalogy*); or we might, on the other hand, try ourselves to do the work of postmodernism, accepting as a premise that traditional philosophy, with its search for foundations and its representational theory of truth, is passé, over, done. But in both these accounts the work of postmodernism is defined only negatively, by what it rejects in the past and so by what it is not. This common and negative starting point, it seems to me, discloses an important feature of postmodernism, although perhaps not a feature that it recognizes in itself. It also points to the general thesis I shall be arguing here: that one thread of discourse has in the history of philosophy been continually, repeatedly, postmodernist. How this is so turns out to be important for understanding both the history and the present of philosophy, on the one hand, and the phenomenon of postmodernism, on the other.

Let me rehearse a composite and thus bland, but also standard, account of the history of philosophy, as postmodernism in such figures as Heidegger, Derrida, and Rorty impatiently looks back at it. We mark off here the approximate distance between Plato and Hegel in a circle with a perimeter twenty-four hundred years long. At the center of this circle is a motivating distinction between, on the one hand, the apparent world—loose, disjointed, occasional; and, on the other hand, a second world that appearance both conceals and discloses, one that includes the apparent world and has enough left over to explain why the apparent world looks as it does without actually being it. The claim of displacement made by this second world, together with the related claim of truth as a form of representation, draws on an apparent variety of powers: the role of a logos or god or causality that determines aspects of everything else; the idea of substance—an underlying stuff (or two or three) that is then somehow differentiated into a greater number of things; the doctrine of a soul or mind that is as invisible and active as the body it animates is palpable and inert. What in these numerous accounts appears at first as a genuine variety in the history of philosophical thought, however, may be interpreted formally as no more than a series of variations on a single theme, that of hierarchical displacement: appearance subordinated to reality, plurality to the One. And just this suspicion—that it is the will to displacement, the desire for a center and then for a representation of that center, which has motivated the history of philosophy—is the starting point of the postmodernist diagnosis of that philosophical history. It is with this diagnosis, moreover—the moment of "rupture," to use Derrida's term—that the supposed will for truth or wisdom in the history of philosophy is revealed as no more than a disguise for nostalgia, a form of wistfulness and, finally, of self-deception. We must, then, learn to think of the traditional discourse of philosophy rather as expression than as idea; as manifestation, not assertion. There is no real object or source driving the process, only other expressions and manifestations that philosophers have consistently reified, finding objects where there were in fact only reflections or traces.

Now it might well be argued that this revisionist history is based on fragmentary, even uncertain evidence (we know, after all, that suspicion may be a pleasure in itself). And it is, I think, a matter of fact that none of the several versions of philosophical deconstruction that support the efforts of postmodernist philosophy has come close to explaining why the history of Western thought should have gone astray as deeply and consistently as it has been alleged to, in what amounts to a falsification not much slighter than the fault of original sin—and like it, too, apparently passed on as transgression to every following generation. But no matter, for this is history as the postmodernist imagines and so, we may suppose, lives it; and so there, again, at the alleged core of that history, the aspiration for authority, for structure, for beginnings, species, essences, categories, centers, natures, explanations, causes, divisions—all of these reflecting a malady that we now, postmodernly, are in a position to overcome. At least we can cure the symptoms, but that is all, we are told, that there is to the malady (since there are no centers any place, not even in illness). And we cure these, moreover, mainly by the recognition that they *are* symptoms (an unusually docile malady, that). So speech, for Wittgenstein, is reconceived as a part, not a contrivance of the organism; the ghost in the machine, for Gilbert Ryle, turns out to be only the cogs and levers that anybody not frightened by the sight of blood will find for himself if he has the courage to look inside. For Sartre, human nature is precisely the absence of any such nature; for Derrida, discourse is about discourse, and even then, more about its absence than its presence—in any event, not about subjects and certainly not about objects. The motivating image here is also of a circle, but undifferentiated now, deliberately antihierarchical and thus verging on the possibility that everything is itself only by being everything else as well, that distinctions of any sort are suspect, unnatural. Given this starting point, even to ask the simple question "What now?" is already to beg the question, since it retrieves, from the past, ideological commitments to a "what" (things) and to a "now" (the present and thus whatever the present is not); and although these may be evoked by the headiest of nostalgias (our own), they too must be suspect.

There are, it seems to me, two possibilities open to postmodernist thinking beyond this point, the one consistent but self-defeating; the other inconsistent, revisionary even of the starting point in its conception of history, but nourishing at least a hope of survival. We can think of the difference between these as a difference between two theories of time. On the first (consistent) one of these accounts, the linear conception of time that has dominated Western history is alleged to be part of the problem. Lines imply beginnings and ends; they also imply continuity, inferring from the reality of a past the probability of a future. If, then, as this first version of postmodernism maintains, we are not entitled to such claims, then time must be *dis*continuous, unmotivated—and we are talking here of separation not only between periods of time (years or generations) but between moments or instants, where even personal identity becomes an arbitrary and mystifying fiction, where proper names or the meanings of common terms cannot count on reidentification either. Not just institutional or corporate continuity is denied here, since then continuity might still occur for individual persons or objects; regularity or repetition *as such* is suspect, whether as a feature of institutions or as a characteristic of actions or even of persons.

It can, I think, be reasonably objected to this (consistent) version of inconsistency that there is little in the appearances of culture that we take most seriously—in ethics or law, in science, in the arts—that accords with it: one has only to consider the phenomenon of "style" (of individuals or groups) to recognize the dependence of expression on the assumption of continuity. Repetition is in fact a condition of style—perhaps, as Freud argues, of the mind itself—and the sacrifice of cultural or human anatomy would be a high price to pay for a new theory, no matter how enticing on other grounds. To be sure, the phenomenon of style itself—the way it domesticates novelty, its reliance on categories that then pass themselves off as nature—has been accused of an all too easy nostalgia, but this objection itself has a price. To replace even the superficiality of which the ascription of style is often guilty with the supposed neutrality of stylelessness is to threaten nature and not only art (and this does not yet assume a notion of "natural" style, although there is arguably some point even to that). We would find ourselves then in a domain of pure contingency, where the purpose of the artist would be mainly to defeat expectations, to deny reference, and thus to reiterate continually the absence of continuity. Dadaism, surrealism, and the so-called experimental novel have in fact been partial attempts to move in this direction, and without judging them in other ways we recognize a crucial feature common to them all: much of their power comes from the expectations they work to defeat. Like the jujitsu wrestler, they get strength for their throw from their opponent's rush: without that, they have no more power than he has by himself. They flourish, then, by contrast, by reaction; although this may be a way into the future, it hardly promises survival there (it is also, of course, itself a form of continuity, since it presupposes the past). Moreover, the philosophical or theoretical past that postmodernism (on this first view) simply writes off had at least an unmistakeable productive corollary in poetry, science, social institutions. The theoretical present that postmodernism claims for itself has as yet had only marginal consequences of this sort (Yeats and Pound were reactionaries politically and arguably poetically as well, but the practice of postmodernist theory has hardly produced poetic imaginations to rival theirs). Hegel suggested that philosophy's Owl of Minerva would fly only at dusk. Perhaps, as postmodernism now intimates, he was mistaken; perhaps criticism, theory, philosophy, can anticipate rather than follow such objects of experience as literary texts or paintings. But even then, they need not be identical to the latter—and so we feel the strain when postmodernist critics and theorists represent their own work as itself displacing the art about which they theorize. (The outcome has been no more successful, it seems to me, when the artist has presented *his* work as theory).

Still, there is no assurance that the second, contrasting version of postmodernism I have proposed, since it disputes the alleged rupture in the history of Western thinking, will do better than the first. Such a revision, it might be argued, would forfeit not only a potent criticism of the past but also the new beginning in the present that might be extracted from that criticism. But it is precisely this sense of a beginning, it seems to me, that can best be sustained by rejecting the former. Here, in the interest of postmodernist survival, I appeal to a military analogy—but irenically, hoping to beat the swords of deconstruction into the ploughshares of pragmatism. The analogy is in the distinction between a conception of *strategy*, on the one hand, in which it is ends or goals or principles that are asserted, and the idea of *tactics*, on the other hand, where it is means, even beginnings, that are sought only in order to serve the context that evokes them. Postmodernism has characteristically placed itself in opposition not only to particular strategies in one or another of the traditional theoretical and critical systems but to the possibility of strategies altogether. What happens to strategists, on this account—here the analogy to military history is pointed—is ossification, reification. Generals, we know, are constantly preparing to fight the war just past (this is true even if they have been victorious, but especially if they have been defeated). And the strategic ends are still more implacable: only the incidental names of the enemy change over time, and even then, in cultural warfare, not by much. Looking out on the debris of the battlefield, we might well willingly say with the postmodernist, "Enough and more than enough, no more: only tactics, now—the response to a moment, and always in a context, *always* in the spirit of contingency—that is, with the present always in part absent, a celebration, in effect, of mortality itself."

Here we note the beginning of a small deceit as it grows, like most deceits, from a small truth. That rupture in the history of Western philosophy, the diagnosis and then rejection of logocentrism: may we not suspect that the claim for this breach is itself open to suspicion? Do we not have, in the distinction between strategy and tactics, a weapon to be turned against the *reading* of history as well as against history itself? My thesis can be put in two parts: first, that the traditional discourse of metaphysics, now supposedly ruptured once and for all, was itself—notwithstanding its high talk of God, substance, soul, logos—a sequence of tactical variations that only came to be seen (by advocates and critics alike) as committed to strategic ends. Its own intention reflected a design that was contextual and not transcendent, historical and not atemporal, practical and not theoretical. And second, that the postmodernist critique is itself also a tactic in the tradition of those other tactics, not a strategy to end all strategies, as it has often (again by advocates no less than by critics) been represented.

These are large claims to make good on, and I do not mean that the ascription of such a tactical impulse to the history of philosophy is easily substantiated or that the impulse is everywhere present (certainly not in the same measure) in that history. I am suggesting, in fact, only the justice of an even hand—that where logocentrism or reification is alleged, we look for the occasion of those charges in the dramatizing eyes of the beholder, among the historians of logos, rather than in the historical texts themselves. For there is considerable evidence in the texts that this mote may be in the eye of the beholder, not in the eyes of their authors. (Ideology, after all, may victimize readers no less than writers.) I can hardly attempt to defend the latter claim for all the texts and philosophers that have been accused of deviant practices (the history of philosophy as written by postmodernists seems to have closer textual affiliations to the Marquis de Sade and Krafft-Ebing than to more standard philosophical sources); but, since the Greeks were on this account originally responsible for the Fall into logocentrism, let me refer to them and in particular to Plato, who is more than only representative here, himself a "paradeigma" of the doctrine of presence. It is easy enough, in reconstructing Plato's dialogues, to regard the questions raised in them as also establishing their answers: What is justice? What is Piety? What is knowledge? What is courage? We hear this catalogue of questions, finding in it the merely assumed existence of the "things" in question, which are thus given life immaculately, without a basis. Around them, the representational world of the philosopher then turns; nothing more, it is inferred, need be added by Plato except for a brief specification in the definition itself. There, in the very questions he asks (and then, of course, unsurprisingly, in his answers to them), we have Plato's theory of Forms: immobile, abstract, otherworldly—patterns to be known and then imitated by the rational self, at once explanations and directives for action.

The one thing missing from this common portrait, it seems, is Plato himself, specifically the act (the motives, the reasons, the practice) of his writing and philosophizing. *Is* the genre of the philosophical dialogue a means of objectification and representation, or even of assertion? Do Plato's dialogues provide definitions or rules—for justice or temperance or courage or piety or whatever—that the reader is then required to pledge allegiance to or to imitate? Is the Good itself quite other than the individual items that constitute the domain of the experience or the implementation of the Good? One need not agree to the flat "No" with which I myself answer these questions to concede its plausibility—and this in itself is enough of a wedge to loosen the rigid distinction that the ideologists of the historiography of philosophy would now have us simply take for granted. It hardly turns Plato into a crypto-Marxist to acknowledge that his eye for the work of the shoemaker, the sailor, the horse-trainer, was the same eye with which he looked for, and even at, the Forms, and which continued to govern that view. What many readers of Plato have done, dogmatically assuming that psychology duplicates ontology, is to read backward from the Forms to experience, rather than the other way round, which is the way that Plato himself almost certainly proceeded and in any event assumed that his reader would.

This account does not deny that the Forms might have taken on a life of their own once Plato had conceived of them, but it is at least a cautionary warning that he (and they) may have found their hands forced by the evidence—that they may have been driven rather than driver. In any event, it underscores the importance of avoiding interpretive placebos (like nostalgia) to explain Plato's allegiance to the Forms, when other less reductive and ad hominem explanations (including even Plato's own) are available. Perhaps the theory of the Forms is not strictly required to account for the possibility of Platonic experience, but Kant's transcendental formulation is surely relevant to understanding the status of the Forms. To be consistently or even occasionally suspicious may well mean that we cannot take philosophers at their own words, but that hardly entails that we should not take their words at all.

One advantage of the account I have begun here is that it suggests the outline for an explanation of the deconstructionist view of the history of philosophy itself—something that Heidegger, Derrida, and Rorty have themselves, it seems to me, given little more to than the benefit of momentary intuitions and a metaphysics of history cobbled together out of those moments. There is no requirement here for a conspiracy theory of history, no need for the simple but invidious contention one finds lurking in the work of these figures that we (or at least they) are simply more astute, more circumspect, more enlightenedly suspicious, than past figures, singly or even together, in the history of Western thought. It turns out, for one thing—what the readers of ancient philosophers, like the readers of the ancient poets, can hardly be surprised at—that the occasions of philosophical experience from which those writers set out in important ways resemble our own. Abuses that occur, moreover—fetishism, for example—may be endemic to the process of thinking itself rather than peculiar to the history of a single-minded ideology. So, for example, the fallacy, in Whitehead's phrase, of "misplaced concreteness," in which the price exacted by abstraction for the power it provides brings with memory (which itself may be, as Nietzsche argued, a human creation) forgetfulness of its own origins. This theoretical version of religious idolatry appears when symbols, signs, constructs, representations, are taken to be things-in-themselves, when their history is repressed. And there is, of course, an irony in the association of this particular fallacy with the deconstructionist view of the history of Western thought: that the latter view, meant to destroy the idols of the past, is true only (or largely) as it is false, when it itself fetishizes history.

One could go further here, incorporating even the rupture announced by postmodernism into the very history it claims to have ruptured. For if we ask now not why the past should have been misread but, more substantively, why it should be held that the history of philosophy is over, finished, that it has, in Heidegger's words, "come to term," we see that declaration too, in all its hyperbole, to be continuous with the past of philosophy itself. Not only is it not the first time that philosophers have seen themselves as starting anew, shrugging free of the past, which they pronounce as over, finished, but this is in fact what philosophers have repeatedly done: Aristotle, Descartes, Locke, Kant, had little "philia" left for their predecessors; they were not more inclined than the more recent and explicit advocates of postmodernism have been to place themselves in a continuous line of indebtedness. The history of prefaces to philosophical writing—Descartes in the *Discourse*, Locke in the *Essay*, Kant in the *First Critique*—is in fact a history of revolt; less nicely, of murder, where the sons pit themselves against the fathers, promising a future that begins with them (the sons), with *their* discourse. That the past is condemned by such figures does not always mean for them that there is (or should be) no future for philosophy (as Heidegger and Rorty propose)—but for them, too, it is the rejection of the past that determines a radically different future.

The impulse here is more than psychological; it is, we may say, philosophical, an appeal to reflection in which the assertion of distance is a prerequisite for the act of discourse itself. The life of philosophy, it may be surmised, is in this sense paradoxical, since we know that the claims of distance, of detachment have (repeatedly) been superseded, upended by history itself as it insists on closing the gap. (Nature may have its vacuums, but not—or not yet—history.) Thus philosophy succeeds only when, if not because, it fails, when it evokes the past by rejecting it in favor of the present, when it wins access to the moment by imagining the whole. The moral that emerges here may seem Calvinist in its anticipation of defeat, but it at least addresses the history of philosophy as a history: to win the partial glimpse that is at most what philosophy can hope for has been in fact to presuppose a rejection of one whole and the desire for another. An original impulse for acceptance, for partiality, promises at worst fetishism or other versions of idolatry, at best a glimpse of pleasure—but little, in either direction, of a habitable world, let alone of the reflections of philosophy. Lionel Trilling suggests that the concept of modernism soon came, in one of its main proponents, Matthew Arnold, to lose its standing as a chronological category: "By [his] definition, *Periclean Athens* is a modern age, Elizabethan England is not." Could we not, then, think of postmodernism in the same way—not simply as a present possibility, now at *this* moment, but a possibility attached to the present, whenever the present occurs?

The historical occurrence of such possibility is not difficult to find. Descartes's eventual claim of certainty in knowledge came neither as a straightforward rejection of his philosophical past nor as a step added to it: he found in the very skepticism that he disputed, because that skepticism could be turned on itself, a ground for its denial and then for personal and, eventually, for systematic certainty. That alteration, we understand, was more than a turn of rhetorical irony; it was a reversal of speculation back on its own means, carrying the force of a "postmodernist" break with its past—provoking, in another now-current phrase, a "paradigm shift" in philosophical discourse and method. Similarly, Kant, responding to Hume's critique of causality, turned the mechanism of cognition inside out, assigning to the subject or knower the power that Hume had cogently found wanting in the object. This, if anything, provides a stronger example still of the way in which the means of discourse, as the poststructuralists who are themselves heavily indebted to the Kantian tradition have insisted, can be turned back on itself, deconstructed. There is, then—although the claim obviously requires much elaboration—a history of such "postmodernist" moments within the history of philosophy. (The concept of *the* history of philosophy itself, one might argue, is tied to another of those moments, in the assertion of philosophical hegemony over time found in romanticism—specifically in the Hegelian account of philosophical time. In that account, too, we note a ready source of the postmodernist fascination with the death of philosophy: as Hegel himself could herald the deaths of art and religion, he might well have appreciated the cunning of history which would then go on to write the obituary of the writer of obituaries.)

But what, then, looking from *this* present, of the postmodernist future in philosophy? For even if the much-qualified version of postmodernism presented here were granted for the sake of argument, there is nothing predictive about it—and we have the constant obligation as well of responding to those thinkers who, standing at the edge, have declared, even cherished, the death of metaphysics, not the beginning of a new version of it but simply the end. There is Wittgenstein for whom, mimicking his compatriot Karl Kraus's words about psychoanalysis, philosophy was the disease it would itself cure; there is Heidegger, according to whom Nietzsche had once and for all settled the traditional philosophical accounts, leaving the slate clean; there is Derrida for whom discourse, writing, is now disclosed as entirely, only, its own object and for whom, then, philosophy, no more than any other addictive science of representation, has a future. Could philosophy survive such confident obituaries?

One way would be toward quietism—in the words of a character out of Unamuno, simply "to catalogue the world and return it to God all in order." There is indeed something of this conservative affirmation of things as they are in the mood of those thinkers themselves, and it is important to keep in mind how they come to this. Consciousness itself, Nietzsche had proposed, could be suspected as a malady—

and with *that* suspicion, it is understandable that tactics no less than strategy should be viewed with a wary eye, that the conclusion might be drawn that there was no place at all to go, that there were no distinctions to stand on, no references to hold to. Pleasure and the will might at first seem likely replacements for truth and understanding, as historically the latter had hardened into abstraction: categories, foundations, disinterestedness had become ends in themselves. But then, too, the former soon become objectified as well, also doctrinaire, punitive: what started as tactic had again become strategy.[2]

I have suggested that this impulse for displacing its past, for repeatedly privileging the present over the past, may be native to philosophy. But looking at the recent present also as a past, we may also see something omitted there, something that philosophers in the tradition were more candid about, even if they could not, any more than the philosophers of suspicion, do anything about it: that philosophy may begin not in suspicion but in the quite different phenomenon of wonder. The difference between those two is much like the difference between fear and anxiety that Kierkegaard wrote about, between the problem and the mystery that Gabriel Marcel distinguished, with each of the former terms reacting to a specific object and the latter being diffused, a general feature of experience. I do not wish here to try to identify the concept of wonder beyond its least technical sense, which still suffices to identify it as a peculiarly postmodernist, and yet constant, feature of philosophy. For wonder, unlike suspicion, is attached to the present, a function of the here-and-now. So far, then, as wonder is a motive of philosophy, it will always be forcing philosophy to begin there, in the present, that is, to start anew—thus, to reject the past even with the full knowledge that this rejection is a function of the present as present, rather than the rejection of a particular past. So we understand the mild irony of a ninth-century Arabian writer, Ibn Qutayba, when he reminds his readers that "God has so ordered it that very ancient was modern in his own time." To which I would add, "And so at least some ancients were also postmodern in their own time."

This may seem to offer a view of the history of philosophy (past and future) that is peculiarly disembodied and formal, with its fate entirely in the hands of individual philosophers (as individuals), attempting as they can to break free of their philosophical pasts and even of the world itself, succeeding at best only in part but willing to try to deceive their readers (perhaps themselves as well) with much larger claims. There is, indeed, a social history of philosophy yet to be written, one that reflects on that history as history and not just as word and that, in doing this, provides a context of meaning for the word that the word cannot do for itself. I suggest, as a link between that unwritten history and my more formal analysis, that philosophy has itself been openly ambivalent about its social status. Nietzsche would write that the idea of a married philosopher was a joke—and we could predict from this the harsh words that he was also to supply about "institutional" philosophy on a larger scale. But philosophy itself seems to have realized well before this challenge occurred that the phrase "institutional philosophy" was close to being an oxymoron, that even if philosophical discourse might arise *in* institutions, it could never be honestly *of* them (which was, of course, the wish of the institutions themselves). One way of understanding the recent proclamations of the end of philosophy, in fact, is as a reaction to the institutionalization of philosophy that occurred mainly in the nineteenth century, associated there with the more general phenomena of bureaucracy and professionalization of which we now, permitting ourselves a guarded optimism, might hope to be the tail end.

I do not mean here to draw an image of the philosopher as characteristically an outsider or an alienated consciousness (insofar as this is true at all, it holds only for a small number of figures in the history of philosophy), but rather to suggest that there is a difference worth building on between institutional philosophy and a conception of philosophy as "polyphonic," in which the voice of the individual philosopher is recognizable as an overlay of many voices brought together. The latter, it seems to me, has in fact been a recurrent feature of philosophical discourse that has only recently been discounted in the now-dominant conception of a "heroic" history of philosophy. As the arts discovered and then celebrated the artist as individual in the Renaissance, so philosophy, tardily, would then in the eighteenth and nineteenth centuries learn to forget the metonymic function that proper names often serve—referring apparently to an individual but standing in fact for a practice. We have recently heard much about the "death of the author" (admittedly proposed by authors who seem willing to observe that phenomenon for everyone but themselves), but it seems likely, in fact, that philosophy in its most powerful moments has long known about that death, even willed it. This is but another way in which proclamations of the "end of philosophy" have been part of its history.

None of this is to claim that even the noninstitutional philosopher will manage to escape the constraints of ideology any more than he can hope to jump out of his skin. (In this respect, Hegel's historicism extends to postmodernist philosophy more radically than Hegel himself allowed, since his historicism ended before philosophy did.) There are always some things that will not be spoken of: repression in its various guises will see to that, and if repression fails, finitude itself will suffice. Thus, philosophical wonder itself in the end will also turn out to be partial, adapted to particular interests and idioms, and so always with an object not quite of the philosopher's own choosing. But there is a difference between speaking *for* a context and speaking *out of context*—and it is the latter, a violation of the taboos of the understanding, that philosophy, when it succeeds, seems to me to accomplish. That retrospectively we can always devise a context in which such violations may be neutralized should be less unsettling than is the dream of those who spend time planning to escape that (or any) retrospection. The denial of ideology is where ideology is in fact most active and most determinant—and like positivism and existentialism, which have attempted to privilege themselves in this way, postmodernism in the fundamentalist version I have criticized here has victimized itself by just such a denial.

Thus, irresolute and absent-minded an answer as it may seem, a plausible response to the question "What now?" is "Go and do it." For as wonder is involuntary, spontaneous, and cannot be coerced, neither can it be anticipated or predicted. There is here, moreover, a theory of time at work which escapes both the lockstep of historical determinism that the standard postmodernist reading finds in the pre-postmodernist history of philosophy and the varieties of discontinuity or randomness that it would itself substitute. Is it so improbable that the present may be new without being *absolutely* other than the past or that it may be indebted to the past without being identical to it? This combination would offer a way of being or thinking *in* the present without yet being quite *of* it; it would also, I think, validate in one way the view of the history of philosophy that postmodernism at its extreme has urged and even make it consistent with what postmodernism has proposed to do in the present.

All this may seem to promise a future that is either hopelessly amorphous or, still worse than that, that bears an uncanny resemblance to the past—that is, a "new" present in which nothing has changed. But consistent with both these alternatives is another one, the "possibility of everything," the postmodernist theme with which this account began and which turns out now to be an illusion (a creative illusion, philosophy's own "Noble Lie") by which philosophy has constantly lived in the past, watching its own tactics turned into strategies, sometimes by itself. What this means for postmodernism is that in it, too, philosophy, waiting again on the new present, will be tactical, moving from the immediacy of particular moments of experience, incited by the moments themselves. What we may look forward to, then, are indeed "conversations," as Rorty names them, although we might hope that they are not limited to the structures that he himself predicts for them. They will—if we are fortunate—be more like Plato's dialogues, Montaigne's essays, Descartes's meditations, Hegel's phenomenologies, Kierkegaard's points of view for his work as author. Like them, but of course also not like them—by as much, at any rate, as those themselves were, are, like and not like each other. Does not this leave things exactly as they had been? What would be *post*modernist about this? But the occasions will be different; the intersections of history, no matter how alike, will be occurring for the first time, and with them the questions of address, of tactics. And more important than these, there is the instrumentality of a past that can be advanced, subverted, or, with the tactics of postmodernism, turned on its side: certainly not for the first time, almost certainly not for the last, but nonetheless. Thus, everything *is* possible—including philosophy when it flatly asserts that not everything is possible. In this way, Aristotle argued for the law of noncontradiction as itself not requiring or even as capable of demonstration. The proof of its ground, even of its possibility, was for him the actuality of everything else around it. There too we may find, if not a foundation, at least the origins of a discourse that has in the past turned out to be philosophical. To demand more than this is to will oneself a victim of the past; for the next step to be taken can only be in coming back once more to the work of philosophy, not in a gift of history that promises freedom with one hand only to withdraw it with the other. Nostalgia, when it is spontaneous, is for the future; anticipation, when it is not merely wistful, is of the past. This is why philosophers would say at first—and then again and again in their history—"Let us begin." Let us, then, begin. Again.[3]

Notes

1. I do not attempt to assess here the numerous, sometimes conflicting definitions of postmodernism; the term, which was originally quite modest in its applications to architecture and to poetry, has become a general term of cultural reference. See, for the historical background of the term, Jerome Mazzaro, "The Genesis of Postmodernism," in *Postmodern American Poetry* (Urbana: University of Illinois Press, 1980), 1–31; also, Marjorie Perloff, *The Poetics*

of Indeterminacy (Princeton: Princeton University Press, 1981), 28–44, and Richard Palmer, "Towards a Postmodern Hermeneutics of Performance," in *Performance in Postmodern Culture* (Milwaukee: Center for Twentieth-Century Studies, 1977). For a more speculative historical reconstruction, see Jean-François Lyotard, *The Postmodern Condition: A Report on Knowledge*, trans. G. Benington and B. Massumi (Minneapolis: University of Minnesota Press, 1984). The contrast that I find between modernism and postmodernism in philosophical discourse is itself part of the thesis argued here.

2. Although coming from a different starting point, this formulation converges on Habermas's objection to postmodernism as a form of *anti*modernism, with its aestheticism a cloak for conservative or reactionary ideology. So, the postmodernists "remove into the sphere of the far-away and the archaic the spontaneous powers of imagination, self-experience and emotion." Jürgen Habermas, "Modernity—An Incomplete Project," in Hal Foster, ed., *The Anti-Aesthetic: Essays on Postmodern Culture* (Port Townsend, Wash: Bay Press, 1983), 14. See also, in the same volume, Fredric Jameson, "Postmodernism and Consumer Society," 114–18; Jameson, associating postmodernism with the genre of the "pastiche," argues still more sharply for the incapacitating social consequences of postmodernism. For a discussion of the background of the aestheticism of postmodernism, see Berel Lang, "The Praxis of Criticism, in *Philosophy and the Art of Writing* (Lewisburg, Pa.: Bucknell University Press, 1983).

3. I am indebted to Forrest Williams for suggestions he has made about a number of points raised in this essay.

Notes on Contributors

CHARLES ALTIERI is professor of English at the University of Washington, Seattle. His works include *Act and Quality: A Theory of Literary Meaning and Humanistic Understanding.*

HARRY BERGER, JR., is fellow of Cowell College at the University of California, Santa Cruz. The essay published here is part of his ongoing work on Plato, some of which has appeared in *Classical Antiquity* (1984), *Representations* (1984), and *Philosophical Forum* (1982).

ANTHONY J. CASCARDI is the author of *The Limits of Illusion* and of *The Bounds of Reason: Cervantes, Dostoevsky, Flaubert.* He is associate professor of comparative literature at the University of California, Berkeley.

ARTHUR C. DANTO, Johnsonian Professor of Philosophy at Columbia University, is the author of *The Transformation of the Commonplace, Narration and Knowledge,* and many other works.

DENIS DUTTON is senior lecturer in the philosophy of art at the University of Canterbury, New Zealand. He is editor of the journal *Philosophy and Literature.*

DAVID HALLIBURTON is professor of English, comparative literature, and modern thought and literature at Stanford University. He is the author of *Poetic Thinking: An Approach to Heidegger.*

DALIA JUDOVITZ is a member of the faculty of French at the University of California, Berkeley. She is the author of the forthcoming study, *Subjectivity and Representation: The Origins of Modern Thought in Descartes.*

BEREL LANG is professor of philosophy at the State University of New York, Albany. He is the author of *Art and Inquiry* and editor of the volume *The Concept of Style.*

PETER MCCORMICK is the author of *Heidegger and the Language of the World* and has recently completed *Fictions, Philosophies, and Poetics.* He teaches philosophy and comparative literature at the University of Ottawa.

ALEXANDER NEHAMAS is professor of philosophy at the University of Pennsylvania. He is the author of *Nietzsche: Life as Literature,* as well as of numerous studies of Plato.

MARTHA CRAVEN NUSSBAUM is professor of philosophy, classics, and comparative literature at Brown University and the author of *The Fragility of Goodness: Luck and Ethics in Greek Tragedy and Philosophy.* A companion piece to the present essay was published in *New Literary History.*

STANLEY ROSEN is Evan Pugh Professor of Philosophy at the Pennsylvania State University. He is the author of *Nihilism: A Philosophical Essay* and of *Plato's "Symposium,"* among other works.

MARY BITTNER WISEMAN teaches philosophy at Brooklyn College and the Graduate Center of the City University of New York. She is the author of the forthcoming volume on Roland Barthes in the Croom Helm series *Critics of the Twentieth Century.*